THE BATTLE OF TRAFALGAR

Painted by C. Stanfield, R.A.

A History of
The Nineteenth Century
Year by Year

BY

EDWIN EMERSON, Jr.

Member of the American Historical Association, New York
Historical Society, Franklin Institute of Philadelphia,
Honorary Member of the Royal Philo-
Historical Society of Bavaria, etc., etc.

WITH AN INTRODUCTION BY
GEORG GOTTFRIED GERVINUS

ILLUSTRATED WITH SIXTEEN COLORED PLATES AND
THIRTY-TWO FULL-PAGE, HALF-TONE CUTS
AND TWO MAPS

IN THREE VOLUMES—VOLUME ONE

NEW YORK
P. F. COLLIER AND SON
MCMI

CONTENTS

VOLUME ONE

VOLUME TWO

VOLUME THREE

LIST OF ILLUSTRATIONS

VOLUME ONE

F<small>OR</small> *invaluable assistance received the author desires to express his indebtedness to Messrs. Andrew D. White, Datus C. Brooks, Maurice Magnus, Waldemar Kaempffert, William G. Brown, and to the most faithful of his helpmates — his wife. Grateful acknowledgment for professional courtesies is also rendered to the officers of the Public Libraries of New York and Boston, of the American Congressional Library, British Museum, and Paris Library, as well as to the librarians of the Universities of Harvard and Columbia and of the Historical Society of New York.*

A HISTORY OF THE NINETEENTH CENTURY

NAPOLEONIC ERA

PREFACE

A SURVEY of the last century reveals it as an age of some great men and many marvellous achievements. As the achievements exceed the giants of the age in number, so, too, they surpass them in grandeur. All the restless activity of a Napoleon or the iron policy of a Bismarck have not wrought upon modern life as did the steam engine. The great inventions and their adaptation to the needs of humanity are the real glories of the Nineteenth Century.

Thus new epochs in the development of man have been brought about by our modern modes of transit and transportation, our steam cars and boats, electric motors, bicycles and automobile vehicles, as well as our new modes of communication by means of the electric telegraph, telephone and phonograph.

Human life, as it exists now among civilized communities, owes still more, perhaps, to our new labor-saving machines and devices. Of these, our various agricultural implements, our sewing machines, typewriters and printing presses are but instances. The comforts of life have been immeasurably increased by the universal adoption of things now termed common and indispensable, such as friction matches, gas lighting, electric light and appliances, or steel pens—as well as modern methods of heating, plumbing and construction. Among the esthetic gains of mankind attained during this same century must be reckoned such results of the study of light as photography or the kindred processes of photo-engraving, electrotyping, lithography, color printing and similar new methods of illustration.

The modern study of light has resulted in other scientific achievements of lasting importance, notably our knowledge of the velocity of light, Spectrum Analysis and the Roentgen Rays. In the study of medicine, to which this last invention has been principally applied, a new era may be said to date from the use of anæsthetics and antiseptics, first adopted during the middle of the last century. A similar impulse to the theoretical study of medicine has been given by the discovery of the functions of the blood corpuscles, the cell theory in embryology, and the germ theory. Of like importance to science are such scientific discoveries as the correspondence between heat and energy, the theory of gases, of molecules and of atmospheric dust, the nebular and meteoric theories in astronomy, and the determination of geological epochs resulting indirectly in Darwin's theory of the Evolution of Species and the Origin of Man. War has been made more terrible by such instruments of destruction as torpedoes, rifled firearms, machine guns, smokeless powder, lyddite and melinite.

So much for a single century's achievements

in science. They outnumber the great inventions
of all the previous centuries within historic times.
The same may be said of some other triumphs of
the past century—notably of Music. No less has
been accomplished in some other arts. The great
masterpieces in painting of the late Middle Ages and
the Renaissance have been rivalled in this century
by the artists of France, England and other modern
schools.

Unlike Music and the Fine Arts, the march of
Modern Literature has been along national lines. It
was a far cry from Haydn to Wagner, or from David
to Millet, yet it seems no further than the intervals
of intellect that lie between Keats and Kipling,
Kant and Nietzsche, Schiller and Sudermann,
Pushkin and Tolstoi, Alfieri and Annunzio, or
Chateaubriand and Zola.

The years between the men representing these
two extremes of various literary developments are
filled with illustrious names. Well could Browning
sing:

> "And did you once see Shelley plain,
> And did he stop and speak to you,
> And did you speak to him again?
> How strange it seems, and new!"

What is true of the Letters and Art is true of
almost every other phase of human attainment in
the Nineteenth Century. Since Napoleon, Nelson,
Pitt and Wellington, down to Garibaldi, Cavour,
Kossuth, Bismarck, Moltke, Gladstone and Krue-
ger, there has been a constant succession of famous
captains, sailors, statesmen, philosophers, inventors

and other great men, whose biographies alone would fill many more volumes than this history.

It is the pride of Americans that their hemisphere has contributed its share, and over, to the sum-total accomplished by the world since the death of Washington. In the roll-call of the great men of this age few names stand forth more brightly than those of Jefferson, Bolivar, Lincoln, Grant, Farragut and Lee, or those of Fulton, Ericsson, Morse, Edison, Diaz and Dewey.

Considerations such as these have entered largely into the preparation of this work. To them must be ascribed the apparent preponderance given to the part played by America in the history of the world during the Nineteenth Century. When a similar work was undertaken by Gervinus, the great German historian, he laid the responsibility for modern statecraft and ideals of government at the feet of America. Had he lived to complete his work, his pen might have traced the great story of the rise of nations during the last fifty years. Since the great civil war, which established the union of the North American States, the world has seen the rise of a national Italy, Japan, Germany and the Slavic States, and of colonial empires, like those of India, Australia and Africa. The attempt of the small Boer Republic to start a similar national movement in South Africa could not have failed to impress an observer like Gervinus as but another inevitable symptom of the times. He it was, too, who predicted the opening of the Far East as a result of these modern tendencies.

The Empire of Japan, since it faced about to adopt the latest benefits of Western civilization, has indeed become the Land of the Rising Sun. Of her eastern neighbors across the China Sea, on the other hand, Matthew Arnold's lines on the Alexandrian conquest still hold true:

> "The brooding East with awe beheld
> Her impious younger world.
> The Roman tempest swell'd and swell'd,
> And on her head was hurl'd.

> "The East bow'd low before the blast
> In patient, deep disdain;
> She let the legions thunder past,
> And plunged in thought again."

Matthew Arnold's as well as Gervinus' prediction, strangely enough, has been fulfilled at the very close of the Nineteenth Century. Now that the century has ended, the eyes of men have turned from the new world in America to a newer world in ancient China.

EDWIN EMERSON, JR.

New York, December, 1900.

AN INTRODUCTION

HISTORY OF THE NINETEENTH CENTURY

BY GEORG GOTTFRIED GERVINUS

(Translated by MAURICE MAGNUS)1

———————

THE HISTORY of the European States during the Christian Era forms as inseparable a
whole as that of the Greek Peninsula and
its colonies in Antiquity. In both eras the same Forms of
Law and
forms of law and order are revealed in their course Order in
Christian
of inner development. These laws are the same Era and
Antiquity
which repeat themselves at large in the history of
the entire human race. From the despotism of the
Orient to the aristocratic States of Antiquity and
the Middle Ages, founded on slavery and serfdom,
and from them to the policy of the Western States
still in development, there is a regular progress

---

¹ This famous essay was written as an introduction to Gervinus's
projected history of the Nineteenth Century. He was then a professor of history at Heidelberg. As soon as the pamphlet appeared,
in 1853, Gervinus was placed on trial for high treason. He declined
to plead in his own behalf. In behalf of his work he declared in
court: "The charge, though it appears directed against me, is in fact
an accusation against Providence, or let us say History, which cannot be condemned."—Gervinus was convicted and sentenced to four
months in prison and his work was burned. The "Introduction"
immediately became a classic in Germany and throughout Europe.

of intellectual and civil freedom—first from one to that of the few, and from them to all. But where States have completed their cycle of existence one may again observe from the height of their development a corresponding decline of culture, of freedom and power, from the many to the few, and from them to one alone.

It is this law which is found in every part of history, in every mature independent State, likewise in the group of States mentioned above. England, notably in its later development, has given the pattern of a mixed constitution. William Pitt, one of England's greatest statesmen, found the chief value of the unwritten constitution in its preservation of all the different forms of government—monarchy, aristocracy and democracy—while avoiding the evils of each.

Those advanced views on policy and religion, which some intuitive and prophetic minds held in Germany at the beginning of the Reformation, were not really realized until the establishment of the American Constitution. Certain changes had been effected in the English Constitution which led to a similar end, but in a different way—that of realizing existing circumstances and gaining all from them. Both in England and America popular government worked well—the fortune, power and freedom of each competing for a prize which consisted in the glory of their own constitution.

The growth of the English Constitution was not the outcome of a regular system. But those who filled out the inefficiencies knew how to do the work in such a way as to bring their own views into evidence, and yet to remain in harmony with their predecessors. It took centuries to build up such a constitution, but every period contributed its best material and labor.

No modern State has passed through such a normal history as England—the different phases of State development have nowhere else been so clearly defined. The old Teutonic constitution under the patriarchal monarchy appears nowhere so fully developed as with the Anglo-Saxons; and no race has left such treasures of law books and literature of its first period of State formation. The feudal system was nowhere so finished and perfect from its beginning, nor so strong and lasting for such a period of time, as in Normanic England; no other aristocracy has shown itself as capable as the English. Royal despotism has nowhere else used its powers, both at home and abroad, with so much benevolence, nor shown itself so reluctant to use its prerogatives as in England. In no other country than England, in fine, have the people so strengthened the State with their individual force and also gained so much political influence. Thus, when the constitution was to be amended in 1688, no one could be found to suggest even a curtailment or an omission of the existing elements of State—all having proved their utility. The people were not envious of the large estates of the nobility which the republic wanted to divide by an Agrarian law. They felt secure in their industry, to the large development of which they had been driven by the fact that

The old Teutonic Constitution

The People and the Nobility

the land was almost exclusively in the hands of the nobles. And again the nobility willingly granted to the people a share in their privileges. The State fostered their industries as well as their increasing power in the lower House of Parliament. They knew then how indispensable taxes and credit were to the State. In their leisure, and knowledge of State affairs, the great nobles felt secure of their influence. The two classes were not separated by the advantages or disadvantages of birth, but were united by family ties; their interests were not politically opposed, but each formed a body of men divided only by the natural differences of political purpose for which they were formed. Both classes agreed in the expedient of a monarchical head over three united states, at that time without a common legislation. Accordingly they retained the monarchy, restricting only some of the royal privileges. The monarchy in return received the throne from Parliament, and thereby renounced its claim to divine origin. Therewith fell all royal claims to special rights above the rights of others. The position of the King, Lords and People rather rested on the basis of an acquired and acknowledged right, and each saw in the right of others a confirmation of their own. In this they remained faithful to the character of those times when revolutions were only undertaken in defence of those that were wronged— or to restore ancient rights. The well-balanced influences of these powers of the State, the manly and political character of those in administration, depended upon the equality of their rights. Their

Restrictions on the Monarchy

different callings acted as a safeguard against political degeneration, which, according to Aristotle, is produced by appropriating the offices of State to serve individual purposes on the narrow ideas of rank.

It is in this mixed constitution that the different classes of the people appear side by side, each possessed of peculiar privileges; while the elements are so thoroughly blended that History stands up and points to the English Commonwealth as her The Commonwealth masterpiece. It is the constitutional form of the State in its most perfect and natural development— where the constitution has continued through all ages, where no essential has been lost in the material of its history, where the old customs by a wonderful adjustment have been adapted to the wants of the new, while the experience of a mature political science has been superadded. Where one will discover in it the perfection of the old Anglo-Saxon, another will discern the perfection of the class institutions of the Middle Ages.

The separation into corporate bodies is still retained in English habits of life, in their society, as well as in the constitution. The different classes and powers of the State, with their respective interests, resemble great blocks of stone wherewith the edifice of the State is constructed with extraordinary solidity. It is hard to tell which of the two gives the particular character form and name. If we consider the prerogatives of the government, the royal veto, the power and strength which it lends in the relations with foreign powers, we feel as if the State

were monarchical. If we view the Church, which
with a royal pope at its head endeavors to effect a
national standard in matters of faith, as Catholicism
endeavors to effect general conformity, we stumble
on the theocratic element. If we survey the whole
public spirit, the conservative nature of its policy,
the character of those to whom the administration
is intrusted, the privileges, customs and habits of
the representatives of this people, the English State
appears essentially aristocratic. If we reflect that
the consent of the people is required for their own
taxation, the chief influence seems to reside in the
community at large. So, too, if we still further
examine the institutions and relations of society
in detail—the activity and independence of private
life, the decentralization of the administration, the
self-government of the people, the absence of bu-
reaucracy, the entire freedom of person and property, the system of the land defences, the rights of
meeting and of the press, everything seems to be
democratic. It is likewise pure democracy that the
chief power should reside in the Commons, and
that the people by controlling the crown through
its Parliament should assert its own sovereignty.
Yet no people speak less of their sovereign power
than the English, or have a more genuine loyalty
for their monarchy. No State depends more upon
the traditions of the past and no people insist more
on aristocratic conservatism. It is the Englishman's
boast. that his constitution is open to all progress,
and is plastic to the influence of every great idea,
every experience and every demand of necessity.

*English
Customs*

*Democ-
racy vs
Monarchy*

No one is more jealous than the Englishman of the safety of his person and property from the usurpations of the State; yet there is no State of modern times constructed more on the model of antiquity, where the individual lived for the State, and sacrificed to it his personal will and private interests. This gives an exclusive narrow self-interest and strictly national character to the English nation. Still, no people have proved themselves more capable of showing regard and forbearance toward foreign nations, even in their defeat. These reconciled contradictions, this varied unity and continued harmony resulting from the happy mixture in the character of the people and the external State institutions are the actual worth and merit of the English State policy, the source of its power and the pledge of its freedom. This compound nature is also the reason why it is theoretically difficult to comprehend and to do justice to this State and its institutions, and why, practically, it has remained without a true counterpart in spite of many copies.

This constitution, in truth, is not fit to be a formula for any other State. It may only serve as a model to a people of equally strong patriotic feeling, and desirous of making the same use of old and new institutions, a people capable of forming a constitution that would be in its nature and attributes the same, equal in worth to the English, yet most unlike it in form.

The English democracy in the time of the first Stuarts had already begun to turn their attention

toward emigration. They hoped that on the free
soil of America, unperplexed by monarchical and
aristocratic privileges, habits and power, they might
raise the edifice of a new State and a new Church
Colonial
Tendencies in their own simple style. Shortly after the time
when Spain had lost her influence in Europe by her
successive defeats in the wars with Germany, the
Netherlands, and England, a Teutonic element settled in the north of Spanish-America imbued with
the desire not to permit Spain and the Catholic
Church to rule absolutely in the New World.
Nowhere else were the habits and character of
Teutonic and Romanic culture in more striking
contrast than in the drama of the new life which
unfolded itself here.

In the vast tracts of the Spanish and Portuguese
colonies the old spirit of the Middle Ages was expressed in all its original barbarity and its degra-
Spanish
Conquests   dation of mankind. Spanish despotism with the
narrow spirit of its religion was here transplanted—
a ready-made hierarchy with all its external pomp
and inward crudeness, and in its train a feudal aristocracy bent on conquest, covetous and inhuman.
There mercantile industry and mental activity were
excluded, while conformity in Church and State,
under which both Indian and negro suffered, spread
over this part of the New World. The reverse took
place in the north. Since the beginning of the
Seventeenth Century people of the Teutonic races,
chiefly Germans, Dutch, Swedes, and English, the
latter of the Saxon blood, gathered here. They
were for the most part Protestants of the clearest

dye, notably **Puritans** and Quakers. No viceroy with monarchical institutions was admitted here. On the contrary a true republican spirit prevailed among the colonists, and not only among those who had emigrated without royal consent, but even with those who came provided with charters and accompanied by governors. The hierarchy never reached here, the English noble and the Flemish patrician only made feeble and short-lived attempts to transplant their institutions. The feudal usages and all the habits of the Middle Ages were behind them —the New Era with its intellectual growth, with its commercial industry, and with its equality of rights had sprung into being. The slow natural process of development into a national life lasting centuries was a matter of a few years here. Its independence permitted commerce closely to follow the primeval occupations—hunting, fishing and farming.

The emigrants had the close and exclusive spirit of Teutonic reserve which forbade them to form connections with the Indians, whom they regarded as being incapable of accepting humanity. Withal they were conscientious enough to purchase the land fit for their uses from the natives, instead of taking possession of the country as a grant from the Pope. In contrast to the conformity of the one dominion of Spanish-America, a varied world composed of numerous petty States grew up here, and its diversity was a singularly apt expression of the conditions of the south and the north before the emigration from Europe.

The Spaniards, coming from vast domains at

home, found great Indian States already established in Mexico and Peru. It was therefore absolutely necessary to overthrow these with an extensive colonial State in order to assert their authority.

The English in the north, who had come few in numbers and wide apart in time, found petty tribes of Indians scattered over the country—unconnected, weak in numbers and in power. The colonists were therefore quite free to follow their Teutonic bent,

European Prototypes

living apart in small varied communities. Thus Massachusetts became a theocracy on the pattern of Geneva; Maryland a feudal princedom; Carolina a realm of eight lordships with a landed aristocracy; Virginia an English province with high-church institutions; Rhode Island and Connecticut democracies; Pennsylvania a cosmopolitan Quaker republic, which in its commencement opened an asylum to the world; and New Amsterdam a Flemish town with a well-ordered patrician municipality. In their gen-

English Ascendency

eral development the States followed England. Unobserved in the beginning they formed their constitutions freely according to their demands. During the era of the English Commonwealth the spirit of democracy planted itself securely. Under the Restoration it suffered much injury and danger to self-government and property, with charters and privileges. After 1688 each separate State returned to its previous institutions. Throughout all these first varying fortunes of the colonies it may be remarked that freedom of action and democratic development continued to prosper. This can only be attributed to one cause—that those institutions which hinder the progress of the State and Church, the hierarchy and the aristocracy, did not reach them from Europe. They prospered exactly in proportion as the one remaining engine of oppression—Monarchy—found no occasion or opportunity to assert itself. That the republican spirit of the colonists would rebel against any free exercise of Monarchy, when they realized its inability to interfere with independence, was already prophesied by certain wise men at the beginning of the Eighteenth Century. The principles of the first emigrants, their customs and struggles, had for the first time firmly established democracy. The Puritans had fled from the tyranny of Church and State in Europe, impelled by principle. They came to America determined not to allow the home government to lay claim to the possessions they had paid for. They came, after the example of the Greek colonies, to maintain free and general intercourse with the mother country, but resolved to oppose every interference in their government and their religion. They resented any attempt at legislation by a distant Parliament to which they could send no representatives. In 1646 Massachusetts regarded her relations with England in the same light as the Hanseatic towns did theirs to the German empire, and this fundamental principle of independence increased more and more with the numbers and power of the colonists. The same spirit of democracy, which grew so rapidly in the State, entered also into the affairs of the Church, where, however, it moved slowly and not without hindrances. Necessity decided the former case, but the latter depended

Democratic Spirit

Growth of Independence

entirely on their education and culture. In some
few States, such as Carolina, New York, and Maryland under the philanthropic Lord Baltimore, all re-
ligions were tolerated from the beginning, although
equal privileges were not granted. Virginia still
required conformity to the High Church; even
amid the Puritans of Massachusetts Calvinistic intolerance excluded every other creed from the State
and persecuted the Baptists and Quakers by exile

Puritan
Intoler-
ance
and execution. Roger Williams, in accordance with
this principle, urged liberty of conscience in Massachusetts and a separation of Church from State matters. But he was obliged to flee, and in 1636 he
founded a small new society in Rhode Island on
the principles of entire liberty of conscience and the
uncontrolled power of the majority in civil rights.
This also became the constitution of Connecticut.
Principles and theories of political and ecclesiastical
freedom were here brought into practice in the government of a small community before they were
taught in the schools of philosophy in Europe.
It was prophesied that the democratic attempts to
obtain universal suffrage, a general elective fran-

Religious
Tolerance
chise, annual elections, entire religious freedom and
the Miltonic right of schism would be of but short
duration. But these institutions have not only maintained themselves here, but have spread from these
smallest of States over the whole Union. They superseded the aristocratic commencement of Carolina
and patrician New York, the high church of Virginia, the theocracy of Massachusetts and the monarchy throughout America. They have given laws

to a continent, and, dreaded for their moral influence, they stand in the background of every democratic struggle of Europe.

The purely Saxon, purely democratic constitution of the United States stands in direct antithesis to the Normanic-Saxon constitution of England. The Puritans when they emigrated brought with them ideas, more or less clearly defined, of the edifice of their constitution, and carried them into practice without hindrances. The last completion after the Declaration of Independence was only the fulfilment of the first thought. No antiquity, no tradition, no history or experience devised a plan for them or fettered them to existing materials. Aristocracy and hierarchy were left behind in Europe; the royal and parliamentary government of England was rejected. Common-sense and the natural instincts of the simplest consequence led here to the completion of a new edifice in a rising State, apart from all existing State organizations. They ventured, though with admirable prudence, on the great trial of extending it over an immense region, in spite of the prophecies which, in their small beginnings, promised them only a temporary success. It was not a question here how different classes might be brought into relationship with one another, and how all might enjoy equal rights. In the first outbreak of the Revolution, the Americans appealed to their charters and self-created institutions and endeavored to defend them as conceded rights, but, at the separation, they ceased to look for justification for their rebellion. Had they still urged their claim to ex-

The American Constitution

New World Ideas

isting relations, they would have had to begin by
acknowledgment of their chief relation to the mother
country, which they were on the point of exchang-
ing for independence. They scorned, therefore, to
demand rights and freedom which they claimed
natural and universal, and thus acted as much in
conformity with the earliest principles of Protestantism as with those of the latest theories, which
France had sent into the world a short time before
the rebellion of the colonies. The American Bill

The Bill of
Rights
of Rights in 1776 began with an acknowledgment
of the natural rights of man, of which no form of
government can deprive him, of his freedom and
independence, his claim to the enjoyment of life
and liberty, of the means for the acquisition of
property and wealth, and for the attainment of fortune and safety. The people were entitled to change
or depose any government which denied these universal rights to man, by which clause they justified
the separation. By the introduction of universal suffrage they pronounced the great democratic maxim
that the government is the legal expression of the
people's will. This did not produce a mixed consti-

Universal
Suffrage
tution composed of several parts united into one, as
in England, but a single symmetrical State-union of
the utmost simplicity. It is not the skilful administration of the many different elements which is the
boast of the American constitution, but the perfect
fulfilment of a logical sequence, deduced from one
single principle—freedom, or the right to obey only
the law, and equality—the duty of one and all to
obey the same law. There was, therefore, no neces-

sity to level ranks, power, pretensions, influence or privileges, as there only existed one society and one class from which all particular rights and privileges were abolished. Power, which, in the hands of the few, has often led to arbitrary rule, and, in the hands of the many, to privileges, was equally distributed as the right of all. One Blending of Classes right insures one common practice. The rich adopted the tone of the middle class, to which the poor aspired, and from whose customs and for whose convenience the law was actually made. Old and new institutions had not here to be reconciled with one another in the spirit of progression or conservatism. Everything in this State of the Future is new; everything is already in progress and built upon innovations. The picture of an ancient incorporated State, of a strict, exclusive nationality, is not presented to us, but a society originating from all parts of the world, with the greatest adaptability of government, of a cosmopolitan nature.

The North American Republic is not one great nation, but a federal union, in which each separate State strives to obtain the sovereign power, while within them again individuals claim the utmost independence of the government. The feeling of Political Individuality individuality, the characteristic feature of modern times and of Protestantism, has here maintained its rights. The State exists more for the individual than the individual for the State. The institutions of the State are in the service of personal liberty. The freedom of man is more important than his duties as citizen. The widest field upon which the claims of man and the claims of the State have contended, and yet always contend—the Church—is here entirely withdrawn from the State, and nothing remains as a ground on which to legislate, and concerning which the government and the individual can dispute, but general principles. The panorama of a new State, such as had never existed before, lies now unrolled before us after an interval of one hundred years.

A New State

This new State, by its astonishing achievements in fortune and power, has suddenly surpassed all others, and the boldest political ventures have succeeded, in spite of all sceptics. The government of the people, even when scattered over immeasurable tracts of country, has shown itself to be compatible with order and prosperity. An apparently improvised constitution is adapted to the maintenance of old, confirmed usages. The free exercise of religion goes with piety; the reverse of military pretensions with a warlike spirit. An ever-increasing population brought together by haphazard appears imbued with patriotism rooted in freedom. The general government is administered by officials and representatives, often chosen from the poorest classes, with comparative economy and thrift. The resulting prosperity, combined with the simplicity of the constitution, which is clear to the plainest understanding, has made a model of both State and Constitution which the discontented and lovers of freedom of all nations strive to emulate. The American Declaration of Independence in 1776 has become the creed of the liberalism of the world.

The Creed of Liberalism

After a compromise constitution had been established in England, and when the Declaration of Independence by the American colonies had been followed by a purely republican constitution in the
United States, both began to exercise an influence
across the sea upon the European continent and to
react upon the Romanic races. At the very period Results on
Europe
when the English colonies prepared for separation,
however, some new tendencies appeared in history,
which interrupted, magnified and involved the hitherto simple course of affairs.

Previous to this, war and peace both had been
largely a result of religious differences. Even when
the issue was one of national moment, or when it was
ostensibly a struggle for power between hostile States,
religious questions were still deeply involved in them.
This simple relation of the European people toward
one another, this long-lasting cause of dispute in
history, was lost in the wars which arose after the
independence of the English colonies in America.
The interests of commerce and territorial expansion
took the place of those of religion and dictated the New
Issues
laws and policy of States, settled the occasions of war
and revolutions and prescribed the articles of am-
nesties and treaties of peace. Religion likewise no
longer lay at the root of the political struggles in
America, but commercial and international principles, which were largely borrowed from abstract
philosophical theories. They proclaimed the advent of a new agent in politics, the influence of
Science and Literature.

This altered position of nations, these new and

potent forces in the history of the world, are the
first signs that the bitter hostility caused by religious differences and the political principles which
had exclusively belonged to either division of the
great European people, had lost their power. The
immediate consequence was, that as soon as the independence of America was established, the great
movement for freedom passed from there over to
France and tore down religious bigotry and despotism in the greatest of Romance races.

The March
of Free-
dom

During Spain's encounter with the Teutonic races,
the clash of Catholicism with Protestantism, France
had found herself, if not exactly in a central position, in a suspended state of balance between the
diverging tendencies which led to the hostility of
the north and south. It seemed as if it were her
vocation to prevent a lasting superiority of either
party, just as if the Teutonic and Gallic-Roman
elements of the race had alternately fought for it.
France felt the necessity to repress the overgrown
power of Spain, even if it had to be in league
with Protestant States; but as soon as England
grew to be a dangerous neighbor by this alliance,
France considered herself bound to return to her
connection with the Catholic powers. When
Charles V. drove the French out of Italy, the
House of Valois united with Landgraves Philip
and Maurice of Saxony against Spain. In the
Sixteenth Century, France joined Spain in an alliance against England, and three years later allied
herself with England against Spain. Henri IV. continued to keep on good terms with both the Protes-

The Bal-
ance of
France

tant and Catholic powers. The former changes recommenced under Richelieu, and while in league with England against Spain, he laid schemes with Spain and the Pope for an attack on England, and at the same time formed an alliance with Sweden against Spain and Austria. By this shifting policy, France French Vacillation had been frequently saved from Protestantism, as in the time of Maurice of Saxony and the period of Gustavus Adolphus, when Protestantism gained so much ground. But Protestantism was promptly suppressed by Louis XIV. when it ceased to be a source of danger and alarm. To the cause of freedom in France it has always been detrimental for her rulers to side with Spain or to follow the lead of Spanish policy, whereas her temporary alliances with England and Protestantism have proved beneficial, not less so in the times of Henri IV. than in those of Louis Philippe. This perpetual vacillation produced the reverse of constancy in the political and religious character of the people as in that Effects on the People of their government. Throughout the later history of France, the strangest discords occur in the principles of her government, in the administrative bodies of the State, and in the different factions either in politics or in literature. Absolutism had its democratic freaks, and Democracy its despotic propensities. Literature wavered between pagan free-thought and monkish bigotry. Poets praised republican virtues with a servile muse, Parliaments fluctuated between cringing flattery and vulgar uproars. The clergy preached to-day the divine right of princes and to-morrow the sovereignty of the people. The

Jesuits taught democratic principles in matters of State and despotism in those of dogma. This play

Latter-day
Influences of alternate extremes may be observed in all the relations of France down to the present day.

The prosperity of the colonies of the New World at the beginning of the Eighteenth Century caused a change in the condition of those States from which they had proceeded. Shipping was carried on far more extensively and underwent great improvements. Maritime commerce seemed to promise to become more lucrative than that by land. The connection of the two hemispheres multiplied human wants as well as the means of satisfying them; it increased the materials for industry and spread its happy results. Vast commercial relations were established to equalize demand and supply, superfluity and want. Industry and trade became sources of wealth to the middle class, and, therefore, a stimulus to individual exertion which had never before existed. They also became the sources of the nation's wealth, and, therefore, the first object to be considered in politics and government. This was

New World all the more the case, since, by the altered condition
Tendencies of the world, the growth of the States, and the complicated relations of all the affairs of life, the resources which formerly had provided for the exigencies of the government, such as crown-lands and land-taxes, sufficed as little now for the expenses of the State as the feudal military service for its defence. In this new aspect of affairs it became a question which nation would apply its skill and industry to the greatest advantage. France discov-

ered this later than all her neighbors, and roused herself, finally, under Richelieu and Louis XIV. Then she endeavored to make amends for her delay by improvements in her navy, by new commercial industry and by her attempts at colonization. An Awakening for France to warn.

The policy of the Spanish kings had always turned to an aggrandizement of power and dominion, and for this purpose they required the most unlimited authority and the disposal of all the resources of the State. This system of government, both at home and abroad, repressed the ancient love of freedom in the people. Those means from which other nations, in the altered condition of the world, derived their abiding strength, checked all intellectual and commercial activity. The Spanish settlements were made in the spirit of this despotic policy. They were conducted and regulated by the government. To add to her splendor, Spain took possession of enormous tracts of land, which the emigration of a thousand years could scarcely people. Grants of land were made only to native Spaniards, and the mother country exhausted her The Example of Spain, which was already weakened by the expulsion of the Moors and the Jews. The settlers looked for gold, for rapid gain, for indulgence, not for labor. Incitement to all active energy was stifled. Spanish commerce declined, as agriculture had long ago declined under the thraldom and privilege of class. With the failure of home profits, trade ceased or passed into the hands of strangers. With the

poverty of private individuals came the weakness of
the State, which was required to grant the convoy
of great fleets to private galleons laden with gold,
when it had not a ship for the defence of its coasts.
The situation of the colonies, the luxuriant world
of the tropics, which needed little human aid for
its productions, favored the indolent inclinations
of the Southern settler. Religious bigotry impeded
the growth of home rule and active independence
of mind. Even where it assumed an appearance of
humanity, it promoted only the material advantage of the foreigner, without avoiding the decline
of morals at home. Thus, because the inhuman
monopoly of the importation of black slaves into
the Spanish colonies was a scandal to the Catholic
Church, the trade was given over into the hands
of foreigners, and finally, by the Assiento of 1711,
resigned wholly to the English, who reaped from it
an immense profit both for their own commerce and
for that of their colonies.

Spanish Mistakes

With the Teutonic and democratic colonies all
this was reversed. Spain discovered the new world,
but the Teutonic race tilled its soil. Under them
everything conduced rather to the energy and culture of each member of the State than to the acquisition of territorial power. The State as such did
little for the colonization of America. The colonists took possession of only a few tracts of land for
their settlements. They were not like the lower
gentry which emigrated from Spain, but were the
middle class from the country and towns, a class
which was unknown in the Romanic States. Emi-

British Colonists Profit

grants from all the world were at liberty to settle down beside the Englishman. The greatest profit fell to the most industrious. Enjoyment was sought in labor. The climate and soil, which resembled that of the home they had abandoned, sharpened rather than blunted their exertions. The habits of the north, the vigorous spirit of Protestantism, the assiduity of the Teutonic races, everything contributed to favor great commercial activity at home New World and in the colonies. From it arose a degree of prosperity and political importance in the middle class of which history affords no previous example.

New World Activity

In the colonies, the French Jesuits in Canada performed wonders of conversion and martyrdom, but the planters of Louisiana did nothing which could be compared to the miracles performed by Anglo-Saxon activity. The French planter never exhibited the daring spirit of the Anglo-Saxon pioneer, who penetrated into the depths of the forest and conquered the wilderness for cultivation. Unlike the Spaniard in the South, he found no excuse for indolence in the relaxation of the tropics. The fault here was with the men, who were not accustomed to think and act for themselves in the free life of a community. In addition to this, the French settlers assumed a hostile attitude toward England from the commencement. The French settlers in North America surrounded the English colonial cities in the rear and on either side. They instigated the Indians to attack them, and, by a more rapid increase of their settlements, they hoped at some future time to advance from

Anglo-Saxon Daring

the rear upon their coasts. However, this prospect of gaining advantage over the English colonies by their superior position was soon frustrated by the indifference and incapacity for colonization of the French themselves. The first half-century of the

Colonial Impotence of Latin Race French settlement in Louisiana did not exhibit one-tenth part of the population nor of the results which were produced in that time in New England. This fact only stirred up more jealousy between France and England, which already derived too much nourishment in their religious differences, in their diverse origin and in the geographical proximity of the two countries.

This jealousy, which soon led to war, proved of material service in laying the foundation of freedom in North America. If the French settlers had succeeded in establishing themselves there in great numbers, the English would probably, from the dread of French rule, have consented to remain faithful to the mother country under any condition.

French Hostility Turned to Account As there was no hope of this, France conceived the thought of weakening England by a separation from her colonies; and they, as soon as they saw France change from an enemy into an ally, threw off their regard for the mother country and set themselves free—an aim they had kept in view ever since the parliamentary government in England laid its hand on them. England herself, by her foreign colonial policy, had given the chief pretext for this alliance with France and even with Spain of her rebellious colonies.

However the whole scheme and commercial

activity of the English colonies might differ from those originating with Romance races, yet the practice of the English government had essentially agreed with that of the latter. They all maintained that the mother country had the exclusive right to trade with the colonies, to subject them to a commercial code and to treat them as a means to their ends. Every other nation was debarred from trading with them; the foreign merchant was treated as a privateer. By this measure he became such, and the prize was allotted to him whose boldness and activity dared the most, and accordingly fell to the energetic Englishman. From the time of the Assiento, in 1711, the English wrought havoc on Spanish-American commerce by a shameless system of smuggling, for which the importation of the negro furnished a pretext. About the time of the conclusion of the thirty years' truce, the merchants urged upon the English government a war with Spain on the subject of the exclusive system of monopoly which they themselves practiced at home. England was opposed to Spain in the great naval expeditions against Carthagena and Panama, in 1741 and 1742, the object of which was the separation of Mexico and Peru from the mother country, as Spain had once opposed England in the time of the Invincible Armada. Both armaments came to a like inglorious end. The world already trembled before the naval power of England, and France consulted with Spain on a compensation by the English colonies, even at the risk of her own. The great naval war of 1755 confirmed this project

Narrow Colonial Spirit

English Privateering

in the eyes of France even more than in those of Spain. France was punished for it by the loss

The Loss of Canada of Canada and of her navy. The English influence during that period was rising in the East Indies, and England appeared as much resolved to assert her supremacy at sea, as Spain had once been to assert hers on land. In pursuance of these projects, Parliament was as despotic as any monarchy in its measures both at home and abroad. England contended against the republican movements in her colonies with the same means that an absolute monarchy might have used. The importation of negroes was encouraged to diminish the numbers of dangerous white freemen. No doubts were entertained concerning Canada, as the presence of the French there kept up the loyalty of the colonies to the mother country. But when the Americans had already succeeded in laying the plan for a

British Encroach- ments federal constitution which plainly announced their views of a possible independence, and when fear of the French after the wars of 1755 could no longer restrain them, Parliament, instead of trying to attach them by offering conciliatory measures, adopted a still more oppressive line of conduct than that which had already excited the discontent of the colonists. The British Parliament, in which the Americans were not represented, and which was even ignorant of their affairs, since the revolution of 1688 had gradually invested itself with supreme authority over the colonies and their usages. It insisted that the final decision in matters of jurisdiction must be referred to England. The colonies were treated only as a commercial establishment. Commerce among themselves or with foreign nations was forbidden, and all industry was suppressed. This excited so much discontent about the middle of the Eighteenth Century that wise men prophesied the approaching separation. But no one as yet had conceived the idea of imposing a tax upon the colonies. In 1764, when this innovation was first attempted in the form of a stamp tax, systematic resistance began. The first open rupture was occasioned by a tax on tea. The Colonial Congress of 1774 commenced by a Declaration of Rights, in which they announced their intention of maintaining all existing relations, and in which they rehearsed and vindicated their old privileges, following the example of the English in their declaration of rights to William III. Yet they shrank from the name of rebellion. But as oppression grew regardless, so also grew the desire for independence in the colonies. Formal independence was declared in 1776. The injustice of decrees levied to satisfy the covetous desires of the mother country had irritated the Americans; the folly of wavering resolutions had inspired them with courage; the last brutal procedure, which Fox called the scalping tomahawk measure, ended all hesitation. The year 1782 gave the colonies their independence. France had declared war on England in 1778—all the naval forces in the West failed England, and those of the East disputed her usurped rights of the sea. But there was a considerable difference in the position of England at that time compared with former rulers

[margin note: Colonial Taxes]

[margin note: American Independence]

of the world under similar circumstances. The

British
Sympathy greatest men of the English Parliament had contin-
ually been opposed to the taxation of the colonies
for the benefit of the English treasury—they had
rejoiced in the insurrection and prophesied its victories. Parliament early adopted their views and
refused to prolong the war indefinitely as the Spaniards had done in the Netherlands. England was
no more weakened by the loss of her colonies, which
gave so much satisfaction to France, than she was
by the closing of the Continent under Napoleon.
On the contrary, the full development of her internal
strength and her judicial administration now really
began. That to which she chiefly owed the greatness of her commerce, and the power it communicated to her government—the active energy of the
people—no war could destroy. This was strengthened indeed by the greater freedom of the State and
the now untrammelled trade with North America.

Old Colo-
nialSystem
condemned The result of it was the sentence of doom on the old
colonial system. The separation of the Spanish
colonies was a natural sequence to the liberation
of North America. The patent errors of the prevailing commercial system were clearly demonstrated and denounced by all. The first great path
to free commercial intercourse was opened, which
was followed by succeeding generations. A new
road had been opened to political freedom, for
which new possibilities arose in the foundation of
the new American States.

The foreign aid of France had helped to complete
the independence of the United States, a turn of

affairs which would not have been thought possible during the reign of Louis XIV. The influence of the intellectual movement which had taken place in France since that time added to the internal State development which the new federal government adopted. These two facts led to the entire overthrow of the old French constitution.

The theories of Rousseau were first brought into practice in the American constitution as the principles of a new code of politics. The combination of new theories of government with their realization after the independence of the American colonies accelerated the reaction of the movements for freedom in the Old World upon these results. When, in the Sixteenth Century, France was obliged to strengthen herself to the utmost possible unity, on account of the menacing power of Spain, so now, when she was exposed to similar dangers during the Revolution, she was obliged to apply the same policy for her preservation. Both the moderate constitutional monarchy of Louis XVI., and the Dictatorship, showed themselves either unwilling or unable to meet the alarming confederacy of European princes. The Reign of Terror was first needed to collect the whole effective force of the country. Later on, the universal empire and military despotism were required to fight the great nations of the east with their own weapons.

The emancipation of all those that are oppressed and suffering is the vocation of the Nineteenth Century. The force of this idea has been victorious over mighty interests and deeply-rooted institutions, which may be perceived in the aboli-

Influence on France

French Regeneration

Ethical Purpose

tion of serfdom and villanage in Europe and in the liberation of slaves in America. This is one of the greatest features of the time. The strength and belief of conviction, the power of thought, the force of resolution, a clear view of the object pursued, endurance and self-sacrifice, are all enlisted on the side of the people, and give this historical movement the character of Providence which cannot be resisted.

It is this character we recognize in all the movements of the age, even those not appearing periodically. The history we propose to narrate was divided into three movements, which appear to be impelled by a higher power, and in turn have shaken a great part of the world to its foundation. They follow one another almost in geometric progression. The same progression which we have observed in time, people and country may be observed also in the direction of the movement itself. The course of freedom, as we have seen since the Reformation, has been chiefly in the regions of the north among Teutonic races until it reached America, where it found its natural limits. From that time it moved

Modern Movements

back toward the east. Its landing in France was difficult to effect; the whole of the east of Europe and even the free west opposed the new importation —but it secured its first footing. The movements of the twenties passed over from South America to Spain, from Italy to Greece, in regular line toward the east. The July revolution procured soil for freedom in France, and it breathed again in Spain, in Belgium, and in Old England—it endeavored even to reach Poland. In the year 1848 the Continent was shaken to its centre, and the revolution penetrated the stronghold of Conservative principle, even as far as Prussia and the Balkans. In this history we shall above all see the hand of Providence in these movements.

The resources of the United States, sufficient for their own supply, and their refusing all other nations the right of occupation in America as proclaimed in the famous Monroe Doctrine, will in time TheMonroe Doctrine restrict the amount of emigration from Europe, and limit the commerce of the West. In an equal proportion the increasing decay of the East will invite to a renewal of the old commerce and civilization of Asia.

To effect this, the freedom of the continental nations of Europe is required, if the advantages which these prospects open are not to be lost to those whom they most concern. This eastern course of the principle of political freedom, which history seems so confidently to predict, will be fulfilled.

A HISTORY

OF

THE NINETEENTH CENTURY

YEARS OF FORECAST

A T THE END of the Eighteenth Century the civilized world, though distracted with wars and revolutions, found time to spare for quarrels about the beginning of the new century. Two parties disputed the question then, as they did a hundred years later. One held that the Nineteenth Century began with January 1, 1800, the other maintained that it would not begin until after the last day of that year. Those that clung to the first view were known as the "Ninety-niners" —chief among whom were the German poets Goethe, Schiller, and Jean Paul Richter. The philosophers of the so-called Age of Reason disputed this view almost to a man. Thus, the savants of the French Academy put themselves on record in opposition to this theory, as did the ablest scholars of England. On New Year's Day, 1800, even the London "Times" thundered against the heresy of "Ninety-nine." At best this was but an academic discussion of mere momentary interest amid the startling events that crowded one upon another in those days.

Death of
Washing-
ton   In the New World the revolutionary period came
to an end with the death of its master spirit, George
Washington. In his farewell address, issued when
he declined the Presidency for a third term, Washington had left a solemn legacy to his countrymen
to avoid foreign entanglements, holding it to be
"the true American policy to steer clear of permanent alliances with any portion of the foreign
world." In pursuance of this policy, Washington
had not hesitated to break with France. When the
new French Republic became embroiled in war with
England, he issued a proclamation of neutrality.
Washington's efforts, while productive of immediate evil, wrought ultimate good. They saved the
young American Republic from entering into a long
and costly war at a time when his country's greatest
need was peace and the establishment of a solid
national credit.

Then began the wonderful development of the
western prairies, while a new impulse to industry
and commerce in the Southern States was given by
Whitney's invention of the cotton gin. By the
time the capital of the nation was transferred from
American
Develop-
ment   Philadelphia to the city of Washington, the American people were well started on the way to prosperity.

Upon Washington's successor, John Adams, fell
the immediate brunt of the new American policy.
The first prospect was war with France. Throughout the European wars, brought forth by the French
Revolution, the United States were in the position
of a feeble neutral between aggressive belligerents.

Whatever turn the tide of war might take, American commerce was sure to suffer. Jay's treaty with Jay's Treaty Great Britain had brought some amelioration by providing for a commission to pass upon claims of American citizens for loss or damage sustained by reason of the illegal capture or condemnation of their vessels. The concessions obtained from England only provoked the privateers of France to further outrages. The American commissioners sent to France were not received by the Directory. At last they reported that immunity from attack could only be bought with money. President Adams, substituting the letters X Y Z for the names of the French agents, sent a full report of their demands to Congress. The people of the United States were at once aroused, and acting upon Pinckney's passionate declaration, "Millions for defence, not one cent for tribute!" forthwith armed for war. A new navy department and marine corps were created, Maritime War with twelve frigates were fitted out, and letters of marque France granted to privateers. Altogether a navy of thirty-eight stanch vessels was called into being. "Hail Columbia" became the popular song of the day.

The first conflicts were in West Indian waters. Captain Decatur, commanding the "Delaware," captured the French privateering schooner "Croyable." Renamed as the "Retaliation," she was presently recaptured by the French. In February, 1799, the American frigate "Constellation," commanded by Captain Truxtun, near the island of Nevis, defeated and captured the French man-of-war "Insurgente." David Porter, then a midshipman, with eleven

American seamen brought in the prize, single-
handed. The American squadron in the West
Indies, while cruising for French prizes, improved

the occasion by suppressing the piracies of the
troublesome picaroons of the West Indies. Nearly
a year later, on February 3, 1800, Captain Truxtun
added to his laurels and those of the "Constellation"
by beating the French frigate "Vengeance" to a
standstill off the island of Guadeloupe. Previous
to this, Captain Little of the "Boston" had defeated
and captured the French corvette-of-war "Berceau."
In all, some ninety French vessels, carrying altogether more than seven hundred guns, were captured during the war, and a great number of American ships were retaken. By the close of 1800 the
purposes of the war had been accomplished. Bonaparte, who had just come into power, willingly
granted redress to the United States.

Napoleon Bonaparte had weightier problems on
his mind than the prosecution of a harassing guerilla warfare on water against a distant race of sailors. For his own part, Bonaparte had learned his
first bitter lessons of the sea when the French fleet
of seventeen vessels that had carried his army to
Egypt was destroyed by Nelson in the battle of the

Nile, on the first day of August, 1798. Another
French fleet of nine vessels, attempting to reach the
coast of Ireland early in September of the same year,
likewise fell into the hands of the British. Ruinous
as these strokes of war were to the French in Egypt,
who thus found themselves cut off from all succor,
General Bonaparte pursued his conquest of Egypt.

After defeating the Mameluke horsemen under the shadow of the Pyramids, he marched into Syria, stormed Jaffa, and pushed on to St. Jean d'Acre, after massacring his prisoners. Here again English ships under Sydney Smith spoiled his plans. After a siege of two months, during which the French succeeded in beating off an overwhelming number of Turks that came to the relief of Acre, Bonaparte had to retire baffled from the ruined walls of the ancient stronghold. This ended his project for the subjugation of the Orient. Years afterward he confessed that Sir Sydney's defence of Acre had made him miss his destiny. For Bonaparte, further stay in Egypt was fruitless. His brilliant defeat of the Turks in the second battle of Aboukir did not change the situation. Before this battle, General Bonaparte had received urgent tidings from his brothers in France. Then and there he resolved to return to Europe. Leaving his army in the lurch at Cairo, under the command of the brilliant Klèber, he embarked secretly at Alexandria on October 6, 1799, and made a run for France. Pursued by British cruisers and beaten about by storms, the ship that bore him finally landed him at Saint Raphau, near Fréjus, after a voyage of thirty-six days.

During Bonaparte's absence, disaster threatened the young French Republic. Russia, Austria and England were leagued against her. In Italy the Russian general, Suvaroff, had beaten the French in a series of brilliant battles. In the final battle of Novi, General Joubert, one of the most promis-

Battle of Pyramids

Battle of Aboukir

ing of French generals, had fallen at the head of his troops. The so-called Parthenopean republic of Italy fell with him. Less decisive campaigns

Weakness of French Government

were waged in Switzerland and Holland where the French generals, Masséna and Brune, succeeded in holding their own against an English and Russian army under the Duke of York. The varying issues of so many campaigns had their serious effect on the political fortunes of the men who composed the Directoire government in France. They were all civilians and were accordingly disliked by the army. Internal dissensions leading to frequent overturns of the Cabinet had further weakened their hold on the people. All France yearned for a strong man.

About this time came the reports of General Bonaparte's victories at Mount Tabor and Aboukir, together with a false account of the fall of St. Jean d'Acre. France went into frenzies of delight. Political agitators, instigated by Napoleon's brothers, Joseph and Lucien, inveighed against Bonaparte's continued "exile," and petitions were made to the Council of Five Hundred to revoke the successful general's "deportation." Now came the news that General Bonaparte had landed on the

Bonaparte Returns to France

coast of Provence. It seemed like a miracle. "I was sitting that day," wrote Béranger in his autobiography, "in our reading-room, with thirty or forty persons. Suddenly the news was brought in that Bonaparte had returned from Egypt. At the words every man in the room started to his feet and burst into one long shout of joy."

From the moment Bonaparte set foot on the soil

of France he was her master. As he flew from
Fréjus to Paris by means of fast relay stages, all
the countryside welcomed him with open arms. In
Lyons they gave a hastily prepared play in his
honor, entitled "L'Héros d'Egypte." Arrived in
Paris, Bonaparte's first visit was to Gohier, the Welcome
in Paris
newly elected president of the Directory, an intimate
friend of Josephine Bonaparte, his wife. The next
day the Directory received the young general in
state and exonerated him from blame for abandoning his army in Egypt. Siéyès, the strongest member of the Directory, at once went over to the new-
comer, and himself prepared the *coup d'état* which
was to drive his fellow directors from office. Bonaparte first fought shy of him, but presently came to
terms. It was arranged that a Triumvirate should
be formed with Napoleon Bonaparte at the head.
The details of the plot were intrusted to Napoleon's
brother Lucien, now president of the Council of
Five Hundred, aided by Talleyrand, Fouché, and
the generals Murat and Lannes.

On the morning of November 9, or the 18th Bru- The 18th
Brumaire
maire according to the revolutionary calendar, a
crowd of generals and officers met at Napoleon's
house. At the same time certain members of the
Council held an early meeting of the Assembly and
passed a decree giving General Bonaparte command of all the troops in Paris. They then adjourned the Council to St. Cloud outside of Paris.
General Bonaparte, escorted by his military
friends, at once took charge of the troops that
had been adroitly stationed at the various com-

manding points of the city. The new decree was read aloud and he was acclaimed as chief by the host of officers who brandished their swords before him. Those of the directors who were in the plot resigned, and the others were put under arrest. When the deputies met on the next day in St. Cloud, they wasted their time by administering new oaths of allegiance to each member of the Assembly. Lucien Bonaparte addressed them from the President's chair until Napoleon appeared upon the scene. The Council of Ancients received the dictator in silence. When he entered the Chamber of Five Hundred he was greeted with a roar of fury. Some deputies tried to drag Lucien from his chair while others surged toward Napoleon. Then he beckoned to his soldiers, and General Murat ordered the grenadiers to fix their bayonets. The deputies took to their heels and the hall was cleared. At midnight Bonaparte, with the two former directors, Ducos and Siéyès, took the oath of office as consuls, their joint consulate to last three years.

The Coup d'Etat

Bonaparte, now barely thirty-one years old, speedily made himself absolute master. His fellow consuls were such only in name. When the Abbé Siéyès drafted a constitution with certain terms which might have acted as a check on the First Consul, Napoleon brushed the flimsy fabric away with a stroke of the pen. "Was there ever anything so ridiculous?" he exclaimed. "What man of spirit would consent to hold such a post?" As Siéyès said, after one of their first meetings, "Behold, gentlemen, we have a master. He means to

Bonaparte First Consul

do everything; he knows how to do everything, and he has power to do everything."

In the new French Constitution of 1799, as con- _{Constitu-} ceived by Siéyès and amended by Napoleon, all executive, administrative and judicial powers were conferred on the First Consul as head of the State. A system of centralization came into force which has remained in France to the present day. Its basis was universal suffrage, carefully pruned by letting the power from above select its appointees from the host of candidates chosen by popular vote. All governing and judicial officers were appointed, with all their subordinates, by the central government, and were directly responsible to it. These officers were divided into ranks as strict and absolute as those of the army. In its rational order, regularity of function and apparent stability, the new government was a vast improvement on the old, and could not fail to confer great and rapid benefits upon disordered France. It was a working government from the start, and its work was accomplished so smoothly and thoroughly that it relieved the common people from all need of taking a share in it. On December 15, the new Constitution was offered to the French people for acceptance or rejection with this famous concluding phrase: "Citizens, the Revolution is fixed to the principles which commenced it. It is finished." The new harness was accepted by a popular plebiscite of more than 3,000,000 yeas against 1,567 nays. Thus France passed from a distinctly democratic government to the most absolute rule yet imposed upon her.

So rapidly was popular government relinquished that within a year no one raised a hand when the First Consul quietly removed the very authors of the new instrument, his fellow consuls, Siéyès and Ducos, and appointed Cambacérès and Lebrun in their place. By means of life-senatorships the former consuls were paid to sink into instant obscurity. To Siéyès, the covetous abbé of the Revolution, the hereditary estate of Crosne was granted in addition.

Bonaparte appoints new Consuls

In the words of a contemporary epigram—

"Siéyès à Bonaparte a fait présent du trone
Sous son pompeux débris croyant l'ensevelir.
Bonaparte à Siéyès a fait présent du Crosne
Pour le payer et l'avilir." [1]

Corvisart

When Bonaparte selected Dr. Corvisart for his physician he little knew that he thereby gave a new impetus to the modern science of medicine. Dr. Corvisart somewhat surprised the First Consul by tapping his chest by way of examination. With characteristic shrewdness, Bonaparte recognized the advantage of scientific test over guesswork, and engaged Corvisart to be his regular adviser.

For fifteen years Jean Nicolas de Corvisart had practiced chest tapping, getting little but abuse from his fellow practitioners, but now the new method came into instant vogue. Thus was laid the foundation of modern physical diagnosis in medicine.

---

[1] "Siéyès to Bonaparte made a present of a throne
Thinking to raise himself upon its stool.
Bonaparte to Siéyès made a present of Crône,
Thus the priest was paid and made a fool."

1800

BONAPARTE'S first acts were conciliatory. Bonaparte's He drew around him the leaders of all parties Conciliatory Acts and men of high talents: if they showed themselves submissive they were rewarded with public honors. Thus he honored Volta, the inventor of the new voltaic pile, and La Place, the great astronomer. Volta, La Gaudin, the greatest financier of France, was intrusted with the public moneys, and, encouraged by Napoleon, founded the Bank of France. Tronchet and two of the most eminent lawyers of the Revolution were appointed at the head of a commission to codify the laws. Aided by Napoleon they drew up an admirable civil code which was afterward known as the "Code Napoleon." It was the first The "Code Napoleon" working code effected in France, and has stood as a standard of its kind throughout western Europe and the Latin countries since its adoption.

Equally well calculated was the First Consul's indulgence for the ancient enemies of the Revolution—the Royalists and the Clergy. Thus he restored the freedom of religious worship. All those emigrants who had not actually borne arms against their country were invited to return. More than Return of the Emigrants 150,000, most of whom were priests, responded. Bonaparte in person went to the Temple Prison to set the political prisoners free. In those early days of his rule great moderation was also used with the Vendean nobles and Breton peasants who had risen in arms against the Revolutionary government. A Proclamation of Amnesty for those who laid down their arms was issued on Christmas Day.

Peace Overtures

On the same day Napoleon, with his own hand, wrote courteous letters to the King of England and to the Emperors of Germany and Russia. Diplomatic steps were also taken to conciliate the King of Prussia and the Pope.

In his letter to George III. of England, Napoleon asked: "Are there no means of coming to an understanding?" The rest of the letter was given over to praises of peace.

Paul I. of Russia Won

The only monarch who gave a willing ear to Napoleon's offers of friendship was Paul, the Czar of Russia. This eccentric ruler publicly drank to the health of Consul Bonaparte and surrounded himself with portraits of the successful general. Suvarov, the Russian general who had won such signal victories over the French, was sent into disgrace. The Czar's friendship for the exiled Bourbon prince, Louis XVIII., and for his ally, England, became lukewarm and then cold.

The Austrian government contented itself with politely declining to entertain Napoleon's overtures to the German Emperor. When the Austrian ambassador ascertained that Napoleon had no intention of restoring the territory yielded by Austria in the recent treaty of Campo Formio, the imperial government at Vienna begged to be excused on the plea that it could not negotiate peace without consulting its allies.

England, under the guidance of the younger Pitt, **England's Reply** bluntly rejected all offers and avowed its intention to continue the war until the Bourbons should be restored to the throne of France. It was a curious State paper which Lord Grenville transmitted to Count Talleyrand, Napoleon's Minister for Foreign Affairs:

"DOWNING STREET, *January* 4, 1800

"SIR—I have received and laid before the King the two letters which you have transmitted to me. His Majesty, seeing no reason to depart from those forms which have long been established in Europe for transacting business with foreign States, has commanded me to return in his name the official answer which I send you herewith. I have the honor to be, with high consideration, sir, your most obedient, humble servant, GRENVILLE."

The letter itself recited that "the best and most natural pledge of the reality and permanence of peace would be the restoration of that line of princes which for so many centuries have maintained the French nation in prosperity at home and in consideration and respect abroad. Such an event would have at once removed, and will at any time remove, all obstacles in the way of peace."

Great Britain's curt reply was like a blow in the **Effect on France** face to France. Frenchmen of all parties burned to avenge the insult. At one stroke Napoleon had all France arrayed behind him. The cause of the Royalists waned from that day. In January their leaders, De Chatillon and d'Antichamp, signed conventions of peace with General Hédrouville on the Loire. By the middle of February followed the submission of the Royalist Chouans of Brittany and Normandy. Other chiefs in the Vendée were beaten by General Brune. The Prince of Condé entered British service. The remaining rebels were proclaimed as outlaws, and a price was set on the heads of the leaders. Count Louis de Flotte, who was taken alive, was shot by Napoleon's orders. The rank and file were quickly enrolled in the army and sent away to the frontiers.

Bonaparte enters the Tuileries Napoleon celebrated his complete suppression of the Royalists by installing himself in the former royal palace of the Tuileries. To veil the significance of this step, his first entry into the Tuileries was made on the occasion of an imposing memorial service in honor of the death of Washington. The speaker of the day drew a comparison between Washington and Bonaparte, giving the preference to the latter. In obedience to Napoleon's orders no mention whatever was made of Washington's brother-in-arms, Lafayette.

The Egyptian Fiasco Relieved of internal dangers, the First Consul was able to turn his attention to those outside of France. Disquieting news was not lacking. By an irony of fate General Klèber's indignant remonstrance to the Directory against the treatment meted out to him by General Bonaparte fell into the hands of the First Consul. Napoleon was the more annoyed at Klèber's complaints as he knew them to be true. He, too, while in Egypt, had written to the Directory that

unless reinforcement reached him he would be compelled to sue for peace. Now he found himself at a
loss how to avert the sure disaster impending over
his ambitious projects in the East and over those
that had followed him to Egypt to execute them.
His relief expedition was bottled up by the British
fleet before Brest. Instead of reinforcements Napoleon despatched a letter to Klèber assuring him of
his full confidence, and therewith left him to his fate.

One of General Klèber's appeals for help had
fallen into the hands of the English. It encouraged
them to repudiate the previous agreement to let the
French evacuate Egypt unmolested. On January
18, Lord Keith, commanding the British fleet in
Egypt, called upon General Klèber for an unconditional surrender. The French general communicated the text of the British demands to his troops
and gave out this rally: "Soldiers, such insults can
only be avenged by a victory. Forward!" The
French, early next morning, fell upon the sixty
thousand Turkish soldiers encamped on the ruins
of Heliopolis and completely routed them. Cairo
was recaptured. While strengthening the French
position in Cairo, General Klèber was assassinated
by an Arab cutthroat. The command fell upon an
incapable subordinate, General Menou. From that
time the evacuation of Egypt by France became
inevitable.

Battle of Heliopolis

In the meanwhile the war between Austria and
France was reopened. To provide for it the consuls
revived the Revolutionary measure of general con-
scription. Every male citizen over the age of eigh-

War with Austria

teen and under the age of sixty was called into the army. A reserve corps of 60,000 recruits was thus raised and placed under the command of the First Consul. Through his foreign agents Napoleon levied tribute from Genoa and Hamburg, and tried to force loans from Holland and Portugal on the security of their own jeopardized territory. By the spring of 1800 France was ready to strike.

Toward the end of April a French army under Moreau crossed the Rhine and seized the town of Freiburg. A series of bloody fights followed. The plan for opening the campaign, as arranged between Moreau and Napoleon, was to make a feint against the corps of Keinmayer and the Austrian right; and, having thus drawn Kray's attention to that quarter, to concentrate the French centre and left upon the imperial centre, break through the Austrian line, cut off their communication with the Tyrol and Italy, and force them to the banks of the Danube. On May 3, General Moreau defeated the Austrians and Germans under Kray at Engen, near the falls of Schaffhausen. Nearly 20,000 men fell on both sides. On May 5, the Austrians and Bavarians, five miles from there, were beaten in another battle at Moeskirch. They lost 7,000 killed and wounded, 1,500 prisoners, and a part of their stores. On May 9, the loss of a third battle at Biberach near Ulm cost Kray 4,000 men and all his stores. On May 11, the French generals Lecourbe and Ney took the small town of Memmingen after a fierce assault, in which some 5,000 fell on either side. The Austrians, having suffered four bloody

Margin notes: Moreau seizes Freiburg — Engen — Moeskirch — Biberach — Memmingen

reverses within eight days, fell back on Ulm. After
a short respite this city was wrested from them by
the French, who swam the river and treated them
to another bloody fight at Hochstaedt on the famous ^{Battle of} Battle of Hoch-staedt
old battlefield of Blenheim. Five thousand pris-
oners and twenty cannon were surrendered to the
French.

During this time General Masséna, who had
fought so well in Switzerland, had taken charge
of the French army in Italy and was hemmed in Siege of Genoa
at Genoa. Napoleon, instead of taking measures
to relieve the garrison by sending an army along the
coastwise roads on which he had won such successes
before, determined to deliver a counter stroke in the
rear of the Austrian army. This could only be
done by crossing the Alps.

Leaving the government in Paris to his colleagues
he took charge of the new army of the reserve and
manœuvred with it in various directions. He deceived Masséna as well as the Austrians. All
thought that he would surely descend upon Genoa.
The Austrians accordingly drove the French back
upon Genoa, and its harbor was blockaded by an
English fleet.

In the third week of May, after Marescot and his
engineers had prepared the way, Bonaparte sud- Napoleon crosses the Alps
denly took the main body of his army over the
Great St. Bernard Pass, while smaller detachments
crossed over the passes of the Little St. Bernard,
Simplon, St. Gotthard, Mont Cenis and Mont
Genevre. The march, though toilsome, presented
no extraordinary difficulties, till the leading column

arrived at St. Pierre: but from that village to the summit it was painful and laborious in the highest degree. A hundred men were harnessed to each gun, incased in a hollow log, and they were soon relieved.

Ford of St.
Bard

The worst obstacle encountered was at the mountain ford of St. Bard, which commanded the only passable road. Here the men had to pass in single file over a goat path high above the fort. The whole passage of the Alps was accomplished in four days without any serious mishap or confusion. This has always been accounted one of the most brilliant military feats. of modern times, surpassing the ancient Alpine exploits of Hannibal and Julius Cæsar.

The advance guard of the French army poured down into the plains of Piedmont before the Austrians could dispute their entrance into Italy. Old General Mélas, who had pursued a French division to Nice, hurried to Turin with a few thousand Austrians. From Turin he sent word to General Ott, whom he had left before the walls of Genoa, to raise the siege of that city and come to his support with all his men. Ott could not tear himself away from

Fall of
Genoa

so sure a prey. Before Masséna struck his flag on June 5, fifteen thousand of the people within the walls of Genoa had died of hunger. Masséna's stubborn resistance served the purpose of keeping the Austrian forces divided. It cost them nearly as dear as a defeat.

Napoleon, instead of marching on Genoa, as was still expected of him, turned to the east and thrust himself between the Austrians and their strongholds in the rear. Lannes defeated one Austrian force at Montebello. Murat took care of another. Nothing Battle of
Montebello remained for Melas but to escape to Genoa or make a bold break through the French lines. The arrival of Ott's forces, at last, making his numbers slightly superior to those of Napoleon, encouraged the aged Austrian leader to stake all on a pitched battle.

On the 12th of June Napoleon advanced westward from Milan and Piacenza, through Stradella. So anxious was he lest Melas should make good his escape that he detached a division of 6,000 under his special favorite Desaix, who had just arrived from Egypt with his aides-de-camp, Savary and Rapp. They were to head off any possible movement toward Genoa. Early next morning the Austrians came forth from Alessandria and attacked the French at Marengo. Their onslaught was so impetu- Marengo ous that it carried all before it. At the end of seven hours' fighting the French forces were in full retreat. Tired out, the aged Austrian general rode back into Alessandria to despatch tidings of his victory. The pursuit of the French was left to General Zach.

Far in the distance, nearly twenty miles away, Desaix's division had halted at the first sound of the cannon. As the distant booming increased, Desaix turned his column and countermarched for Alessandria, on the double quick. He had covered half the stretch when he was met by a despatch rider from Napoleon summoning him to the relief. Further couriers urged him to the utmost haste. At last his panting vanguard arrived upon the battlefield at sunset, only in time to meet their retreating comrades.

Desaix galloped up to his commander and said:

"I see that the battle is lost. I am afraid I can do no more for you than to secure your retreat."

"Not so," replied Napoleon. "Charge with your column! The disordered troops will rally in your rear."

Such was Napoleon's own version in after years. Others, at the time, said that Desaix on his own motion offered to retrieve the fallen fortunes of his chief.

Whatever he may have said, Desaix at once placed himself at the head of his first two half-brigades and charged into the victorious Austrians.

Death of Desaix He was shot through the heart, but his men charged on. At this moment Colonel Kellerman, with eight hundred French dragoons who had halted behind a wood, dashed furiously into the Austrian flank as it swept forward. The Austrians wavered and broke. Desaix's main body and rearguard fell upon them. French detachments from all sides returned to the fray. Melas' victory turned into defeat for Zach. He surrendered with 5,000 Hungarians.

Melas was so upset by the unexpected reverse that **Armistice with Austria** he sued for an armistice under humiliating terms. All Austrian fortresses in Northern Italy west of the Mincio were abandoned to the French. After the battle Napoleon wrote: "All the chances of success were with the Austrian army." Referring to Desaix he said, "Victory at such a price is dear."

To Kellerman he said curtly, "You made a good charge." In Paris, French consols rose from 29 to 35 points. Before the 18th Brumaire they had stood at 11. Napoleon returned to Paris.

The Austrian people were dismayed at the disastrous turn taken by their war with France. But the Ministry of Thugut stood firm. On the day the news of Marengo reached Vienna, Thugut in a formal treaty accepted England's offer of a money-subsidy to prolong the war. Yet, in deference to public clamor, and to gain time, Count St. Julien was sent as an envoy to Paris to ascertain the French terms for peace. They tried to patch up a naval armistice with England, but the negotiations fell through. In the middle of September, the garrison of Malta, having been entirely reduced by famine, capitulated, on condition of being sent to France and not serving again until regularly exchanged. The noble fortress, with its unrivalled harbor and impregnable walls, was permanently annexed to the British dominions. The English also made themselves masters, in the course of this year, of Surinam, Berbice, St. Eustache and Demerara, Dutch settlements in the West Indies and on the mainland adjoining them. The Austrian emperor finally was constrained to apply for an extension of the armistice on land. For this concession he had to yield Munich and Ingolstadt to the French in Bavaria. In the end Count St. Julien's arrangements were repudiated. The gain in time was turned to no material advantage by the Austrians. In all, they had 230,000 soldiers in the field. The French maintained five

Capitulation of Malta

Dutch Losses

strong armies, numbering altogether 250,000 men.
They controlled the Rhine, Alps, Upper Danube
and the Po. The portfolio of the French war department was placed in the hands of Carnot. Discontent at this state of affairs grew so acute in
Hungary and Austria that the Thugut Ministry
had to resign.

Thugut
Ministry
Resigns

In the month of November, Napoleon announced
the conclusion of the armistice, and on the 28th of
that month both parties were prepared to fight.

Archduke Johann, a youth of eighteen, now took
command of the Austrian army in the valley of the
Inn. Moreau held the high plateau of Munich and
the banks of the Isar. The young archduke had a
pet plan of surrounding the French and cutting off
their supplies. As soon as the armistice expired,
on the third day of December, during a heavy fall
of snow, he manœuvred his army into the rough
country around Hohenlinden. Moreau waited until
the Austrians, amid fatal confusion, had penetrated
into the heart of the forest and had become entangled
with some of his skirmishers. The Archduke, it was
said, believed them to be the French rearguard and
began to rejoice over his easy victory. Then Moreau
fell upon the bewildered Austrians with his whole
force from front, flanks and rear. The slaughter
was appalling. Ten thousand Austrians were taken
prisoners, among them three general officers. Eighty
cannon and two hundred caissons were among the
loot. The scattered remnants of the Archduke's
army were chased across the rivers Inn, Salza and
Traun straight to Vienna. They tried to make a

Hohen-
linden

stand at Herdorf and again at Schwanstadt, but were only the more thoroughly routed.

This overwhelming victory made a deep impression on the men of that day. It moved the English poet Campbell to write this poem, which has become a classic:

HOHENLINDEN

Campbell's Stanzas

On Linden, when the sun was low,
All bloodless lay the untrodden snow,
And dark as winter was the flow
Of Iser, rolling rapidly.

But Linden saw another sight,
When the drum beat at dead of night,
Commanding fires of death to light
The darkness of her scenery.

By torch and trumpet fast arrayed,
Each horseman drew his battle blade,
And furious every charger neighed,
To join the dreadful revelry.

Then shook the hills with thunder riven,
Then rushed the steed to battle driven,
And louder than the bolts of heaven
Far flashed the red artillery.

But redder yet that light shall glow
On Linden's hills of stainèd snow,
And bloodier yet the torrent flow
Of Iser, rolling rapidly.

'Tis morn, but scarce yon level sun
Can pierce the war-clouds, rolling dun,
Where furious Frank, and fiery Hun,
Shout in their sulphurous canopy.

The combat deepens. On, ye brave,
Who rush to glory, or the grave!
Wave, Munich! all thy banners wave!
And charge with all thy chivalry!

Ah, few shall part where many meet!
The snow shall be their winding sheet,
And every turf beneath their feet
Shall be a soldier's sepulchre.

In the same time the three other French armies
had won laurels of their own. On the day of Hohenlinden, General Augereau gained an important
advantage near Bamberg. General Macdonald, undismayed by the rigors of winter and a series of disastrous avalanches, crossed his army over into Italy
across the dizzy heights of the Spluegen Pass, and
beat back his enemies.

Passage of Spluegen

Vienna was struck with terror. Archduke Charles
took command of the army and tried to infuse new
courage into his troops. On viewing the French position before Vienna he was quick to sue for an armistice. It was concluded at Steyer on Christmas Day.
By its terms the Austrians practically agreed to the
provisions of the former treaty of Campo Formio,
which they had repudiated earlier in the year. Beyond that they gave up additional territory, relying
on Moreau's promises of restitution. William Pitt,
sensible of Austria's alarming situation, released the
German emperor from the terms of his alliance with
England.

Treaty of Steyer

Napoleon showed himself disposed to be lenient
with his vanquished foe for the sake of peace. The
kingdom of Naples was saved for the moment by the
intercession of the Czar of Russia. Napoleon also
concluded definite peace with the United States,
and entered into negotiations with Spain for the
retrocession of Louisiana. England was now left

alone in her struggle with France. Not only had
her allies fallen off, but new enemies had arisen.
In distant India, Seringapatam had to be taken at ^{Fall of Ser-} the point of the sword. Emperor Paul of Russia,
exasperated by the Duke of York's mismanagement
of the Anglo-Russian attack on Holland, and piqued
at England's blockade and seizure of the Isle of
Malta, of which he styled himself the Grand Master, had gone over to Napoleon. On September 9,
the Czar seized all the English vessels in his ports
and imprisoned their crews. His quarrel was seconded by the other Northern kingdoms, which
strove to resist the harsh measures of the British at sea. Foremost among them was Denmark,
which had just lost the frigate "Freya," on account
of her captain's refusal to submit to British search.
Late in 1800 the Armed Neutrality of 1780 was revived in this new Northern Maritime League, the Northern
Maritime
conventions of which were signed, on December League
16, by Russia, Sweden, Denmark, and, later, Prussia. Gustavus IV., the young king of Sweden,
convoked a Riksdag to raise money. Its sessions
were so stormy that he never repeated the experiment. On his own authority the king mortgaged
the Swedish city of Wismar to the Duke of Meck-
lenburg for one hundred years for the sum of two
million dollars. The determination of the League
to resist the seizure of French goods on board their
own merchantmen was received by England as a
general declaration of war.

Such was the close of the Eighteenth Century.
Great changes had occurred throughout Europe as

War with
England

the result of the incessant wars of the last decade.
In England, owing to the increased annual expenditure of £60,000,000 for the war, the debt of the
nation had doubled, rising from £244,000,000 to
£484,000,000. The British navy had been nearly
doubled in strength and now numbered eight hundred vessels with 120,000 fighting men. On land
the fighting strength of Great Britain had grown
from 80,000 to nearly half a million. These bur-

British
Resources

dens could not have been borne but for a corresponding increase in British trade. The imports
and exports together had grown from forty to seventy million pounds sterling. Yet it is to be noted
that during the last year of the Eighteenth Century
the Bank of England paid out no coin. The poor
harvest of 1799 resulted in famine prices. In London and elsewhere the poor people rioted for bread.
One poor devil, discharged from the army, attempted
to assassinate the king.

In Paris, too, an attempt was made to blow up the
First Consul with an infernal machine. It served
as a pretext to banish a number of inconvenient
Jacobins. Cerachi and Demerville, two determined
Jacobins, charged with inciting the plot, and St.
Regent and Carbon, who were actually concerned
in it, were sentenced to death and executed. The
old French debt had been repudiated, and a new

French
Finances

debt contracted for fifty-five millions. The expen-
ditures of the first year of the Consulate amounted
to twenty-two millions. This paid for an aggregate
army of nearly a million men in the field. On the
other hand, the French navy had been reduced by

one-half and was still dwindling. The tricolor had been chased from the seas by the combined efforts of British and American sailors. A relief expedition for Egypt was bottled up at Brest. The foreign trade of France was practically extinct. All Europe, in fact, had suffered immeasurably from the long war.

Across the seas, in America, on the other hand, the new century opened serene and full of bright hopes for the future. The last Presidential election *American Affairs* under the old electoral system had brought only a passing cloud. It was held in the fall of 1800. Thomas Jefferson, of Virginia, and Aaron Burr, of New Jersey, were the candidates of the Republican-Democratic party against the Federalists John Adams and C. C. Pinckney. The contest was practically decided in May, 1800, when the Legislature of the State of New York was found to have a Republican majority. Four years previous, the State of New York had given most of its votes to Adams. At this election Jefferson and Burr tied with 73 votes each, while John Adams only got 65 votes. For a long time Congress, which had the decision, stood even for Jefferson and Burr. Thirty-one tie ballots were taken. At last Jefferson received the votes of ten *Jefferson defeats* States, leaving four for Burr and two blank. Under *Burr* the old law Burr as the next strongest candidate was declared Vice-President. A grave peril to the young country was thus averted. Burr never got over this disappointment. The tragedies of his later life were largely due to the resentments begotten in him by the failure of more legitimate ambitions.

Jefferson
takes the
Oath of
Office

Thomas Jefferson took the oath of office in the new Capitol, ridiculed as a palace in the woods. The building stood on a hill in the city of Washington, then nothing but a straggling village of a few hundred inhabitants. It provoked comment at the time that Jefferson, who preferred republican simplicity in all things, wore "long pantaloons, an innovation of the French Revolution."

Painted by Wilhelm Kaulbach

GOETHE IN WEIMAR

1801

THE BIRTH of the Nineteenth Century was most elaborately celebrated at Weimar. During the year 1800 the two poets, Goethe and Schiller, had experienced a change of heart in regard to the true beginning of the century. Now they were at last in accord with their patron Carl August, the Duke of Weimar. The young poet, Leo von Seckendorf, who was afterward killed in battle, was most enthusiastic. He wanted the New Year to be celebrated by special productions of the latest dramatic works of Goethe and Schiller, with musical performances of Haydn's new "Creation," and Gluck's "Iphigenia." But the Duke took the defeat of the Germans at Hohenlinden so ill that he was in no mood for merrymaking. Shortly before New Year Schiller had to write to Goethe at Jena: "The Duke, so we have been informed, a few days ago, gave it to be understood that he is very much opposed to our proposed centenary festivities. You know what this means. . . . In God's name let us bury ourselves in our poetry and try to produce things from within, as we have so little success in producing from without."

Goethe was not so easily foiled. He was translating Voltaire's "Tancred" at the Duke of Weimar's summer castle at Jena. He had with him Friedrich

Beginning of the Century

Interest of German Poets

Wilhelm Schelling, the great German philosopher, then but in his twenty-fifth year. A few days before their return to Weimar, about Christmas time, Goethe wrote to Schiller, "I shall bring Schelling with me so as to have a strong support for our centenary plans." The Duke gave in. A record of the event is preserved in an entertaining letter of Schiller to Koerner, the father of the poet who

Festivities at Weimar later lost his life in the wars. In the afternoon of January 1, 1801, Haydn's "Creation" was sung and the Duke's players at the court theatre gave a mask written by Goethe for the occasion. A masquerade ball at court finished the evening. Some of the most enlightened spirits of Germany were present. Goethe, who was then in his prime, was hailed as Olympian Jupiter. In the throng of maskers were the poets Schiller, Herder, Wieland and Von Seckendorf. With them were Schelling, the philosopher, Hufland, the great physician, and Heinrich Steffens, the learned Dane. Among the ladies were the Duchess Louise, the lively Dowager Duchess Amalie, with the beautiful Frau von Stein, Amalie von Imhof, the poetess, Corona Schroeter, the singer, and Henrietta Jageman, the tragedienne, with Goethe's latest favorite, the lovely Countess von Egloffstein. It was a notable gathering. Next day Goethe had a falling out with his oldtime

Illness of Goethe friend Frau von Stein, and was taken seriously ill. For a long time he lay unconscious and the best physicians of Germany were summoned to attend him. All literary Germany held its breath until the crisis was safely over.

More lasting tributes to the new century were the opening ceremonies of the Peace Conference at Luneville and Pitt's final accomplishment of the Union of Ireland and England. This event was Union of England celebrated in London and Dublin by the ringing of and Ireland bells, salutes of guns and the hoisting of the new imperial standard over the Tower. To accomplish this great result Pitt had promised to remove those . obnoxious laws against Roman Catholics that drove Ireland into rebellion in 1798. Now one hundred Irish members were taken into the Commons and free trade between England and Ireland began.

The terms of the treaty agreed to at Luneville Peace of Luneville changed the map of Europe materially. First of all the cessions wrested from Austria at Campo Formio were confirmed. All German territory on the left bank of the Rhine was ceded to France. The German princes who lost by this arrangement were to be indemnified with other possessions taken from Italy, the Free Hanseatic cities and other weak landholders. It meant the disintegration of the old German Empire. The net loss to Germany was 25,180 square miles with nearly 3,500,000 inhabitants. The provisions for indemnity proved an apple of discord. For years afterward a horde of German princelings haunted the antechambers of Bonaparte, outbidding one another with concessions and bribes. Spain lost Parma and Louisiana. Tuscany was merged with Parma. Formal recognition was given to the French foster Republics of Batavia, Helvetia, Liguria, and the Cisalpine Republic.

Peace of
Florence

The Peace of Luneville was followed by treaties
at Madrid; and the Peace of Florence, between
France and the kingdom of Naples, was concluded
on March 28, after a number of Italian cities had
been overrun by the French army. Naples ceded
her principalities in central Italy and undertook to
close her ports against all vessels of Great Britain
and her ally, Turkey. Thus Napoleon took up a
new weapon of offence against England's shipping—
the Continental Embargo.

In England, meanwhile, the days of the younger
Pitt's ministry were numbered. Early in the year
the first United Parliament of Great Britain and
Ireland met in London. Pitt tried to carry out his
promise to remove all political disabilities from the
Irish Catholics. This met with George III.'s opposition. Powerless to move a ruler who staked his

Pitt
Resigns

soul on the letter of his oath of coronation, Pitt
resigned. With him went Grenville, Dundas (later
Lord Melville), and Windham. The new Prime
Minister was Addington, the Speaker of the House
of Commons.

Addington's Cabinet found themselves with a
general declaration of war on their hands. Willy-
nilly they had to prepare for hostilities. An embargo had been declared on the ships of all the
northern powers. The French army in Egypt was
still unsubdued and a French fleet lay watching
for a chance to go to its relief. On March 8 a

Battle of
Aboukir

British fleet under Sir Ralph Abercrombie debarked
18,000 troops at Aboukir. On March 13 a battle
was fought with the weak French army under

Menou, in which the French were worsted. **On**
March 17, Sir Sydney Smith, the hero of the Siege
of Acre, seized the lake of Madieh and reduced the
forts of Aboukir. On March 20 a pitched battle
was waged between 15,000 Englishmen and 9,000
Frenchmen. Abercrombie, the British commander,
was mortally wounded. The French lost heavily
and were thrown back upon Alexandria and Cairo. _{Siege of Alexandria}
A large Turkish army landed at Aboukir and the
French were invested in Alexandria.

At home another British fleet was preparing to
strike a blow at Russia. All was changed by the
sudden death of Emperor Paul of Russia. This _{Death of Paul I.}
eccentric monarch had ruled but four years. Of
late his conduct had excited general comment.
Thus, on December 30, 1800, the St. Petersburg
"Court Gazette" contained the following item:

"His Majesty, the Emperor, perceiving that the
European powers cannot come to an accommodation,
and wishing to put an end to a war which has raged
· fourteen years, has conceived the idea of appointing
a place to which he will invite the other potentates
to engage together with himself in single combat on
lists which shall be marked out; for which purpose
they shall bring with them, to act as their esquires,
umpires and heralds, their most enlightened ministers and able generals, as Thugut, Pitt and Bernstorff. He will bring on his part Count Pahlen and
Kutuzov."

Kotzebue, the famous dramatist and political
writer of those days, published this comment: "It
is not known whether this rumor can be depended

upon. Meanwhile it does not seem altogether without foundation, as it bears the mark of what has often been imputed to him."

Emperor Paul's Vagaries The Czar's next surprise was to order Louis XVIII., the French pretender, to leave his refuge at the Russian town of Mitau. At the same time he cancelled the handsome annuity granted to the Bourbon prince. About the middle of March the Czar gave to his minister a warrant for imprisoning or banishing the Czarina, his wife, and his two sons, Alexander and Constantine. Count Pahlen showed the warrant to the two princes and said: "Your father is ruining the country and himself. He will now destroy you if this is to be borne." He suggested that something must be done to stop the Czar's course. The Czarovitch left all to him. On the night of March 24 thirty of the most influential members of the court, after a long carouse, forcibly entered the Czar's bedroom. They demanded his abdication. While wrangling over this matter, Prince Zubov, one of the former favorites of Empress Catherine, got into a violent dispute with The Czar's Assassination the Czar. Seizing a chair he struck the Emperor down. Then the others jumped on the prostrate Czar and beat and strangled him to death. Next morning Alexander announced in an imperial proclamation that his father had died of a stroke of apoplexy. After his coronation the assassins were advised to leave court and went into retirement.

Paul's death came just in time for Russia. On March 12, a British fleet of eighteen ships of the line, four frigates and a number of gunboats,

amounting in all to fifty-two sail, left Yarmouth
under the command of Sir Hyde Parker. Nelson
went with him as his first flag-officer. The immediate objective point was Copenhagen. They bore
with them a British ambassador who had instruc- England's
tions to allow Denmark forty-eight hours wherein to terms to
Denmark
accept Great Britain's terms and withdraw from her
engagements with the other northern powers. This
done, the Russian fleet at Revel was to be attacked.
In anticipation of what was coming, Danish troops
seized the free port of Hamburg and closed the
mouth of the Elbe to British ships.

The Danish navy, at this time, numbered twenty
ships of the line, fit for service, and fourteen
frigates. Sweden had eighteen ships of the line,
with fourteen frigates. Together with the Russian
ships at Revel, St. Petersburg and Cronstadt, there
were some eighty sail of the line and fifty frigates
available for sea service against England. But they
were widely scattered. On March 19 the British
envoy rejoined the fleet off Elsinor. His demands
had been rejected. This amounted to a declaration
of war. On March 30 the British fleet entered the
sound. Next night was employed in soundings.
Sir Hyde Parker, in accordance with Nelson's suggestions, directed him to make a front attack on Designs
against
Copenhagen with twelve ships of the line and all Copenhagen
the smaller vessels, while he himself was to menace
the crown batteries and four Danish ships on the
inner line. The Danish battle front, composed of
anchored ships, floating batteries and coast defences,
was one mile wide. Of the six hundred and twenty-

eight Danish guns, three hundred and seventy-five could be brought into action on the engaged side. The approach was covered by a large shoal called the Middle Ground.

At half-past nine in the morning of April 2, Nelson weighed anchor. Three of his ships of the line soon ran aground. Their place was taken by several frigates that had to suffer dearly for their gallantry. By noon the battle was at its height. Manœuvring had ceased and all depended on gunnery and sheer endurance. At one o'clock the signal-lieutenant of the "Elephant" reported that the admiral had thrown out No. 39, the signal to discontinue the fight. Nelson was pacing his quarter-deck and took no notice of the report. The signal-officer met him at the next turn, and asked if he should repeat the signal. Nelson asked if his own signal for close action was still hoisted. "Yes," said the officer. "Mind you keep it so!" said Nelson. Nelson continued to tramp his quarter-deck, the thunder of the battle all about him, his ship reeling to the recoil of its own guns. The stump of his lost arm jerked angrily to and fro, a sure sign of excitement with him. "Leave off action!" he said to his lieutenant; "I'm hanged if I do." "You know, Foley," he said, turning to his captain, "I've only one eye; I've a right to be blind sometimes." And then putting the glass to his blind eye, he exclaimed, "I really do not see the signal!" He dismissed the incident by saying, "D— the signal! Keep mine for closer action flying!"

Battle of Copen-hagen

Nelson's Insubordi-nation

By two in the afternoon most of the Danish guns had been silenced and the flagship "Danebrog" was in flames. One hour later nearly all of the floating defences had been destroyed or had struck their flags. The shore batteries were still unharmed, as were the Danish ships hovering under their protection at the mouth of the harbor. At this point, Nelson sent in a flag of truce, and thus gained a valuable respite wherein to save his grounded ships. It is still a matter of dispute whether the use of the white flag in this case was a *bona fide* act of humanity, or a *ruse de guerre*. Whichever it was, Nelson succeeded in the difficult manœuvre of withdrawing his injured ships during the long interval that the gig with the flag was pulling to and fro between the Danish batteries and Sir Hyde Parker's flagship four miles in the offing. In the end the Danish king agreed to an armistice.

Nelson obtains Terms

The result of the battle was to lay the front of Copenhagen open to bombardment. Under this threat Denmark was driven to consent to a long armistice, which gave the British admiral a free hand for his attack on the Baltic. The value of this service was never adequately understood by Sir Hyde Parker or the British authorities at home.

On the same day that the British fleet forced the passage of the Sound, the Prussian Cabinet made a formal demand on the regency of Hanover, to permit the occupation of the Electorate by the Prussians, and disband a part of their own forces. As this proposal was supported by an army of twenty thousand men, the Hanoverian government was com-

Prussia seizes Hanover

pelled to submit; and Hanover, Bremen and Hameln
were occupied accordingly. At the same time, the
Danes took possession of Hamburg and Lubeck, so
as to close the mouth of the Elbe against English
commerce; and, on the other hand, a British squadron, under Admiral Duckworth, reduced all the
Swedish and Danish islands in the West Indies.
Three weeks later, Nelson's measures were ap-

Nelson Sustained proved in this chilling note from the British admiralty office. "Upon a consideration of all the circumstances, his Majesty has thought fit to approve
the armistice." Very different is the verdict of the
greatest naval authorities on this subject. They all
agree in declaring Nelson's service on this occasion
as admirable in the highest degree. His fellow admiral, Lord St. Vincent, wrote at the time: "Your
lordship's whole conduct, from your appointment
down to this hour, is the subject of our constant
admiration. It does not become me to make com-
parisons. All agree there is but one Nelson."

The news of the Russian Emperor's death, which
arrived during the naval armistice with Denmark,
gave a wholly different cast to the situation. The
Czarovitch was known to incline toward England.

Alexander releases British Seamen Now that he was on the throne, one of Alexander's
first measures was to release the British seamen
imprisoned by his father. This order was issued on
the 7th day of April. Four days later, the northern
powers were surprised to find that the British fleet
had entered the Baltic Sea. To pass the Kögge
Shoals, the heavy guns on the three-deckers had
to be transshipped. Sir Hyde Parker was now re-

called and Nelson placed in full command. He Nelson in
Command had orders to suspend hostilities if Russia followed up the release of British sailors with the suspension of her embargo on British ships. Still Nelson attempted to intercept the Russian fleet at Revel, but Parker had delayed too long. The Russian ships had sailed away the day before. After all it did not matter, since peace was now in the air. On April 17, Russia and Prussia had agreed to cease warring on England. On May 17, the Czar ordered the re- Peace with
Russia lease of all embargoed British ships. On June 17, a convention at St. Petersburg settled the points in dispute. It was conceded by Russia that a neutral flag should not cover an enemy's goods, whereas England agreed to respect *bona fide* neutral shipments. Sweden and Denmark were not expressly included in this convention, but they of necessity followed the example of Russia. The Danish government agreed to evacuate Hamburg, and restore the free navigation of the Elbe, and both Sweden and Denmark raised the embargo. Great Britain adopted corresponding measures; and Prussia took an early opportunity to withdraw her troops from Hanover. Thus was dissolved, in less than six Northern
Maritime months after its formation, the most formidable League
Dissolved confederacy that had yet been arrayed against the maritime power of England.

Napoleon sent Duroc to St. Petersburg to counteract the influence of Great Britain, but his ambassador accomplished little beyond a flattering reception. For France, during this interval, a new annoyance had arisen in the West Indies. Early in the year,

the island of San Domingo had been thrown into ferment by the high-handed acts of a negro military
chieftain known as Toussaint L'Ouverture.   Pre-

tending to act in the name of France, Toussaint,
heedless of the protests of the French civil commissioners, annexed other portions of the island that
had been ceded to Spain in the treaty of Basle five
years before.   In July, 1801, the negro leader had
himself acclaimed governor for life.   A new constitution was promulgated abolishing slavery and all
distinctions of color.   Free trade was adopted.   The
landed estates belonging to Frenchmen not residing
on the island were confiscated.   To his French re-
monstrants, Toussaint replied haughtily: "I am the
Bonaparte of San Domingo.   The colony cannot
get along without me."   Napoleon was constrained
to gather a naval force wherewith to recapture the
lost colony.   To make so distant an enterprise a
safe venture, a disproportionately formidable fleet
had to be assembled, for British cruisers were scour-
ing the sea.   With the bad tidings from San Domingo came the news of a fierce sea fight of two

squadrons of French and English ships off Algesiras
in the Bay of Gibraltar.   The French were trying
to reinforce Cadiz.   With the help of the Spanish
land batteries, the French rear-admiral, Linois, succeeded in capturing one of Admiral Saumarez's big
ships, the "Hannibal," that had grounded under
the Spanish guns.   Saumarez withdrew to Gibraltar.
Linois, having been reinforced with five Spanish
ships of the line and another Frenchman, came out
into the bay.   The British attacked after dark and

the fight lasted through the night. The French man-o'-war, "Formidable," beat off three British ships. In the dark two of the largest Spanish ships, the "Real Carlos" and "San Hermenigeldo," taking each other for enemies, set fire to one another and blew up. The French "St. Antoine," was captured.

Throughout the summer all England had been aroused by the menace of invasion because of the French gatherings of troops and ships at Toulon, Dunkirk and elsewhere. Coastguards were picketed all along the shore, and a British volunteer army called into service. When Admiral Ganthaume succeeded in taking a French squadron into the Mediterranean, in his attempt to succor the French in Egypt, the alarm grew. This was not abated when Ganthaume returned to Toulon after capturing three small English war vessels and the "Swiftsure," a ship of the line, carrying seventy-four guns. Early in August Nelson made an unsuccessful dash at the French flotilla off Boulogne. By the middle of the month he reappeared with eight ships of the line and a dozen or more frigates. The engagement that ensued was indecisive. By October both countries were heartily tired of the war. The various modes of prosecuting a war of offence were exhausted. One thorn in the side of both belligerents had been removed when Lord Keith brought about the French evacuation of Egypt by undertaking to ship their army back to France on his own vessels. This was accomplished early in September to the satisfaction of both sides.

Threatened Invasion of England

French evacuate Egypt

Preliminary peace negotiations were entered into at London on the first day of October. Previous to **Coercion of Portugal** this, Portugal purchased a treaty with her powerful neighbors by ceding to France one half of Guiana, paying twenty millions of francs for the support of the French troops, confirming Olivenza with its territory to Spain, and closing her ports against all English ships, whether of war or of commerce.

On October 18, another secret treaty with Spain was signed at Madrid, by the terms of which Louisiana once more changed hands. In England, the implacable Pitt and Nelson were among those who approved the conciliatory policy of the new Ministry. **Peace of London** try. Peace was ratified in Parliament, on October 10, by a majority of ten to one. It was agreed that hostilities with France should immediately cease by land and sea; that Great Britain should restore its colonial acquisitions in every part of the world; Ceylon in the East, and Trinidad in the West Indies, alone excepted; that Egypt should be restored to the Porte, Malta and its dependencies to the order of St. John of Jerusalem, the Cape of Good Hope to Holland; the integrity of Portugal was to be guaranteed, the harbors of the Roman and Neapolitan states evacuated by the French, and Porto Ferrajo by the English forces. The news of the definite signing of the treaty at London made French consols go up from forty-eight to fifty-three. In the same year, peace treaties were concluded between France and Turkey, France and Bavaria, France and America, France and Algiers, and France and Russia.

1802

IN ENGLAND the threatening phantom of foreign invasion had been laid at rest. The British "Annual Register" thus records the beginning of the year: "It was the opinion of a Results of Peace in England vast majority of the British nation that the year 1802 commenced under circumstances highly auspicious. . . . It was universally understood that the income tax, a burden which the bulk of the nation had rather impatiently borne, was now to be withdrawn, and that vast reductions were to take place in our military and marine establishments." The last part of this promise was actually fulfilled, much to the disgust of Sheridan, who spoke against these measures in Parliament. He said that the country had failed in every object for which it had plunged into war. Instead of checking the aggrandizement of France, Great Britain had raised her to such a height as to endanger the existence of all. He saw the immense power of France now consolidated, all her continental enemies subdued or won over to her interests. For his part his fears and alarms began where those of the Ministry had ended. Mr. Sheridan was scarcely heeded. Pitt, for the moment, silenced all opposition by support- The Opposition silenced ing his successors in office. Even Nelson arose in the House of Lords to say that the possession of the Island of Malta and of the Cape of Good Hope were of little consequence to England.

The next thing to take up the attention of Parliament was the petition of the British printers and booksellers asking for a release from the heavy duties on paper. In their petition they recited that by the additional duties levied on paper "the progress of literature and the encouragement of genius had been equally fettered." Parliament agreed to a reduction of the paper tax on the ground that the tax "struck directly at the very existence of English literature."

The true makers of literature scarcely stood in need of such encouragement. Unlike France, the leaven of the new age in England, as in Germany, had called forth a fresh harvest of brilliant writers.

Romantic Movement in Literature The English romantic movement in literature was in full bloom. To be sure, Burke, the great Parliamentarian, Cowper, the poet, and Burns, the Scottish bard, had just died, but their names were in every one's mouth. The stirring events of the *Impetus of German Letters* French Revolution, together with the sudden brilliant rise of literature in Germany, where Goethe, Schiller, Richter, Wieland, Herder, and the great philosopher Kant were vying with each other in new productions, acted as a spur to the writers of England. Coleridge turned from his translations of German plays and ballads to write his "Rime of the Ancient Mariner." Walter Scott sought inspiration for his revivals of medieval chivalry by translating Goethe's "Goetz von Berlichingen."

Sheridan, at the same time, translated Kotzebue's "Pizarro." The next years brought Tóm Moore's Revival of British Poetry "Anacreontics," Campbell's "Poems," Coleridge and Wordsworth's lyrics, Southey's "Thalaba," the prose masterpieces of Charles Lamb and Thomas DeQuincey, with Paley's "Philosophical Essays." In 1802 Scott brought out his "Minstrelsy of the Scottish Border," while the works of Chaucer were revived by Godwin, Shelley's friend. The same year saw the establishment of the "Edinburgh Review" and of Rees' great Cyclopedia.

Nowhere else in the world was there such an outpour of literature. In Italy the death of Alfieri, the dramatic poet, left a void. In France the only writer of note was Chateaubriand. Art, too, languished. In France the painter David stood alone. Canova, the Italian rival of the Danish sculptor Thorvaldsen, had just finished his famous group of Theseus. Napoleon made haste to summon him to Paris.

The First Consul, after concluding his various peace treaties, continued to play the game of world politics on a grand scale. Before the end of January Napoleon caused the Cisalpine Republic to call a convention at Lyons. The 300 delegates had to cross the Alps in midwinter. Napoleon, proceeding there with Josephine his wife, had himself proclaimed president of the Italian Republic. A constitution like that of France was adopted. The acceptance of a similar constitution was imposed upon the Batavian Republic of Holland. On March 25, a formal treaty of peace was concluded at Amiens Peace of Amiens between France, Holland and Spain on one side, and Great Britain on the other. France kept possession of the Austrian or Flemish Netherlands, the left bank of the Rhine, the greater part of Italy and Switzerland and that vast tract of territory on the Gulf of Mexico known as Louisiana. England kept none of her new possessions, excepting Ceylon wrested from Holland, the Island of Trinidad taken from Spain, and a new slice of India won from the conquered Hindu prince, Tippoo Sahib. San Domingo for the moment was restored to France by General Leclerc's early victories over the blacks under Toussaint. The same fate befell the negro colonies of Guadeloupe and Martinique.

Religious Concordat in France

On April 8, the final adoption of the religious Concordat arranged with the new pope, Pius VII., was celebrated in the Church of Notre Dame de Paris by a grand Te Deum in honor of the re-establishment of public worship. Throughout France the priests turned from foes into loyal supporters of the new government. At the same time forty-four articles of the Protestant cult were sanctioned by law. This caused bitter dissatisfaction among the old Republicans. The country at large hailed the re-establishment of religion with joy. At the

Return of the Emigrees

end of the month came another act of amnesty for the Royalist exiles, though Napoleon's efforts to make the Count de Lille renounce his rights to the throne of France had failed. All but one thousand of the proscribed royalists were permitted to return. Their lands, seized by the State, were to be returned to them if not exceeding a certain area, but

not so their hereditary privileges over canals, highways or other public institutions. As a result of
these measures a great number of exiles returned
from England, and with them came a host of travellers eager to visit the land that had so long been
closed to them. The British Embassy in Paris was
reopened.

Napoleon's next measure was to reorganize the French
French educational system. On the first of May, Internal Reforms
an act was passed governing secondary schools.
Thirty of the best *écoles centrales* were reorganized as *lycées*, where the pupils were drilled and
trained in semi-military fashion. To bind these
new schools as closely as possible to the State,
6,000 pupils, called "wards of the nation" were
to receive free education. Most of these were the
children of deserving soldiers. Technical and special schools were also founded. Education, which
up to 1790 had been in the hands of the clergy,
became a prerogative of the State. On May 8, a
decree of the Senate extended Napoleon's Consulate ten years beyond the original term of ten years
in recognition of his services to France. Napoleon
accepted the honor in these words: "Fortune has
smiled upon the Republic. But Fortune is inconstant. How many men whom she has showered
with her favors have lived more than a few years?
The interests of my happiness and of my good fame
demand a termination of my public life so soon as
general peace is assured to the world. But you say
that I owe my country another sacrifice. I will
make it."

Order of
the Loyal
Legion

A few days afterward the Order of the Loyal Legion was established, not without determined opposition in the Chamber. The two Tribunes Savoie-Rollin and Chauvalin denounced the measure as a monarchical institution. On the next day the Chamber passed a law re-establishing slavery in the West Indian colonies restored to France by the Treaty of Amiens. This goaded the blacks of San Domingo to further desperate resistance.

The Revolution of Hayti

General Leclerc and Admiral Villaret-Joyeuse had landed their expedition at Samana. Leclerc first tried to win over Toussaint by a friendly letter from the First Consul, and offers of bribes sent him through his own sons, who had been brought from school in France. The attempted restoration of slavery made the blacks reject all proposals. On the night after the French troops landed, the negroes burned the French settlement at Cape François, now Cape Haytien. Of 800 houses but 60 escaped. The blacks carried their war into the mountains. Revolting cruelties were practiced on both sides. Yellow fever came to the aid of the blacks. Then General Leclerc again tried diplomacy. The two black leaders, Dessalines and Christophe, were won by false representations. Next he induced Toussaint to come to a conference at Gonaive. Toussaint was seized and deported to France. There he died of neglect in the dungeons of Chateau Joux. General Leclerc, with the bulk of his army, remained to fall a prey to the ravages of yellow fever.

On June 25, the final treaty of peace between

France and Turkey was concluded. It assured free navigation in the Black Sea to French ships, and French Peace with Turkey in some other respects was found to be inimical to England. Similar conventions were established with the Deys of Algiers, Tunis and Tripoli. On August 3, the French Senate revised the constitution of the year VIII., so as to extend the term of office of the consuls for life. To the First Consul Bonaparte Consul for Life was given the former royal prerogative of executive clemency. The troublesome Tribunes were reduced from one hundred to fifty. Lafayette, who opposed the suspension of political liberties and of a free press, was retired from public life. Napoleon accepted his new honors in these words: "Senators! the life of a citizen belongs to his country. The French people wish mine to be entirely consecrated to them. I obey their will." It was in those days of general reforms that an ample supply of fresh running water was secured to Paris by aqueducts from the River Ourcq.

Toward the end of the year most internal questions were settled for France, and Napoleon once more felt the need of reaching out. In September a decree of the French Senate "reunited" the Island of Elba with France. Next, the Italian province of Piedmont was annexed to France. On October 9, French troops occupied the Duchy of Parma upon New French Annexations the sudden death of the Duke, Don Ferdinand de Bourbon. On October 21, General Ney, at the head of 12,000 French soldiers, entered Switzerland to suppress the disorders that had been brought about by Napoleon's agent. Already the canton of Wallis had been detached, ostensibly to form an independent republic, but really to secure to France the control of the Simplon Pass into Northern Italy. The British ambassador in Paris alone protested against these breaches of the peace. Napoleon silenced him with the proud declaration, "It is recognized in Europe that Italy, Holland, and Switzerland are at the disposal of France."

No part of Napoleon's diplomacy was more ably conceived or better carried out than the negotiations with the German princes intrusted to Talleyrand. Diet of Regensburg, or Ratisbon All through the years 1801 and 1802 a Diet at Regensburg deliberated over the changes imposed upon the German empire by the treaty of Luneville. The proverbial antagonism between the various German States and princes played its usual part. In the summer of 1801 Prime Minister Montgelas of Bavaria had signed the first of those treaties which made Napoleon the arbiter of Germany. Two months later a secret treaty between Alexander and Bonaparte admitted Russia to a share in the reorganization of Germany. Equilibrium was to be maintained between Austria and Prussia. Beyond that the Czar stipulated for the advancement of his own relatives on the thrones of Wurtemberg, Bavaria, and Baden. One after another the German princes settled with their patrons for a share in the spoil. On June 3, a secret agreement between France and Russia embodied all of these arrangements, and Spoliation of Germany the spoliation of the ancient German empire was a settled fact. The Diet of Regensburg in its final conclusions, known as the Reichsdeputationshauptschluss, solemnly ratified the provisions by which forty-two out of forty-eight free cities, and all the ecclesiastical states lost their independence. Only six free cities remained—Hamburg, Bremen, Lubeck, Frankfort, Augsburg, and Nuremberg. All the landed property of the Church was confiscated. The free Universities, too, lost heavily. Most of the former feudal States were wiped off the map. For Germany as a nation the destruction of these innumerable petty principalities was a distinct gain. A constant source of discord was done away. The national feeling of the German people grew in unity and strength.

Growth of German National Feeling

During the same year, in October, 1802, the decisive battle of Poona in India changed the fate of the Mahratta empire. The united armies of Sindia and the Peishwa were defeated by Jaswant Rao Holkar, an illegitimate pretender to the Mahratta throne. Peish Baji Rao fled for his life to the western coast, and escaped on board an English ship to the port of Bassein, about twenty miles to the northward of Bombay.

Mahratta Wars

Baji Rao was paralyzed by the disaster. Another Peishwa was set up by Jaswant Rao Holkar at Poona, and Baji Rao saw nothing before him but ruin. In this extremity he agreed to sign the obnoxious treaty, provided the English restored him to his throne at Poona. Accordingly the treaty of Bassein was concluded on the last day of December, 1802.

Treaty of Bassein

1803

THE DESIRE for peace led Addington's government in England to remain inactive until
the French aggressions in Holland, Italy
and Switzerland became accomplished facts. Even
**Napoleon
renews
quarrel
with Eng-
land** then Napoleon was the first to renew the quarrel.
In January, Talleyrand, urged by his master, complained to the British ambassador of the hostile
articles in the English newspapers. Lord Whitworth made a countercharge against Napoleon's
official organ, "Le Moniteur." Then Talleyrand
called for an explanation of Great Britain's delay
about evacuating Malta. On January 13, the "Moniteur" published Sebastiani's report on the mission
that the First Consul had intrusted to him in the
East. The report, which filled eight columns of the
"Moniteur," contained a very complete account of
the resources and possible allies available for a new
**French
Designs on
Egypt** conquest of Egypt. The exact number and disposition of the British in the East were given with those
of the Turkish forces, estimated altogether at 19,000
men. They were declared to be, "not an army, but
a collection of men, badly armed, undisciplined, and
worn out by debauchery." In conclusion, it was
stated that "six thousand French would suffice to
reconquer Egypt."

This threatening manifesto resounded in England like a war cry. The British ambassador in Paris henceforth became intractable on the subject of Malta. On February 13, Lord Whitworth attended a state function at the Tuileries. He was violently accosted by the First Consul. When he tried to reply, Napoleon exclaimed: "I suppose you are going to speak of Piedmont and Switzerland. They are mere trifles. You ought to have thought of this during the peace negotiation. You have no right now to complain." Lord Whitworth transmitted the conversation verbatim to his government. Two days later the "Moniteur" published the government's annual report on the situation of the Republic to the legislative body. Referring to England, Napoleon's mouthpiece said: "Be the success of intrigue what it may in London, it will not drag other nations into its net. The nation asserts with just pride that England, single-handed, is unable to cope with France."

It was a cry to arms. On March 8, King George, in a message to the House of Commons, informed Parliament that he had thought it expedient to adopt additional measures for the security of his dominions. Discussions of great importance between his Majesty and the French government, it was set forth, induced him to rely on the assistance of Parliament to adopt such measures as the honor and interest of the English people required. On March 10, followed a royal proclamation calling the militia into service. Two days afterward, the First Consul summoned Lord Whitworth to the Tuileries, and loudly assailed him: "So you are bent on war." Turning to the other ambassadors he shouted: "The English are bent on war, but if they are the first to draw the sword, I shall be the last to sheathe it. Since Britons do not respect treaties, we shall cover them with black crape." Next day Napoleon despatched confidential couriers to Alexander of Russia and to the King of Prussia to induce them to make common cause with him. Negotiations were opened to sell French Louisiana to the United States of North America for eighty million francs.

French War Preparations

On March 25, a law was passed in France which placed 120,000 new conscripts under the colors. During the French parleys with England it had been explained that the naval armaments at Toulon and Brest were made to take possession of Louisiana. Previous to this Bonaparte, in a confidential communication to England, had laid stress on the importance of Louisiana for keeping the United States in check. President Jefferson, receiving intimations of this, protested against such a proceeding. In America, the presence of General Leclerc in the West Indies with so large a force was regarded as a menace. Napoleon's sudden need of money in 1803 changed all that.

The United States Threatened

Four nations—France, Spain, Great Britain and the United States were concerned in determining the boundaries of this territory. It was finally agreed that American Louisiana should extend from the Mississippi along the thirty-first parallel to the Gulf of Mexico, thence along the Red River up to the Arkansas, and thence north with the mountain chain to the forty-second parallel of latitude. The region practically included the present States of Louisiana, Arkansas, Missouri, Iowa, Minnesota, Kansas, Nebraska, Colorado, the Dakotas, Montana, Wyoming and Indian Territory. The official discussions over the various lines lasted for years. In the meanwhile, Napoleon yielded all the French territory in dispute, aggregating more than a million square miles, with 85,000 mixed inhabitants, for the sum of $11,250,000, to be paid in six per cent bonds, payable fifteen years after date. For the United States, Messrs. Monroe and Livingston concluded the terms of the purchase on April 30, 1803. In the autumn the United States took peaceable possession. *The Louisiana Purchase*

The purchase of Louisiana was the greatest event in Jefferson's administration. The power of the Mississippi was no longer a matter of dispute. Very aptly did Mr. Livingston say to the French ministers as they arose from signing the treaty: "We have lived long, gentlemen, but this is the noblest work of our lives." Napoleon said: "This will forever strengthen the power of the United Sates." Among the American people this was not so clearly recognized. Jefferson's administration was severely assailed by critics who declared that the new territory was a barren wilderness which would never be worth the price. Previous to this, during Jefferson's first term, the new State of Ohio had been taken into the Union. *American Expansion Denounced*

Two other notable American achievements undertaken in that year were Chief-Justice Marshall's reorganization of the American law, and the war against the Barbary pirates. For some time the Moorish pashas along the Northern coast of Africa had exacted tribute from all American shipping that came within their reach. The American government consented to pay a subsidy to exempt American ships from these exactions. In 1801 Captain Bainbridge, commanding the "George Washington," took the money to the Dey of Algiers, and was ordered by him to convey the Dey's own tribute to the Turkish Sultan to Constantinople. At the request of the American Consul, Bainbridge consented, but expressed a hope that the "next tribute might be delivered from the mouths of his guns." In the same year the Sultan of Tripoli clamored for more tribute. He tried to enforce his demand by acts of war. An American squadron was sent to the Mediterranean under Captain Dale. The Dey of Algiers came to terms. Not so the Pasha of Tripoli. The first engagement of note was fought in the fall of 1801, off Malta, between Lieutenant Sterrett, commanding the twelve-gun schooner "Enterprise," and the war polacre "Tripoli." The corsair struck her colors after a two-hour fight. She discharged another broadside when the American vessel came into close range. "Sink the damned treacherous Moor," shouted Sterrett. His gunners raked the enemy fore and aft, shot away her mizzenmast and killed fifty of her Arab crew. At last the pirate captain threw his flag into the sea and begged for mercy. All his guns and small arms were thrown overboard. The "Tripoli" was sent home under a jury mast and jibsail with the compliments of the American navy. The "Enterprise" had not lost a man.

In July, 1802, the "Constellation," under Cap- ^{Sea Fights} tain Murray, fought nine gunboats off Tripoli and drove five of them ashore. Next summer a Tripolitan cruiser of twenty-two guns was driven into a bay seven leagues east of Tripoli. The "John Adams," under Captain Rutgers, and the "Enterprise," under Lieutenant Isaac Hull, stood in and gave battle at close range. In three-quarters of an hour the enemy's flag came down. The Americans tried to take possession, but the Tripolitan met them with another broadside and then blew up with all aboard. In 1803 the American squadron in the Mediterranean under Commodore Preble numbered nine ships. The "Philadelphia," under Bainbridge, captured a Moorish corsair. Commodore Preble entered the harbor of Morocco and brought the Sultan to terms. The "Philadelphia" soon after chased the pirate into the Bay of Tangiers and ran upon a reef. She was surrounded by gunboats and Captain Bainbridge had to surrender. Among the ^{An American Brig captured} prisoners were Lieutenant Porter, James Porter, Jack Jones and James Renshaw, of future fame. Three hundred American seamen were sold into slavery. The "Philadelphia" was floated and refitted, with her thirty-six guns, as a corsair. While in prison Captain Bainbridge managed to send home a secret letter written in lime juice, in which he suggested that the ship might be retaken. Lieutenant

Decatur's
Moorish
Exploit

Decatur acted upon the suggestion a few months later. In the Moorish ketch "Mesticah," captured by himself, this gallant officer slipped into the harbor of the enemy one night. Pretending to be a Maltese merchantman that had lost his anchors he made fast to the former "Philadelphia." The instant the two ships came abeam, Lieutenant Decatur gave the order: "Boarders away!" His disguised seamen swarmed over the side of the brig. The pirates were cutlassed and driven overboard. Decatur, with the help of his midshipmen, Morris, Lawrence, McDonough and Laws, fired the former Yankee brig. By the light of the burning ship the Americans sailed for the mouth of the harbor. Within half an hour the "Philadelphia" blew up. The ketch got away safely without the loss of one man and was joined by the American ship "Siren" waiting outside. Decatur was made a captain by Congress and his crew were rewarded. The ketch was renamed "Intrepid," in honor of the event.

Nelson's
opinion of
Decatur's
Exploit

Lord Nelson characterized it as "the most bold and daring act of the age." The Dey of Tripoli vented his rage by casting Bainbridge and his officers into deeper dungeons. The war continued unabated.

This little pirate war, while full of stirring exploits, was of slight importance compared to the impending world-war between France and England. On May 13, the British ambassador had been ordered to withdraw from Paris. On May 22, the French Senate declared all British travellers in France prisoners of war. French troops under Gen-

eral Mortier immediately invaded Hanover. As the French invade Hanover
hereditary elector of this principality, King George
of England had attempted to save his domain by
declaring neutrality for Hanover. All England
took to arms. Wordsworth's vigorous sonnets in
behalf of Switzerland and Holland were followed
by this clarion cry:

> No parleying now. In Britain is one breath.
> We are all with you now, from shore to shore.
> Ye men of Kent, 'tis victory or death!

In June a royal message informed Parliament that
Holland had been drawn into the campaign and
more armaments were called for. The whole number now raised in Great Britain was 103,000 men.
Further war measures were passed early in July.
On July 20, Napoleon issued a decree in Antwerp
excluding all vessels that had even touched at a
British port. It was the beginning of his famous
continental embargo against English shipping. Continental Blockade begun
Admiral Brui was placed in command of a small
French naval force for the avowed purpose of in-
vading England. Great Britain retaliated by de-
claring a blockade on the waters of the Elbe and
Weser, Genoa and Spezzia, and Havre-de-Grace.
More than a hundred prize vessels were captured
by the English before the middle of June. Things
were at this pass when Emperor Alexander of
Russia, on August 19, offered to mediate between
England and France. Great Britain refused to ac-
cept mediation unless the French first evacuated
Hanover. About this time another insurrection

Rebellion in Ireland broke out in Ireland under the leadership of Napper Tandy, Redmond and Emmet, who had come from France. Lord Kilwarden, Chief-Justice of the King's Bench, was murdered in the streets of Dublin. It took several months to quell the rebellion. The chief rebels were brought to trial and condemned to death. England in turn tried to stir up trouble among the Royalists in France. In November, Portugal, England's former ally, after a secret treaty with Spain and France, declared neutrality.

The British Admiralty despatched a fleet to the West Indies to take a hand in the struggle going on in San Domingo. Here the news of Toussaint's captivity and death had been followed by renewed disaffection on the part of his fellow leaders, Des-

The Horrors of Hayti

salines and Christophe. They were joined by Sans Souci, another negro chief, and Bellair with his Amazonian wife. These two were captured and tortured to death by the French. Henceforth the war degenerated into unspeakable horrors. The bulk of the French army was down with yellow fever. The survivors were driven back into the chief towns. Both sides sank into savagery. Bloodhounds were imported from Martinique wherewith to hunt down the luckless negroes, and whole shiploads of captives were killed. In the fall of 1802 General Leclerc died of fever. His successor, General Rochambeau, ventured an open battle with the blacks and was driven back to Cape Haytien. In exasperation the French massacred their prisoners. The blacks in turn gibbeted all the French officers they had taken.   Neither side asked nor gave mercy. Jerome Bonaparte was glad to return to France. A British Fleet takes a Hand At this point the British squadron hove in sight and blockaded the French at Cape Haytien.   The situation became intolerable.   General Rochambeau thus commented on it in later life: "Pressed almost to death by absolute famine, wretchedly feeding on our horses, mules, asses, and even the bloodhounds, we had no way to escape the poniards of the enraged negroes but by trusting our fate to the sea."

During the last days of November the French, after a final assault by Dessalines, capitulated first to the negroes, and then, fearing a general massacre, to Commodore Loring of the British squadron.   Five French vessels that tried to escape without surrendering were caught.   General Noailles alone got French Capitulate in Hayti away.   The force taken by the British numbered 8,000 troops, three frigates and seventeen merchantmen.   That was all that was left of the total French expedition of 36,000 men that had been sent to the West Indies.   Altogether 80,000 human beings had lost their lives within the space of two years.

French San Domingo declared its independence and became the Republic of Hayti.   The other colonies of France and Holland also suffered severely by the war.   A squadron under Sir Samuel Hood successively captured St. Lucia, St. Pierre, Tobago, Berbice, Demerara, and Issequibo.   During this time French agents succeeded in stirring up trouble in England's colonies in the Far East.   While the British were straining every nerve to resist Napoleon's projected invasion of England, they were dis-

Troubles in India tracted by incessant insurrections and border wars in India. The great Sultanate of Mahratta had split up into a federation of warlike chiefs, who were forever overrunning their borders. In their armies they employed many French officers. After the subjugation of Tippoo Sahib a series of treaties were concluded by various Hindu princes, Lord Cornwallis and the Marquis of Wellesley. In 1802 the Mahrattas, after defeating the Peishwa of Poona, became threatening, and Lord Clive prepared for emergencies at Hyderabad by gathering an army of 19,000 men and five hundred guns. In 1803, General Wellesley was directed to restore the deposed Peishwa. By a march of sixty-two miles in thirty-two hours he reached the city of Poona. An attempt was made by some of the Mahratta chiefs to turn their territory over to France. Admiral Linois, who arrived at this juncture with a French squadron, failed in his demonstration. The troops he landed at Pondicherry were taken prisoners. The arrival of reinforcements and the opportune death of the Nizam of Hyderabad strengthened England's position in Northern India. In the autumn of 1803, General Wellesley defeated the

Defeat of the Mahrattas Mahrattas and stormed Ahmednuggur. The Marquis of Wellesley's brother, the future Wellington, earned his spurs in this campaign. The fort of Djalnapoor was taken in September. On September 23, another bloody battle was fought at Assaye,

Wellington in India in which Colonel Arthur Wellesley had the supreme command. Though outnumbered by ten to one, and quite overmatched by the Mahratta artillery, he won the day by a series of wild charges. One-third of the British were slain. Finally, after 15,000 of the enemy had been killed, the Mahrattas were put to rout. For his share in this victory Colonel Wellesley received a sword of honor from Parliament. Meanwhile hostilities had broken out in the province of Bombay. The town of Baroach was stormed by the British under Colonel Woodington, and his victory was followed by the conquest of Chimapeer. In the east, the British troops stationed in Bengal and Madras stormed the fortress of Barbutty. Perron, a Frenchman placed in command of 15,000 Sindias, suffered a defeat in front of Allyghur. On September 4, the fort itself was stormed and Perron was taken prisoner. General Lake pushed on and attacked a large Hindu army under the French general, Bourgnieu, in front of Delhi. The Hindus lost 3,000 men and 68 guns. The French officers surrendered, and Peishwa Allum of Delhi accepted British suzerainty. General Dudernaigne surrendered Mathura in October. By the end of that month the Mahrattas made a determined attempt to recapture Delhi. On October 27, General Lake's cavalry was defeated at Lashwaree. Colonel Vandeleur, the leader, was killed. The British infantry, coming up, renewed the attack with great loss. Major-General Ware was killed, and General Lake and his son were wounded. Two thousand Hindus and a large number of elephants were captured. On October 29, General Wellesley defeated the Mahrattas at Arghaum and captured thirty-eight guns with all their elephants. The stronghold

Perron defeated

Surrender of Delhi

of Dammergaun was taken early in December with great slaughter. After these events the Rajahs of Berar, Sindia and Bhonsla came to terms. They en-
British Ac-
quisitions
in India
gaged never to enter into another treaty with Frenchmen and yielded all their territory in Northern Hindustan between the Jumna and the Ganges. All the forts in the Deccan were given up. The war in India had lasted altogether five months. During its course the natives of the Island of Ceylon were likewise subjugated and brought under British rule.

While Great Britain thus had her hands full, King George III. succumbed to a temporary attack of insanity and had to be put in a strait-jacket. In Paris the "Moniteur" published this comment: "Why are we at war? Because the English people have no one to conduct their affairs but a mad king and a prime minister who is like an old nurse." Napoleon, himself, was inspecting the camp of in-
Preparing
to invade
England
vasion at Boulogne. Frenchmen were reminded of the glorious deeds of Joan of Arc, and new songs were composed on the descent into England. The poets were publicly rewarded by Napoleon. Not so Madame de Staël, who about this time ventured to return to France from her recent exile. "Inform her," wrote Bonaparte to Regnier, "that if at the end of five days she is still in France, she will be conducted to the frontier by the gendarmerie. The arrival of this woman, like that of a bird of ill omen, has always been a signal of some trouble. It is my intention that she shall not remain in France."

Together with the poet Chateaubriand, who had been sent to Switzerland by Napoleon, Madame de

Staël had helped to start the French romantic movement in literature. The literary career of this
gifted daughter of Necker began with her "Lettres
sur J. J. Rousseau." Conviction led her to oppose
Bonaparte, whom she enraged with pinpricks of
irony. Upon her second banishment from France
she went to Germany, which, as was then said,
"ruled the kingdom of the air." There she sought
out the literary celebrities at Weimar. Goethe put
her off on Schiller. This poet put her off on Wilhelm Schlegel, the critic, who helped her gather
the material for her celebrated book on German
institutions, "L'Allemagne."

The exile of Madame de Stael was followed by
a reorganization of the French Institute, which
practically reduced that body to a nullity.

1804

THE new year opened amid general feverish preparations for war. At Boulogne, Napoleon had gathered a flotilla of flat-bottomed ships and an army of 120,000 veterans, who were constantly drilled in the tactics of embarkation. It was only necessary for Napoleon to be master of the Channel for a few hours to make the descent upon England a reality. Meanwhile Englishmen were distracted by the growing opposition to the government at home and the alarming mental condition of their king. Parliament asked for explicit information on the subject. This led to prolonged debates between the Ministry on one side and Fox, Pitt and Canning on the other. Finally the House was informed that the king was in a fair way to recovery. The opposition returned to the attack on the subject of naval defence. Pitt practically moved a vote of censure of the Admiralty. Defeated in this, Fox next opposed a government bill to increase the regular army at the expense of the volunteer system. The government won by a majority of fifty-five, but Addington's Ministry was so shaken at these repeated onslaughts that late in April the Cabinet resolved to resign. On May 8, Pitt was once more called to power. Fox was left out of his Cabinet.

During the interval, Napoleon put the finishing strokes to the foundation of his Empire. Some time previous to this Fox had written to his nephew that the rumor was current that Bonaparte would soon proclaim himself Emperor of the Gauls. The impending war with England was favorable to the enterprise. By way of prelude an elaborate plot on the First Consul's life was discovered by the police. George Cadoudal, a Breton gentleman, was suspected of negotiations with the Count of Artois and the English government to murder Bonaparte. Suddenly the French secret police made a number of arrests. Cadoudal was brought to trial and executed. On April 6, Pichegru was found strangled in prison. Captain Wright, the commander of the vessel which brought Pichegru to France, was murdered in prison. General Moreau, the hero of Hohenlinden, was tried for high treason. Jury trial in his case was suspended, and Thuriot, one of the associates of Robespierre, was placed in charge of the prosecution. Of the forty-seven prisoners, twenty were condemned to death, five sentenced to imprisonment, and the rest acquitted. Moreau was sentenced to two years in prison. "I only wished to pardon him," said Napoleon to the judges. Judge Clavier rejoined: "But who will pardon us?" Armand Polignac, one of the prisoners, was spared from death only by the intercession of Josephine Bonaparte. Moreau's sentence was commuted by Napoleon, who banished him for life. The unfortunate general with his wife betook himself to America.

Conspiracy against Bonaparte

General Moreau Banished

In the principality of Baden, twelve miles from the French frontier, there remained the Duke of Enghien, one of the Bourbon princes. He was said to be implicated in the conspiracy. On March 15, a troop of French soldiers made a dash across the border and arrested the prince in his house at Ettenhein. He was taken by Savary to the Fort of Vincennes, where a grave had already been dug for him. On the night of his arrival he was court-martialled and shot. His body was scarcely cold when the French Senate, at the suggestion of Napoleon's chief of police, Fouché, hastened to gratify the First Consul's ambitions: "You are founding," they said, "a new era, but you ought to make it last forever. Splendor is nothing without duration. Do not delay, great man, to accomplish your work! Render it immortal like your glory! You have rescued us from the chaos of the past. You make us blessed with benefits of the present. Guarantee for us the future!"

Bonaparte begged for time wherein to consider this offer of a crown. While he was considering, the rest of the world awoke. At the news of the Duke of Enghien's death a thrill of horror seized the princes of Europe. Chateaubriand, the poet, resigned his office as ambassador in Switzerland. The court of Russia put on mourning. The Russian chargé-d'affaires in Paris lodged a formal protest against the execution of Enghien and the invasion of German territory. Napoleon, on the other hand, issued orders to the German States to expel all French Royalists and English subjects from their

Execution of Duc d'Enghien

Effect on Europe

dominions. The British ambassador at Munich received his passports. Other German princes hastened to execute Napoleon's orders. The Austrian Minister told the French ambassador that his master "understood the necessities of politics." But at the Diet of Regensburg official protests were raised against Napoleon on the part of Russia and Sweden. Prussia immediately allied herself to Russia in a secret treaty in which both agreed to declare war "on the first encroachment of the French government upon the States of the North." Napoleon answered Russia's protest with a cutting allusion to the unpunished death of the late Czar. "The complaint now raised by Russia," he wrote, "leads us to ask whether, when England was meditating the assassination of Paul, if Russia had been informed that the conspirators were assembled one league from her frontier, she would not have hastened to seize them." At the same time Talleyrand was instructed to recall the French ambassador from St. Petersburg. Count D'Ouvril, the Russian ambassador, was instructed to leave Paris unless four points were granted: 1. The French evacuation of Naples. 2. A convention on Italian affairs. 3. An indemnity for the King of Sardinia. 4. French evacuation of Northern Germany. These demands were not granted. "I do not wish for war," wrote Napoleon, "but I do not fear it with any one. . . . I will suffer no interference in France."

[sidenote: Russia and Prussia against France]

[sidenote: An Ultimatum to France]

For the moment, France was allowed to accomplish her own destiny. On May 18, Napoleon accepted the French Senate's offer of hereditary empire. Cambacérès, the regicide, first saluted him with the title of Majesty. "I accept," said Bonaparte, "the title which you believe to be useful to the glory of the nation. I hope that France will

Napoleon made Emperor

never repent of the honors with which she endows my family. At all events, my spirit will no longer be with my posterity on that day when they shall cease to merit the love and confidence of la grande nation." A procession of Senators, accompanied by trumpets and kettledrums, announced the event to the people of Paris. The act was ratified by means of lists to which the people signed their names. The affirmative votes numbered 3,572,329, as against 2,509 negatives. The succession was to be in the male line, the Emperor having the privilege of adopting the children of his brothers, in default of which, or of direct issue, the crown was to go to Joseph and Louis Bonaparte. The consular constitution was amended by an imperial decree. Cambacérès and Lebrun, the two outgoing consuls, were made arch-chancellor and arch-treasurer. Napoleon's two brothers became grand elector and grand constable. Their sisters were princesses.

Bonaparte's Lieutenants Rewarded

Eighteen marshals of the empire were created. They were Murat, Masséna, Kellerman, Soult, Brun, Lannes, Ney, Moncy, Jourdan, Augereau, Bernadotte, Mortier, Davoust, Bessières, Junot, Le Febvre, Perignon and Lessurier. Of the illustrious leaders of the Army of the Rhine, none were honored. Moreau was disgraced, and Lecourbe, his right hand, with Macdonald, had to shun Paris. Moreau's house and estate were given to two of

Napoleon's generals. A new nobility was created and the Order of the Legion of Honor was enlarged. An imperial court was established at the Tuileries.

"Whoever," says Madame de Staël, in speaking of these days and events, "could suggest an additional piece of etiquette from the olden time, propose a new reverence, a novel mode of knocking at the door of an antechamber, a more ceremonious manner of presenting a petition or folding a letter, was regarded as a benefactor of the human race. The code of imperial etiquette is the most remarkable authentic record of human baseness that the history of the world contains." *French Imperial Etiquette*

The new dynasty was recognized at Vienna and Berlin. Two months after the assumption of the imperial title by Napoleon, Francis II. of Austria raised the dominions of the House of Hapsburg to the dignity of an empire in place of the dismembered ancient German empire, of which he had been the nominal head. In distant Hayti, the negro leader, Dessalines, assumed the title of Emperor Jean Jacques I. *Austria made an Empire*

His neighbors, the people of the United States, viewed these proceedings with indifference. The interminable naval warfare between Great Britain and France had increased American shipping nearly fivefold. The little war against the Barbary pirates still lingered on, and several attempts were made by Commodore Preble in the Mediterranean to bring Pasha Yusuf of Tripoli to terms by bombarding his harbors. Finally General Eaton, the American Consul at Tunis, brought about an alliance between the

American forces and those of Hamet, who was then commanding an army of Mamelukes against the Turks in Upper Egypt. From the other side, Turkey was threatened by the Servians, who threw off the Turkish rule under the leadership of Czerny Georgos.

Death of Alexander Hamilton

At home the American people had been deeply shocked by the killing of Alexander Hamilton, the great Federalist, in a duel with Vice-President Burr. President Jefferson's first term was drawing to a close. Aaron Burr, who had been defeated in obtaining the Presidency the last time, foresaw that Jefferson would be renominated, and that he would fail again. While holding the office of Vice-President, he became a candidate for the governorship of New York, hoping to strengthen thereby his candidacy for the Presidency. The powerful influence of Hamilton prevented Burr's election. Burr sought a quarrel with Hamilton and challenged him to a duel. On the morning of July 11, on the heights of the Hudson, opposite New York, he shot Hamilton dead after Hamilton had declined to fire. Duelling came into disfavor in America from that day. Burr was indicted for murder and sought refuge in the South. After the expiration

Aaron Burr Disgraced

of his Vice-Presidency, he conceived a plan to found a Western Empire composed of the southernmost States of the Union and Mexico. Thomas Jefferson was re-elected.

By the death of Alexander Hamilton, America lost one of her great statesmen. He was born in the West Indies, of English and French parentage.

Having been sent to school in New York, he joined
the American Revolution at the age of seventeen.
He served early in the Revolutionary war as a cav-
alry officer and later on General Washington's staff.
At the end of the war he married the daughter of
General Schuyler. Next he served in the Conti-
nental Congress and the Constitutional Convention.
Soon he became the leader of the Federal party
in New York. Of the eighty-five papers in the
"Federalist," more than fifty were written by him. The Feder-alist Papers
In 1789 he entered Washington's Cabinet as Secre-
tary of the Treasury. When war broke out with
France, he was made Inspector-General. In poli-
tics he was the opponent both of Jefferson and Burr.

Another famous man who died during this year Death of Kant
was Immanuel Kant, the great German philosopher.
His metaphysical doctrines belonged to a closely
connected system of reasoning begun by Hume
and ended by Hegel. As an ethical thinker he
first achieved fame at Königsberg in 1781. The
existence of an authoritative moral law (his so-
called "categorical imperative"), he contended, im-
plied immortality of the soul and the existence of
a power above. The theory is best put forward
in Wordsworth's famous "Ode to Duty." Kant's
teachings excited persistent controversies throughout Germany. His doctrines were summed up in
his "Critique of Pure Reason" (1781), "Critique
of Practical Reason" (1787), and "Critique of the
Faculty of Judgment" (1790). When this philosopher died, it could be said of him that the whole
of his life had conformed to his teachings.

In contrast to this, the latest utterances of Napoleon conflicted oddly with his acts. On December
1, the French Senate presented to Bonaparte the results of the plebiscite by which he was elected Emperor. Next day Napoleon and his wife, Josephine were solemnly crowned as Emperor and Empress in the Cathedral of Nôtre Dame. Pope Pius

Napoleon
crowned
Emperor

VII. officiated. When the Pope reached for the
crown Napoleon snatched it out of his hands and
placed it on his own head. In his first imperial
proclamation to the Senate, Napoleon said: "If
death do not overtake me in the midst of my enterprises, I hope to leave to posterity a memory
which shall serve forever either as an example or
as a reproach to my successors. .... I do not desire to increase the territory of the Empire. I have
no ambition to exert influence in Europe. No other
State shall be incorporated in the Empire under my
rule." Referring to his foreign relations he said:
"The spirit of Catherine the Great will watch over

Threats
against
Russia

the counsels of Alexander. He will remember that,
situated far from France as he is, he could neither
reach us nor disturb our peace."

The close of this year was marked by an absolute
rupture between Spain and Great Britain. Spain
had been in a measure compelled to purchase peace
from France by the payment of a large subsidy,
the amount of which was kept carefully concealed
from the British Cabinet. When the facts were
learned, the English Minister in Madrid remon-
strated against the payment of such money. It
was not long after discovered that a squadron of

Spanish line-of-battle ships were equipped and ready to sail for Ferrol, where a French fleet awaited their junction, and that the Spanish vessels would put to sea the moment that four Spanish frigates, with the subsidy on board in specie, should arrive from America. The British Cabinet immediately issued orders to Lord Nelson in the Mediterranean, Lord Cornwallis on the Brest station, and Admiral Cochrane off Ferrol, to prevent the sailing of both the French and Spanish squadrons; they also directed each of the three naval commanders to detach two frigates to cruise off Cadiz, and intercept the homeward-bound treasure-ships of Spain. Four of the six British frigates soon fell in with the four Spanish ships off Cadiz. The Spanish commodore declined to submit to an equal force, and a naval engagement was fought. It ended in the blowing up of one of the Spanish ships, and the capture of the other three, with ten millions of dollars on board.

Seizure of Spanish Treasure Ships

The capture of these frigates, before any formal announcement of hostilities, produced the result which might have been anticipated; to wit, a declaration of war by Spain against Great Britain.

Spain declares War on England

1805

IT has remained a subject for conjecture to this day whether Napoleon's preparations for invading England were serious or intended only as a feint. At all events he proceeded so earnestly at Boulogne that all the world anxiously awaited the blow. To Napoleon it afforded an excellent excuse for keeping large bodies of troops on their feet ready for instant action. It was at this time that Napoleon perfected his new military system. He divided his army, in the first instance, into corps of from twenty to thirty thousand men, each of which was intrusted to a marshal of the Empire. Again he separated these corps into four or five divisions, under the command of generals who received their orders from the marshal. In this way, the generals became familiar with the qualities of their officers and the officers with the capacity and disposition of their men; an *esprit de corps* was formed, not only among the officers of the same regiment, but among those of the same division and corps. Early in January, after Admiral Villeneuve had succeeded in taking a French squadron out of Toulon past the ever-watchful cruisers of Great Britain, only to be pursued to the West Indies by Nelson —Napoleon explained to his privy council that

Napoleon's Military Reforms

the Boulogne encampment was maintained but to hoodwink the continental neighbors of France. He justified his expenditure of thirty million francs, for twenty thousand artillery horses and the like, by the fact that he was now able to throw an army into the field within twenty days —one month earlier than Austria could mobilize her artillery. Yet the preparations at Boulogne were so thorough that Napoleon could afford to bide his time for a favorable opportunity to make a dash across the Channel after all. Whichever way he turned he did not mean to be caught napping.

France ready for Instant Mobilization

When Austria, under the promise of more subsidies from England, started to reorganize her artillery service, Napoleon curtly told the Austrian ambassador in Paris that he and his marshals looked forward to eating their Christmas dinner in Vienna.

Austria Forewarned

Early in 1805 the Czar had sent special envoys to London to arrange for a coalition against France. Napoleon at the same time wrote another personal letter to George III. of England. It ran in this wise:

"SIR AND BROTHER—Called to the throne of France by Providence, my first sentiment is a wish for peace. France and England abuse their prosperity. . . . What can your people hope from war? To form a coalition with some powers of the Continent? The Continent will remain tranquil. A coalition can only increase the preponderance and continental greatness of France. . . . If your Majesty will but reflect, you must perceive that the war is without an object, without any worthy

Final Correspondence with England

result to yourself. . . . Is not the world large enough for our two nations to live in it? . . . I trust Your Majesty will believe in the sincerity of my sentiments and my wish to give you every proof of them.   NAPOLEON."

Lord Mulgrave, the British Foreign Secretary, sent a reply the concluding sentences of which read thus:

England's reply

"Conformably to his desire for the future safety and tranquillity of Europe, His Majesty feels it impossible to answer more particularly to the overtures that have been made to him till he has time to communicate with the powers on the Continent with whom he is engaged in confidential relations, and particularly with the Emperor of Russia, who has given the strongest proofs of his wisdom, the elevation of the sentiments with which he is animated, and the living interest which he takes in the safety and independence of the Continent."

Napoleon transmitted his correspondence to the Prime Minister of Spain, and wrote to the Emperor of Austria of the intended accession of his brother Joseph to the crown of Italy. Napoleon himself journeyed to Italy, after a rapid tour along the Rhine to Aix-la-Chapelle, ostensibly for the purpose of visiting the tomb of Charlemagne. In Italy he and Josephine revisited the scenes of his campaigns and held a grand review upon the battlefield of Marengo.

Napoleon visits Italy

On January 24, England declared war with Spain for placing her forces at the disposal of France. Early in March, Napoleon informed the French

Senate that he would accept for himself the crown of Italy. The Pope left France and returned to Rome, foiled in his efforts to regain his lost temporal powers.

About the same time Jefferson and Clinton took the oath of office as President and Vice-President of the United States. On March 5, General William Eaton, the American Consul at Tunis, started out from Alexandria on his overland expedition against Yusuf, the usurper of the throne of Tripoli. With General Eaton went a picked body of Mameluke horsemen, Greek mercenaries and a number of Egyptian fellahs. They traversed the Desert of Barca in a long march of over a thousand miles, and finally arrived before the Tripolitan harbor of Derne. An American fleet opportunely arrived before the harbor at the same time. Their ships bombarded the castle, and American seamen were landed to help General Eaton and his motley followers. They stormed Derne on April 25. Yusuf sued for peace. On June 4 a treaty was concluded between the United States and the last of the Barbary pirates. The American prisoners at Tripoli were set free and the pirates relinquished all claim to further tribute.

Thomas Jefferson Inaugurated

Americans storm Derne

In the meanwhile England had to wage more wars in India. Jaswant Rao Holkar and his general, Ameer Khan, the former allies of Sindia and the Mahrattas, stirred up another war with General Wellesley, the British High-Commissioner. Holkar was defeated in a series of bloody battles by General Lake. In the first of these General Fraser, com-

Another Mahratta War

manding the British cavalry, lost his life. In the end Holkar had to take to the mountains, and India, for the moment, was pacified.

In spring a treaty had been signed between Great Britain and Russia to stop further encroachments by Napoleon. King Gustav of Sweden gave his **Napoleon crowned King of Italy** immediate adhesion. Three weeks later Napoleon was crowned King of Italy. The Austrian dependency of Genoa was annexed to Italy. This last act, premeditated by Napoleon for many years, brought Austria into the coalition. The allies against **Third Coalition against France** France now included England, Russia, Austria and Sweden. Great Britain undertook to pay subsidies to all the members of the coalition. France could count on the South German States and on Spain. The King of Prussia remained aloof in the hope of obtaining Hanover.

By the middle of summer the political horizon was surcharged with electricity. Napoleon wrote to Talleyrand: "All my news from Italy is warlike. Indeed Austria no longer observes any conceal**Napoleon's Opening Move** ment." On August 13, Napoleon, through Talleyrand, demanded the withdrawal of all Austrian troops to Bohemia, so as to leave him a free hand against England. Otherwise he threatened immediate hostilities. On the same day he issued urgent orders to Admiral Villeneuve, who had returned to Ferrol from the West Indies, to join the squadron at Brest and to strike the English at all hazards. "If with thirty ships my admirals fear to attack twenty-four British," he concluded scathingly, "we may as well give up all hope of a navy."

Villeneuve at once got to sea with twenty-nine ships of the line. As he sailed, the hesitating admiral wrote to the French Minister of Marine: "The enemy's forces, more concentrated than ever, leave me little other resource than to go to Cadiz." So it turned out. Meanwhile Napoleon wrote this prophetic letter to Talleyrand:

My squadron sailed August 14 from Ferrol with thirty-four ships; it had no enemy in sight. If it follows my instructions, joins the Brest squadron and enters the Channel, there is still time. I am master of England. If on the contrary my admirals hesitate, manœuvre badly, and do not fulfil their purpose, I have no other resource than to wait for winter to cross with a flotilla. That operation is risky. Such being the case, I hasten to meet the most pressing danger. I raise my camp here by September 23. I shall have in Germany 200,000 and 25,000 in Naples. I march upon Vienna, and do not lay down my arms until I have Naples and Venice. Then I shall have no more to fear from Austria."

Admiral Villeneuve, discouraged by adverse winds and an indecisive action with some British ships under Sir Robert Calder, took his fleet to Cadiz. A small British squadron, commanded by Collingwood, took care of it there until reinforced by Calder's squadron, which followed the French from Ferrol. Other British ships joined the blockade from the Mediterranean. With twenty-six ships of the line, Collingwood held the French securely blocked until the end of September. Then Nelson arrived from England and took command. Napoleon's hopes of invading England, if ever genuine, were ended for good.

Napoleon received the news of Villeneuve's fatal blunder with an outburst of rage. War on land was his only course henceforth. On August 24, he summoned General Marmont and gave him secret French marching orders. Marmont's army corps left Bou-
Armies on
the march logne next day. On the same day Napoleon wrote to Talleyrand: "My decision is taken. My movement is begun. Three weeks hence I shall be in Germany with 200,000 men." By the end of August the whole French army was in movement. Napoleon himself remained at Boulogne under the pretence of preparing to embark for England. Not until September 24 did he leave France. Then the Emperor fairly flew to join his army. On the 26th he was at Strasburg. The whole army crossed Napoleon
crosses the the Rhine, and on October 7 the united French forces
Rhine struck the Danube below Ulm. "You have won the war with your legs," said their delighted leader. Marmont's corps of 20,000 had marched for Mainz. Bernadotte, with the 20,000 who had held Hanover, Prussian boldly abandoned the North, and crossing through
Territory the Prussian territory of Anspach, joined Marmont.
violated Thirty thousand soldiers of the Southern German States threw themselves into the arms of the first comer. This swelled the French army to 200,000 men. By the time the Austrians threw an ill-mobilized advance force of 60,000 into Bavaria, the soldiers of Bavaria and Wurtemberg had already joined the French at Stuttgart. Bernadotte occupied Munich.

The Austrian general, Mack, stood at Ulm with 45,000 men waiting for the 50,000 Russians under Kutusov, who were to reach him by October 10. The Russians were several days behindhand. Meanwhile the French with four army corps crossed the Danube nearly a week before they were expected. The left wing of the Austrians was turned and the Austrian forces in the Tyrol were thus cut off. Bernadotte's and Ney's divisions pushed in between General Mack and the slowly advancing Russians, while Marmont swung around to the Austrian rear. Ney, Soult and Lannes advanced their three army corps from Donauwoerth, while Murat, with his cavalry, made a dash along the banks of the Danube. The concerted movement was executed by Napoleon's seven marshals with admirable precision. Ney rolled up the Austrians under Archduke Ferdinand at Gunzburg and again at Elchingen. Three thousand prisoners fell into his hands. Soult overran Augsburg and took Memmingen, with 4,000 prisoners. Murat overtook General Werneck's battalions marching out of Ulm and threw them back into the city, taking 3,000 prisoners. From all sides the Austrians were thrown into Ulm. There they were completely surrounded by overwhelming numbers, and, as it were, suffocated. On October 20, Mack surrendered with 23,000 Austrians, without ever a chance to fight a pitched battle. Napoleon could write to Josephine:

French cross the Danube

Russian Army cut off

Gunzburg, Elchingen, Memmingen

Surrender of Ulm

"During all the days of the week I have been drenched with rain and my feet have been nearly frozen. To-day I have had some rest. I have fulfilled my designs. I have destroyed the Austrian army by simple marches. I have taken 60,000 prisoners, 120 guns, 90 flags, and more than 30 general officers. I am content with my army. We have lost but 1,500 men, two-thirds of whom are merely wounded. I now go in pursuit of the Russians. They are undone. Adieu, my Josephine. One thousand loving words to you."

On the day after this brilliant success the French arms elsewhere suffered irretrievable disaster. Before quitting France, Napoleon had given orders for the French fleet to enter the Mediterranean to help the French army under St. Cyr to strike at Naples. *Villeneuve disgraced* At the same time there was to be a change of command. "As Villeneuve's excessive pusillanimity will prevent him from undertaking this," wrote Napoleon to Decrès, "we will send to replace him Admiral Rosily, who will bear letters directing Villeneuve to return to France and give an account of his conduct." On the approach of Admiral Rosily, Villeneuve, getting wind of his mission, determined to strike a blow on his own behalf. On October 18 he wrote to Decrès: "I will sail hence to-morrow if circumstances favor." The next day *He sails forth for Battle* his fleet weighed anchor. Nelson, waiting far outside, at once made sail for the Straits of Gibraltar to bar the entrance to the Mediterranean. Early on the morning of October 21 thirty-three French and Spanish ships of the line with five frigates and two brigs headed due south for the Straits. The two British columns were nearly a mile apart, sailing parallel according to Nelson's prearranged plan of battle. Nelson was on the "Victory," with seventy-four guns, commanding twelve ships on the right. Collingwood on the "Royal Sovereign" headed_ fifteen ships on the left wing. The French and Spaniards steered south in five columns, two of which were detached to windward under Admiral Gravina. Cape Trafalgar loomed up twelve miles in the distance. Nelson hoisted the signal: "England expects every man to do his duty."

To the British double column advance the French opposed a long line, close-hauled, so as to curve away from the point of attack. Admiral Villeneuve was almost in the centre on the "Bucentaure," an eighty-gun ship, and Vice-Admiral Alava was but a few ships from him on the "Santa Anna." Both British columns made for the middle of the French line, Nelson's flagship heading for the "Bucentaure," while Collingwood made a dash for the "Santa Anna." "Let us do something to-day that the world will talk of hereafter," said Collingwood. So far did the "Royal Sovereign" outsail, or rather outdrift, the rest of the fleet, that Collingwood entered the enemy's fire three-quarters of a mile ahead of the rest at noon. For fully half an hour he had to support the combined fire of the enemy's ships quite alone. "See!" cried Nelson, as he watched his progress, "see how that noble fellow Collingwood carries his ship into action!" and Collingwood at the same time observed to his officers, "What would Nelson give to be here!" Collingwood's first broadside raked the "Santa Anna" from stern to stem. Her decks ran with blood. Then the "Royal

Battle of Trafalgar

Collingwood opens the Fight

Sovereign" luffed up close to her chief antagonist, and side by side with the "Santa Anna" she fought off the enemy's ships that closed in upon the two. At last Collingwood's next-in-line came up with the "Royal Sovereign," and together they sank or captured twelve of Admiral Alava's sixteen ships forming the rear line. Nelson, at the head of his squadron, did not reach the "Bucentaure" until half an hour after his right wing was in full battle. Nelson's flagship raked the "Bucentaure," but a ship close to leeward blocked her way. A furious close-range fight followed between the "Victory" and the "Redoubtable." The English broadsides were stronger, but the French swept the "Victory's" decks with their musketry. Of the French crew of 643 but 35 were left, and they kept up the fight. At half-past one Nelson was struck by a bullet fired from the Frenchman's rigging. He fell on the deck mortally wounded. As his ship trembled under the thunder of her continued broadsides, Nelson exclaimed: "Ah, Victory, Victory, how thou dost rack my brain." "They have done for me at last," he said. While they carried him down to the cockpit he covered his face and epaulets with a handkerchief, lest the news of his injury should discourage the fighting sailors. When they brought him news that fifteen of the enemy's ships had been taken, he whispered: " 'Tis well, but I bargained for twenty." Lord Nelson died a few moments after the "Achille" and the "Intrepide" had blown up.

Perez Galdos, in his "Episodios Nacionales," has

"Victory" and "Re-doubtable"

Death of Nelson

given a realistic picture of the scenes within the Perez Galdos's pen picture
gloomy recesses of the great Spanish four-decker,
"Santissima Trinidad," as the British ships hung
on her flanks and wasted her with their fire: "The
English shot had torn our sails to tatters. It was
as if huge invisible talons had been dragging at
them. Fragments of spars, splinters of wood, thick
hempen cables cut up as corn is cut by the sickle,
fallen blocks, shreds of canvas, bits of iron, and
hundreds of other things that had been wrenched
away by the enemy's fire, were piled along the
deck, where it was scarcely possible to move about.
From moment to moment men fell—some into the
sea; and the curses of the combatants mingled with
groans of the wounded, so that it was often difficult
to decide whether the dying were blaspheming God Particulars of the Fight
or the fighters were calling upon Him for aid. I
helped in the very dismal task of carrying the
wounded into the hold, where the surgeons worked.
Some died ere we could convey them thither;
others had to undergo frightful operations ere their
worn-out bodies could get an instant's rest. It was
much more satisfactory to be able to assist the car-
penter's crew in temporarily stopping some of the
holes torn by shot in the ship's hull. . . Blood
ran in streams about the deck; and, in spite of the
sand, the rolling of the ship carried it hither and
thither until it made strange patterns on the planks.
The enemy's shot, fired, as they were, from very
short range, caused horrible mutilations. . . The
ship creaked and groaned as she rolled, and through
a thousand holes and crevices in her strained hull

the sea spurted in and began to flood the hold. The 'Trinidad's' people saw the commander-in-chief haul down his flag; heard the 'Achille' blow up and hurl her six hundred men into eternity; learned that their own hold was so crowded with wounded that no more could be received there. Then, when all three masts had in succession been brought crashing down, the defence collapsed, and the 'Santissima Trinidad' struck her flag.'' When the French flagship struck, she was taken possession of by a tiny boat's crew from the ''Conqueror,'' consisting of three marines and two sailors. The marine officer coolly locked the powder magazine of the Frenchman, put the key in his pocket, left two of his men in charge of the surrendered ''Bucentaure,'' put Villeneuve and his two captains in his boat with his two marines and himself, and pulled off in search of the ''Conqueror.'' In the smoke and confusion, however, he could not find that ship, and so carried the captured French admiral to the ''Mars.''

Capture of Villeneuve

French and Spanish losses

By two in the afternoon the enemy's fleet was cut in two. Altogether the French and Spaniards lost eighteen ships. At five in the evening Admiral Gravina retreated to Cadiz with the remnants of the allied fleet. Only five French ships got away. Admiral Villeneuve and the Spanish Rear-Admiral Cisneros were taken prisoners. Admiral Gravina and Rear-Admiral Alava were wounded, and the French Rear-Admiral was killed. Villeneuve, later, committed suicide. Four of the French ships that escaped shortly afterward fell a prey to the British

Villeneuve commits Suicide

off Cape Vilano. After a four hours' fight between Commodore Strachan and the French Rear-Admiral, Dumarois, they struck their colors.

Napoleon took pains to suppress all reports of this disastrous battle in France. In a subsequent message to the Corps Legislatif he thus referred to it: "We have lost some ships by storm after a battle imprudently undertaken." As a matter of fact the battle of Trafalgar at one stroke destroyed the sea power of Spain and of France. Its conse- quences have lasted to the present day. *Far-reaching results of Trafalgar*

In Italy the command of a French force number- ing 90,000 men had been given to Masséna. The Austrians confronted him with their strongest army numbering 75,000 under Archduke Charles. Face to face, on the opposite banks of the Adige, the two armies waited only for the signal of attack. Masséna, hearing how favorable matters stood in Germany, resolved to strike simultaneously with Napoleon. On October 18 he crossed the Adige, but encountered such a murderous fire from the Austrian trenches that, after securing a lodgment, he had to fall back. On October 20 the French army crossed the river a second time and stormed the heights of Valpantena and St. Michael amid great slaughter. On October 30, upon the news of the surrender of Ulm, Masséna attacked very vigor- ously all along the line. A bloody battle followed at Caldiero, in which both sides suffered severely. In the end 3,000 Austrians were made prisoners. A detached column of 5,000 under Hillinger like- wise had to surrender to the French. Archduke *War in Italy* *Battle of Caldiero*

Charles, after obtaining a short armistice, fell back and began a steady retreat toward Vincenza and Venice. The French followed step by step. All attempts to reinforce him from the Tyrol were frustrated.

In Germany, Napoleon followed up the surrender of Mack by sending his cavalry under Murat after the detached Austrian battalions, with instructions to come in touch with the approaching Russian column. Kutusov, the Russian general, fell back over the Danube. Murat failed to engage him, but pushed on to pluck the easy prize of Vienna. His victorious squadrons rode through Vienna on November 13. As a result of this tactical mistake on the part of Napoleon's brother-in-law, Mortier's advance columns under General Gazan were almost annihilated by the Russians. Murat received peremptory orders to leave Vienna and attack the Russians on their right flank in Moravia. In a stubborn fight at Hollabrunn the Russian general, Bagration, held the French long enough to prevent the Russian flank from being turned. The Russian reserve of 45,000, under Generals Bennigsen and Essen, came up and joined forces with Kutusov and the remnants of the Austrian armies. Napoleon, standing at Brunn with 80,000, found himself confronted by an army of 100,000 allies. To protect his flanks, Napoleon had to extend his army far into Bohemia, Hungary, and down to the Alps. Behind him in Italy, Russian and British forces had landed at Naples to throw the French out of Taranto.

At this critical moment the Prussian prime minis-

Capture of Vienna

Allies join forces

ter, Von Haugwitz, appeared at Napoleon's head- Threatening Prussian demands
quarters. By way of reparation for Bernadotte's
march through Prussian Ansbach, he demanded
immediate evacuation of all recent French acquisitions. Otherwise Prussia stood ready to join the
allies with an army of 180,000 men. As it was,
the King of Prussia had already shown his temper
by permitting the Russians to march through Prussian Silesia. For Napoleon, it became all-important
to hold the Prussians off, if only for a few days.
To gain this time he sent Von Haugwitz to Talleyrand at Vienna with private instructions to that
master of diplomacy to prolong his proceedings
with the inconvenient envoy as long as he possibly
could. In the interval all might be won by a bold
stroke of fortune.

In the camp of the allies the youthful Czar of Alexander's Generalship
Russia felt equally impatient. Alexander burned
to measure his imperial generalship against that
of the Corsican upstart, and, forthwith, General
Weyrother was ordered to draw up a plan of battle.
The allies, in their plan of attack, meant to turn
the right flank of the French army, to cut them
off from Vienna and drive them to the Bohemian
mountains. They sought to effect this by one
of the most hazardous operations in war—a flank
march in column in front of a concentrated enemy—
and that enemy Napoleon. Accordingly, early on
December 1, they moved forward in five columns
obliquely across the French position, while the reserve, under Grandduke Constantine, occupied the
heights in front of Austerlitz. The moment that

Napoleon saw this manœuvre undertaken, he exclaimed, "That army is mine!"

His vanguard was at once withdrawn to lure on the Russians. For the sake of better concentration, Napoleon fell back behind Brunn, where Bernadotte and Davoust could the more readily join him with their army corps. The Russians harassed the right flank of the French. To detach the Russian forces still further, Napoleon, on the eve of battle, extended the end of his right flank in the direction of Tellnitz. The Russian general fell into the trap. While turning the distant French flank he denuded the centre of the allied battle line. Napoleon had planned to strike the allies in their weak centre. The better to accomplish his purpose he meant to take them by surprise. Upon the approach of the allies, early next morning, Marshal Soult, who held the French centre, was ordered to fall back from the heights of Pratzen. This was done. The Russian vanguard hastened to climb the heights and waited for the rest to come up, while the French concentrated in the valley below. All was hidden in the mists of winter.

At nine o'clock the haze blew away and the sun rose glorious above the heights—the famous "Sun of Austerlitz." It was Napoleon's lucky day, December 2, the date of his coronation. As soon as the fog lifted, Soult's columns dashed up the hill and stormed the heights. The Russian guns, just unlimbering on the crest of the hill of Pratzen, were turned against the allies. At the point of the bayonet their infantry was driven down the steep slope and threw the Russian reserve columns into inde- scribable disorder. The struggling mass of allies came under the shot and shell of their own captured batteries on the hill, while the French horse artillery dashed to other points of vantage. The Russian guards made a brave stand in the plain, but they were overwhelmed by Soult's compact corps charging down the hill. Soult pierced the centre and cut the allied army fairly in two. All the French reserve cavalry under Murat crumpled up the Austrian left wing. For a while the right flank still held its own. The Russian horse-guards repulsed the French grenadiers-à-cheval and cut their way through them to the foot of the eminence, where Napoleon stood directing the battle; but the combined forces of Soult, Lannes and Davoust were too much for them. Napoleon's aide-de-camp, Rapp, was wounded, and the Russian prince, Ruppin, was taken captive during this encounter. Whole battalions were bayoneted by the French. The bridge at Aujezd broke under the weight of fleeing Russians. Other large bodies of allies broke through the ice of Lake Satcha, which was burst by means of French artillery fire. Several thousand were drowned or taken prisoners. Elsewhere six thousand Austrians perished, and 20,000, most of whom were Russians, were taken alive. All the stores and ammunition of the combined armies fell into Napoleon's hands. "I had previously seen some lost battles," says an eye-witness of this frightful scene, General Langeron, "but I had no conception of such a defeat." The

Emperor
Francis
comes to
terms

young Czar wept as he rode away from the scene of the disaster. After him went all that was left of the Russian army. The Austrian emperor sought out Napoleon at his headquarters and sued for terms. Thus ended the battle of The Three Emperors.

Prussia
changes
front

Through Von Haugwitz at Vienna, Prussia, instead of attacking Napoleon, entered into a secret treaty with the conqueror at Schoenbrunn. Napoleon remarked: "Voilá un compliment dont la fortune a changé l'adresse!" Prussia's reward for this change of front was to be the dominion of Hanover. Ten days after the departure of Haugwitz from Vienna, Austria made peace with France at Pressburg. Napoleon's threat that his marshals would eat their Christmas dinner in Vienna was fulfilled. Austria had to give up 28,000 square miles of territory, with three and a half million inhabitants. Venice and Dalmatia went to France; the Tyrol and the free cities of Augsburg and Nuremberg to Bavaria, which was elevated to a kingdom together with Wurtemberg. Prussia obtained Hanover, but lost Neufchatel in Switzerland to France, and Anspach to Bavaria. The treaty of Pressburg was followed by Napoleon's famous proclamation against the House of Naples: "We have pardoned," it ran, "that infatuated king, who has thrice done everything to ruin himself. Shall we pardon him a fourth time? Shall we a fourth time trust a court without faith, without honor, without reason? No! It is incompatible with the repose of Europe and the honor of my crown." Once more Napoleon

Peace of
Pressburg

Venice
taken from
Austria

South
German
Princes
rewarded

was master of Europe, with none to dispute his sway but England.

The year 1805 was a sad one for Germany in other respects. During this year the poet Friedrich Schiller died at Weimar in his forty-fifth year. He was then in the midst of a Russian historical play, "Demetrius." Schiller was one of the brightest stars of German literature. In his convictions he was pre-eminently an idealist like Shelley, and, like him, he was a master of lyric expression; and this at a time when the German language was still in an uncouth and crude stage. As a historian, unlike most German scholars, he was distinguished rather by his command of facile and lucid prose than by the thoroughness of his research. Idealist that he was, his philosophical studies made him a clear thinker. Thus, as early as 1794, he gave this forecast of the main results of the French Revolution, then at its height: "The French Republic will pass away as suddenly as it arose. It will pass into anarchy, and this will end in submission to a despot, who will extend his sway over the greater part of Europe." Schiller began his literary career as a revolutionary. While serving as a regimental surgeon in Stuttgart, he wrote "The Robbers," a wild, rhapsodical play, the performance of which created a tempest in a teapot. Schiller was called to account for it and left Stuttgart as a fugitive. The next few years were spent at Mannheim, Leipsic and Dresden in great poverty. With the aid of his old friend, Koerner, Schiller found his way at last to Weimar, where he was kindly received. Goethe

Death of Schiller

Schiller's forecast of Napoleon

secured for him an appointment as professor of history at the University of Jena, a post which Schiller held until his death. In his capacity of historian he wrote "A History of the Revolt of the Netherlands" and an elaborate "History of the Thirty Years' War," which is still a standard.

His last Works

From 1795 to 1800 the poet wrote his finest ballads and his most finished drama, the trilogy of "Wallenstein." In the following years, spent mostly at Weimar, he produced "Mary Stuart," "The Maid of Orleans," "The Bride of Messina," and "William Tell," the last and most successful of his plays.

1806

ON January 1 of this year the reigning princes of Bavaria and Wurtemberg assumed the royal crown. From Schoenbrunn in Austria Napoleon dictated a decree deposing the Bourbon family in Italy: "La Dynastie de Naples a cessé de regner." The Queen of Naples fled to Palermo in Sicily, where her court was protected by the guns of British cruisers. *House of Naples dethroned*

In England the opponents of the government opened the year by asking for an inquiry into the causes of the disasters to the British policy abroad "so far as they were connected with the conduct of the Ministry." The motion, though read in both Houses of Parliament, was never brought to a vote, owing to the severe illness into which the Prime Minister had fallen after the disaster at Austerlitz. On January 23, William Pitt died in the forty-seventh year of his life. The death of Nelson, with the disasters of Ulm and Austerlitz, following so closely upon one another, were too much for Pitt's failing health. The dying statesman's exhortation to Emperor Francis, written after the surrender of Ulm, is one of the most soul-stirring appeals to be found in English diplomatic correspondence. "Austerlitz killed Pitt," wrote Wilberforce in his diary. *Death of Pitt*

" 'Roll up that map,' he said in a hollow voice, as he pointed to a map of Europe which hung upon the wall. 'It will be useless for ten years to come.' " While in the stupor of death Pitt rallied for a last time. Those that bent over him caught a faint murmur: "My country! How I leave my country!" The bearer of a great name, he had made it even more illustrious. During his lifetime he exerted a powerful influence over the destinies of his country and of Europe. For twenty-three years he presided over the councils of Great Britain. He showed his chief ability in the management of the internal affairs of his country, particularly in the regulation of its finances. But for his resolute creation of a national sinking fund based on the increment of compound interest, England would have been unequal to the financial burdens of her gigantic war against the power of Napoleon. The union of Ireland to England was Pitt's crowning stroke. In external affairs he was singularly unfortunate. His blunt letters to Napoleon are a case in point. Almost all his political reverses came from that source. Had he lived, his recent disastrous foreign policy would probably have foundered his administration before the close of Parliament. Lord Grenville, who succeeded Pitt in office, took Mr. Fox into his cabinet to act as Secretary of Foreign Affairs. For the moment Mr. Fox had to follow in the footsteps of his predecessor. After Pitt's death, Parliament voted a sum of £40,000 to pay the dead statesman's debts, and decreed that he should be buried by the nation in Westminster Abbey. The

The Younger Pitt's achievements

city of London voted to erect a public monument
to Pitt at Guildhall.

On the same day, the French Senate decreed that
a public monument should be erected to "Napoleon le Grand." The young Italian sculptor Canova
was intrusted with this task. A few days later the
last remnants of the French navy under Leissègues
were destroyed in the bay of San Domingo by a Sea-fight
off San
British squadron, under the command of Admiral Domingo
Duckworth. After a fierce sea-fight, lasting several hours, two French ships were blown up and
three surrendered. Next, the French Vice-Admiral Other
naval
Linois, returning from India, fell into the hands of encounters
the British with one ship of the line and one frigate.
The "Cannonnière," another French ship of the line,
was captured off the Cape of Good Hope. French French
paralyzed
at sea
commercial shipping was annihilated. Henceforth
Napoleon had only his land forces to count on. In
the first week of February he sent an army of invasion to Naples under Masséna, and his brother
Joseph was made King of the Two Sicilies. Napoleon announced it at the opening session of the
Corps Legislatif. His address contained the following characteristic sentences:

"I have avenged the rights of the weaker States.
The royal House of Naples has lost its crown forever. Italy from end to end now forms a part of
our great empire. Frenchmen, I have not been
deceived in my hopes. Your love more than the
acquisition of rich territories is my chief glory.
Henceforth nothing shall be done that is not essential to guarantee the glory and safety of my
peoples."

Simultaneously with this, Joseph **Bonaparte**, very much against his will, was proclaimed King of Naples and Sicily. Napoleon's other brothers, Louis and Jerome, were likewise disposed of. Louis, in the face of his protest, was selected for the throne of Holland. "If you have not been consulted in this affair," wrote Napoleon to his brother, "it was because a subject cannot but obey." Jerome, who had married a Miss Patterson of Baltimore, was ordered to give up his wife and child to marry a princess of Wurtemberg, with whom to reign over the projected kingdom of Westphalia. When Pope

Pius VII. demurred to this divorce, Napoleon wrote brusquely: "Your Holiness is sovereign of Rome, but I am her Emperor. . . I am accountable to God, who has chosen my arm to re-establish religion. . . It is not by sleeping that I have reorganized religion in France in such a manner that there is no other country in which it is productive of so much good, or where it is so much respected." To his cousin, Cardinal Fesch, Napoleon wrote: "1 do not intend the court of Rome to mix longer in politics; I shall inform the Pope in a very few words. If he does not acquiesce, I shall reduce him to the same condition in which he was before Charlemagne." Napoleon's stepson, Eugene Beauharnais, married Princess Augusta of Bavaria and was made Prince of Upper Italy, while her former betrothed was united by force to Stephanie de Beauharnais, Napoleon's mistress. To this system of grand fiefs

Napoleon added a number of lesser sovereignties which he distributed at will among his relatives and favorites. His sister Elise received Lucca and Piombino; Pauline Bonaparte obtained the Duchy of Guastalla; Marshal Berthier got the Principality of Neufchatel; Murat was made Grandduke of Clèves-Berg; Lebrun became Duke of Piacenza; Bernadotte received Ponte-Corvo, and Talleyrand, the former bishop, became Prince of Benevento. The Venetian States alone formed twelve additional fiefs.

Napoleon's most gifted brother, Lucien, alone held out. He had angered his brother by marrying Madame Jouberteau, a lively lady of Paris, at a time that Napoleon wished him to marry the Queen of Etruria. "I wish to place all my brothers on thrones," wrote Napoleon, "yet you, who ought to second my wishes, whom I love, your only delight consists in running after this woman." Several attempts at reconciliation failed. Finally, when one of Napoleon's go-betweens proposed to Lucien to make peace with his brother by putting away his wife "at least for a time," Lucien ended all negotiations in a letter which ended with the famous line: "I glory, sir, in being ignorant of the language which you employ." After this Lucien was expatriated.

Lucien Bonaparte defiant

During the war of 1805 the internal affairs of France were going from bad to worse. The annual expenses for the year 1805, according to Gaudin's reports, were 894,000,000 francs. On starting for the front of war, Napoleon remarked to his new minister, Mollien: "Our finances are in a bad state. It is not here that I can restore them to order." After the battle of Austerlitz all this changed.

French financial reforms

The enormous French army was quartered outside of France at the expense of other countries. From the contributions levied on Austria and Southern Germany a "Caisse militaire" was formed and intrusted to Mollien for the especial benefit of the soldiers of the empire. Triumphal arches to the army were erected at the Carrousel and the Etoile; the bridge of Austerlitz was laid across the Seine, and columns were raised, cast from the bronze of the enemy's cannons. "The belles-lettres and arts are about to take a soaring flight," wrote Napoleon, as he issued decrees for the completion of the museum of the Louvre, the restoration of the Pantheon to religious worship, and the construction of a "Tribunal of Commerce" on the site of the Church of La Madeleine. New streets were opened, among them the handsome Rue Rivoli and Rue de la Paix. The foundation of the new University of France was postponed until later. The most lasting of all these home measures was the great code of civil procedure. It was promulgated a few days after the death of Tronchet, the celebrated legal defender of Louis XVI., who had helped to frame the new code. It went into effect by the end of the year.

Other internal reforms

The Code Napoleon

The "Code Napoleon," as it has come to be called, was so admirably constructed that it soon became the organic law of the land. It swept away the last remnants of feudalism and established the equality of all French citizens before the law. The freedom of divorce, one of the innovations of the French Revolution, was abolished, and in its place came a strict legal recognition of the responsi-

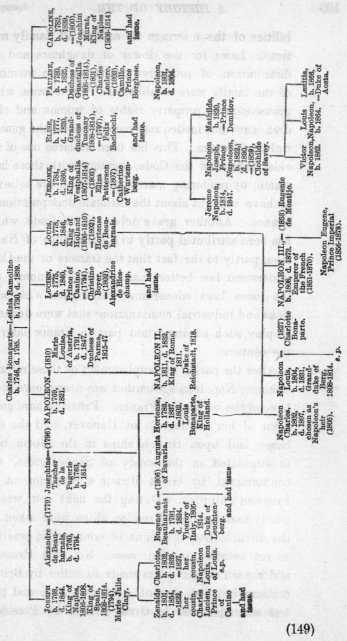

THE FAMILY OF NAPOLEON

Charles Bonaparte—Letizia Ramolino
b. 1746, d. 1785. b. 1750, d. 1839.

JOSEPH, b. 1768, d. 1844, King of Naples, 1806-1808, King of Spain, 1808-1814, (1794) Marie Julie Clary.

Alexandre = (1779) Josephine Tascher de la Pagerie, b. 1763, d. 1814.
de Beauharnais, b. 1760, d. 1794.

(1796) **NAPOLEON,** b. 1769, d. 1821. = (1810) Marie Louise, of Austria, b. 1791, d. 1847, Duchess of Parma, 1815-47.

LUCIEN, b. 1775, d. 1840, Prince of Canino, =(1794), Christine Boyer, =(1802), Alexandrine de Bles-champ, **and had issue.**

LOUIS, b. 1778, d. 1846, King of Holland (1806-1810), =(1802), Hortense de Beau-harnais.

JEROME, b. 1784, d. 1860, King of Westphalia (1807-1814), =(1808) Eliza Patterson =(1807) Catherine of Wurtem-berg, **and had issue.**

ELISE, b. 1777, d. 1820, Grand-duchess of Tuscany (1808-1814), =(1797), Felix Bacciochi, **and had issue.**

PAULINE, b. 1780, d. 1825, Duchess of Guastalla (1808-1814), =(1801), Charles Leclerc, =(1803), Camillo, Prince Borghese.

CAROLINE, b. 1782, d. 1839, =(1800), Joachim Murat, King of Naples (1808-1814), **and had issue.**

Zenaide Charlotte, b. 1801, d. 1839, =1822, her cousin, Charles Lucien, Prince of Canino **and had issue.**

Charlotte, b. 1802, d. 1839, =1827, her cousin, Napoleon Louis, son of Louis. *s.p.*

Hortense, b. 1783, d. 1837, =1802, Louis Bonaparte, King of Holland.

= (1806) Augusta of Bavaria. Eugene de Beauharnais, b. 1781, d. 1824, Viceroy of Italy, 1805-1814, Duke of Leuchten-berg. **and had issue**

NAPOLEON II., b. 1811, d. 1832, King of Rome, 1811, Duke of Reichstadt, 1818.

(1827) Charlotte Bonaparte. *s. p.*

Napoleon Charles, b. 1802, d. 1807, chosen as Napoleon's heir (1805).

Napoleon Louis, b. 1804, d. 1831, Grand-duke of Berg, 1806-1814.

NAPOLEON III., b. 1808, d. 1873, Emperor of the French (1851-1870). =(1853) Eugenie de Montijo.

Jerome Napoleon, b. 1814, d. 1847.

Napoleon Joseph, Prince Napoleon, b. 1822, d. 1889, =(1859) Clothilde of Savoy.

Mathilde, b. 1820, =Prince Demidor.

Napoleon Eugene, Prince Imperial (1856-1879).

Victor Napoleon, b. 1862.

Louis Napoleon, b. 1864.

Letitia, b. 1866, =Duke of Aosta.

bilities of the marriage tie and of all family relations. Laws for the dower of daughters and the
distribution of property among all the members
of the family were established. These laws, while
protecting the property rights of women and children, gave but inadequate recognition to the general
rights of woman. This has been declared one of the
chief defects of the Code, together with those laws
which, by rendering marriage difficult, are believed
to have brought about the ultimate depopulation of
France. Another grave defect in the Code, which
has been attributed partly to the influence of Napoleon, partly to the fact that the framers of the Code
understood law better than political economy, are
the loose laws concerning workingmen's associa-
tions and industrial combinations that were destined
to play such an important part in France later in
the century.

British
Naval Em-
bargo
    After the partial accomplishment of these reforms
at home, Napoleon's attention was drawn once more
beyond the borders of France. Prussia's announcement of her annexation of Hanover, and the embargo laid upon British ships in the North Sea,
as stipulated in the treaty of Schoenbrunn, was
counteracted by Great Britain's embargo on all
Prussian shipping. During the next few weeks,
nearly four hundred Prussian ships were taken by
the British, but the right of confiscation was not
as yet enforced in their case. Not only Prussian
and French shipping was made to suffer by British
cruisers, but also that of America. A formal protest was addressed to Great Britain by President

Jefferson. The main points of this State paper are thus summed up in the British Annual Register for 1806: "The forcible impressment of American seamen into the British navy, so the United States contended, was a practice derogatory to the honor of their flag and inconsistent with their rights as an independent nation. While it lasted, there could be no real friendship between Great Britain and the United States. So intolerable an abuse could not be endured by an independent State unless from inability to resist the injury." Great Britain did not heed the protest. On April 25 the feeling between the two countries was aggravated by the killing of an American seaman named Pierce, by a stray shot from the British cruiser "Leander," within sight of New York. The captain of the "Leander" was permitted to go unpunished. President Jefferson issued a proclamation excluding the "Leander" and her two convoys from all harbors of the United States. In New York the citizens held an indignation meeting at the Tontine coffee house, and had the captain of the "Leander" indicted for murder. The New York rabble clamored for war. Yet war with England was not to be lightly undertaken. As John Randolph said in one of his speeches at the time: "I will never consent to go to war for that which I cannot protect. I deem it no sacrifice of dignity to say to the Leviathan of the deep: 'We are unable to contend with you in your own element, but if you come within our actual limits, we shall shed our last drop of blood in their defence.'" Finally a treaty was

Impressment of American sailors

The "Leander" affair

Attempts at adjustment

draughted between Lords Holland and Auckland on one side and Messrs. Monroe and Pinckney on the other, in which an attempt was made to regulate these abuses. But President Jefferson, finding England's concessions inadequate, withheld his ratification.

About the same time that the British squadron before New York was excluded from American ports of entry, the United States stopped all trade with Hayti. Though this was done at the bid of Napoleon, whose ministers had written that "Com-

San Domingo out-lawed

merce with San Domingo must not continue," the true motive for this unusual measure lay in the Southern slave-holders' execration of the successful revolt of the negroes in San Domingo. The latest outrage in that quarter was a massacre of all the remaining French colonists at Cape Haytien, per-petrated under the orders of Dessalines. In the end the so-called Emperor was himself assassinated.

Early in the year the American Secretary of State, Madison, had been seriously embarrassed by an abortive filibustering expedition against Spain. The moving spirit of this enterprise was one Fran-cesco de Miranda, a Spanish revolutionist, who had gained personal access to Madison. Another Ameri-can statesman was more deeply interested in Miran-

Burr's am-bitious projects

da's plots; this was Aaron Burr. Finding Miranda too impetuous, Burr dropped him and entered into a project with the British Minister in America and others to separate the Western and Atlantic States and seize Spanish territory in Florida and Mexico wherewith to form a new empire of the South. In

pursuance of this plan, Burr made a hurried trip
through the southwest, and tried to gain adherents
to his plans. From Great Britain Burr demanded
a promise of naval aid and a credit for £110,000.
Burr and his fellow conspirators talked so freely
that the plan became known to the Spaniards.
Marquis Yrujo, the Spanish Minister, informed his
government of all the main details of the plot, which
he characterized as "almost insane." Burr's wild
scheme at this time was to introduce his fellow conspirators into Washington and there to seize the
President, Vice-President and president of the Senate, together with the public funds and Capitol
defences. With this end in view, Burr made overtures to General Wilkinson, chief commander of the
American army, Commodore Truxtun, and to General Eaton, the hero of Derne. Andrew Jackson
was likewise approached. President Jefferson, when
apprised of the plot, showed himself inclined to
give Burr liberal leeway. By midsummer, in 1806,
Burr had accomplished all that could be done in
the East and betook himself westward. In Ohio,
Burr induced Blennerhassett, an Irish gentleman of
means, to throw his fortunes in with him. Blennerhassett started to raise troops and armaments for
the enterprise on his island estate. Meanwhile the
Spanish Minister had written to the governors of
the Spanish Floridas and to the Viceroy of Mexico
to keep their eyes on Burr. In Ohio and Kentucky
Burr's project for disunion aroused intense opposition. Even one of Blennerhassett's servants frankly
said to Burr: "If you come up our way the people

*A chimeri-
cal con-
spiracy*

Colonel
Burr haled
to court

will shoot you!" Finally the district-attorney of Ohio made formal charges against the conspirators. Burr appeared in court seconded by young Henry Clay and was acquitted. At last President Jefferson took action. On October 22, he ordered gunboats to proceed as far as Fort Adams and called for Burr's arrest upon the commission of any overt act. His letter began in this wise: "During the last session of Congress, Colonel Burr, who was here, finding no hope of being employed in any department of the government, entered into a scheme to separate the Western from the Atlantic States and to erect the former into an independent confederacy." Burr was again arraigned in court, Henry Clay pledged

Aaron Burr
acquitted

his own honor on his friend's innocence, and Burr was once more triumphantly acquitted by a grand jury. A public ball was given in his honor. Then President Jefferson issued a proclamation against "sundry persons conspiring against Spain," and ordered them and all their property to be seized. The expedition at Blennerhassett's island fled down the river. Burr escaped from Nashville and floated down the Mississippi only to surrender in the end.

While the South was still in a turmoil over Burr's enterprise, a peaceful mission, far more lasting in its effects, had just been accomplished. In

Lewis and
Clarke's
Explora-
tion

September, Lewis and Clarke had returned from a trip of exploration into the new western territory of the United States upon which President Jefferson had sent them. They had been absent nearly two and a half years, and had travelled over eight thousand miles in boats, on horseback and on foot.

They had worked their way up the Missouri until they reached the gates of the Rocky Mountains near the present city of Helena in Montana. Thence they floated down the Oregon River to the Pacific Ocean. Their full report of their travels was a revelation of the boundless possibilities of the newly acquired territory of Western North America.

In the meantime, the war between England and France was lagging on in a half-hearted fashion. Englishmen at home were too much occupied with the impeachment proceedings against Lord Melville on charges that he had misappropriated public funds to take very active interest in matters abroad. Finally Lord Melville was acquitted. Mr. Fox was inclined to enter into more peaceful relations with Napoleon. Thus he sent word to the French Emperor of a plot for Napoleon's assassination that had been unfolded to him. Talleyrand returned the compliment with a graciously worded message of appreciation. This exchange of courtesies presently led to direct parleys on the subject of peace. They were carried on through Lord Yarmouth, one of the many British travellers detained in France at the outbreak of hostilities. Talleyrand, speaking for Napoleon, expressed his readiness to give up Sicily. While the parleys lasted peace had been made to appear even more desirable to Napoleon by a bloody defeat inflicted upon the French under General Regnier by Sir John Stuart, at St. Euphemia or Maida, in Calabria. The battle was fought on July 6, between 7,000 Frenchmen on one side

Lord Melville impeached

British peace overtures

Battle of Maida

and 4,800 Englishmen on the other. Both sides advanced to the attack with fixed bayonets, but at the first shock of meeting the French vanguard broke and their whole force was thrown into disorder. The French lost 4,000 men in the rout, while the English had only 45 men killed and 282 wounded. All Calabria rose in revolt against the French, and the province was drenched with blood, until the last of the French garrisons had been driven from the country. The capture of Gaeta by Massena more than counterbalanced these reverses. The surrender of Gaeta, after its severe siege under the Prince of Hesse, cut off communications with the disaffected northern provinces of the kingdom of Naples. Some 16,000 of the besieging army were set at liberty to act against the Calabrians. With their help, Calabria was finally reduced to subjection, but for many months that part of Italy was plunged into a bloody bandit war. Hordes of galley slaves and convicts under the notorious Fra Diavolo and Pane di Grande kept up a stubborn struggle. It was waged on both sides with a ferocity that recalled the horrors of San Domingo.

Napoleon's covert offer to cede Sicily to England was communicated to the reigning house of Spain, the rightful owners of that province. Spain took alarm the more as the enmity of England had been brought home to her by the recent temporary capture of her South American colony of Buenos Ayres by an English fleet that had been sent to seize the Cape of Good Hope, and by the appearance of a formidable British squadron under Lord St. Vincent

[margin notes:]
Revolt of Calabria

Fall of Gaeta

Calabrian horrors

British capture Buenos Ayres

off Lisbon. Godoy, the Spanish Prime Minister, went to England to negotiate a secret treaty.

The Emperor of Russia, whose troops had seized the mouth of the Cattaro when the French were about to occupy it, influenced by other counsels, now decided to withdraw his forces. In pursuance Russian peace overtures of this new policy he sent Count D'Ouvril to Paris as a peace commissioner. The conclusion of the preliminaries of the peace with Russia, on August 15, completely changed the tenor of Napoleon's negotiations with Fox. He would no longer hear of yielding Sicily, not even to the Spanish Bourbons. Instead of that he offered to return Hanover to King George of England. This offer came upon the heels of Napoleon's formal announcement of the Confederation of the Rhine formation of his new Confederacy of the Rhine. By the terms of this confederacy, as arranged in July, fourteen German princes seceded from the German Empire and entered into a league with France. Besides the three sovereigns of Bavaria, Wurtemberg and Baden, the new confederation included the new Prince Arch-Chancellor of Dalberg, the Elector of Hesse-Darmstadt, the Duke of Nassau, the French Grandduke of Berg, the Prince of Salm-Salm and others. They entered into a defensive and offensive alliance with France in perpetuity and agreed to furnish an army of 63,000 men to be incorporated into the French army of 200,000 still standing in Southern Germany. Within a week after this announcement, Francis II. of Austria, who had been despoiled of all his German fiefs, relinquished his vain title of German Emperor.

End of
Holy Ro-
man Em-
pire

The Holy Roman Empire, so-called, was dissolved. The French Minister informed the members of the ancient German Diet that the Emperor, his master, no longer recognized the Germanic constitution, though he recognized the sovereignty of each of the German princes considered individually. The old town of Regensburg, where the Diet met, was ceded to Bavaria. The German princes had been induced to join hands with Napoleon, partly through fear and partly by the new accessions to their realms, which Napoleon consented to grant them.

The announcement of this new powerful league caused consternation among those German States that had not been included in it—most of all at Berlin. The King of Prussia had reason to be alarmed. In the north, the King of Denmark seized this opportunity to declare "Holstein forever separated from the German Empire," and annexed it to Denmark. More alarming still were the significant manœuvres of the French army evacuating Austria. When the French columns left Bohemia and Moravia, they did so in oblique marches that brought them between the Palatinate and the banks of the Weser. This placed General Augereau, with a French reserve corps, at Frankfort, a convenient central position. An official betrayal of Napoleon's offer of Hanover to England brought matters to a point. Prussia began to mobilize her army. Russia, taking alarm at the French preparations for a northward move, on August 15 broke off all proposals for peace. England, through her ambassador at Berlin, confirmed the report of Napoleon's

Prussia
takes
alarm

Hanoverian bargain. This put an end to all peace negotiations between Talleyrand and Fox. It was the last stroke in Fox's career. He died on September 13. Thus, within a few months after his illustrious rival, another of the most eminent statesmen of England passed away. The most prominent feature of this great man's character was his love of liberty and hatred of oppression.

Death of Fox

Napoleon ascribed England's change of policy to the death of Fox. To anticipate the inevitable coalition forming against him, Napoleon issued an ultimatum to Prussia. He refused to evacuate Germany unless Prussia agreed to put a stop to the mobilization of her army. Failing to receive a satisfactory reply by October 8, he threatened immediate hostilities. In Germany public opinion, long pent up, burst forth in great violence against Napoleon. His destruction of the Holy Roman Empire had wounded German patriotic sensibilities. Popular murmurs arose and patriotic pamphlets against the French appeared on all sides. One of these, entitled "Germany in the Depths of Degradation," the work of Genz, was published by Palm, a bookseller of Nuremberg. On August 5, Napoleon wrote to Berthier: "My cousin, you have, I presume, arrested the booksellers of Augsburg and Nuremberg. I intend them to be brought before a military commission and shot within twenty-four hours." In obedience to these instructions Palm was at once arrested and shot. The unfortunate bookseller met death with a simple fortitude that made him a popular martyr among his countrymen.

French ultimatum to Prussia

Execution of Palm

War spirit in Berlin   In German song and story public feeling against the French rose high. In Berlin the war party, headed by Queen Louise, got the upper hand. The officers of the guards whetted their swords on the stone steps of the French embassy. Philosophical writers like Fichte and popular poets like Arndt stirred up the people by their appeals to patriotism. The Prussian regular army, proud of its achievements under Frederick the Great, burned to prove its mettle against the foreign invaders. Only Frederick William III., the King of Prussia, hesitated. While he took council with his cautious Cabinet,

Napoleon goes to the front   Napoleon hurried to Mainz at the rate of sixty miles a day. From there he flew to the front at Carlsruhe.

The hostile forces stood facing each other in central Germany. The Prussian army numbered 130,000 men, under the command of the aged Duke of Brunswick, with a staff of inexperienced princes and old officers like Mollendorf, grown gray in service.

Conservatism of Prussian army   The soldiers were armed and drilled according to the precepts in vogue at the time of Frederick the Great. They were well disciplined, but had no other incentive to drive them on but brutal corporal punishment. Promotion from the ranks was unheard of. All the officers' commissions were held by the nobles. The French army, on the other hand, was commanded by youthful officers throughout. Every man in the ranks was made to feel that he carried a marshal's baton in his knapsack. Napoleon had taken pains to equip all the branches of the service with the most modern arms and ac-

coutrements. Under the stress of constant active French army up-to-date
service in the field, the whole French army had
been reorganized from top to bottom. Everything
down to ordinary tactics had been brought up to
date. In strategy, Napoleon and his marshals could
be presumed to be immeasurably superior to their
antagonists. To the French leaders advancing from
campaign to campaign the art of war had become
almost second nature. Where their opponents deliberated, they acted. All were firm believers in
Napoleon's maxim: "The strength of an army,
like the power in mechanics, is estimated by mul-
tiplying the men by the rapidity. A rapid advance
augments the morale of the army, and increases its
means of victory. Press on!" The events of the
next few weeks made all this plain. The Prussians, Prussian dilatory tactics
instead of taking the offensive, as was counselled
by Scharnhorst, one of their few young generals,
remained in their original position on the banks of
the Saale. There they waited for the commencement of hostilities. On October 5, three days before the expiration of the period set in Napoleon's
ultimatum, six French army corps advanced simultaneously into Saxony. They marched in the form
of a large square. The Prussian general, Blücher,
commanding a detached corps of Prussians, made
haste to join the main army. The Prussian reserve,
under Prince Eugene of Wurtemberg, moved too
late to catch up in time. On October 7, Napoleon
was in Amberg. In contemptuous allusion to the
blunders of the old Prussian generals he said, "They
will make frightful fools of themselves, those old

Napoleon's
rapid
advance

wigs.'' The next day the French army made a rapid advance in three divisions. By their movements the left wing of the Prussians was exposed to the attack of the whole French army. While the vanguard of the Prussians fell back, the extreme end of the left flank was turned by the French. Davoust, with 33,000 men, overran the Prussian stores at Hof, and made for their base of supplies at Naumburg.

The Prussians met the concerted French advance by advancing their central army corps under Prince

The opening fight

Hohenlohe. On October 9, the two vanguards came in touch. Marshal Lannes, by forced marches, brought his whole army corps to bear down upon the firing line. Prince Louis Ferdinand of Prussia advanced with a brigade of crack cavalry over the bridge at Saalfeld. His troopers, proud of their former prowess, were eager to distinguish themselves. The French fell upon them in overwhelming number. The Prussians put up a furious fight, but were overthrown and utterly routed. Prince

Death of
Louis Ferdinand

Louis Ferdinand was killed in action. With him fell six hundred of his troopers. ''Diable! That will make an impression upon them!'' said Lannes, when they showed him the dead prince, riddled with bullets.

As soon as Napoleon arrived in Gera, he divined the position of the Prussian army, and gave orders to his marshals to swing their divisions around to the west, while advancing north toward the Prussian flank. By October 12, Murat's cavalry had already penetrated to Naumburg, the Prussian base of supplies. Threatened in their rear, the Prussian general staff was seized with consternation. After endless consultation, they decided to retreat. By the time they came to this decision, Davoust's corps had already passed the dangerous defiles of Koesen and was advancing toward the Prussian centre. Further back, near Weimar, marched General Ruechel with 30,000 Prussians, while Prince Hohenlohe's former van was transformed into a rearguard, covering the Prussian retreat.

On the night of October 13, Napoleon, from the crest of the Landgrafenberg, beheld the camp fires of the Prussian rearguard at Jena. He determined to strike on the morrow. All that night was spent in getting the French artillery up the Landgrafenberg. Napoleon himself lighted the way with a torch. Lannes's corps hastened to occupy the foothills. Bernadotte's advance corps was despatched parallel with the Prussian line of retreat. Ney and Soult hurried up in all-night marches, to fill the place left by Bernadotte's division, while Murat's cavalry was summoned from afar. All night long endless columns of troops were toiling to reach the firing line. At last Napoleon snatched a few hours of sleep at one of the camp fires. At dawn he was up and rode with Lannes through the lines. The soldiers, shivering in the ranks, waited impatiently for the command to advance. Under cover of the morning mist the army was ranged in final battle order. The guards remained stationed at Napoleon's headquarters.

At six in the morning, Lannes's corps poured down

the hillsides. The Prussians, who had watched the distant torchlights flickering up and down the Landgrafenberg all night long, were ready for the fight. The whole vanguard came under fire. Prince Hohenlohe believed he had but one French army corps to deal with and determined to crush it with his whole force. Lannes's corps suffered severely. Of the other French divisions only that of Ney was within striking reach. At noon, Prince Hohenlohe thought victory was sure and sent this despatch to General Ruechel in his rear. "Send all the force you can to the chief point of attack. At this moment we beat the enemy at all points. My cavalry has captured some of his cannon." Napoleon was on the point of throwing his guards into the battle when Ney's main army descended upon the Prussians, and Soult also came into action with his vanguard. Ney's men stormed the hamlet of Vierzehnheiligen. Soult crumpled up the Prussian left wing and threw the disordered Prussians under the fire of the French batteries stationed on the Landgrafenberg. Hohenlohe realized that he was losing the battle. He despatched an aide-de-camp to Ruechel with this message: "Lose not a moment in advancing with your yet unbroken troops! Arrange your columns that through their openings may pass the broken strands of the battle. Be ready to receive the fierce charge of the enemy's cavalry which is overwhelming our infantry, cavalry and artillery." Hohenlohe's situation was made still worse by the entry of Augereau's corps in the line of battle. General Sujet broke through the woods of Isslerdorf and cut off the Saxon guards on the line of retreat to Weimar. They alone lost 6,000 prisoners. At last Ruechel marched on from Weimar with 20,000 reserves. They were thrown into confusion by the disordered retreat of their comrades.

It was now four in the afternoon. Napoleon saw that the decisive moment had arrived. He ordered Murat's cavalry, which had just come up from its all-night ride, to charge the Prussians. Twelve thousand horsemen dashed down the slope straight into the confused masses of Prussian infantry. Everything went down before them. The battle was over. Murat's squadrons chased the fleeing Prussians along the road to Weimar. The rest of the French army followed. At dusk the French horsemen met the straggling hordes of the Prussian main army, which had gone to pieces at Auerstaedt.

While the Prussian right and centre were thus Battle of Auerstaedt engulfed, their left, under the personal command of the King, his aged field-marshal, the Duke of Brunswick, and General Mollendorf, were engaged by Davoust's division. The loss of the Prussian supplies at Naumburg had left most of the troops without provisions. Many of the soldiers had eaten nothing for the last two days, and Blücher's cavalry had to go without fodder. Early in the morning, while Napoleon was attacking at Jena, General Schmettau was sent forward to secure the mountain passes of Koesen. The Prussian squadrons found they were too late. Fighting began at Hassenhausen. Hidden under a heavy mist, the

French vanguard appeared as a formidable army, the more so since the French infantry, forming in squares, fought off the first fierce onslaughts of the Prussian cavalry. In the fog and confusion, several batteries of Prussian horse artillery were ditched. The main body of the Prussian cavalry under Blücher now tried a general assault, but in the haze their horses were hindered by the roughness of the country. The incessant fire of the French skirmishers created havoc among them. They never got within sabre-reach of the French. In the confusion some squadrons came under the fire of the Prussian batteries posted on their flank. They raised a cry of treason and galloped to the rear.

On the extreme right the Prussian dragoons succeeded in flanking the French, but the Prussian infantry was so slow to follow that Davoust had time to throw his reserves under Morand into the intrenched village of Hassenhausen. Here the French held off the Prussian infantry. At last the fog lifted and the generals on both sides could see how the battle stood. The Duke of Brunswick brought some field batteries into action, but their scanty ammunition gave out. In exasperation, the aged field-marshal ordered a general assault, and himself took the lead. Riding at the head of the famous regiment of which the late Prince Louis had been the colonel, the old general could be seen by the entire battle front charging into the French. The whole Prussian line followed. Their vanguard got into the village, but were shot to pieces in the churchyard. In the thick of the charge the Duke Death of Duke of Brunswick of Brunswick fell, shot through the head. The Prussian ranks were disheartened by a report that their King had been killed. At this point, Davoust made a counter-attack with all his cavalry. The Prussians broke and fell back under a heavy artillery fire. At Auerstaedt they came to a standstill, and the reserves were called into battle. It was nearly noon. The King of Prussia himself assumed command. As he rode through the lines the Prussian ranks raised a cheer and rallied.

Davoust's third division, under Friant, was trying to outflank the Prussians on the left near Poppel. Past this village ran the highway to Weimar, the Prussian line of retreat. The King took alarm and threw his reserves under Arnim in the direction of Poppel. This weakened the Prussian line at Auerstaedt. Davoust drew his two remaining divisions together, and, shattering the Prussian bri- The Prussians routed gades, seized their position at Auerstaedt. The centre of the battle shifted to Poppel. Here the Prussian rearguard stood its ground, while the bulk of the army retreated toward Weimar. The French tried to storm the hills on the other side of Auerstaedt, but were repulsed by a murderous fire from the heights. The Prussians followed up their success by a bayonet charge and threw the French back into Auerstaedt. But the King was anxious to reach Weimar, hoping there to join forces with his centre and right under Ruechel and Hohenlohe. Of their terrible fate he knew nothing. So orders were given to retreat, and fall back on Weimar. At

Double re-
treat to
Weimar

Weimar, the Prussian battalions, fleeing from two battlefields, were mixed up in inextricable confusion. Darkness came. It brought no relief to the vanquished. From both sides the French pursuers were upon them. Marauders from their own ranks seized the transport wagons and increased the horror of the night by their drunken excesses. The Prussian King with his staff narrowly escaped Murat's dragoons. He fled in the gloom of night, plunging through forests and rivers, until, utterly worn out, he found a safe retreat at Charlottenburg. From there he fled toward the Russian frontier.

Prussian
losses

In this disastrous twofold battle, the Prussians lost 20,000 killed and wounded, and 30,000 prisoners, with 260 guns. Twenty-six of their general officers were taken. The Duke of Brunswick and General Schmettau were killed. Prince Henry of Prussia and General Ruechel were severely wounded. The French losses, according to their official reports, were 1,100 killed and 3,000 wounded. Among their killed were one brigadier-general and nine colonels.

Marshal
Davoust
honored

Napoleon raised Marshal Davoust to the rank of Duke of Auerstadt. To honor him still more, he made a public promise to him that he and his troops should be the first to enter Berlin. Davoust rejoined: "Sire, the soldiers of the third corps will always be to you what the tenth legion was to Cæsar." In his official account of the twofold battle of Jena-Auerstadt, Napoleon wrote: "On our right the corps of Marshal Davoust performed prodigies. Not only did it keep the enemy in

check but pursued the bulk of his forces over a
distance of three leagues.   Marshal Davoust has
displayed alike the distinguished bravery and firmness of character which are the first qualities of the
soldier."

While the shattered divisions of the Prussian
army were driven along the Elbe, to fall a prey
to their pursuers one by one, Napoleon established
his headquarters at Weimar.   The Grandduke of Napoleon
Weimar had commanded a division of the Prus-   at Weimar
sian army.   His wife was the sister of Emperor
Alexander of Russia.   The Grandduchess, greatly
agitated, went to meet Napoleon as he rode into the
devastated city—the Athens of modern Germany.
"Madame, you see what war is," said Napoleon.
That was his only comment.   Weimar, with the
other Saxon States, was spared.   To the captive Saxony
Saxon officers, Napoleon said: "I know not why spared
I am at war with your sovereign.   He is a wise,
pacific prince, deserving of respect.   I wish to see
your country rescued from its humiliating dependence upon Prussia.   I am ready on my part to give
you a pledge of my disposition toward you by
setting you all at liberty, and by sparing Saxony.
All I require of you is your promise no more to
bear arms against France."

On October 28, General Mollendorf, with his fleeing corps of 16,000 Prussians, surrendered to Murat.
Among the prisoners were Prince August of Prussia, the Prince of Mecklenburg-Schwerin, and General Tauenzien.   Later the prisoners were liberated
by a bold charge of hussars led by Lieutenant von

Napoleon
enters
Berlin

Hellwig. On the same day Berlin was taken. Napoleon, riding in his faded gray cloak at the head of his resplendent marshals, made a triumphal entry into the city. He established himself at the royal palace, where the apartments of Queen Louise had been left in disorder. While at Berlin, Count Hatzfeld, the governor of the city, got into trouble through clandestine correspondence with the absent king. Napoleon ordered him to be shot, but pardoned him when the condemned man's wife threw herself at his feet. Heinrich von Buelow, who had counselled against the war, was delivered to the Russians, whom he hated, and was beaten to death by his Cossack escort. Previous to this Napoleon

Takes
Frederick
the Great's
Sword

visited the tomb of Frederick the Great. The sword of Frederick, suspended above the tomb, was placed in his hand. Napoleon regarded it thoughtfully and said: "I would not exchange this sword of Frederick for millions. I will send it to the Invalides. My old soldiers will regard with religious reverence a trophy which has belonged to the most illustrious captains of history." General Rapp suggested that Napoleon keep it himself. The Emperor gave his aid a look, and said haughtily: "Have I not a sword of my own?" All the memorial standards taken from the French and Austrians in the Seven Years' War were shipped to France, together with the stone column that commemorated Frederick's victory over the French at Rossbach.

A fortnight later the 13,000 Prussian reserves were scattered by Bernadotte at Halle, and were

Painted by G. Richter   By permission of Berlin Photographic Co., N. Y.

QUEEN LOUISE

XIXth Cent., Vol. One

driven into the strong city of Magdeburg. There ^{Fall of Magdeburg} Von Kleist capitulated to Ney. The town of Erfurt surrendered next with 14,000 men. The stronghold ^{Erfurt} of Kustrin fell without a blow. Blücher and York ^{Kustrin} at Luebeck and Radkan, after sustaining a fierce ^{Luebeck} siege until hand-to-hand fighting occurred in the streets, were forced into submission. Of the Prussian army of 150,000, only Estocque's division of 15,000 remained. They crossed the frontier to join the Russian army approaching through Poland.

Northern Germany, from the Rhine to the Oder, lay at the feet of the conqueror. Napoleon called for a war indemnity of 150,000,000 francs from Prussia and her German allies. The dominions of Hanover, Hesse, and Brunswick were forcibly annexed to France. From Berlin, Napoleon issued ^{Berlin decree} a decree prohibiting all intercourse with Great Britain. Englishmen and English property wherever found were to be seized. Confiscations were made at Hamburg. The harsh provisions of this decree, so Napoleon declared, "should be regarded as a fundamental law of the French Empire, and her allies, till England recognized the law of war to be one and the same by sea and by land, and in no case applicable to private property or to individuals not bearing arms, and until she consented ^{Continental blockade} to restrict the right of blockade to fortified places actually invested by a sufficient force." The issue of this decree caused consternation in the commercial centres of the Continent. Deputations were sent to Napoleon from Hamburg and other seaports. They informed Napoleon that "these measures

Ruin of trade

would involve them in universal bankruptcy and banish commerce from the Continent." He replied: "So much the better. The bankruptcies in England will be more numerous and you will be less able to trade with her." As it turned out, the decree could not be enforced sufficiently to make it effective. The world owes to this decree the extraction of sugar from beet-root, invented by a Frenchman. The decree of Berlin was followed by another authorizing the levy of 80,000 new conscripts in France, to form a national guard. On November 25, Napoleon hastened to the province of Posen to arouse Poland against the Russians. Some 60,000 Polish peasants rose in arms. Russia issued a formal declaration of war, beginning thus: "The Lord on high will take our just cause under His protection." At the same time a Turkish army advanced to the Lower Danube. General Sebastiani, the French ambassador at Constantinople, had at last aroused the Sultan to this act of open hostility. The Russians had to detach 80,000 men to meet the new danger, and the Austrian army of observation likewise turned eastward. Austria had reason to feel concerned, for the Ottoman Empire then, as so often after this, seemed on the verge of dissolution. The Russians, under Michaelson, were overrunning Moldavia, Bessarabia and Wallachia, after they had occupied Bucharest. The Servians, under Czerny Georgos, had driven the Turks from their land and laid siege to Belgrade. Egypt was in a state of anarchy. Mecca and Medina were in the hands of the Wachabees. Bagdad had

become independent. A French army lay in wait
in Dalmatia, and a British squadron of seven men-
of-war under Admiral Louis was cruising in the
Dardanelles. In Constantinople the Janizaries were
so discontented over the introduction of European
tactics in the Turkish army that a palace revolt was
regarded as imminent. Yet Turkey somehow managed to survive.

During the last days of November, Napoleon began his advance against the Russians. Bennigsen's
column of 60,000 was pushed back on Pultusk. Operations
in Poland
Ney and Bernadotte's division moved eastward over
the river Weichsel or Vistula. Davoust and Lannes
occupied Warsaw and swung their divisions northward. In the centre, the divisions of Soult and
Augereau advanced amid constant skirmishes as
far as Golymin. Lannes's corps pushed on to Pultusk to cut off the Russians from the Narev. Soult
and Bernadotte were to cover a possible Russian
retreat on Ostrolenka. On Christmas Day the Russian right wing became engaged with Bernadotte's
forces at Moehrungen and was pushed back under Moehrungen
heavy losses on both sides. Bernadotte's attempt
to outflank the Russians failed.

The next day Lannes attacked Bennigsen's centre
at Pultusk, thirteen leagues north of Warsaw.
Simultaneously Napoleon sent the divisions of
Augereau with Murat's cavalry against the Russians under Buxhovden at Golymin, six leagues Golymin
away. The Russians stood their ground so well
that the fight at Golymin lasted all day, with heavy
losses on both sides. General Rapp, Napoleon's

aide-de-camp, was severely wounded. In the end the Russians retreated in good order. At Pultusk equally bitter fighting on both sides only resulted in a drawn battle. For eight long hours Lannes's veterans had to sustain the murderous fire of the Russians while standing in a deep morass. Lannes himself succumbed to the strain and had to relinquish the command. At nightfall Bennigsen took the Russian army across the Narev without serious hindrance from the French. After this double disappointment, Napoleon's army went into winter quarters. The closing days of the year brought famine and wretchedness to the French soldiers camping on the frozen marshes. Bad weather made the roads impassable for the transport wagons. The Russians had destroyed everything for miles around, so that food and provender were very scarce. The distress was so great that a number of the starving soldiers committed suicide. Napoleon betook himself to Warsaw. There the Polish nobles and patriots gave him an enthusiastic welcome as their deliverer. One of the first to greet him was Countess Valevska, a Polish beauty. Her efforts to win the French Emperor to her country's cause ended in a love affair. She was induced to follow Napoleon from camp to camp, and finally to Paris. Later she bore him a son, Alexander, who distinguished himself under the second empire. Yet Napoleon gave a deaf ear to all entreaties for Poland. "I like the Poles," he said, "their enthusiasm pleases me. I should like to make them an independent people; but the cake has been shared by too many. When the

(margin note) Winter hardships in Poland

(margin note) Napoleon in Warsaw

match is kindled who knows where the conflagra-Doubts as to intention may stop. My first duty is toward France. tion re-
garding
Poland
I must not sacrifice her interests for Poland. In
short, we must refer the matter to the universal
sovereign—Time." It is doubtful, at best, whether
Napoleon ever intended to free Poland. At that
time he could not afford to arouse the enmity of
Austria with her army of observation in his rear.
To the entreaties of Polish deputations he made this
final statement: "I have not come here to involve
France in new quarrels. I am not in want of thrones
to give away."

1807

THE OLD YEAR had scarcely run out before the civilized nations had begun to feel the effects of Napoleon's staggering blow to commerce. Late in December, General Armstrong, the American Minister in Paris, asked Talleyrand for an explanation of Napoleon's decree so far as it affected American trade. He received no satisfactory reply. All was deferred to the French Emperor lying in distant winter quarters at Warsaw. The new year opened with international commerce at the mercy of the two most powerful nations—France and England—now locked in deadly conflict. On January 7, the British Ministry responded to Napoleon with a retaliatory measure. The bill related that King George "felt himself bound to retort upon the French the evils of their own injustice, and therefore has ordered that no vessel shall be permitted to trade from one port to another, both which ports shall belong to or be in possession of France or her allies." This bill proved a blow to American commerce. It deprived American ships of the right to sail from one European port to another. From the point of view of the more enlightened British Whigs, the bill, though drafted by a Whig Min-

[margin note: Results of Continental blockade]

[margin note: British retaliatory measures]

[margin note: Effects on American shipping]

ister, was really a concession to King George and Tory prejudices. The Whigs denounced it as against common-sense and good political economy, a measure in line with the violent aggressions of Pitt. For three weeks the debate raged in Parliament before the bill was finally passed. It was the last important measure of Grenville's so-called Ministry of "all the talents"—a Ministry more liberal than England was destined to see for a generation.

As an immediate result of this bill, the United States were estranged from England. Jefferson repudiated the new treaty concluded by Monroe and Pinckney without even submitting it to Congress. A few weeks previous to this the French Minister had written to Talleyrand: "If I am to judge by the talk and countenances of the general people, this Congress wil' be more favorable to England than the last was. Already its leader, under the President's own invitation, shows a benevolent disposition toward the British government." Jefferson himself wrote to Monroe at the Court of St. James: "No two countries have so many points of common interest and friendship, and their rulers must be great bunglers indeed if with such dispositions they break them asunder. England may, by petty larceny thwartings, check us on the ocean, but she cannot seriously retard us." Now all this was changed, and a feeling of exasperation set in which was destined to bring the two countries into conflict.

For the moment, President Jefferson was too engrossed in other affairs to take any decisive act. The exciting trial of Aaron Burr for trea-

[sidenote: United States estranged from England]

[sidenote: Aaron Burr tried for treason]

son was just getting under way, and the political
enemies of the President were beginning to bait
him. Without such distractions, Jefferson's natural inclinations were against war. "The present
administration," said he, "has taken up a new
system of defence—it is that of saving the public
money. This system is new and was not known in
Federal times. We have not gone on increasing
taxes like our predecessors." This was the truth.
With the help of Gallatin, the Secretary of the
American financial reforms Treasury, the administration had succeeded in paying off twenty-four millions of debts. Still the rev-
enues grew. Eppes, of Virginia, the President's son-
in-law, said in Congress, "If there is any principle
which ought to be hooted at in a Republican government, it is that to preserve peace we should be
prepared for war. Sir, it is this very principle
which is the source of all the miseries of Europe."

In his message to Congress, Jefferson called for
a broad system of internal improvements, a national system of roads and canals, a national university and the organization of a national militia to re-
Jefferson proposes opposition of slave trade place the regular army. The most striking feature
of his message was the proposed abolition of all
slave trade. "I congratulate you, fellow citizens,
on the approach of the period when you may interpose your authority constitutionally to withdraw as
citizens of the United States from all further participation in those violations of human rights which
have been so long continued on the unoffending inhabitants of Africa, and which the morality, the

reputation, and the best interests of our country have long been eager to proscribe.''

It was a reform worthy of the new spirit of the age. In England, Parliament at this very time was debating a bill to put a stop to all slave trading with Africa. In Russia, Emperor Alexander freed the Russian serfs in the Baltic provinces. Jefferson's proposed prohibition of the slave trade threw a vivid light on those sectional differences in America, which were destined to lead to secession and civil war. Under the act, a cargo of a forfeited vessel was to be sold on behalf of the United States government. The cargo of a slave ship consisted of negroes. Rather than see this done, Sloan of New Jersey offered an amendment in Congress that every forfeited negro should be entitled to freedom. Upon this amendment a debate arose which waxed exceeding hot. The Southern representatives, almost to a man, opposed it. The debate was adjourned, resumed, and adjourned again. It was further imbittered by a motion of Smiley of Pennsylvania to make the importation of negroes a felony punishable by death. ''All the people in the Southern States are concerned in slaves,'' retorted Early, the chairman of the committee in charge of the bill. ''By them it is not considered as criminal. I will tell the truth—a large majority of the people in the Southern States do not consider slavery as even an evil.'' The Quaker amendment was rejected by a majority of ten. Bidwell of Massachusetts next moved, ''That no person shall be sold as a slave by virtue of this act.'' On this

[margin note: Emancipation of Russian serfs]

[margin note: Premonition of American Civil War]

amendment the House of Representatives tied, sixty to sixty. The speaker by his vote threw out the amendment. When other similar amendments were proposed, Early made this significant statement in behalf of the South: "We want no civil wars, no rebellions, no insurrections, no resistance to the authority of the government. Give effect to this wish and do not pass this bill as it stands."

Randolph of Virginia asserted that the coastwise prohibition touched the right of private property and expressed fears, "Lest, at a future period, it might be made a pretext of universal emancipation. I had rather lose all the bill, I had rather lose all the bills of the session, I had rather lose all the bills passed since the establishment of the government, than agree to the provisions contained in this slave bill. If ever the time of disunion between these States should arrive, the line of severance will not be between Eastern and Western, but between slave-holding and non-slave-holding States. All that I ask is that the North shall remain neutral, that it shall not erect itself into an abolition society." Yet the bill prohibiting the slave trade went through. President Jefferson approved the measure.

The opposition against Jefferson's administration was largely strengthened by this. The proceedings against Burr helped to place Jefferson in an awkward position. The conspiracy of Burr had been a more episode amid many more vital questions that stirred the American people. While New Orleans was convulsed by Burr's attempted coup d'état in

[margin: Seeds of discord sown]

[margin: Burr a source of embarrassment]

that city, the rest of the country refused to believe that the former Vice-President was so insane as to expect a dissolution of the Union. For this general apathy Jefferson himself was largely responsible. He had long belittled the importance of Burr's conspiracy, and he permitted General Wilkinson to remain in command of the American army after it had become evident that this general suffered himself to become involved in Burr's schemes. Wilkinson saved himself by turning against Burr. Gen. Wilkinson's treachery To understand Wilkinson's conduct, Americans must look into the archives of the crown of Spain. On January 28, 1807, Yrujo, the Spanish Minister to the United States, wrote to Cevallos in Madrid: "According to appearances Spain has saved A Spanish view of it the United States from the separation of the union which menaced them. This would have taken place if Wilkinson had entered cordially into the plans of Burr. This was to be expected because Wilkinson detests his present government, and the separation of the Western States has long been his favorite plan. The evil has come from the foolish and pertinacious perseverance with which Burr has persisted in carrying out the wild project against Mexico. Wilkinson is entirely devoted to us. He enjoys a considerable pension from our King. . . . Failure of Burr's attempt would have left Wilkinson like the dog in the fable with the piece of meat in his mouth—that is, he would lose the honorable position he holds at home, and the generous pension he enjoys from the King. These considerations, secret in their nature, he could not explain to Burr.

When the latter persisted in an idea so fatal to Wilkinson's interest, nothing remained but to take the course adopted. By this means he assures his pension, and will allege this as an extraordinary service, either for getting it increased or for some generous compensation. On the other hand, this proceeding secures his distinguished rank in the military service of the United States. In such an alternative he has acted as was to be expected; that is, he has sacrificed Burr in order to obtain, on the ruin of Burr's reputation, the advantages I have pointed out." On one point Yrujo wrote from positive knowledge. The general-in-chief of the American army was in the pay of Don Carlos IV. He took a pension of $2,000 a year in consideration of secret services. For twenty years these services had been rendered and the pension had Jefferson's been paid. By supporting Wilkinson, Jefferson support of Wilkinson lost the last support of such men as John Randolph and Chief-Justice Marshall. From the first arraignment of Burr in January, until the last day of his trial at Richmond in October, the proceedings against Burr seemed a matter of secondary importance compared with the discomfiture of the President of the United States. Burr, who was himself Burr's trial no mean lawyer, was defended by the ablest counsel a State affair of the American bar—Edmund Randolph, George Washington's attorney-general; John Wickham, the famous Virginia wit; Benjamin Botts, an unusually thoroughgoing attorney, and Luther Martin, who had made a great name for himself by his defence of Justice Chase. On the government side,

the death of Attorney-General Breckenridge left an
irreparable loss. Cæsar A. Rodney, his successor,
left the prosecution of Burr to District-Attorney
Hay and his associates, William Wirt and Alexander McRae, the Lieutenant-Governor of Virginia.
From the very outset Chief-Justice Marshall decided against the government. In one of his early
opinions he blamed the administration for neglect
of duty: "Several months have elapsed since this
attempt occurred—if it did occur. More than five
weeks have passed since the opinion of the Supreme
Court has declared the necessity of proving the fact
if it exists. Why is it not proved? To the Executive Government is intrusted the important power of
prosecution of those whose crimes may disturb the
public repose or endanger its safety. It would be
easy in much less time than has intervened since
Colonel Burr was alleged to have assembled his
troops, to procure affidavits establishing the fact."
Jefferson's reply to this censure from the Supreme
Bench gives a glimpse of the general condition of
the country in those days. "In what terms of de-
cency can we speak of this? As if an express
could go to Natchez or the mouth of the Cumber-
land and return in five weeks to do which has never
taken less than twelve!" Chief-Justice Marshall's
ruling, that the President of the United States could
be subpœnaed in court as a witness, stung Jefferson
to the quick. He wrote to the District-Attorney:
"The leading feature of our Constitution is the independence of the legislative, executive and judiciary
of each other; and none are more jealous of this

President Jefferson criticised

Chief-Justice Marshall's censure

than the judiciary. But would the executive be
independent of the judiciary if he were subject to
the commands of the latter and to imprisonment for
disobedience?" The judge upon the bench retorted
cuttingly, "It is apparent that the President's duties
as chief magistrate do not demand his whole time
and are not unremitting." Jefferson gave way to a
burst of anger. "I have heard," he wrote in another
letter, "that my predecessor, General Washington,
sometimes decided things against his council by
dashing and trampling his wig upon the floor.
This only proves what you and I knew, that he
had a better heart than head." Justice Marshall
appointed John Randolph, Jefferson's political opponent, as clerk of the grand jury. Randolph made

General
Wilkinson
implicated every effort to fasten Burr's guilt on Wilkinson,
but failed. The motion to indict Wilkinson was
lost in the grand jury room by a bare majority
of two. Randolph wrote in a letter, "Perhaps you
never saw human nature in so degraded a situation
as in the person of Wilkinson before the grand
jury. And yet the man stands on the very summit and pinnacle of executive favor, while James
Monroe is denounced." Throughout the trial feeling ran very high, especially in Richmond and the
South. "As I was crossing the court-house green
to the Eagle Tavern," wrote an eye-witness, "I
heard a great noise of haranguing some distance
off. Inquiring what it was, I was told it was

Andrew
Jackson
and Burr a great blackguard from Tennessee, one Andrew
Jackson, making a speech for Burr, and damning
Jefferson." Finally Judge Marshall struck the

prosecution dumb by a ruling which excluded the testimony of Blennerhassett against Burr: "Because such testimony, being in its nature merely corroborative and incompetent to prove the overt act in itself, is irrelevant until there be proof of the overt act by two witnesses." After this ruling of the court, the prosecution abandoned the case and the jury entered a verdict of "not guilty." *Aaron Burr acquitted*

Jefferson made elaborate preparations to impeach the Supreme Court, but, in truth, nothing was to be feared. The days of Jefferson's power and glory were passing, while Marshall was only at the threshold of his illustrious legal career.

While this cause célèbre was on the boards in the New World, another more tragic State trial had drawn to a close in Vienna. General Mack and several of his unfortunate fellow officers were court-martialled for their disastrous blunders during the last Austrian campaign against Napoleon. General Mack was unanimously sentenced to death, but Emperor Francis remitted the sentence. The Prince of Auersperg, who had neglected to destroy the bridge at Vienna, though he had received positive orders to do so, was condemned to imprisonment for ten years. Several other officers were punished, but in most cases the Emperor softened their sentences. *Austrian generals punished*

In Paris, questions of more lasting importance were settled by the great Sanhedrim, a convention of seventy-one Jewish rabbis and notables which sat for over a year under the leadership of David Sinzheim and Furtado. As a result of their delib- *Jewish Sanhedrim of Paris*

erations they issued a rescript for Jewish guidance
in the spring of 1807. The Mosaic dispensation,
while recognized as absolute in religious matters,
was declared inapplicable to mundane affairs, since
the Jews had ceased to exist as a nation. Polyga-
mous marriage as practiced by the patriarchs was
forbidden. Marriages between Christians and Jews
were recognized. Jews called to military service
were exempted from religious observances conflicting with military duty. Usury, in particular, was
denounced as a crime against law and religion.

Napoleon, during this interval, had been held in
check in his winter quarters on the distant Vistula.

The cam-
paign in
Poland
His soldiers found themselves in a worse situation
than ever before. The winter was severe and the
wretched state of the impoverished country made
campaigning atrocious. All supplies had to be
brought from interminable distances and over
roads that were all but impassable. In Silesia,
the Prussian strongholds of Breslau, Brieg and
Schweidnitz had to be reduced by long sieges.
The Russians under the command of Bennigsen

Sufferings
of French
soldiers
held their ground tenaciously. By the end of January, Marshal Ney's corps had suffered so severely
that he resolved to strike northward for better winter quarters at Koenigsberg. A Prussian division
of 10,000 under Estocque stood in his way. At the
news of Ney's movement, Bennigsen marched his
whole army out of cantonments. He hoped to overwhelm Ney's 12,000 men with his 56,000 Russians.
Napoleon at once broke up his winter quarters at
Warsaw and marched, with his guards and the

divisions of Soult, Augereau and Davoust. Bernadotte, who stood at Elbing, received his marching orders too late to fall into line. The corps of veterans, hitherto commanded by Lannes, was left behind to cover the banks of the Narev. Bennigsen, finding his flank threatened, had to give up his pursuit of Ney, nor could he prevent the latter from getting in touch with the French main army. The Ney opens hostilities Prussian column, engaged with Ney's forces, remained detached. On February 7, Bennigsen gathered all his available forces to withstand the French at Eylau. The first to arrive were Murat's cavalry and some of Soult's mounted squadrons. Together they attacked the Russian line and captured Prussian Eylau. At nightfall a solid mass of Russian infantry stormed the town with the bayonet and sent the French squadrons flying. Prince Eugene of Wurtemberg tells in his memoirs how hideously the raucous battle cry of the Tobolski regiment rang in his ears during that night. Under cover of the darkness the main army with Napoleon came up and ranged itself in battle line. The divisions of Ney and Soult formed the left wing, while Augereau with the guards and Murat's cavalry behind them held the centre. Davoust's columns marching overnight were to form the right wing. It was a dark night and bitterly cold. Eylau lay on a slight rise of land extending two or three miles, skirted by a vast bleak plain on which the snow blew in drifts. Upon the ridge the Russians posted all their artil- Advantage gained by Russians lery and the bulk of their infantry, 80,000 strong. Before them in the plain 70,000 Frenchmen bivouacked in the snow. At midnight Napoleon snatched an hour's sleep on a camp-stool. Before dawn he made his last dispositions.

The battle opened on both sides with prolonged artillery fire at pointblank range. The effects of this cannonade were fearful. Whole regiments of St. Hilaire's corps were mowed down by grape-shot. The Twenty-fourth French regiment of the line, consisting of 3,600 veterans under Colonel Semèle, was wiped out. Napoleon and his guard established themselves in the churchyard of Eylau. From there Napoleon ordered the corps of St. Hilaire and Augereau to lead the advance against the Russian left. Marshal Augereau, shaking with fever, had himself strapped to his horse and galloped up the slope at the head of his division. In the face of a blinding blizzard the French standards were lost to sight among the whirling snowflakes. During the storm, which lasted three-quarters of an hour, Augereau's column missed its objective. Napoleon ordered Murat to ride to their rescue with some of his squadrons. Suddenly there was a rift in the storm. From all sides the Russians fell upon Augereau's stray columns. The Frenchmen were shot down with grape and canister and fell a prey to the spears of the Cossacks. Marshal Augereau went down with his horse, and his troops fell all around him. The Fourteenth regiment of the line, rallying to its standard, was cut down almost to a man. Through the struggling mass dashed the yellow hussars of Novgorod. They cut their way up to the very wall of the graveyard in which Napo-

Battle of
Eylau

leon stood watching the battle through his field glass. "Save the Emperor!" cried the members of his staff as they scrambled on their horses. But Napoleon did not stir. At an order from him, the Old Guard, under their colonel, Dorsenne, threw themselves between their Emperor and the Russians and broke the force of the cavalry attack. At the same instant Napoleon's scarlet horseguards swooped down on the Russian Hussars and carried them down the hill in a running fight. General Corbineau was killed by a shell while he was receiving orders from the Emperor. Young Captain Auzoni of the Guards, one of Napoleon's favorite officers, died kissing his hand to La Belle France.

At this point Murat thundered into the breach with eighty squadrons of cavalry. Colonel Hautpoul, who led the charge, was the first to fall. This assault of 10,000 troopers in full career has remained one of the famous traditions of the French army. As a strategic manœuvre it cannot be pronounced a success. All it did was to bring the battle to a standstill! At least such is the verdict of Prince Alexander of Wurtemberg, who saw it with his own eyes. In and about the town of Eylau, the fighting was so fierce that the Russians used the bodies of the dead for barricades. Marshal Murat and his chief lieutenant, Count Lasalle, had to fight for their lives, sabre in hand. Fighting from street to street and from house to house, the French at last succeeded in retaking Eylau.

On the right, Davoust drove the Russians from

Murat's memorable charge

Serpallen to Saussgarten, .and thence as far back as the village of Kuschitten. There he was stopped short by the sudden appearance of a division of Prussians under L'Estocque, who had succeeded in joining the Russian main army despite Ney's diver-

Prussians save the day

sion. With bugles blowing and drums beating, the Prussians threw themselves into the fight and drove back Davoust's division. At nightfall Ney's detachments came up on the road from Schmodetten just in time to stop the retrograde movement of the French right wing. It was dark, and the snowy plain was strewn with the dead and dying. As Marshal Ney rode upon the battlefield he shuddered and said, "What a massacre—and without any issue."

It was in truth a drawn battle. The French army had suffered so fearfully that Napoleon could not have kept his positions any length of time before a resolute foe. As it turned out, he prevailed by dint of sheer tenacity. General Bennigsen, in disregard of the entreaties of General Knorring and Tolstoi, who wished to renew the fight on the morrow, fell

A drawn battle

back during the night. In the face of this voluntary retreat of the enemy, the weakened French forces were yet in a mood to fall back across the Vistula. On the day after the battle, Napoleon wrote: "It was a very bloody affair. The field of battle remained in our hands. Though a great many men were killed on both sides, our situation renders my loss the more sensible. . . It is possible that in order to get quiet winter quarters I shall remove to the left bank of the Vistula." To

Josephine, Napoleon wrote: "I send you one line, _{Napoleon's version of it} my love. You must have been very anxious. I have beaten the enemy in a memorable battle, but it has cost me many brave men. Corbineau was killed by a shell. It gave me great pain. Allemagne was wounded dangerously. My horseguards covered themselves with glory. The country is covered with the dead and wounded. This is not the pleasant part of war. One suffers and the soul is oppressed to see so many victims. The inclement weather constrains me to return to my cantonments, but all this will soon end. I have repulsed the enemy and compelled him to abandon his projects."

Some idea of the frightful loss of human life on The losses both sides can be gained from the official report of of Eylau Chief Surgeon Larrey of the French army. In the space of one square league, the surgeons counted more than 10,000 dead soldiers and the carcasses of 5,000 horses. Forty-eight hours after the battle, there were still upward of 5,000 wounded Russians lying unattended on the snow. The wounded had to be carried on long trains of sledges to the field hospitals at Thorn. The French surgeons observed with astonishment that long exposure to cold did not seem to affect the wounded Russians. The extent of the losses was never accurately stated. A German historian estimates them at 40,000, including subsequent deaths from wound fever. At the time, both Bennigsen and Napoleon issued misleading bulletins to bolster up their claims to victory. In bulletin fifty-eight of La Grande Armée, the French conceded the loss of 1,000 killed and 5,700 wounded. Of these 1,090 were rendered unfit for further service. Four general officers and six regimental colonels were among the fallen. The loss of one French eagle was admitted. The enemy's losses were given as 12,000 killed, 15,000 prisoners, 45 guns and 18 standards. General Bennigsen, in his

letter to Czar Alexander, written on the night after the battle, gave a very different account. He assured the Czar that the enemy had been completely defeated; that a thousand prisoners and twelve standards, which he had the honor to send to his imperial majesty, had fallen into his hands. He had been attacked, he stated, on the centre and both wings by Bonaparte in person, who, however, had been beaten back at all points and everywhere defeated. Napoleon's imperial guards had attacked the Russian centre three times, and had as often been repulsed. Several columns of French infantry and regiments of cuirassiers had been destroyed. The loss of the Russians he believed might exceed 6,000 men, but that he might estimate without exaggeration the loss of the enemy at more than 12,000.

The plain soldiers who saw things their own way knew better. Thus a Russian officer of dragoons, whose letter has been preserved, wrote home from

Tilsit three days after the battle: "For these three days we have been asking one another on which side the victory lay. This question may appear singular, but in truth it is impossible for us to tell which of the two armies did the greater mischief to the other." One of Napoleon's bulletins, assigning

the credit for the victory to the Emperor's brother-
in-law, Marshal Murat, gave rise to much discontent in the French ranks. Marshals Lannes and
Augereau, the sorely wounded, dared to give voice
to these murmurings, and were sent to the rear in
disgrace.

One week after the battle of Eylau there was
another bloody fight at Ostrolenka. It was fought Ostrolenka
between the Prussian General Von Essen on one
side and Generals Suchet and Oudineau on the
other. Thanks to their better manœuvring, the
French won and drove the Prussians back from
the banks of the Narev. Here, too, the losses
were out of all proportion to the gain. General
Suvarov, a brother of the famous Russian field-
marshal, was killed, and the French lost General
Campana and two colonels. The Cossacks, under
their fiery Hetmann, rescued a number of their
wounded, and were in turn taken prisoners. When
Napoleon learned of the combat and the casualties
it entailed, he ordered the fifth army corps to cease
active operations. The Russians retreated in good
order to Koenigsberg, though Murat's cavalry followed them almost to the walls of the city. Under
stress of the severe winter weather, both armies
went into cantonments and waited for spring.

The ninth and tenth corps of the French army
alone continued their operations in Silesia. With
the aid of the Poles, the Prussians were driven into
their strongholds. The French invested Sweidnitz, Prussian
strong-
Kosel, Neiss, Graudenz, Colberg, Stralsund and holds
invested
Dantzig. Had Bennigsen been equal to a diversion

with his Russian army at Koenigsberg, effective siege operations against these cities would have been impossible. Without such interference, Marshal Lefebvre was able to concentrate 30,000 men around Dantzig. At the same time Napoleon ordered new levies of troops from Poland, Germany, Holland, Spain and France. Little Switzerland even had to furnish 16,000 men under pain of forfeiture of all her treaty rights. An excuse for these additional armaments was furnished by the attitude of England. The successful resistance of the Turks to Michaelson's Russian army on the Danube, induced England to make a demonstration in that direction. Admiral Duckworth's fleet was

British fleet before Constantinople

called from the coast of Spain to the Dardanelles to give weight to the remonstrance of Ambassador Arbuthnot in Constantinople. On February 28, Arbuthnot insisted on the dismissal of General Sebastiani, Napoleon's envoy to the Sublime Porte. On the Sultan's refusal, Arbuthnot joined the British fleet, and war was declared. Duckworth sailed through the Dardanelles and anchored off the Sultan's palace in the Bosphorus. The British admiral was held off by pretended negotiations inspired by Sebastiani. Presently he found that

Admiral Duckworth driven off

heavy batteries had been mounted against him, under the fire of which he was compelled to leave the Bosphorus and sail once more through the Dardanelles. The British squadron had to sustain a heavy fire from the strong shore batteries at the Straits, aided by Turkish ships anchored there. The Turks lost one line-o'-battle ship, four frigates,

Painted by E. Meissonier

"FRIEDLAND, 1807"

three corvettes and one brig. The English suffered only in their rigging and complements. Altogether, forty-two British sailors were killed and two hundred and thirty-five were wounded. The British squadron sailed to Egypt and took the city of Alexandria.

Napoleon exulted in Turkey's success. To the Sultan he wrote: "You have shown yourself a worthy descendant of Selim and Soliman. You have asked me for officers: I send them to you. Generals, officers, soldiers, arms of every kind, even money, I place at your disposal. You have only to ask. Ask plainly, and whatever you ask shall be sent forthwith. Make friends with the Shah of Persia, who is also the enemy of the Russians. Persuade him to remain firm, and vigorously to attack the common enemy." Before Selim III. *Sultan Selim deposed* could enter fully into these schemes he was deprived of his throne by a palace revolution. The Janizaries raised his nephew, Mustapha IV., to the throne.

It was now the immediate object of Napoleon to secure complete command of the countries he had overrún. To do this he had to reduce the Prussian *Prussian strongholds reduced* fortresses that still held out on the Vistula and the Oder. The Russians, determined to harass the French in every way, engaged them in a series of sharp actions. On February 26, a Russian detachment of 10,000 marched against Braunsberg, the most advanced of the French cantonments. General Dupont of Bernadotte's division met the Russian attack. At the point of the bayonet the Cossacks

were repulsed and thrown over the river Parsarge.
Two thousand of them were taken prisoners, with
sixteen guns. On February 24, Baron Korff next
occupied the town of Peterswald with a Russian
column. General Leger Belair, hastening thither,
attacked the town at daybreak and defeated the
Russians in a sharp fight. General Korff surrendered with his staff and a full battalion of
his guard. After the affairs of Peterswald and
Braunsberg, Napoleon moved his headquarters
from Osterode to the Castle of Finkenstein, that he

Hardships
of winter
campaign might be nearer to Graudenz and Dantzig. Some
idea of the hardships of the winter there may be
gathered from this letter of Napoleon to his brother
Joseph at Naples: "The officers of our staff have
not undressed for these two months, and some not
for four months past. I myself have been a fortnight without taking off my boots. We are amid
snow and mud. Without wine or bread, eating
potatoes and mule flesh, making long marches and
countermarches without any kind of comfort, we
fight in general with bayonets and under grape.
The wounded have to be carried in sledges, exposed to the cold, two hundred miles away."
While thus engaged, Napoleon received the news
of the death of his little nephew, Charles Napoleon,
a son of Louis and Hortense, whom he had wished
to make his heir. The siege of the Prussian cities
was pursued with relentless vigor. Troops were
brought from as far as Spain, and heavy artillery

Sturdy
resistance
of Colberg was dragged over hundreds of miles. Graudenz and
Colberg, under the gallant command of L'Homme

de Courvière, a French refugee, and Gneisenau, an old-fashioned Prussian soldier, held out until the bitter end. Count Kalkreuth, with the flower of the Prussian army at Dantzig, showed himself less sturdy. The old Hanseatic city was defended by double rows of fortifications, ditches and inundations, with the Fort of Weichselmunde on the other side of the harbor. The garrison numbered 18,000 men. On March 8, the siege was begun, and was The siege conducted through sixty-five days under the skil- of Dantzig ful leadership of the French military engineers Chasseloup and Larevoisiere. On April 24, the French, having assembled all their artillery, commenced the bombardment. After sustaining a heavy fire for several days, the garrison made a sortie, but were beaten back in three successive attempts to rush the French parallels. King William of Prussia and Grandduke Constantine determined to relieve the city by sea. Accordingly, two Russian divisions embarked in a fleet of sixty-six transports at Pillau. Napoleon, hearing of this, sent his reserves under Lannes to reinforce Lefebvre before Dantzig. By a forced march from Marienburg, the French managed to arrive on the day that the Russians were landed at Weichselmunde. On May 15, the Russians attacked a Futile French detachment of General Schramm that was diversions holding a fort opposite Weichselmunde. In a hard fight lasting several hours, the Russians were thrown back into Weichselmunde by a combined attack of the French forces under Marshals Lefebvre and Lannes. Simultaneously with this stroke at Dantzig, the whole length of the Russian line facing Napoleon demonstrated against the French outposts stationed on the Alle, Parsarge, Vistula, Narev, Boug, and at Ostrolenka. They were repulsed at all points. The British brigantine "Dauntless," which attempted to sail into the harbor of Dantzig with Russian and Prussian officers aboard, came under the fire of the French batteries and musketry, and had to surrender. An attack on the strong French post at Pultusk, undertaken by a column of 6,000 Russians under General Turkov, likewise failed. On April 19, the French proceeded with all their forces to make a combined assault on Dantzig. In the face of this movement, General Kalkreuth agreed to capitulate the city on condition that the whole garrison be paroled with all the honors of war. On May 27, the Prussians marched out of the city nine thousand strong, with General Kalkreuth at their head. All the rich stores and eight hundred pieces of artillery fell to the French. Napoleon was able to distribute one million bottles of wine among his soldiers. The Russian garrison at Weichselmunde followed suit with a surrender at discretion. The fleet that had brought them escaped to Pillau with General Kaminskoi, the Russian lieutenant-general. Owing to the advance of a Swedish army under General von Essen, and an English expedition under General Clinton, the siege of Stralsund had to be raised by the French. They were forced to evacuate Swedish Pomerania. During their retreat, the French lost 3,000 prisoners, among them twenty

Dantzig capitulates

Siege of Stralsund raised

officers. The Swedes pursued so hotly that they extended their line too far, and were caught at a disadvantage after crossing the river Pirne. Marshal Mortier suddenly turned on them with his division and seized the bridges. Two Swedish posts were overthrown and a third column under General Cardell was cut off. General Kronfeld, a Swedish commander-in-chief, was wounded by grape-shot. The next day a detached column was overwhelmed at Neckarmunde, and another Swedish post at Demnin was captured. Seventeen hundred prisoners were taken, together with seven guns. The Swedes had to fall back over the Pirne. General Kronfeld, finding himself at the mercy of the French, entered into an armistice, by which the Swedes bound themselves not to give further succor to the allies. On April 29, it was agreed between Von Essen and Marshal Mortier that the truce should hold for one month. The King of Sweden, on news of this, hastened to Stralsund. General Kronfeld, who concluded the first truce, had to resign his commission. But General Von Essen was made Governor-General of Pomerania and the terms remained in force.

Sweden forced to a truce

After the opening of spring, when the ice of the rivers had melted, and the roads became passable, Bennigsen grew restless in his intrenched camp at Heilsberg, near Koenigsberg. He gave up his wise policy of harassing the French advance lines and took the offensive. As once before, he could not resist risking a descent upon Ney's exposed position. Ney's corps occupied an isolated advance post at Gutstadt in the midst of screening forests.

Bennigsen attacks Ney

On June 5, the Russians suddenly advanced on several points at once. Two of these attacks, at Spandau and Lomitten, were only feints to hold off the detachments of Bernadotte and Soult, but the third at Bergfried was a bold manœuvre to cut off Ney's corps from the rest of the French army. The Russian columns under Sacken and Gortshakov did their part so clumsily that Ney was able to beat a steady retreat, contesting point by point until he reached Deppen. There, in a masterly rear action, he made his way across the Parsarge.

Ney's clever retreat

Having lost this battle, the Russians had to retrograde in their turn. The bulk of the French army was marching to drive them back, and their right was already outflanked. Bennigsen fell back on his camp at Heilsberg, where he lay strongly intrenched on both sides of the Alle. Here he resolved to give battle. On June 10, the advance troops of Soult, Lannes, Davoust and Murat's cavalry debouched before the camp. They did not advance to the attack until late that evening. Soult's corps was the first to assail. It was beaten back by a murderous fire from the Russian trenches. The successive assaults of Murat and Lannes fared no better. General LeGrand, who threw one of his regiments into a redoubt, was so overwhelmed with grape that he had to give up his advantage. The fight lasted far into the night. At last the French gave it up. The next morning it was found that nearly 10,000 Frenchmen had fallen before the Russian trenches. Soult's corps in particular suffered enormous losses. The Russian casualties were

Battle of Heilsburg

comparatively light. Napoleon abandoned further frontal attacks on Heilsberg, and started to out-flank Bennigsen and make a rush for Koenigsberg. To do so he had to risk seeing his communications cut off, but he reckoned rightly, for when Bennig-sen learned that the French were streaming past his flanks, he burned all his bridges over the Alle and broke up camp at Heilsberg. Both armies made for Koenigsberg, descending the river on either bank. For three days they marched thus in parallel col-umns. The Prussians under L'Estocque reached The race for Koe-nigsberg Koenigsberg first, though harassed on their flank by the vanguards of Murat and Davoust. Behind these marshals came the divisions of Soult and Lannes, followed in turn by the corps of Mortier, Ney, and Napoleon's guard. Bernadotte's division, under the temporary command of General Victor, brought up the French rear. Napoleon's only de-sire was to take Koenigsberg before Bennigsen could find refuge there. The prospect for this was fair, since the Russians, on the other side of the Alle, were marching on a road that followed all the windings of the river. Bennigsen, on the other hand, could count on reaching Koenigsberg in time to prevent a premature capitulation of that city by the Prussians. Napoleon felt no apprehensions that his long-drawn-out column might be attacked en route, since the Russians to do so were bound to cross the river. Yet Napoleon took the precaution to order Lannes's troops to cover Friedland and Friedland the first objective Wehlau, the only points at which the Russians could cross for an attack. Bennigsen, too, had his

eye on those points. He feared that the French, in
their turn, might there attack his left flank and cut
him off from the Pregel and Koenigsberg. By
crossing first, he hoped he might catch the long-
extended French line unawares, and roll up Lannes's
vanguard upon the rest of the army.

On the evening of June 13, a strong detachment
of Cossacks crossed the river, and riding into Friedland drove out an advance outpost of French hussars, who had ridden into the town. At three
o'clock in the morning the Russians crossed the

Time
lost by
Russians

river. So much time was spent in marching the
various columns over the bridges, that half of
the Russian artillery was left behind. As a consequence, Bennigsen's first attack, instead of overwhelming Lannes's detached division by one stroke,
was carried out but feebly. A fraction of the Russian army only came into play, and Lannes was
able to prolong the fight. The French veterans
hastily intrenched themselves at Posthenen, and
fought like lions against overwhelming odds. Mar-

Lannes's
strong
stand

shal Lannes, recognizing the danger of the position, sent despatch after despatch to the Emperor,
ten miles away. Napoleon thought, at first, that
the attack on Lannes was merely a Russian
demonstration to safeguard the river crossing
against the French. He could not believe Bennigsen capable of jeopardizing the whole of his
army in such a place. Yet he sent orders to all
the nearest columns, marching parallel with him,
to press on to Friedland. While he hastened to
the scene with the old guard, Ney's division and

Mortier's corps, with Grouchy's Polish cavalry
had already come to Lannes's assistance and established themselves at Heinrichsdorf. There they
were hard pressed. The Russians bore in on the
French at every point. It was afternoon when the
Emperor with his staff galloped into Posthenen.
General Oudinot, his face black with powder, rode
up on his bleeding horse and cried, "Make haste,
sire! My grenadiers are at the last point." Napoleon rode up to the crest of the hill and overlooked
the field. When he saw the Russians hemmed in
by a bend of the river, and thought of his own
divisions marching up on every side, a gleam of
joy lighted up his features. "This is the 14th
of June," he said; "the anniversary of Marengo."
Then he dictated his dispositions for the battle as Battle of
he would have done at the beginning of the combat. Friedland
It was in reality a second battle that was about to
begin. One of his officers ventured to suggest a
postponement of the attack until all the French
troops had arrived. "No, no!" retorted Napoleon,
"one does' not catch an enemy twice in such a
scrape." Lannes and Mortier were ordered to retain their central position, with Murat and Bes-
siere's cavalry divisions on their left. Ney's corps
pushed up on the right, supported by General Victor
and the imperial guards. As Marshal Ney wheeled
on his horse to assume command of the French right
flank, Napoleon grasped him by the arm. "There
is the goal," he said, pointing to Friedland. "Make
for it without a look behind you. Break into that
Russian mass, whatever the cost. Seize the town

and hold the bridges. Never mind what happens on your right, on the left, or in the rear; I and my army will attend to the rest."

Ney went to carry out his desperate attack. In plain sight of the army he led his men straight into the Russian centre. As Napoleon caught sight of him galloping proudly at the head of his troops, he exclaimed, "Behold, there goes our lion!" Ney's vanguard was first engaged by a horde of Russian Cossacks, but Latour-Maubourg rushed in with his dragoons and drove them back. At a mill-pond close to the walls of Friedland, Ney's advancing column was met by a corps of Alexander's imperial guards, the choicest troops of the Russian army. They charged the French with their bayonets and crumpled up Brisson's division. His regiments fell back on the other brigades, and Ney's entire column wavered and fell back. General Dupont saw the danger, and rushed his reserves through Ney's broken lines. The Russian guards were stopped in their onslaught, and driven back on Friedland. Ney rallied his troops, and with his united forces stormed the flaming town. The Russians were cut down or thrown into the river, and the bridges were burned. Prince Gortshakov, commanding the Russian right, now found himself between the victorious French troops at Friedland and the divisions of Lannes and Mortier in the centre. Retreat across the bridges was cut off. Fighting desperately all the way he led off his troops along the bank of the river, while his Cossacks hunted for fording places. At the moment of Ney's assault upon Friedland,

Russian centre attacked by Ney

Ney's brilliant charge

Napoleon ordered thirty-six guns of Sernarmont's
artillery to cover the French advance with a steady
hail of grape and canister. He led the second line
at the head of his guards and Victor's division.
Murat's cavalry with Bessières's cuirassiers charged
into the Russian columns and utterly overwhelmed
them. Several thousand Russians were caught on
this side of the river, and found themselves at the
mercy of the French crossfire. Others were trampled under foot by the rush of the cavalry squadron, or were drowned in the river. Several regiments surrendered. When night fell, the French
had won at all points. Napoleon had achieved another decisive battle, worthy not only of Marengo,
but of Austerlitz and Jena as well.

The Russians lost at Friedland nearly 20,000 men Losses of
Friedland
in killed and wounded. The French lost scarcely
half that number. As usual the official bulletins
vied with each other in misrepresentations. Ben-
nigsen, in his letter to the Czar, pretended that he Bennig-
sen's ex-
planation
had only sent his infantry to take possession of
Friedland, so that his troops might march in security. The infantry was attacked, he supported
them, and thus was drawn into battle. He gave
his total losses as 8,000, with sixteen pieces of cannon. Napoleon's bulletin was in his best vein: Napoleon's
bulletin
"Soldiers, on the fifth day of June we were at-
tacked in our cantonments by the Russian army.
The enemy mistook the cause of our inactivity. He
perceived too late that our repose was that of the
lion. In a campaign of ten days we have taken a
hundred and twenty guns, seven flags, and have

killed, wounded or taken prisoners 60,000 Russians. We have taken from the enemy all his magazines, his hospitals, ambulances, the fortress of Koenigsberg, with 300 vessels, which were in that port laden with all kinds of military stores, and 160,000 muskets, which England was sending to arm our enemies. From the banks of the Vistula we have come with the speed of the eagle to those of the Niemen. At Austerlitz you celebrated the anniversary of my coronation. At Friedland you have worthily celebrated the battle of Marengo."

After the battle General Victor was elevated to the rank of Marshal. Koenigsberg was occupied by the troops of Marshal Soult. The strongholds

Prussian forts surrender

of Neisse, Glatz and Kosel capitulated, one after another. Only Graudenz and Memel still held out

End of the war

for Prussia. The war was over.

On his entry into Tilsit, a little town on the river Niemen, Napoleon received a letter from the Czar of Russia. Alexander proposed an armistice until he could arrive for personal conference. Marshal Kalkreuth, on behalf of the Prussian army, asked for the same. The truce was granted. The first interview between the emperors was appointed for June 25.

On the appointed day Napoleon ordered three rafts, richly carpeted and surmounted by splendid pavilions, fluttering with flags, to be moored in midstream. The two armies were drawn up on the shores of the Niemen. At the stroke of one, cannons roared and regimental bands played, as each Emperor, accompanied by a few officers, stepped into a boat on his own side of the river. The imperial suites, gorgeously apparelled, followed The meeting at Tilsit in other boats. The main raft was intended only for Napoleon and Alexander. Napoleon reached the raft first, and immediately crossed it to receive Alexander stepping from his boat. In the sight of the armies the two Emperors embraced. A multitudinous shout arose from the soldiers drawn up on either bank. The first words which Alexander uttered were: "I hate the English as much as you do. I am ready to second you in all your enterprises against them." "In that case," replied Napoleon, "everything will be readily arranged and peace is already made." So much for Napoleon's own account of the interview. It lasted two full hours. Certain it is that Napoleon, by his charm of manner, fascinated the youthful Czar. In later years Alexander said: "Never did I love any one as I loved that man." It was agreed between them to neutralize the town of Tilsit, so that they might meet frequently and at their leisure. As Napoleon wrote to Alexander in one of his notes at that time, it was his intention "to pass in one moment from open war to the most friendly relations." Accordingly the two Emperors met, dined together, entertained one another, and reviewed the French, clad in each other's insignia. William III. of Prussia hastened to Tilsit anxious to plead the cause of his own country. He was regarded as something of a marplot. Queen Louise, who came later, cut a very different figure. "The Queen of Prussia," said Napoleon, "in spite of my address and utmost efforts, Queen Louise arrives

constantly led the conversation. She returned at
pleasure to her subject and directed it as she chose,
but still with so much tact and delicacy that it was
impossible to take offence. Had she arrived earlier,
it might have had much influence upon the result
of our negotiations. Happily she did not make her
appearance until all was settled. It is plain that
she has been the real sovereign of Prussia for the
last fifteen years." Queen Louise made a strong
effort to have Napoleon withdraw some of the hard
conditions imposed upon Prussia. When she found
that she had failed, she said to Napoleon: "How
much I should admire you, sire, were you as mag-
nanimous as you are powerful."

Later, when he had handed her into the carriage,
she burst into tears.

Napoleon's report of the Czar's confession of resentment against England was not inherently im-
probable. There was ground for resentment, for
the reason that the British Ministry had failed to
pay Russia the subsidy of £6,000,000 which it had
granted to Austria. Apart from this there was a
well-defined movement in Russia for the annexation of Finland, then possessed by the King of Sweden, one of England's allies. Napoleon readily
entered into this, and also agreed to leave Russian
Poland under the yoke of Russia. Only Prussian
Poland with Warsaw and Posen were incorporated
into the federation of the Rhine, while Russia acquired the former Prussian province of Bialistok.
With the exception of dismantled Prussia, all Germany entered into the alliance with France. The

Marginal notes:
Queen
Louise
pleads for
Prussia

Settle-
ments of
Tilsit

King of Saxony, as a reward for his complete change of front, received the new duchy of Warsaw, and was elevated to the rank of king. Hesse, Brunswick, and all former Prussian provinces west of the Elbe were molded into the new kingdom of Westphalia, which was given to Napoleon's brother Jerome. *Jerome, King of Westphalia* Prussia retained only one-half of her former territory, with but six million subjects. She had to agree to pay an indemnity of twenty million francs. Her army was restricted to 60,000 men. Under the new arrangement her frontier lines left *Prussia shorn of power* her a prey to French invasion from the West. The city of Dantzig benefited by the rearrangement in so far as it was restored to the rank of a free city. Alexander lost practically nothing. He agreed to evacuate Moldavia and Wallachia, and gave formal recognition to the new-fledged royal titles of Napoleon's three brothers. For the future, the two Emperors made some sweeping secret arrangements. Turkey was to be despoiled of Montenegro and the Ionic isles. Sweden, Denmark and Portugal were to be treated as enemies if they did not agree to join the continental blockade against England. In case *Continental blockade extended* the King of Sweden clung to England, as was to be foreseen, Finland was to be wrested from him forthwith and incorporated as a Russian province. Alexander bound himself to act as an ally of France against England, if peace were refused by that power. The peace of Tilsit was fully ratified on July 9, in a final convention at Koenigsberg. Peace with Prussia was formally declared and terms were made for a French evacuation of Pomerania and Silesia, after

Prussia should have begun the payments of her war
indemnity.

Napoleon
returns to
France Napoleon returned to France. He was received
with the roar of cannon, and once more became the
object of the most extravagant adulation. The President of the French Court of Appeals delivered an
address of welcome, in the course of which he said:
"Our victorious Emperor has never desired anything but peace. He has ever presented the olive
branch to those who have forced upon him the laurels of victory. Napoleon is above human history.
He belongs to the heroic age. He is above mere
admiration." Napoleon in turn said: "Let us now
turn to trade and manufacture. I have had enough
of the trade of General. I shall now resume with
you that of First Minister. I will recommence my
great reviews of affairs, which it is time to substitute
for my great reviews of armies." The state of public affairs in France warranted such an utterance.
The new armaments called for by Napoleon's prolonged campaign in Prussia had caused consternation among the French peasants. The expense of
the war had sapped the resources of the country
both in products and in men. The stoppage of
commerce by the continental blockade struck all
branches of production sterile. Public credit was
shaken and French consols were at an alarmingly
Need of
internal
reforms low ebb. Napoleon called a Council of State to
inquire into the causes of the evil, and the proposed
remedies. The suggestion to refurnish the palaces
of bishops and prefectures, so as to give work to the
poor, did not commend itself to Napoleon. Yet he

ordered his apartments in the Tuileries to be refurnished, and cautioned his wife and sisters to confine their purchases to the public workshop for military supplies. He decreed that 500,000 francs a month should be advanced to the manufacturers who were in difficulties, on condition that they should continue in operation. The launch of this loan drew attention to the country's need of commerce, for the goods thus acquired spoiled on the hands of the State and had to be got rid of. On the other hand, not enough was manufactured in France to clothe even the army. Thus Bourrienne, Napoleon's private secretary, records in his diary that the bulk of the French army was supplied with shoes and clothing smuggled into France from England. The financial distress spread to the neighboring countries. Holland was hard hit. Louis Bonaparte, reigning there as king, sided with his stricken subjects and declined to raise 50,000 Dutch conscripts for his brother. Louis, on the other hand, was quick to raise money for the sufferers of Leyden, when a powder ship blew up in the harbor of that city and destroyed 200 houses and killed 150 men, among them the celebrated Professors Luzac and Kleit. At this Napoleon was moved to wrath: "Have you so completely lost your head as to forget what you owe to me? Do you want to force me to express my great displeasure publicly? Aid my troops! Make a large levy of conscripts! A prince who passes for good in the first year of his reign is a prince who will be ridiculed in his second. When a king is said to be a good man his reign is unsuc-

Condition of French manufactures

Distress in Holland

cessful. The first thing that you ought to do, and that I require of you to do, is to raise a subscription for me."

Immediate results of peace

After the Peace of Tilsit came a sharp change for the better. Confidence was restored in Paris, and French consols rose to a higher point than ever before.

While things stood thus in Europe, the people of England were comparatively tranquil. The danger of a foreign invasion once removed, they

Relief in England

experienced a relief very similar to that which followed the destruction of the Armada, two hundred years before. As in Elizabethan times, colonial conquest, commerce and letters flourished side by side. While Coleridge, Wordsworth, Moore, Crabbe and Charles Lamb were giving their best works to the world, Byron, then still a lad, was stirred to attempt his first poetic flight. During his leisure hours at school and college he had written

Byron's early poetry

occasional verses, which appeared at Newark in 1807, in a little volume entitled "Hours of Idleness." Boyish and weak as these verses were, they scarcely deserved the weighty scorn with which the "Edinburgh Review" pounced upon them. Stung in his pride, Byron retorted with his "English Bards and Scotch Reviewers," a long poem full of scathing invective and satire. It showed his contemporaries that this stripling author of puny versicles, when aroused, could slash about him with a pen dipped in gall. In this poem, Byron fell foul of nearly all the English poets of the day—Southey, the poet lau-

reate, Wordsworth, Coleridge, Scott and **Moore.**
The stanzas on Wordsworth were the best.

> "Next comes the dull disciple of thy school
> That would apostate from poetic rule,
> The simple Wordsworth, framer of a lay
> As soft as evening in his favorite May;
> Who, both by precept and example, shows
> That prose is verse, and verse is merely prose."

For British commerce, the recent annihilation
of Spanish trade with the West Indies and the
acquisition of the rich Dutch colonies at Curacoa
and at the Cape of Good Hope opened a flourish- Financial
reforms in
ing field. Lord Petty's finance reform, undertaken England
early in the year, brought about a total redemption
of £152,348,529 in national debts.   The daily purchase of £96,000 of floating stocks alone amounted
to a redemption of £17,422,000, or a sum but little
short of the whole loan for the public service during the preceding year.   These financial successes
made Sir Spencer Percival, the Chancellor of the
Exchequer, the leader for the nonce of the new
Portland Ministry which had replaced "All the
Talents" in April.   Sir Spencer's mouthpiece was
George Canning, the foreign secretary, who soon
overshadowed his rival, Lord Castlereagh.   All
these gentlemen were Tories of the most conservative stamp.   Sydney Smith, who delighted to ridicule them in his witty Peter Plymley letters, said
of Percival that he had the head of a country
parson and the tongue of an Old Bailey lawyer.
Canning, the most gifted member of the Cabinet, Canning's
change of
long ago had turned from an ardent revolutionist front

into a rabid anti-republican. This change of mind, coming so early in his life, gave rise to a Whig sarcasm that "men had often been known to turn their coats, but this was the first time that a boy had turned his jacket." By the time Bonaparte overthrew the French Republic on the 18th Brumaire, Canning was in a mood to exult in the change. "Huzza! huzza! huzza!" he wrote to a friend, "it is the lasting ridicule thrown upon all systems of democratic equality that makes the name of Bonaparte dear to me. Henceforth republican and fool are synonymous terms."

Canning now held that Napoleon's course absolved England from ordinary rules of morals. To fight Bonaparte with his own weapons had become the rallying cry of Englishmen. The first acts of the new administration showed what was meant by this famous phrase. Weak neutral powers, which yet were England's rivals in commerce, were the first to suffer. Such were Denmark and the United States.

Coercion of
neutrals

Early in 1807, the British squadron happened to lie off Hampton Roads, in Virginia, watching for some French frigates that had taken refuge at Annapolis. In spring a whole boat's crew of the British sloop-of-war "Halifax" deserted and made off to Norfolk. The commander of the "Halifax" was informed that his men had enlisted on the American frigate "Chesapeake," then preparing for a cruise to the Mediterranean. The British Minister at Washington at the same time made complaint that three deserters from the British

Case of the
"Chesa-
peake"

frigate "Melampus" had enlisted on the "Chesa‧
peake." The Secretary of the Navy instituted an
inquiry, and found that these men were native
Americans who had been improperly impressed
into British service, and were, therefore, not subject to reclamation. Admiral Berkeley, commanding the British North Atlantic Squadron, issued an
order to all his captains to search the "Chesapeake"
for British deserters whenever they might meet her
outside of the three-mile limit. The "Chesapeake," owing to various delays, did not drop
down the Potomac until June. When she tried
to fire the customary salute while passing Mount
Vernon, it was found that her ammunition would
not fit her guns. At Hampton Roads, Captain
James Barron, the newly appointed commodore of
the Mediterranean Squadron, assumed command,
and on June 21 the "Chesapeake" started on her
cruise. Sailing under a fair wind, she passed
the British cruisers "Bellona," "Melampus" and
"Leopard" at Lynnhaven Bay. The "Leopard"
stood out to sea after the "Chesapeake." While
dining in his cabin, Commodore Barron caught a
glimpse of the "Leopard" through a porthole, and
remarked that her movements appeared suspicious,
but that she could certainly have nothing to do
with the "Chesapeake." At half-past three the
"Leopard" came down before the wind, and,
rounding to about half a cable's length to windward, hailed the "Chesapeake," and said she had
despatches for the Commodore. Barron returned
the hail: "We will heave to, and you can send

American sailors impressed [margin note]

The "Chesapeake" sets sail [margin note]

your boat alongside." The fact that the "Leopard"

manœuvred to windward was not taken exception to, since British commanders had long been in the habit of arrogating unto themselves the windward position as a sort of maritime right. The lieutenant from the "Leopard" came aboard and delivered to Commodore Barron a written copy of the British admiral's order respecting the alleged deserters on board the "Chesapeake," with this note from his immediate commander: "The captain of the 'Leop-

ard' will not presume to say anything in addition to what the commander-in-chief has stated, more than to express a hope that every circumstance respecting them may be adjusted in a manner that the harmony subsisting between the two countries may remain undisturbed." Commodore Barron, after some reflection, wrote out the following reply: "I know of no such men as you describe. The officers that were on the recruiting service for this ship were particularly instructed by the government through me not to enter any deserters from his Britannic Majesty's ships, nor do I know of any being here. I am also instructed never to permit

the crew of any ship that I command to be mustered by any other but their own officers. It is my disposition to preserve harmony, and I hope this answer to your despatch will prove satisfactory." The British gig pulled away, and Commodore Barron, after consultation with Captain Gordon, gave orders to have the gun deck cleared. The captain of the "Leopard," as soon as he had received Barron's reply, edged nearer and hailed the

"Chesapeake": "Commodore Barron, you must be aware of the necessity I am under of complying with the orders of my commander-in-chief." It was plainly seen that the British crew were at quarters. Barron repeated the order to clear for action without drumbeat. The men were hurried to their quarters. To gain time Barron shouted through his trumpet. "I do not hear what you say!" The British captain repeated his hail, and Barron again replied that he did not understand. For answer, Captain Humphreys fired a shot across his bow. Another shot followed. A few moments afterward the "Leopard" poured her whole broadside into the "Chesapeake" at pointblank range. Commodore Barron was wounded where he stood on the gangplank, but continued to hail the "Leopard" while his own men were getting their guns ready. The "Leopard's" fire lasted fifteen minutes. In all there were seventy discharges, three American sailors were killed, eighteen wounded, all three masts badly injured and twenty-two round shots entered the hull of the "Chesapeake." Then Commodore Barron, bleeding from his wound, ordered his flag to be hauled down. As it touched the taffrail, the third lieutenant of the "Chesapeake" managed to fire one gun by means of a live coal which he brought from the galley in his fingers.

Murderous fire of British

"Chesapeake" hauls down her flag

The boats of the "Leopard" came alongside and the crew of the "Chesapeake" were mustered by the "Leopard's" officers. The three deserters from the "Melampus" were taken, and one, Jenkin Ratford, the ringleader of the British deserters from

the "Halifax," was dragged out of the coal hole.
At seven in the evening the British officers left the
ship, and Commodore Barron reported to the captain of the "Leopard": "I consider the frigate
'Chesapeake' your prize and I am ready to deliver her to any officers authorized to receive her."
Captain Humphreys replied immediately: "Having
to the utmost of my power fulfilled the instructions
of my commander-in-chief, I have nothing more to
desire, and must in consequence proceed to join the
remainder of my squadron."

American surrender refused

Without a flag, disgraced and humiliated, the
"Chesapeake" returned to Hampton Roads, with
her crew smarting under an insult that was never
forgotten or forgiven by Americans. The American
people were thoroughly aroused. The citizens of
Norfolk, for want of anything better, destroyed the
water casks of the British squadron. The mayor
of Norfolk forbade all intercourse with the British
squadron in Lynnhaven Bay. The British commander retaliated by threatening to blockade Norfolk. President Jefferson approved the action of
Norfolk's mayor. He issued a proclamation beginning thus: "Hospitality under such circumstances
ceases to be a duty, and the continuance of it
would tend only to bring on a rupture between the
two nations." The United States cruiser "Revenge"
was sent to England with despatches demanding a
complete disavowal, the restoration of the impressed
seamen and the recall of Admiral Berkeley. Minister Monroe was instructed to communicate the incident to Russia. Congress, as the only body em

An insult to the nation

Jefferson threatens war

powered to make war, was called into session. In regard to the unfortunate commodore, who was involved in this disgrace, an immediate court of inquiry was ordered on the "Chesapeake." Among the judges sat Captain Decatur, one of Barron's harshest critics. Commodore Barron was courtmartialled for neglect of duty in failing to prepare his ship for action, and for surrendering without having fired a shot. He was convicted and sentenced to suspension from rank and pay for five years. In later years, he was refused an active command. In the end, Commodore Barron challenged Captain Decatur for his vindictive attitude toward him and shot him dead in a duel.

Commodore Barron disgraced

The British captain, on the other hand, came out with colors flying. Admiral Berkeley hastened to give him his formal approval. "So far as I am enabled to judge," he wrote in a letter dated on the day of American independence, "you have conducted yourself most properly. I hope you mind the public accounts that have been published of this affair as little as I do. We must make allowances for the heated state of the populace in a country where law and every tie, both civil and religious, is treated so lightly." The three American deserters from the "Melampus" were sentenced to receive five hundred lashes each. Jenkin Ratford, the British deserter, was hanged from the foreyard arm of his own ship, the "Halifax."

In England the people warmly approved Admiral Berkeley's measures. Thus the "Morning Post," the chosen mouthpiece of the British Foreign Office,

Englishmen exultant

published this comment: "America is not content with striking at the very vitals of our commercial existence, she must also, by humbling our naval greatness and by disputing our supremacy, not only lessen us in our own estimation, but degrade us in the eyes of Europe and the world. . . . It will never be permitted to be said that the 'Royal Sovereign' has struck her flag to a Yankee cock." And again: "A few short months of war would convince their desperate politicians of the folly of measuring the strength of a rising but still infant and puny nation with the colossal power of the **British comments** British Empire." The London "Times," in a similar vein, declared that "The Americans could not even send an ambassador to France—could hardly pass from New York to Staten Island without British permission." In view of this temper of the English people, the British Foreign Office, while expressing regret for the occurrence, preferred to put off Mr. Monroe's demands for redress until popular feeling should have subsided. For the present Mr. Canning had a far more pressing enterprise on hand. As soon as the British Ministry had been informed of the portent of Napoleon's negotiations with Alexander at Tilsit it was decided to despatch a large naval expedition to Copenhagen. **Denmark the next victim** Denmark was to be forced away from an alliance with France. On July 26, a fleet commanded by Lord Gambier sailed from the Downs. The expedition consisted of some twenty ships of the line and forty frigates and transports, carrying 27,000 men under Lord Cathcart. A diplomatic agent

went along, with instructions to require the surrender of the Danish fleet as a temporary security
for England. The unfortunate Danes, by reason
of their enterprise as shippers and traders, found
themselves between two millstones. Denmark was
the only neutral power the control of whose shipping was necessary for the success of Napoleon's
designs against English commerce. On August 2, Threats from either side
he sent orders to Bernadotte at Hamburg: "If
England does not accept the mediation of Russia,
Denmark must declare war on England, or I will
declare war on Denmark." Bernadotte was ordered
to hold his troops ready for an instant invasion of
Denmark. Great Britain's ugly message to Denmark was intrusted to Jackson, the former British
Minister to Berlin. This was the same Jackson
whose appointment as Minister to the United States
had been opposed by Rufus King, on account of
Jackson's notorious ill-temper. In obedience to his
instructions, Jackson sought out the Danish Prince
Royal at Kiel, and had a stormy interview with
Bernstorff. The Danish Prime Minister treated the
British demands as a direct insult to Denmark.
The Prince Royal likewise refused to countenance
British interference with Denmark's international
relations. Jackson's manner of presenting Great Jackson's mission
Britain's ultimatum came in for severe criticism.
Thus Lord Eldon, who said in private that the
story made his heart ache and his blood run cold,
related in after life what old King George thought
of the matter. When Jackson returned to London
and was presented at court, King George asked:

Jackson's
interview
with the
King
"Was the Prince upstairs or down when he received you." "He was on the ground floor," replied Jackson. "1 am glad of it," exclaimed the old king. "For if he had half the spirit of his uncle [King George III.] he would have kicked you downstairs." As a result of Jackson's threats of coercion, Prince Christian sailed immediately for Copenhagen, whither Jackson followed him. On August 13, Jackson was informed that the Prince would not see him again, and that his Ministers had no authority whatever to conclude any arrangement upon terms at all compatible with Jackson's instructions. The British envoy at once got his passports and joined the fleet lying outside Copenhagen. Two days later, the British transports landed 20,000 soldiers at Vedvec and the city was invested on the land side. Copenhagen was utterly defenceless. Outside of Elsinor Castle there was not a battalion under arms in all Denmark. Not a gun was mounted on the ramparts. To man the defences, volunteers had to be raised among the populace. The ships in the harbor lay at anchor without a sail

Bombard-
ment of
Copenha-
gen
flapping. On September 2, the bombardment of Copenhagen was begun. For three days the field batteries on land and the British fleet in the harbor poured an unceasing fire into the helpless city. In a very short time several blocks of houses were on fire. At the end of a three days' bombardment half of the city was in ashes and nearly 2,000 noncombatants lay buried in the smoking ruins. The British took possession of eighteen Danish ships of the line and all the war frigates, and stripped the

dockyards of their stores. Denmark lay prone before England. All Danish merchant vessels that happened to be in English waters were confiscated with their cargoes to the value of £10,000,000. In distant India the flourishing Danish factory at Bengal was swept into England's pouch.

The bombardment of Copenhagen affected Europe as did Napoleon's execution of the Duke Enghien. The King of Denmark at once addressed a procla- *Proclamation by King of Denmark* mation to all friendly powers. These were the most striking passages: "All Europe is acquainted with Denmark's unceasing neutrality during this period of disturbance and war. This state of peace and tranquillity is suddenly annihilated. The Danish government saw the English ships of war on its coast without even a conjecture that they were to be employed against Denmark. The English court then declared to the court of Denmark in the most overbearing manner that Denmark was to deliver up all her ships of war to the British government. This opening, as offensive in the manner of presentation as in the demand itself, left no room for negotiation. Placed between danger and dishonor, the Danish government had no choice. Cut off *Resentment against England* from all means of defence we were forced into the unequal contest. Let impartial cabinets judge of the results. Even in England every noble and generous mind must disown this act of violence which deforms the character of a virtuous sovereign and will ever remain a scandal in the annals of Great Britain."

Denmark immediately entered into an alliance

with Napoleon. Emperor Alexander of Russia revived the northern embargo against English shipping in a proclamation in which he said: "The attack of England on Denmark was an outrage in which history, so replete in acts of violence, has no equal. Russia will have nothing to do with England until satisfaction shall have been given to Denmark." England's high-handed acts at sea left

British retaliatory measures

her without a friend save Portugal. Her policy of retaliation was enforced all the more relentlessly. Following upon the attacks on the "Chesapeake" and Copenhagen, the British cabinet issued a decree which prohibited all neutral trade along the entire European sea-coast from Copenhagen to Trieste. Only the Baltic ports were left open. No American vessels should be allowed to enter any port in Europe from which British vessels were excluded. These rigorous measures were taken upon the recom-

Orders in Council

mendation of a parliamentary committee which had declared that the distress in the West Indies was due to "the facility of intercourse, under the American flag, between the hostile colonies and Europe, by means of which the whole of their produce was carried to market at charges little exceeding those of peace, while the British planter is burdened with all the inconvenience, risk and expense resulting from the state of war." After November 11, 1807, any American vessel carrying any cargo was liable to capture if it sailed from any port not under British control. American commerce was to be turned perforce into exclusively English channels.

America, like those other hapless neutrals, Denmark and Portugal, was caught between the two
grinding millstones of England and France. Only Oppression of neutrals
her greater distance from Europe saved her from
a fate similar to that of the others.

A characteristic note of the time has been preserved in one of the letters of the American Minister at Paris. It was written after Napoleon's first
diplomatic reception at the Tuileries on his return
from the campaign in the North. After telling how
roughly the French Emperor accosted the Danish
and Portuguese Ambassadors within the hearing
of their colleagues, General Armstrong goes on:
"These circumstances go far to justify the whisper Letter of American Minister at Paris
that begins to circulate, that an army is organizing
in the South for the purpose of taking possession of
Portugal, and another in the North for a similar
purpose against Denmark. Under the influence of
this suggestion, the Danish Minister, asking me
aside, inquired whether any application had been
made to me with regard to a projected union of
all commercial States against Great Britain. On
my answering in the negative he remarked: 'You
are much favored, but it will not last.'"

The Danish Minister was right. Shortly after
Napoleon's orders forced the governments of Denmark and Holland to close their ports, the Emperor
wrote to Decrès: "France cannot regard flags which
enjoy no consideration as neutral. That of America, however exposed it may be to the insults of the
English, still has some sort of existence. Those of
Portugal and Denmark exist no longer." When

General Armstrong protested against the condem‐
nation of an American cargo that had been wrecked

off Morlaix, Napoleon responded sharply: "Since
America suffers her vessels to be searched, she
adopts the principle that the flag does not cover
the goods. . . . Why should Americans not
equally suffer their vessels to be searched by
French ships? France recognizes that these meas‐
ures are unjust and subversive of national sover‐
eignty, but it is the duty of nations to resort to
force and to declare themselves against things which
dishonor them and disgrace their independence."

The American people, aroused as they were over
the "Chesapeake" affair and the West Indian block‐

ade, were coming to the same conclusion. Gallatin,
the Secretary of the Treasury, began making his
economic preparations for war. Congress, at the
behest of President Jefferson, voted $1,854,000 for
additional gunboats, harbor fortifications and shore
defences. The navy was left as weak as before.

Among the various proposals for the national
defence was one for building submarine torpedoes.
It came from Robert Fulton of New York. On

July 20, 1807, in pursuance of the experiments
which the government had authorized him to make,
Fulton, with one of his torpedoes, blew up the hulk
of a large brig in New York harbor. This exploit
did not produce a favorable impression on the gov‐
ernment, as the torpedo locks missed fire several
times, and the explosion did not occur until sev‐
eral hours after the time announced to the spec‐
tators crowding the New York water front. The

torpedo in this instance was a copper case two feet long, charged with one hundred pounds of gunpowder with clockwork to set it off. Previous to this, Fulton had offered a submarine boat to Napoleon and to the British admiralty.

Napoleon commissioned Fulton to blow up some British cruisers outside of Brest. When Fulton failed in the attempt, Napoleon lost interest in the project. Then the Earl of Stanhope, the inventor of the Stanhope printing press, who had been interested in Fulton's inventions of a flax-spinning machine and cast-iron aqueducts, persuaded Lord Sidmouth to call Fulton to England. A naval commission was appointed to examine Fulton's scheme for floating mines and torpedoes. On October 15, 1805, Fulton blew up the hulk of a Danish brig in Walmar Roads, in sight of Mr. Pitt's country house. As reported by Fulton in a letter to Lord Castlereagh, the experiment proved a complete success: "Exactly in fifteen minutes from the time of drawing the peg and throwing the loaded carcass in the water, the explosion took place. It lifted the brig almost bodily and blew her completely in two. She went to pieces like a shattered eggshell." An attempt to blow up some French gun brigs in the roads of Boulogne proved a failure. The torpedoes exploded alongside of the Frenchmen and did no harm. Fulton left England in disappointment and returned to America. Here he perfected his model of a steamboat which he had first exhibited before the members of the French Academy on the waters of the Seine. In Paris, Chancellor

Napoleon and Fulton

Forerunner of the torpedo

Livingston of New York had become deeply interested in Fulton's steamboat. He entered into active
partnership with the inventor and had a bill passed
through the Legislature of New York granting to
Livingston and Fulton the exclusive right of navi-
gating steam vessels in the waters of New York.
For a long time this steamboat bill was a standing
subject of ridicule among the legislators of Albany.
Upon his return to America, Fulton and Livingston
began in earnest to build their steamboat. The
engine was furnished by Watt and Bolton in Bir-
mingham, who but five years before had constructed
an engine for the first working locomotive in England. In August, 1807, Fulton's steamboat was finished and steamed out of the shipyard of Charles
Brown in the East River. She was named the
"Clermont," but the people of New York called
her "Fulton's Folly." The "Clermont" was a
schooner-rigged boat of a hundred and sixty
tons, and had a cylinder measuring twenty-four
inches in diameter with a four-foot stroke. The
paddlewheels revolved amidships with no box or
covering. Dry pine wood was used for fuel, which
sent forth thick black smoke with flames and sparks
leaping high above the single funnel. This gave
the ship a terrific aspect, and spread terror among
the superstitious watermen of New York harbor.
On August 11, the "Clermont" made her maiden
trip up the Hudson River to Chancellor Livingston's country-seat near Albany. It was a voyage
of a hundred and ten miles, and took twenty-four
hours, without a mishap. Fulton wrote to his

friend **Barlow** in Paris: "My steamboat **voyage** _{Fulton's success} to Albany and back has turned out rather more favorably than I had calculated. The voyage was performed wholly by power of the steam engine. I overtook many sloops and schooners beating to windward and parted with them as if they had been at anchor. The power of propelling boats by steam is now fully proved. The morning I left New York there were not thirty persons in the city who believed that the boat would ever move a mile an hour, or be of the least utility. While we were putting off from the wharf I heard a number of sarcastic remarks. This is the way in which ignorant men compliment what they call philosophers and projectors. I feel infinite pleasure in reflecting on the immense advantages my country will derive from the invention." Soon the boat was running as a regular packet between New York and Albany. The river men grew to hate her, and several attempts _{Opposition to Fulton} were made to sink the "Clermont." The New York Legislature finally passed an act declaring all combinations to destroy her, or wilful attempts to injure her, public offences punishable by fine and imprisonment. Next the courts were asked for an injunction to restrain Fulton from using his new machine on the Hudson, but with Daniel Webster for a pleader, Fulton won his case. Other steamboats were soon built by Livingston and Fulton, and, in the end, Fulton furnished the city of New York with steam ferries. The newspapers of the time gave scarcely any attention to Fulton's steamboat. Much was said on the other hand about the experi-

Garnerin's
balloon
ments of M. Garnerin, with a newly invented balloon filled with hydrogen gas, the great invention of Lavoisier. After his first ascension in Milan, Garnerin addressed a letter to the newspapers of Paris, in which he disposed of an earlier aeronaut's contentions that the sun and moon lost their brilliancy and gravity in force at high altitudes. After Garnerin's second ascension at Paris late in September, 1807, he was publicly entertained by a scientific society and the officers of a regiment of cuirassiers, whose standard he had planted on a high mountain.

Reforms
in Prussia
While science and inventions were thus progressing in other countries, the Prussian people, chastened by war, were catching up their lost place in the march of civilization. At the recommendation of Napoleon, who disliked Minister Hardenberg for his steadfast resistance to French encroachments,

Ministry
of Stein
Stein was summoned to the head of the Prussian Ministry. To Napoleon he was known only as a skilful financier who was likely to succeed in raising the money for the heavy war indemnities exacted by France. Stein entered into office on September 4, 1807. Four days later his first great legislative measure was launched. It was the abolition of serfdom in Prussia, and of all feudal distinctions between the nobles, burghers and peasants. The family estates were freed from entail. Stein appointed Scharnhorst as president of the military commission, which did away with the enforced military service of the former peasant serfs, and created in its stead a system of universal service with the

colors. To comply at least outwardly with Napoleon's demand for a restriction of the Prussian army to 40,000 men, Scharnhorst devised a short service system, with various reserves, by means of which all citizens could be made to serve their time with the colors. Stein likewise planned to give to Prussia a Constitutional Parliament, modelled after that of Great Britain, with municipal home rule, but succeeded only in establishing the last. Stein's reforms aroused so much opposition on the part of the Prussian nobles, besides incurring the jealous suspicions of Napoleon, that his Ministry was not destined to endure. While it lasted the way was prepared for Prussia's resurrection from the political degradation and gloom to which she had sunk through the events of the last few years.

Stein's reforms

Toward the end of the year, war clouds once more gathered over Europe. England's uncompromising attitude determined Gustavus IV. of Sweden to carry on the war in the North, which had lapsed after the defeat of the Russians and Prussians, and his own armistice at Shlakkov. Outgeneralled by Marshal Brune, the Swedes lost Stralsund and Ruegen, and had to withdraw into the interior. This ended the campaign in the North for the nonce.

Stralsund lost to Sweden

The only remaining neutral in Europe was Portugal. The Regent, placed between the alternative of losing his ancient kingdom or his vast new possessions across the sea, leaned toward England. Napoleon saw his opportunity in Spain by making a bold stroke against Portugal. Portugal's refusal

Predicament of Portugal

to confiscate all English property set the ball roll-
ing. On October 17, General Junot marched from
Bayonne with 27,000 men headed for the Pyrenees.
Ten days later, a secret treaty for the spoliation of
Portugal was concluded at Fontainebleau between
Talleyrand and Godoy, the Prime Minister of
Spain. The King of Etruria was to exchange
his kingdom for a Portuguese province, and
Godoy was to receive the sovereignties of Al-
garvez and Alentejo, in Portugal. All Portu-
guese colonies were to fall to Spain, and King
Charles IV. of Spain was to be recognized as
Emperor of both Americas. Neither the Spanish
Minister, nor the Crown Prince, who intrigued
with Napoleon against Godoy, realized the danger
of the projected French invasion of Spain.

General Junot, with his army of the Gironde,
marching across Spain at the utmost speed, was
welcomed by both government and the people. At
the Portuguese frontier no resistance was encountered. The governor of the Portuguese province
Tras los Montes wrote: "We are unable to entertain you as friends or to resist you as enemies. I
have the honor to be," etc. The French troops
swarmed over the mountains and concentrated rapidly upon Lisbon. At Lisbon, the royal Princes
of Braganza were still deliberating what to do when
they received a copy of "Le Moniteur," printed on
November 13, in which was published Napoleon's
decree: "La Maison de Braganze a cessé de regner
en Europe." After consultation with the British
ambassador, the Regent of Portugal resolved to

Treaty between Talleyrand and Godoy

French invasion of Portugal

maintain the independence of his family by flight Flight of Regent of Portugal across the Atlantic. As the French troops appeared before Lisbon, the Regent with his family embarked on a fleet of sixteen ships. Accompanied by four British convoys under Sir Sydney Smith, and saluted by British guns, the fleet dropped down the Tagus and put to sea for Rio Janeiro. Marshal Junot, a few hours later, occupied the royal palace. The French troops were in wretched condition from their prolonged rapid marches. Cannon were placed in all the streets and the inhabitants were disarmed. Heavy contributions were levied for the support of the French troops. The flower of the Portuguese army was sent to France. The island colony of Madeira was occupied by a British garrison to be held for the Portuguese princes until better days.

In Madrid, Godoy, the Prime Minister, looked forward to receiving his share in the spoil of Portugal, Spanish intrigues but Napoleon had another end in view. Not only Portugal but Spain, too, was to be his prey. For more than a year he had contemplated some such project—since the day in 1806 that Godoy had dared to prepare for war against France, by calling the Spanish people to arms. Godoy's attempt to propitiate Napoleon after the French victories at Jena and Auerstaedt, by sending 14,000 Spanish auxiliaries against Russia, proved a mere sop to the conqueror. Under the circumstances, Godoy's chosen title, the "Prince of Peace," partook of ironical significance. Latter-day historians have come to regard this man as the prince of evil for Spain.

In the autumn of 1807, Godoy stood at the zenith of his power. His full name and titles were Don Manuel Godoy, Prince of Peace, Duke of Alcudia, Count of Evora Monte, Grandee of the first class of Spain, Commander of the Knights of Malta, Knight of the Golden Fleece, Grand Cross Bearer of the Order of Charles III., President of the Council of Castile, Generalissimo of the Spanish armies, High Admiral of the royal fleet, Colonel of the Household Troops, etc. With the exception of his promised principalities in Portugal, all these honors had come to him by the grace of Queen Maria Louisa, one of the Naples Bourbons. She was thirty-four when she first bestowed her favors on Godoy, then an untitled young gentleman trooper of twenty-two. She had him educated and drew

him into all the intrigues of court. Within two years she caused him to be made Colonel of the Guards and procured him a seat in the Council of Castile. When Count Aranda, the former Minister, was dismissed for recognizing the revolutionary government in France, the Queen's favorite was installed as Prime Minister. After an unsuccessful campaign against the French republic, in 1794, Godoy concluded peace and presented France with the Pandora box of Western San Domingo. For this he received the title "Prince of Peace," with large sums from the secret fund of Portugal. The next war was with England, and was even more disas-

trous for Spain. England took the Island of Trinidad, and practically wiped out all Spanish commerce with the West Indies. By this time Godoy was so thoroughly ingratiated at court that nothing could harm him. He was the reputed father of one of the royal princes, Don Francisco de Paula. At the same time he lived in open relations with Donna Josepha Tuda, who bore him several children. Besides this the Queen permitted him to marry the second daughter of Don Luis, brother to the King. The Archbishop of Toledo declined to perform the marriage ceremony, and the outraged grandees of Spain all remained aloof, but the nuptials were duly celebrated in the royal chapel, and the Queen appointed Godoy's mistress as one of her ladies in waiting. When France dragged Spain into a war with Portugal, Godoy was made generalissimo in the field, but sold out to Portugal without ever encountering the enemy. A few years later, when the United States made preparation to secure free navigation of the Mississippi by seizing the Spanish colony of New Orleans, Godoy averted war by secretly deeding Louisiana to France. The next war, brought on by England's seizure of the Spanish treasure ships from Mexico in 1804, resulted in the disaster of Trafalgar. The Prince of Peace expressed himself as satisfied, for he had never approved of this war which threatened Spain with the loss of all her colonial possessions. What remained of the Spanish fleet was sent to Toulon just previous to Napoleon's descent upon Portugal. *Disastrous Spanish policy*

In the meantime, the Spanish king's eldest son Ferdinand, Prince of Asturias, who was virtually banished from court by the disfavor of his mother, carried on a plot of his own with Napoleon. He *Ferdinand intrigues with France* entered into a secret understanding with Empress Josephine's relative, De Beauharnais, the French ambassador at Madrid. On October 11, 1807, Ferdinand wrote an abject letter to Napoleon for the ostensible purpose of congratulating him on his "providential salvation of Europe and the restoration of the tranquillity and happiness of nations." The letter went on: "If those men, who unfortunately surround my father, suffered him to become acquainted with your imperial and royal majesty's real character, it would draw closer the ties which would unite our respective houses. What means could be better calculated to attain this object than that of soliciting from your imperial and royal majesty the honor of giving to me in marriage a princess of your august family. This is all my heart desires, but it is not what is calculated upon by the perfidious and selfish men who surround the King, and who will on the first opportunity mislead him." Godoy, through his spies, had been fully informed of Ferdinand's plotting with Beauharnais, and furthermore of his disposition to seize the reins in case of his father's death, before Godoy might use his powers to place on the throne his own reputed son, Prince Francisco. On October 29, Ferdinand was suddenly arrested and brought before his father on charges that he had plotted against his mother's life. King Charles ordered Ferdinand to be cast into prison and wrote an indignant letter to Napoleon in which he announced his intention to deprive his eldest son of the succession.

This was a misstep. Ferdinand was very popular

Ferdinand's letter to Napoleon

Godoy checkmates Ferdinand

with the mass of the Spanish people, chiefly because
he was known to be an enemy of Godoy, who was
hated by all. On the Prince of Asturias were fixed
all Spanish hopes of reform. There were threatening indications of the popular feeling on the subject,
and Godoy was further alarmed at Ferdinand's reve-
lations of the French ambassador's complicity in
his plans. Godoy thought best to recede from his
extreme position, and prevailed upon the King to
liberate his son, on condition that Ferdinand begged
the King's and Queen's forgiveness. This the Prince
was more than ready to do. On November 5, a
royal manifesto announced the King's forgiveness
of his son. Ferdinand was set free. His friends,
who had been placed on trial as so-called accom-
plices, were acquitted by their judges and left
Madrid unharmed.

Napoleon, while receiving the confidences of both
father and son, had no idea of doing anything for
either, for that would not further his own interests.
The imbroglio at Madrid fitted admirably into his
plans. While the Emperor strove to lull Spain into
security by making an aimless journey to Italy, his
generals at Bayonne received orders to prepare for
a sudden march on Madrid.

During the interval many things happened to
divert the attention of Europe. On December 1,
the King of Prussia, at the behest of Napoleon, cut
off all relations with England. A few days after
ward, Napoleon's brother Jerome formally ascended the throne of his new kingdom, Westphalia. On December 10, the kingdom of Etruria was

Prince of Asturias set free

Napoleon's designs on Spain

relinquished by the Bourbons and French troops occupied the country. On December 17, Napoleon

The Milan Decree

issued a decree at Milan, in reply to the British note of November 11, in which he declared any ship that touched at an English port or yielded to England's demands, thereby lost the protection of her neutral flag, and should be seized as a prize. A blockade was declared against all British possessions. As if in answer, the British Ministry on the following day published King George's response to Russia's protest against the bombardment of Copenhagen. The right of search and impressment, with all other obnoxious British practices at sea, were reiterated as a maritime privilege, the enforcement of which was rendered doubly necessary by Napoleon's acts of usurpation.

American Non-Impor- tation Act

In anticipation of what was coming, the American Congress had already passed a Non-Importation Act, which now went into force, despite the protests of American and English merchants. British trade was seriously affected. Among the forbidden articles were all products of leather, silk, hemp, glass, silver, paper, pictures, prints, woollen hosiery, ready-made clothing, millinery, malt liquors, and so forth. The intention practically was to punish England by a fine of several million dollars for her interference with American transatlantic trade. Under the stress of new restrictive measures threatened by France and England, the United States and France went even further. On December 17, simultaneously with the new French and English decrees, President Jefferson issued a proclamation to Congress calling for a general embargo of all American trade with Europe. In his message he said: "The whole world is laid under interdict by Great Britain and France, and our vessels, their cargoes and their crews are to be taken by one or by the other, no matter to what place they may be destined, out of our own limits. If therefore on leaving our harbors we are certainly to lose them, is it not better as to vessels, cargoes and seamen to keep them at home?"

Within four or five hours after the message had been read, the Senate sent the Embargo Act to the House. The House passed it on December 21, by a vote of 82 to 44. The President signed the bill the next day. For most Americans, this embargo, disastrous as its effects were on American commerce, brought premonitions of the impending war with England.

In Spain, during these same days, the curtain rose on a war that is known to English-speaking men as the War of the Peninsula—to Spaniards as La Guerra de la Independencia. General Dupont's French army corps crossed the Pyrenees in the last days of 1807. The French troops were received with acclamation by the Spanish populace. Spaniards still believed that Napoleon had espoused the cause of Ferdinand and meant to free Spain from the detested rule of Godoy. The French in turn proclaimed themselves as the friends of Ferdinand and protectors of the true Catholic faith.

1808

ON New Year's Day, Napoleon returned to
Paris to execute his designs against Spain.

At the outset of the struggle in the peninsula, Great Britain's military power consisted of
more than a thousand warships—to wit, 250 sail of
the line, 261 frigates, 258 brigs and 300 sloops-of-
war. The British army, numbering some 200,000

Resources
of France
and Eng-
land

men, was held in small esteem by the French.
The French navy, what little was left of it, in
land-locked harbors, was despised by the British.
Of French soldiers there were nearly a million
under arms. By a new decree of January 21, another levy of 80,000 men was added to this. Spain,
at this time, had a population of about thirteen
millions. The Spanish soldiers had been distributed by Napoleon in different parts of the world,
some serving under Junot in Portugal, others in
Germany, and some on the frontier of Sweden.

At the opening of 1808 two French army corps
had entered Spain in the wake of Junot's first
army of the Gironde. They numbered 53,000 men.
The second army of the Gironde, under Dupont,

Invasion
of Spain

advanced to Vittoria and thence to Valadolid, while
Marshal Moncy's column, called the army of the
sea-coast, marched along the road from Bayonne to

Madrid. Together they cut off the northern provinces from Madrid and put themselves in possession of the upper Spanish strongholds. A fourth division, under General Duhesme, crossing the Eastern Pyrenees, marched for Barcelona. General Brandt in his memoirs tells how some of the northern fortresses fell into the hands of the French. At Pampeluna the French soldiers, who had been welcomed by the inhabitants, went into quarters near the castle. Every day a file of them went to the citadel with large bags to fetch bread. One day, after a slight snowfall, a number of French soldiers took to snowballing in front of the castle, while their comrades crowded around as if to watch the fun. Meanwhile the French commissary men entered the citadel with their bread sacks, in which were concealed short swords and pistols. Of a sudden they overpowered the guards at the gate, and the mass of apparently idle soldiers near by made a concerted rush into the citadel.

The descent from the Pyrenees

Northern strongholds seized

In Madrid the advance of the French aroused great alarm. King Charles wrote to Napoleon in a tone of friendly inquiry. He received a vague reply that was anything but reassuring. On February 20, Marshal Murat left Paris to assume command in Spain. On March 1, he entered the country with no instructions, but to reassure all parties and commit himself to none. It was now that the Spanish court, expecting to see the French in front of Madrid before another fortnight, resolved to follow the example of the Prince of Braganza, by flight to Mexico. Preparations for the preliminary journey

Spanish court alarmed

to Seville were in progress when Prince Ferdinand's grooms spread a report that Godoy was about to abduct the King in order to continue his own misgovernment. The people of Aranjuez rushed out of their houses and cut the traces of the royal carriage. Quiet was restored when the King gave his word that no journey was intended. That evening he issued this proclamation: "My beloved subjects, calm your perturbed spirits. Know that the army of my dear friend the Emperor of the French is marching through my States with sentiments of peace and amity. The object is to protect the points threatened by the landing of an enemy on the coasts of Spain. My guards have not been called either to defend my person or to escort me on a journey, as some malignant spirits have told you." The next day a mob marched from Madrid to Aranjuez, and called for the blood of Godoy. The soldiers of the royal guard joined them. Godoy's palace in Madrid was sacked. The Prime Minister himself, after lying hid for thirty-six hours, was dragged forth and hurried to the barracks amid blows and curses. On the 19th, the riots recommenced in Aranjuez. The terrified King first issued a decree depriving Godoy of all his dignities, and then abdicated in favor of his son Ferdinand. On March 20, a new king was proclaimed in Madrid. Two days later, Murat rode into Madrid with a vanguard of cavalry, followed by Moncy's corps of infantry. Dupont's division occupied Aranjuez and the Escurial. Here as elsewhere the French soldiers were welcomed by the populace as the

[margin: Riots of Aranjuez]

[margin: Fall of Manuel Godoy]

[margin: King Charles abdicates]

deliverers of Ferdinand. The next day Ferdinand The French in Madrid himself made a solemn entry into Madrid. During the festivities it was noticed that the French troops paid scant attention to the royal pageant. Marshal Murat, while presenting a claim for the famous sword of Francis I. of France, abstained from according any formal recognition to Ferdinand. Murat himself entertained secret hopes that he might be placed on the throne of Spain, as he had longed before to become King of Poland. The enthusiasm of the populace quickly turned into suspicion and ill-will. There was constant friction between Murat's soldiers and the people of Madrid. The late king wrote to Murat that his abdication had been forced and was therefore void. Ferdinand had a conference with Savary, Napoleon's special emissary, to obtain the French Emperor's recognition in person. He was led to believe that Napoleon would meet him half way at Burgos. Accordingly he journeyed northward in company of Savary and his suite. At Burgos they found the Emperor. From all sides Ferdinand received warnings not to Prince Ferdinand decoyed proceed. Some of his noblemen offered to carry him out of danger by sea. At Vittoria the people held up the horses and implored him not to leave the country. Ferdinand was obdurate. Beguiled by a letter from Napoleon, who had proceeded to Bayonne with Josephine, he crossed the Pyrenees and sought out the Emperor there. After a reception and a dinner at a neighboring chateau, Ferdinand was informed by Savary that he was expected to exchange his crown for that of the defunct kingdom of Etruria. For several days the tricked prince

Spanish
Princes
suppli-
cants at
Bayonne
held out. Virtually, he was a prisoner in the hands of Napoleon. He was joined presently by his father and mother, who had come in their turn to sue for favors from Napoleon. Godoy, who had been liberated by Murat, also came to Bayonne. All three overwhelmed Ferdinand with reproaches.

Things were at this pass when the population of Madrid, exasperated by the events of the last few weeks, rose against the foreign invaders. Before this, anti-French riots had already broken out in

The Dos
de Maio in
Madrid
Toledo. On May 2—the famous Dos de Maio, which has since become a Spanish holiday—the people of Madrid went wild at the sight of a carriage in front of the royal palace which was intended to carry the infant prince, Don Antonio, the last member of the royal family, to France. The horses were taken out of the traces and the little prince was snatched from the carriage. At this moment, Murat's aide-de-camp galloped up. He was dragged from his horse and roughly handled till the French guards of the palace came to the rescue. In an incredibly short time the commotion spread through the whole city. French soldiers were struck down on every street, and the military hospital was attacked. Squadrons of cavalry were called in from the suburbs. The great thoroughfare of Alcala, Puerta del Sol and the central square were the chief scenes of slaughter.

At the commencement of the conflict Murat ordered a detachment of 200 men to take possession of the arsenal. Two officers happened to be upon

guard there, by name Daoiz and Velarde. They
pointed a cannon down the street and with the help
of their gunners succeeded in sweeping the street
with grape-shot. Two battalions of French soldiers
had to be ordered up, and finally the small band Massacre
of Madri-
was killed. Several regiments of infantry were lenos
marched through the city in detachments, firing
volleys into all cross streets. Many of the rioters
were shot, others were taken prisoners, and finally
order was restored with the help of the Spanish
garrison which had been confined in its barracks
during the tumult. But at nightfall the peasants
from the suburbs beset the gates. As many as
sixty were shot during the night. On the morrow
it was found that more than five hundred Frenchmen had been killed. In exasperation the French
shot eighty of their prisoners on the Prado. Others
were shot to death in the barracks.

Such was the news from Madrid that reached
Bayonne in the midst of the royal family supplica-
tions for their lost throne. Napoleon curtly informed Ferdinand that if he withheld his abdication
for another day he would be treated as a rebel.
The bearer of this message was Savary, who had
played so prominent a part in the memorable execution of the Duke of Enghien. With the fate of that
luckless prince thus recalled, Ferdinand hesitated Spanish
crown
no longer. His father, Charles, likewise renounced wrested
from
the throne. The crown of Spain was yielded to Bourbons
Napoleon by both father and son. They were dismissed with a couple of country houses near Paris,
and a life annuity of seven and a half million francs.

About the same time that French troops were seizing the Spanish citadels in Pampeluna, Barcelona, Figueras, and San Sebastian, French soldiers were marched into Rome. Their avowed object was to eject from the Vatican the emissaries of those countries that still maintained hostility to France, to wit: England and Sweden. Pope Pius VII. threatened to excommunicate Napoleon. In a papal bull of March 27, the grievances against Napoleon were recited: "For a long time the Holy See has been burdened by the enforced sustenance of the French troops, which have consumed nearly five million scudi. You have deprived us of the duchies of Beneventum and Ponte-Corvo. Now you have invaded the capital itself, and have made us a prisoner in our own apostolic residence." Napoleon replied to the Pope's threat of excommunication by a decree announcing the annexation of the papal provinces Ancona, Urbino, Macerata and Camerino to the kingdom of Italy. The King of Naples, Joseph, was summoned to serve as King of Spain, since his brother Louis had declined that honor.

In northern Europe, too, there was a lively interchange of State papers. Russia declared war on Sweden and seized Finland as per agreement with Napoleon. In a proclamation to the Finns the Czar pledged his imperial word that all the internal affairs of their country should pursue their usual course and be managed according to their ancient laws and customs. The payment of taxes, freedom of religious worship, as well as all other privileges guaranteed by the constitution of Finland, were to remain on

Marginal notes:
French soldiers occupy Rome

Napoleon threatened with Papal excommunication

Finland annexed by Russia

the same footing. Denmark and Prussia followed War in Sweden suit with declarations of war against Sweden. The King of Sweden answered in kind. General Armfeldt at the head of the Swedish army occupied Norway. Great Britain engaged to assist Sweden with a monthly subsidy of £100,000, beginning with January, 1808.

Napoleon, during this interval, collected a body of Spanish notables at Bayonne, composed mainly of the courtiers that had come into the suite of the dethroned king and queen. Joseph was hurried from Naples by the following peremptory letter: "I desire Joseph Bonaparte summoned immediately on the receipt of this letter that you will give the regency of the kingdom of Naples to whomever you like, the command of the troops to Marshal Jourdan, and then start for Bayonne. You will receive this letter on the 19th. You will leave on the 20th, and be here on the 1st of June." Joseph unwillingly complied. Murat, who had set his heart on the throne of Spain, sickened with chagrin and nearly died.

In every part of Spain the people were arming to expel the foreign intruder. On May 20, the same day that Tuscany, Piacenza and Parma were wrested from another Bourbon prince, the abdication of the Spanish Bourbons was announced in the "Gazeta" of Madrid. Napoleon, through this medium, thus addressed the Spanish people: "I have watched your sufferings; I shall remedy them. Your princes have ceded to me their rights to the crown of Spain. I do not wish to reign over your provinces, but I would earn a title to your eternal love and the grati-

Napoleon's
Spanish
pronuncia-
mento tude of your descendants. Your monarchy is old; my mission is to rejuvenate it. Be full of hope and confidence, therefore, and your descendants will preserve my memory, and say, 'He was the regenerator of our country.'"

The effect of this pronunciamiento was magical. The whole country, as by one impulse, rose up in arms. The Mayor of Mostoles, a small village near Madrid, sent out this bulletin: "The country is in danger; Madrid is perishing through the perfidy of the French. All Spaniards, come, and deliver us!"

The news of this spread like wildfire. Carthagena rose against the French on May 22. Valencia, on the next day, proclaimed Ferdinand as the only rightful ruler of Spain. Two days later the mountain district of Asturias, with a population of 500,000, declared war on Napoleon in the name All Spain
up in arms of the royal house. On May 26, Seville and Santander, on opposite sides of the peninsula, joined the movement. The feast of St. Ferdinand, on May 30, was selected as a fitting day for most of the remaining provinces to declare war against the French. Granada, Corunna, and Badajos took up arms; and national juntas were formed. The junta of Asturias sent emissaries to England to ask for aid. One of them was Viscount Matarosa, better known as the Count of Toreno, who has left one of the most faithful records of these events. The junta of Asturias issued a declaration warning Spaniards that their native country, their king, their property, laws, liberties, religion, yea, even their hope for a better world, were at stake. At Valencia every French-

man seen on the streets was killed at sight. In Valladolid the people erected a gibbet before the residence of the Governor of Leon and gave him the choice whether he would join their movement or be hanged. In the country, frightful excesses were committed on straggling French soldiers. The fourteen Spanish provinces all rose against France. The four Basque provinces alone, being overrun by French soldiers, did not join the movement. On June 6, the junta of Seville issued a proclamation in the name of Spain and of Ferdinand. Napoleon was charged with the criminal abduction and terrorization of their king and nobles. His announced intention to impose the French king upon Spain was denounced as the worst "perfidy, fraud and treachery that was ever committed against any nation or monarch by the most barbarous and ambitious kings." "War should not cease," declared the junta, "until Ferdinand and the rest of the royal family be restored to their throne and Spain relieved of the last French soldier." Andalusia was the province that contained the most Spanish troops. They joined the insurrection at once. That circumstance, with the fact that the Sierra Morena, a wild mountain range, runs through that region, made Andalusia the most formidable centre of the rebellion. The Marquis of Solano, commanding a Spanish auxiliary force at Cadiz, was ordered by the junta to seize the French squadron there. He refused and was put to death. His successor ordered Admiral Rosily to surrender, but the French sailed to the middle of the wide harbor,

The people declare war

The army joins the movement

where they were out of reach of guns and awaited
aid from Dupont. Before a week had passed, the
British ministry, through Canning, sent assurances
to Spain that troops and money would be furnished.
Three hundred thousand pounds in Spanish dollars
were sent at once, with a huge quantity of arms and
ammunition. The speedy despatch of a fleet with
a strong landing force was promised at Gijon. Sir
Charles Cotton, commanding the British naval forces
off the coasts of Spain, was ordered to render all possible aid. Within a month, a treaty for offensive
and defensive alliance was signed in Oporto between
the emissaries of England and Spain. "Hitherto,"
cried Sheridan, leader of the Whig opposition,
"Bonaparte has contended with princes without
dignity, numbers without ardor, or peoples without patriotism. He has yet to learn what it is to
combat a people who are animated by one spirit
against him." Tory and Whig alike held that
"never had so happy an opportunity existed in
Britain to strike a bold stroke for the rescue of the
world." On June 15, Napoleon's Assembly of Notables was convoked at Bayonne, and accepted a constitution modelled on that of France. All privileges
of nobility were abolished. The Catholic religion
was declared to be the only one permitted in Spain.
Joseph Bonaparte received royal homage from the
notables, and hastened to cross the Pyrenees. On
July 12, he arrived at Vittoria with a guard of
8,000 Italian soldiers. His best protection was the
forces of General Verdier posted along his route in
Spain. At Vittoria an attempt was made to stop

Joseph's progress, but his guards quickly suppressed the riot. All over the country, in fact, the French were engaged in suppressing uprisings against them. The trained veterans of France Early Spanish defeats easily worsted the insurgents wherever they met them in the open. General Verdier defeated the rebels without trouble at Logrono, Frère at Segovia, Lasalle at Torquemada, at the bridge of Cabezon and before Valladolid, where Gregorio della Cuesta made his troops fight with their backs to the river. The Aragonese bands were scattered at Tudela and Mallen. In all these engagements the French losses were insignificant, while the peasants were butchered right and left. In the east and south of Spain, on the other hand, the French were checked. Moncy, who was to subdue Valencia, had to come to a halt half-way. General Duhesme found himself blocked in Barcelona, and Lefebvre-Desnouettes was held in check before Saragossa, by Palafox. In Andalusia, Dupont had to retreat to Andujar before the armies of Castaños and Granda. The sack of Cordova by his troops, and the pillage of the churches there, was resented on the part of the Spaniards by acts of unexampled ferocity against Retaliation on French soldiers the French. Every soldier found at large was killed by the peasants and the sick and wounded were mutilated. The wells around the French camps were poisoned. The French grew to realize that they had to do with an enemy who neither asked nor gave quarter.

Such was the state of affairs when Joseph entered Madrid. He was proclaimed king on July 20. On

the same day, as it happened, the Janizaries in Constantinople deposed Sultan Mustapha. When they
called for their former Sultan Selim, his dead body

Palace
revolution
in Turkey
was flung before them. His cousin Mahmoud was
made Sultan. In Naples, Murat was crowned King
of both Sicilies in Joseph's stead. During Joseph's
journey from the Pyrenees the scales had dropped
from his eyes. To his brother he wrote: "No one
has hitherto told you the truth. The fact is that
not one single Spaniard comes forward to take part
with me. Fear does not make me see double.

Joseph
Bonaparte
discour-
aged
Since I have been in Spain, I say to myself every
day, 'My life is of little value.' I am not frightened
by my position, but it is unique in history. I have
not a single partisan." The warning was lost on Napoleon. In all this affair with Spain he gave little
evidence of the great genius which had hitherto
distinguished his public conduct. His wonted per-
spicacity and ability to cope with the situation in
advance of the actual event changed into a blind-
ness of which history offers but few examples.
From the start he misunderstood the character of
the Spanish people and of their peculiar warfare.

Napoleon's
blunders
in Spain
Instead of centralizing his forces for a masterstroke, as he had always done in the past, he
scattered them over the whole country in isolated
detachments. So purblind was he that he undertook to direct all military movements from home,
a thing which he himself had so often denounced
as one of the capital errors of war.

Instead of flying to his eagles when they were
hard beset in Spain, the Emperor started on a

leisurely tour of inspection through the southern
provinces of France. In the face of the alarming
information which he had lately received from his
brother and hard-pressed generals, he dictated a
long despatch, in which he reviewed the military
situation as it appeared to him from afar. To each
general he pointed out the line of conduct he should
take. Bessières was praised for his brilliant defeat
of 25,000 Spaniards under Cuesta and Blake at
Medina del Rio Seco, on July 14. With no more ^{Medina del}
than 20,000 men, Napoleon felt sure General Dupont _{Rio Seco}
could take the offensive and overthrow everything
before him. The chances in Dupont's favor were
estimated at more than eighty in a hundred. The
whole situation was summed up in these confident
words: "There is nothing to fear on the side of Marshal Bessières, nor in the north of Castile, nor in
the kingdom of Léon. There is nothing to fear
in Aragon. Saragossa will fall some day, sooner
or later. There is nothing to fear in Catalonia,
there is nothing for the communication from Burgos to Bayonne." To his brother Joseph, Napoleon
wrote: "Be courageous and gay. Never doubt of
complete success."

On the day these despatches were dictated in ^{Dupont's}
France, Napoleon's favorite, Dupont, whom he had _{defeat}
selected for the next marshalship, suffered a disastrous defeat at Baylen, and capitulated with his
whole army of 20,000 men. The battle of Baylen
was the worst reverse suffered by French arms on
land in all the many campaigns waged since 1792.

After Dupont's troops had pillaged Cordova for

three days, they fell back to Andujar before an army of 8,000 Spanish regulars and 20,000 peasants led by Castaños. So despondent was Castaños of success that he embarked his heavy artillery at Seville, intending to sail to Isla de Léon if Dupont advanced against him. Instead of that, Dupont sent to Madrid for reinforcements. His letter to General Bel-

Predica-
ment of
French on
the Morena liard was intercepted. In it he wrote: "We have not a moment to lose in quitting a position in which we cannot subsist. For heaven's sake send us prompt reinforcements with medicines and liniment for the wounded. For the space of a month, the enemy has intercepted all our ammunition wagons and the provisions sent from Toledo." When Castaños read this despatch, he took heart and determined to intercept all reinforcements. The relieving column that Belliard sent out was too small, and gave up all attempts to reach Dupont after much desultory fighting in the defiles of the Morena. A detachment of 500 Frenchmen, which was sent to make a junction with the relieving column, was cut off to a man by the smugglers of Granada. Dupont saw the Spanish forces growing daily in numbers, while his own raw recruits dropped under the summer sun of Spain. Of his men, 600 lay sick with no medicines or ambulances in sight. After severe fighting on July 16, in which the French found themselves hampered by their immense wagon trains containing the loot of Cordova, Dupont determined to fight his way through. On the 19th of July, at three in the morning, the French army moved out from the ferry of Mengibar over the Guadalquivir River. They numbered 20,000 men. The Spaniards facing them had a division of 9,000 under Lieutenant-General Reding, a Swiss, and 25,000 more under Castaños, De Compigny, La Penña and Jones. One-half of their fighting men were peasants. The brunt of the engagement that ensued fell on Compigny and Reding. The first shock of the French was so furious that the Spanish vanguard suffered fearful losses. But the infantry of the line held its ground and their artillery was so well served that forty French guns were dismounted. The French advances in the face of a galling fire were renewed throughout the forenoon, Battle of Baylen and in the end Dupont himself led a general assault on the Spanish batteries. At this point, another Spanish division under General La Penna arrived and bore in on the French from another quarter. The Swiss regiments serving under the French colors went over to the Spaniards. At noon, Dupont, wounded and despairing, sent a white flag with a request for an armistice wherein to arrange for a capitulation.

While the generals on both sides were conferring, Vedel brought a French division from Guaroman, where he had halted for several hours within hearing of the roar of battle. Coming upon the Spanish rear, he attacked Reding's division and captured two guns with about fifteen hundred prisoners. Then an aide-de-camp from Dupont ordered him to cease firing. Surrender of all the French troops was demanded. Vedel expressed his preference for a joint attack on Reding, and like counsel was given by

General Privé. Dupont suggested, by way of compromise, that Vedel give up his Spanish prisoners
and retire out of their reach. Thereupon the Spanish generalissimo, Castaños, threatened Dupont with
a general massacre if Vedel were not recalled. Under orders from Dupont, Vedel came in and surrendered. Eighteen thousand Frenchmen laid down
their arms on a Spanish promise that the officers
were to be paroled and their baggage left undisturbed, while the common soldiers were to be returned to France. Villontreys went into the Morena, and gathering up the French detachments
as far as Toledo, brought them in as voluntary
prisoners. The capitulation, shameful in itself, was
shamefully broken. The French troops, instead of
being returned to France, were imprisoned in galleys. Others were exported to the desert island of
Cabrera. A number were so maltreated that they
died, and at Labrixe more than eighty of the paroled officers were shot down on the market-place.
Dupont himself, with all his staff, was allowed to
return to be court-martialled in France, but General
Privé, who had protested against the surrender, was
left in the hands of the Spaniards.

Marshal Moncy was no more successful in Valencia than Dupont in Andalusia, though he escaped
capture and succeeded in reaching Madrid after
heavy losses. His attempt to take Valencia by
storm had resulted disastrously. Of his division
of 15,000 men, only 10,000 returned, with 150 wagons carrying the wounded. The Spaniards sent
1,500 of his men to Carthagena.

Margin notes:
A shameful surrender

Spaniard's breach of faith

Marshal Moncy's losses

The campaign of Aragon was equally glorious ^{Campaign of Aragon} for the Spanish patriots. Saragossa, then a city of 50,000, had risen against the French two hours after Napoleon's proclamation was read aloud by the town crier. Palafox, an officer of the guards and one of Ferdinand's retinue who had escaped from Bayonne, assumed command. He was aided by Tio Jorge and Tio Marin, two simple citizens.

Surrounded by a low brick wall, Saragossa presented no regular defences and possessed very few guns, but the houses were massively built and the great monasteries and convents, forty in number, served as citadels. The Convent of San José, covered by the torrent Huerba, and Monte Torrero, a high hill, served for towers. Palafox was beaten in a succession of preliminary fights in front of Saragossa, when Lefebvre with his French army was marching on the heroic town. By the middle of July, the French drove Palafox from the olive groves and country houses between the convents of San José and Monte Torrero. The city was closely ^{Defence of Saragossa} invested. Two French companies penetrated into the street of Santa Engracia. The French could have taken the town had the soldiers not feared an ambush and retired. During the night, the citizens threw up defences and put the whole city in condition to withstand assault. In the meanwhile, Palafox recrossed the Ebro at Pina, and joining Baron Versarge at Belchite, gathered some 8,000 scattered Spanish insurgents. With them he gained the Xalon in the rear of the French and made an attempt to relieve Saragossa by a diversion from that quarter. While still on the march his forces were routed by two French regiments. Lefebvre, during the interval, took Monte Torrero by assault. Palafox with his beaten troops hastened back to Saragossa and entered the city just in time to see the French storm the convents of San José and of the Capuchins. Both convents, though occupied and fortified by the French, were *again* relinquished by them. Presently Lefebvre received orders to join Bessières on the Ebro with one of his brigades. General Verdier remained in command with 10,000 French soldiers. This general, though harassed by small bodies of insurgents all around him, pressed the siege more closely. During July the French made several successful assaults on the gates of El Carmen and the Portillo. It was on one of these occasions that Augustina Saragossa, a young woman of twenty-two, is said to have leaped on a cannon and to have discharged it in the face of the enemy, after which she recorded a vow that she would serve the battery until the bitter end, be it her own death or the relief of Saragossa. She was decorated with a medal and henceforth received the full pay of a regular gunner. Shortly after this the besieged Spaniards tried to retake Monte Torrero. Nearly one thousand Spanish regular soldiers succeeded in fighting their way into the city. The French, too, were increased to 15,000 by the arrival of two veteran regiments. On August 3, the city was bombarded by all the French batteries from morning to night. The Spanish powder magazine was blown up. The next day the Convent of Santa Engracia

was stormed by the French. A detachment of
French soldiers got into the old Moorish quarter
and terrible street fighting ensued. Soldiers, citizens, monks, women and children took part in the
hand-to-hand struggle, and the French were assailed
on all sides. A squadron of French cavalry charged
through the narrow streets. They got entangled in
the Arco de Cineja, a crooked street with archways,
and were cut to pieces. During the tumult the hospital for the insane was set on fire and the maniacs
rushed out into the thick of the fight. In another
part of the city, the French had been victorious, but
lost all by stopping to plunder. The Saragossonese
set fire to the convent of San Francisco and drove
the scattered French into the fire. At close of day
the French still held one side of the Cosso, one
of the great thoroughfares of Saragossa, while the
citizens were barricaded on the other side. Here the
most murderous fighting was carried on. The contending forces shot at each other across the street
with muskets and cannon, and gutters were filled
with dead bodies. After several days of this, the
French sent a summons for surrender. They received the laconic answer: "Guerra al cuchillo—
War to the knife!" Slowly the French were making headway when orders came to General Verdier
to raise the siege and to fall back on Larona. The
French retired, pursued by Palafox's forces as far
as to Navarre.

In Catalonia, the small town of Gerona defended
itself with equal success against Duhesme. After
a siege of a fortnight, during which 400 bombs and

hand grenades were dropped into the town on one single night, the French were forced to retreat by a sortie of the Geronese. Duhesme had to fall back on Barcelona, leaving his artillery and ammunition behind him.

At Madrid the news of these disasters caused consternation. King Joseph had reigned but one week when Dupont surrendered at Baylen. Joseph called a council of war. It was proposed to concentrate all the French force at Madrid to fall upon the Spanish armies one by one as they advanced to the capital. But Joseph had enough. He left Madrid on July 29, just nine days after his entry into the city.

King Joseph leaves Madrid

A proclamation was published that "the French army would seek healthier quarters where the air was better and purer drinking water could be obtained." On the same day that Madrid was thus abandoned an English army of 16,000, under Sir Arthur Wellesley (Wellington), landed in Portugal at the mouth of the Mondego, and marched to Leirra, sixty miles from Lisbon. King Joseph in the meanwhile retreated over Vittoria and Segovia to Burgos. This town was made the rendezvous off the whole French army. Before leaving Madrid the French plundered the public treasury and carried off all the crown jewels of the royal family. Thence arose a Spanish saying: "The crown of Spain was too big for Joseph's head, so he put it in his pouch."

Wellington lands in Portugal

In Portugal, Marshal Junot was unable to bring more than 13,000 men into the field against the English. Aware that General Wellesley would shortly be reinforced from the sea, Junot determined not to await a joint attack on Lisbon. He advanced to Vimeiro. There a pitched battle was fought, at the end of which the French retired in good order. Junot's forces could scarcely escape capture, but at this point General Wellesley was replaced by Sir Harry Bourrard. This commander entered into negotiations for a peaceful evacuation of Portugal. In the convention of Cintra, signed August 30, it was agreed that the French troops should be shipped to France at the expense of the British government. A Russian fleet under Admiral Siniavin, riding at anchor in the Tagus, fell a prey to the British. The French, during their embarkation, had to be protected by British bayonets against excesses on the part of the enraged people of Lisbon. Special protests were made against letting the French carry off the rich loot they had gathered while in Portugal. Yet Junot succeeded in carrying away with him the famous manuscript Bible of Belem, which had been presented to the monastery of the Hieronymites by Pope Julius II. In later years these precious volumes had to be bought back by Portugal at the price of 80,000 francs.

Battle of Vimeiro

Russian fleet seized

The convention of Cintra afforded little glory for either side. When on the point of court-martialling Junot for his capitulation, Napoleon learned that the British military had ordered their own generals, Bourrard, Wellesley, Moore, and Dalrymple, to be brought to trial for permitting Junot to escape them.

Convention of Cintra

While Junot's troops were embarking for France,

another more famous embarkation was made in Denmark. There 10,000 Spanish soldiers, enrolled under the French eagles of Bernadotte, with their captain, the Marquis of Romana, revolted against the French and seized the islands of Nyborg and Langland. Having established communication with the English, they embarked on a British cruiser. By the middle of August they were transported to Spain, with arms and ammunition, to join the cause of their countrymen. Of the entire Spanish forces in northern Europe, 8,000 had to be left behind. Romana's exploit won him a generalship in Spain, but in French annals it has gone down as the trea- son of Romana.

The consequences of the French reverses in Spain were far-reaching. It broke the spell that the arms of Napoleon, hitherto invincible, had cast over the spirit of his cowed enemies. In Austria, the Minis- try of Stadion, aided by Archduke Charles, pushed forward the new armaments with fresh vigor. The peasants of the Tyrol, oppressed under the new Ba- varian rule, grew restive. In Prussia the younger elements of the nation began to seethe. "I do not see," said Blücher, "why we should not think our- selves as good as the Spaniards." Stein's Ministry adopted a policy of resistance to Napoleon, and Scharnhorst infused the same spirit into the army. The Sultan of Turkey, apprehensive of new French and Russian aggressions, showed inclination to throw in his lot with England. Even the Dey of Morocco, Ali Mahomet, felt called upon to issue a proclama- tion of sympathy with the Spanish cause: "Arouse,

Romana's exploit

The ex- ample of Spain

Christians! Ah, French dog, why did you give opium to the Christians to effect your entry into their country without exciting apprehension, and to come before long to deprive me also of my throne? Why did you not enter sword in hand, that your objects might be seen, and the Christians might cut off your head? Christians, attack these dogs and defend your kingdom, for the son of my friend Charles! Let Seville be firm and attack that abhorred currish race, and Allah will assist you! Let the Englishmen help likewise! All nations heed this, so ye may know who the French dog is, that all may arise against him with the blessing of Allah!"

A Moorish appeal

In England, the Tories joined with the Whigs in cheering the Spanish revolution. It was resolved to make the most of the foothold gained in Spain by placing a strong army under the command of Sir John Moore. For America the upheaval in Spain meant corresponding upheavals throughout Central and South America. The United States caught the fever. President Jefferson saw in this an opportunity to offset the serious consequences of his policy of non-intercourse with Europe. Negotiations were set on foot to obtain the Floridas from Spain. Napoleon, treating all Spanish possessions as if they were his own, offered to cede Florida to the American Union, on condition that the United States join in his war with England. "War exists in fact between England and the United States," declared Napoleon, in a famous letter, transmitted by Champigny. "It was declared practically when England

Great Britain aroused

Spanish fortunes in America

published her decree against American commerce."
General Armstrong, at the American legation in
Paris, was informed that "should England make
any movement against the Floridas, Napoleon would
not take it ill if the United States moved troops
there for their defence." When Napoleon suffered
disaster in Spain, Jefferson at once saw a new op-

Jefferson's designs on Florida.
portunity for America. On August 9, he wrote to
one of his Cabinet Ministers: "I am glad to see
that Spain is likely to give Bonaparte employment.
Tant mieux pour nous. . . . Should England
make up with us while Bonaparte continues at war
with Spain, a moment may occur when we may,
without danger or commitment with either France
or England, seize this country to our limits of
Louisiana as of right, and the residue of the Floridas as reprisal for spoliation. It is our duty to
have an eye to this in stationing our new recruits
and armed vessels so as to be ready, if Congress
authorizes it, to strike in a moment." Shortly afterward the Cabinet debated the subject. Jefferson
recorded this memorandum of his attitude toward
the Spanish colonies in America: "If you remain
under the dominion of the kingdom and family of

Forecast of Monroe Doctrine
Spain, we are contented; but we should be extremely unwilling to see you pass under the dominion or ascendency of France or England." Here is
to be seen the germ of the famous American attitude
toward the Old World, enunciated in later years by
Monroe. In truth, Jefferson and his Southern supporters cared little for the cause of Spanish freedom. The independence of the Spanish colonies

from European rule in any form was Jefferson's steadfast ideal.   Throughout South America, in Mexico, Cuba, and in the Floridas, meanwhile, the Spanish patriots were eager to do their part for the mother country.   The French settlers were driven out of Porto Rico, Deseada and Maria Galante.   In Cuba, the Spanish governor had difficulty in preventing a massacre of the French at Havana and Santiago de Cuba.   All Florida was seething. Jefferson's non-committal attitude toward this movement gave rise to a suspicion in America that the President was secretly leagued with Napoleon. This lost him many supporters in the North. The New England conscience declared itself with fervor for the Spanish cause.   Northern opposition to the continued immolation of American trade on the altar of Jefferson's embargo grew exceedingly bitter.   A young New England poet, William Cullen Bryant, then barely in his teens, published what he called "The Embargo: a Satire against Thomas Jefferson":

> "And thou, the scorn of every patriot name,
> Thy country's ruin and her council's shame,
>
> . . . .
>
> Go, wretch!   Resign the Presidential chair,
> Disclose thy secret measures, foul or fair;
> Go search with curious eye for horned frogs
> 'Mid the wild waste of Louisiana bogs,
> Or, where Ohio rolls his turbid stream,
> Dig for huge bones, thy glory and thy theme!"

In later life Bryant would have given much to suppress this boyish libel, as unfortunate in its conception as it was lacking in felicity of versification.

Yet Bryant's verses reflected the spirit then prevailing in certain parts of America. The cost of the embargo to the nation had been fearful. At a moment's notice, President Jefferson and his followers in Congress had bidden all ocean commerce to cease. Every ship was withdrawn from the sea and merchants closed their doors. American products sank in value. Wheat dropped from two dollars to seventy-five cents a bushel. Other produce became unsalable, such as cotton, tobacco, rice and timber. Artisans ceased working, laborers dropped their tools and wages stopped. Every imported article rose in price. Thousands of sailors hung idle around the wharves. A British traveller, Lambert, visiting New York in 1808, sent home this description: "The port, indeed, was full of shipping, but they were dismantled and laid up. Their decks were cleared, their hatches fastened down, and scarcely a sailor was to be found on board. Not a box, bale, cask, barrel or package was to be seen upon the wharves. Many of the counting-houses were shut up or advertised to be let, and the few solitary merchants, clerks, porters, and laborers that were to be seen were walking about with their hands in their pockets. The coffee-houses were almost empty. The streets near the waterside were all but deserted. The grass had begun to grow upon the wharves." In the South the effects of the embargo were felt the worst. Tobacco, rice and cotton were almost worthless, yet 400,000 negro slaves had to be supported. Jefferson's own State, Virginia, sunk into stagnation.

Disastrous results of American embargo

Suffering in the South

The President's private family fortune was involved in the general ruin.

By the time Jefferson was ready to hand over the reins of power to his chosen party successor, Madison, the political consequences of the embargo act made themselves felt. New England was lost to Jefferson's party. After the spring elections and during summer, Massachusetts declared for Federalism. Gallatin, who, as Secretary of the Treasury, knew best the difficulties created by the embargo, began to despair. Early in summer he wrote: "From present appearances the Federalists will turn us out by the 4th of March next. I think that Vermont is lost. New Hampshire is in a bad way, and Pennsylvania is extremely doubtful." And again: "If propositions from Great Britain or other events do not put it in our power to raise the embargo before the 1st of October, we shall lose the Presidential election. I think that at this moment the Western States, Virginia, South Carolina, and part of Georgia are the only sound States." Nothing saved Jefferson's party but the fact that the opponents of the government divided their forces between three candidates—Clinton, Monroe and Pinckney. James Madison was elected President and George C. Clinton, as the second strongest candidate, was re-elected to the Vice-Presidency. The Federalist votes had risen from fourteen to forty-seven votes.

American political upheaval

Madison fourth President

The consequences of the embargo, while by no means so disastrous in England, were serious enough to be made the subject of Parliamentary inquiry.

Comments on American embargo

The Ministry was driven to admit that "loss to America was loss to Great Britain, just as the prosperity of the United States had meant prosperity for the mother country." Napoleon took the same view. In his report on foreign relations, September 1, 1808, he expressed approval of the embargo: "The Americans—This people, who placed their fortune, their prosperity and almost their existence in commerce, have given the example of a great and courageous sacrifice. By a general embargo, they have interdicted all commercial exchange, rather than shamefully submit to that tribute which the English pretend to impose on the shipping of all nations."

The aspect of other foreign affairs appeared less satisfactory to Napoleon. The new military reforms that were under way in Austria and Prussia gave rise to serious apprehension. The alliance with Russia likewise seemed shaky. To Emperor Francis of Austria, Napoleon wrote a remonstrance against all attempts at further hostility, with this threatening conclusion: "All that you have now, you have solely through my goodwill." On September 8, he concluded a new convention between France and

Prussia further humbled

Prussia. The Prussian army was reduced from 60,000 to 40,000. The war indemnity still due to France was declared to be 145,000,000 francs. This, in the face of the Prince of Prussia's protest that 19,000,000 only remained to be paid! Until the final payment of the indemnity, Prince William of Prussia undertook to remain in France. The Prussian strongholds of Glogau, Stettin and Kus-

trin were to remain in French hands, garrisoned by
10,000 men at Prussian expense. Such were the
hard conditions imposed at a time that the Prussian
revenues amounted to 386,000 thalers, while the
public expenses ran up to two and a half millions.
Besides this, Napoleon exacted that seven military
roads were to run through Prussia, and the region
around Magdeburg was to be ceded to France.
After this convention had been duly signed at
Paris, the resignation of Stein's Ministry was only
a question of time. Stein had become persona
ingrata with Napoleon since one of his confidential
despatches to the Prince of Wittgenstein had fallen
into the hands of the French. In this letter Stein
wrote under date of August 15, 1808: "The exasperation in Germany increases daily. It must be encouraged and stimulated. The affairs of Spain are
making a profound impression. They prove what
ought long since to have been foreseen," etc. Napoleon had this letter printed in the "Moniteur"
with this comment: "The King of Prussia may be
pitied for having Ministers who are as unskilful as
they are perverse."

Prussian Ministry dismissed

Stein asked for his dismissal. For a while his
Ministry lingered on. On September 11, Napoleon wrote to Soult: "1 have demanded that Stein
be expelled from the Ministry. Otherwise the
King of Prussia shall not re-enter possession of
his States. I have placed Stein's property in
Westphalia under sequestration."

Expulsion of Minister Stein

For Napoleon much depended now on the attitude
of Russia. To clear up the situation, he arranged

for a personal interview with the Czar, to be held at Erfurt. It was to be made a State affair, attended by all the princes of the Confederation of the Rhine. On September 27, almost simultaneously with the establishment of a supreme Spanish junta at Aranjuez, the princes met at Erfurt. The departure of Alexander from St. Petersburg, and of Napoleon from Paris, was calculated to a nicety, so that the two might arrive on the same day. Napoleon took pains to reach Erfurt first in order to welcome Alexander a few miles beyond the town. Throughout the festivities that followed he had Alexander placed at his right to show that he was receiving him on his own soil. All the expenses of this occasion were paid from the French civil list. Die tollen Tage (The mad days) at Erfurt, as the Germans called them, lasted three weeks. Among those who attended were the Kings of Saxony, Bavaria, and Wurtemberg, the Prince Primate, the Archduke of Baden, the Dukes of Saxony, and many minor princes. Emperor Francis of Austria was not invited. Nor did Napoleon heed the hints of Metternich, the Austrian Ambassador in Paris, that he be bidden to attend. To gain some information of what went on, Emperor Francis sent Baron de Vincent, a friend of Talleyrand, to deliver an ostensible letter of goodwill to both the emperors. Erfurt was so filled with notables that a French officer of the guard, so the story has it, once stopped a drumbeat salute to a passing German prince with the words: "Taisez vous, ce n'est qu'un roi!" For the benefit of the invited guests the entire Comedie

The meeting of Erfurt

Française played classic dramas to a pit full of royalties. On the first of these occasions Alexander repeated to Napoleon the line from Œdipus: "The friendship of a great man is a gift of the gods." Of mutual compliments there was no end. In the presence of the Czar, Napoleon decorated the officers of the regiment who had distinguished themselves in the campaign against Russia. Prince William of Prussia was bidden to attend a rabbit hunt on the battlefield of Jena. Napoleon's guests insulted

One of the most interesting events of those days was the meeting of Napoleon and Goethe. The great German poet had just finished the first part of his "Faust." Unlike his contemporaries, Fichte, Schleiermacher, Koerner, Rueckert and Von Arndt, whose writings at this time were all intensely patriotic, Goethe was an open admirer of Napoleon. Bonaparte in his turn admired Goethe. When Bonaparte sailed to Egypt, Goethe's early masterpiece, "The Sorrows of Werther," had accompanied him. In later years the same book served to lighten Napoleon's solitude at St. Helena. The two men, Goethe and Napoleon standing each in his way on the pinnacle of genius and of egotism, met as equals. "Vous êtes un homme, Monsieur de Goethe," said Napoleon as he decorated him with the cross of the Legion of Honor. "Voilà un homme," remarked Goethe to his neighbor. Previous to this, the poet had written a hymn of praise to Napoleon, in which he sang:

> "Doubts, that have baffled thousands, *he* has solved;
> Ideas, o'er which centuries have brooded,
> *His* giant mind intuitively compassed."

A HISTORY OF THE

Goethe found Napoleon, at close range, more admirable than ever. He found that the French emperor knew the classic drama "down to the minutest details." His observations on Werther were the best critique yet vouchsafed to Goethe. To the end of his days, the poet admitted the justice of Napoleon's criticisms. Napoleon's suggestion to Goethe to write a new drama on Julius Cæsar, which might be an improvement on Shakespeare's tragedy, flattered the German poet. Shortly afterward he wrote a letter to Cotta: "I confess gladly that there is nothing more elevating or more gratifying that could have happened to me than this meeting with the French emperor, and the manner of it. Never before have I found so sympathetic a listener, who met me, if I may use the expression, so thoroughly as an equal." Goethe met Napoleon early in October. A week later, at a court ball in Weimar, Napoleon met another famous German poet, Wieland. While the Czar was exciting the admiration of all by his graceful dancing, Napoleon drew the old poet into a corner, and talked to him alone for an hour and a half. An interesting record of this conversation has been given by Wieland: "Napoleon saw, notwithstanding my wretched celebrity, that I was a simple unassuming old man. To leave a lasting good impression on me, at least so it appeared to me, he assumed on the instant that disguise which he knew would accomplish his purpose. In all my life, I never saw a more simple, quiet, gentle and unassuming mother's son of a man. He talked with me like an old acquaintance, as one of his set.

From his utterances on poetry, it was clear to me that he was without deep feeling—our German Gemüth. . . . Though the man was uncommonly friendly and affable with me, it yet appeared to me at times as though Napoleon wore a mask of bronze."

Napoleon's most important interviews, of course, were with Alexander, as were the meetings of Talleyrand and De Champigny with Count Romanzov, the Russian Prime Minister. The Czar, in return for a free hand in Finland and in the Balkans, acknowledged Napoleon's brother Joseph as King of Spain, and agreed to enter into an offensive and defensive alliance with Napoleon in case France were the first to be attacked. Napoleon, at the Czar's request, remitted 20,000,000 francs from the amount to be paid to him by the King of Prussia. Talleyrand, at one of his frequent audiences with the Czar, first broached the subject of the possible divorce of Josephine. With this contingency in view, he voiced Napoleon's suit for the hand of Alexander's sister, but Alexander begged to be excused. Talleyrand improved the occasion by obtaining the hand of the Princess for his nephew, Egmont de Perigord.

Agreement of France and Russia

Josephine's divorce broached

Before leaving Erfurt, the two emperors issued a joint letter to the King of England. It opened thus: "Brought together at Erfurt, our first thought is to yield to the wish and the wants of every people, and to seek a speedy pacification with your Majesty, the most efficacious remedy for the miseries which oppress all nations. . . The cause is to be found in the state of agitation and misery in which the stagnation of maritime commerce has placed the greatest nations. We unite in entreating your Majesty to listen to the voice of humanity silencing that of passions." The letter concluded in the same strain. England's answer to the joint proposals was submitted by Canning to the Russian Ambassador in Paris. The British official note began in this wise: "The King has uniformly declared his readiness and desire to enter into negotiations for a general peace on terms consistent with the honor of his Majesty's crown, with fidelity to his engagements, and with the permanent repose and security of Europe. His Majesty repeats that declaration. . . . If the cause of much misery is to be found in the stagnation of commercial intercourse, although his Majesty cannot be expected to hear with unqualified regret that the system devised for the destruction of the commerce of his subjects has recoiled upon its authors or its instruments—yet it is neither in the disposition of his Majesty nor in the character of the people over whom he reigns to rejoice in the privations and unhappiness even of the nations which are combined against him.

"In the progress of a war, begun for self-defence, new obligations have been imposed upon England in behalf of powers whom the aggressions of a common enemy have compelled to make common cause with his Majesty, or who have solicited his Majesty's assistance and support in the vindication of their national independence. . . . The interests of the Crown of Portugal and of his Sicilian Majesty

Peace overtures to England

Canning's reply

are confided to his Majesty's assistance. With the King of Sweden his Majesty is connected by ties of the closest alliance. With Spain his Majesty, though not bound by any formal instrument, in the face of all the world has contracted engagements no less binding than the most solemn treaties. His Majesty therefore assumes that in overtures for general peace Spain is understood to be a party to any negotiations in which England is invited to engage."

Spain a crucial question

The upshot of the new peace overtures was that France and Russia declined to admit the Spanish "insurgents" to any part in the negotiations. George III. of England issued a formal proclamation announcing the continuance of the war: "We deeply lament an issue by which the sufferings of Europe are aggravated and prolonged. But neither the honor of the crown nor the generosity of the British nation would sanction the abandonment of a brave and loyal people, who are fighting for all that is dear to man; and whose exertions in a cause so unquestionably just we have solemnly pledged ourselves to sustain."

England stands firm

England's interference in the affairs of the Peninsula was at first resented by Portuguese and Spaniards alike. When Sir Arthur Wellesley brought the first British expedition to Spain his services were declined in one port after another, until he betook himself to Portugal. After the Convention of Cintra the Portuguese junta recorded an emphatic protest against the manner of its conclusion. It appeared for a while as if fears of too permanent a

British lodgment were almost as strong as hatred of the French. A late instance of this occurred when Colonel Doyle organized the Spanish prisoners at Portsmouth and sailed with them for Coruña. The prisoners, who had been armed and clothed by England, mutinied and carried the transport to different ports of Spain, whence they went to their homes.

After Joseph's retreat from Madrid, the insurrection of Spain may be said to have ceased as a spontaneous popular movement. Thenceforward it became a war for the military control of the Peninsula, conducted between France and various organized bodies of men, now Spaniards, now Portuguese, now Englishmen. The most picturesque accounts of this warfare may be found in such books as Galdos' "Episodios Nacionales," Blackmore's "Alice Lorraine," or Lever's "Charles O'Malley." When the Convention of Cintra opened a way for operations in Spain, Sir Hugh Dalrymple sent Lord William Bentinck to Spain to arrange a plan of co-operation with the Spanish generals. Associated with him were a number of British military agents whose divergent plans added greatly to the confusion already existing among the Spanish leaders of the war.

A council of most of the generals commanding armies was held at Madrid in the autumn. Castaños, Llama, Cuesta, Infantado and others came. Blake gave his proxy to Infantado, while Palafox was represented by a member of his staff. They could not agree upon a general-in-chief, but decided to unite their forces in the so-called army of the centre.

Peninsular campaign resumed

The Spanish war in literature

Council of generals at Madrid

Even this movement was carried out but partially.
Owing to the factional intrigues and corruption existing among the Spanish juntas, Castaños declared
he would no longer serve under them.   Cuesta was
ready to put the juntas down by force of arms, and
Palafox held himself quite aloof as a successful
Captain-general.   In the end a central government
was vested in the Assembly, and by the advice of
Lord Bentinck and Mr. Stuart, who were authorized
to supply the government with British funds, Castaños was to be appointed generalissimo.   His appointment, however, was deferred on the characteristic ground that when the enemy was driven over
the frontier he might then have leisure to assume
command.   Yet the condition of the Spanish soldiers, ill fed, poorly armed and half naked, was
declared by Mr. Stuart to be "neither calculated
to inspire courage nor to increase enthusiasm."

Napoleon, during the interim, had not been idle.
While he was conversing with poets and princes at
Erfurt, and dangling the olive branch before the
eyes of Englishmen, his armies were marching
southward from the banks of the Vistula, Elbe,
Danube and Rhine—northward from Italy and Dalmatia and from all points of France.   Denmark was
evacuated and 100,000 soldiers of the Empire were
withdrawn from the Prussian States.   The French
garrisons left in Germany were concentrated on the
side of Austria.   The army in Italy was placed
under Prince Eugene de Beauharnais and Masséna.
Murat in Naples was directed to raise a Neapolitan
army wherewith to threaten Sicily.   In France

Dissension of Spanish generals

French armies concentrating

80,000 new recruits, called to arms before their
time, were sent to support the veterans in Spain,
while 80,000 more beardless youths were called to
the colors as reserves. The march of the multi-

Napoleon threatens England
tude was incessant. As the soldiers poured through
Paris, Napoleon addressed them: "Soldiers, I have
need of you. This day, without a moment of repose, I command you to traverse France. The
hideous presence of the Leopard contaminates the
peninsula of Spain and Portugal. In terror he must
fly before you. Let us bear our triumphant eagles
to the Pillars of Hercules. There we have injuries
to avenge."

At the opening of the Corps Legislatif, October
20, the Emperor declared: "In a few days I go to
put myself at the head of my armies, and with the
aid of God to crown the King of Spain in Madrid
—to plant my eagles on the towers of Lisbon." On
the same day Sir John Moore left Lisbon with his
British force to march for Madrid.

French emperor takes command
Napoleon arrived in Bayonne on November 3, and
crossed the Pyrenees at once at the head of 12,000
troops. Within two days he joined his brother
Joseph at Vittoria. By this time the French troops,
immediately available, numbered more than 90,000.
They were distributed at various points under Marshals Moncy, Ney, Bessières, and Generals Saligny,
Dorsienne, Menthion, La Grange and Dunat. The
Spaniards numbered 76,000. Dissatisfied with his
brother Joseph's dispositions, Napoleon at once
took command. While Sir John Moore, with his
British army, was floundering along the wretched

roads of **Portugal** and northern Spain, **Napoleon**
was conducting his military movements with **accus-**
tomed precision and despatch.

The Spanish forces had at last been united under
Castaños. They crossed the Ebro at three points,
and took possession of Lerin, Viana, Capporoso
and other French posts on the left bank of the
Ebro. The French did not oppose Castaños' advance toward Pampeluna any further than was
necessary to mask their own operations. Marshal
Moncy decoyed Castaños well beyond the banks of Castanos
the Allagon and Ebro. Then, suddenly, Marshal alled
Ney, dashing across the river in three separate columns, took the Spanish posts of Lagrona and Col-
chora. He threw the whole army into confusion
and cut off communication between Castaños' main
army and Blake's corps.

In a series of actions during the first week of
November, the Spanish right wing under General
Blake was driven south from Durango to Guenas,
from Guenas to Valmesda, and from there to Espinoza. In the strong position there the Gallican
army made a stand in order to save its magazines Battle of
and artillery, but was routed after two days of Espinoza
fighting. Most of the guns were captured by the
French. General Blake, with the remains of his
broken army, retreated to the mountains of Asturias. Marshal Soult occupied Santander on November 16. The Bishop of St. Anderos took refuge
in an English frigate. Napoleon made his headquarters at Burgos. This town was sacked under
his eyes. An eye-witness has told how he saw a

bivouac fire under Napoleon's windows fed all night with musical instruments.

The Estramaduran army, under Count Belvidere, was lured to a weak position near Burgos, where the French fell upon them in overwhelming numbers. After an all-day fight, this whole army was all but annihilated. The Spanish commander fled to Aranda. The north of Spain was thus laid prostrate. All the rear communications of the French army were safeguarded to Napoleon's generals. Having disposed of these two armies, the French combined their forces against a central army under Castaños. The Spanish vanguards were drawn on to Tudela, and there, on November 23, the main army stood battle. The outcome fixed the fate of the whole campaign.

A concise description of the whole affair was given in the eleventh bulletin of the grand army of the empire in Spain: "On November 23, at break of day, the general of division, Lefebvre, at the head of the cavalry, and supported by the division of General Morlat, forming the advance guard, met with the enemy. His army was found to be in seven divisions consisting of 45,000 men under arms, with its right before Tudela, and its left spread over a league and a half—a disposition altogether faulty. Forty pieces of artillery covered the enemy's line. The Duke of Montebello (Marshal Lannes) caused the centre to be pierced by the division of General Matthews. The general of division, Lefebvre, with his cavalry, immediately passed on the trot through this opening, and, by a quarter wheel to the left, enveloped the enemy. The moment when half the enemy's line found itself thus turned and defeated was that in which General Lagrange attacked the village of Cascante and overthrew Castaños' line. They abandoned the field of battle, leaving behind their artillery and a great number of prisoners. The cavalry pursued the remains of the enemy's army to Mallen, in the direction of Saragossa, and to Terragona, in the direction of Agreda. Seven standards, thirty guns, twelve colonels, three hundred officers, and five thousand troops of the line were taken. No quarter was given to any of the peasants found in arms. Four thousand Spaniards were left dead or plunged into the Ebro. Victory was thus struck home as with a thunderbolt and the league of our enemies is dispersed.''

As a matter of fact, Tudela fell short of Napoleon's expectations, for, thanks to the carelessness or stubbornness of Ney, who rejected Jomini's suggestions to advance at once upon Calatyud, Castaños was able to rally 20,000 of his men at that place. By the battle of Tudela the road was laid open to Madrid. On November 29, the French advance guard reached the foot of the Somosierra. In the strong pass of El Puerto, 11,000 Spaniards, under Don Benito San Juan, were judiciously posted. A battery of sixteen guns planted in the neck of the pass swept the steep road. The Span ish infantry lay in the mountain ridges, one line above the other, with intrenchments at all open parts. A French detachment, sent to attack the

Napoleon's version of victory

French advance on Madrid

advance post of Sepulveda, was beaten back with
loss. Yet the Spaniards retired. At daybreak the
French swarmed over the mountain-side in skirmish
order. Their fire was well returned, and the central
column waited at the foot of the pass, unwilling to
expose itself to the frowning batteries mounted on
the crest. At this moment Napoleon rode into the
mouth of the pass, through the halting ranks of his
infantry. The blue smoke of musketry hung over
the road. In sudden inspiration he ordered the
Polish Lancers of his guard to charge up the mountain-side and take the Spanish guns. Three squadrons dashed up the steep road. As the mass of
crimson-clad wild horsemen swept past the Spanish
sharpshooters on both sides, the Spaniards discharged their muskets and ran toward the summit
of the pass. The first platoon of the Lancers went
down, but the others galloped over them, led by
Kraszynski and Montbrun. The foremost ranks
of the Poles were mowed down by grapeshot, but
before the gunners could reload, the Lancers were
upon them. Leaping their horses over the intrenchments, they took the battery. The Spanish infantry,
drawn up on both sides, took to their heels. Philippe de Ségur, a favorite of the imperial court, was
wounded during the short fight.

This wild charge, rash and almost hopeless from
a military point of view, is one of the most glorious
exploits of French and Polish annals. It could
have been stopped by two good companies of infantry. As it was, an almost impregnable position,
defended by 12,000 men, was abandoned to a few

Exploit of
El Puerto

hundred horsemen. Madrid was now uncovered. On the news of Napoleon's passage of the Somosierra, the central junta left Aranjuez and committed the defence of the capital to the people. Barricades were erected and volunteers enrolled in Madrid. But without any leadership but that of Tommaso Di Morla, the former governor of Cadiz, *The capital unprepared* everything went topsy-turvy. Sand having been found in a number of cartridges and in a powder magazine, the mob lynched the Municipal Administrator, Marquis de Perales. On December 2, the French army appeared in force before the gates. Napoleon called for a surrender. His summons was ignored. The next day French batteries played on the Buen Retiro, commanding the town, while assaults were made on the gates of Alcala, Reccollets, Atocha and Fuen Caril. A breach having been opened, the French division of Villate stormed the Retiro. The Madrileños fell back behind their barricades. Again Napoleon called for a surrender. Morla, with Yriarte, replied by asking for an armistice. The next day Madrid capitulated. Napoleon with his army made a triumphal entry *Napoleon enters Madrid* into the capital. The inhabitants shut themselves up in their houses, and not a voice was raised in welcome of the French. After some excesses of the mob against the French soldiers, Napoleon cancelled all the terms of his capitulation. He notified the paroled Spanish officers that they were prisoners. Sentences of imprisonment were likewise imposed upon the Prince of Castelfranco, the Marquis de Santa Cruz, Count d'Altamira and the Marquis de St. Simon. Other decrees abolished feudal rights, the Inquisition, internal custom regulations, and one-third of all the convents existing in Spain. Napoleon issued a proclamation announcing that if Spain refused recognition to King Joseph he would himself place the crown on his head.

French reforms in Spain

"I shall know how to make myself respected by all rebels, for God has given me strength and the will to surmount all obstacles. From that day will date the prosperity of Spain."

Another decree was in regard to Prussia. The evacuation of Berlin by the French troops was sanctioned, but one Stein, the fallen Prime Minister of Prussia, was declared to be an outlaw and enemy of the empire. His property was confiscated and he was ordered to be apprehended at sight. Stein escaped across the border to Bohemia. As a crowning humiliation to the King of Prussia, he was compelled to pursue with his police, as a criminal, the wisest counsellor he had ever had. While at Madrid, Napoleon learned of the recent palace revolution at Constantinople. The Janizaries had risen again and had strangled Mustapha, the Grand Vizier. Baraiktar blew himself up with his guards.

Stein exiled

Turkish palace revolution

During the latter part of December the French won several handsome victories. At Cardeda, or Llenas, near Barcelona, General Saint Cyr attacked the army of Catalonia. The French troops, though unprovided with artillery or ammunition, routed the Spaniards with the bayonet. On December 21, General Saint Cyr, in a threefold battle at Llobrigat, San Felice, and Molino del Rey, near Barcelona,

French victories in Spain

inflicted a crushing defeat on the Spaniards and took all their artillery and ammunition. Sir John Moore, marching into Spain, learned at Salamanca of the disasters that had overtaken the Spanish army. His own artillery and cavalry did not rejoin him until December. Moore at first decided to retreat to Portugal, leaving an order for Sir David Baird to return to Coruña. At the entreaties of the Spanish general, and of Frere, the British envoy to the central junta, Moore agreed to march to Valladolid, thereby sacrificing his communications with Portugal. Henceforth his base must be Coruña. On December 20, he effected a junction with Baird at Majojorga, which brought his forces up to 25,000 men. Marshal Soult fell back before them beyond Sahagun.

Sir John Moore's manœuvres

Soult's retrograde movement

Napoleon divined the significance of Moore's movement. "Everything leads me to believe," he wrote to Joseph, as he left Madrid, "that they are evacuating Portugal, and directing their line of operation on Coruña. In making this retrograde movement, they may hope to inflict a check on Marshal Soult's corps." Late in December he wrote to Josephine: "I am starting this moment. I am going to outmanœuvre the English. They appear to have their reinforcements and now wish to play the swaggerers." That evening he crossed the Guadarrama in a fearful storm. The snow was so thick that all had to dismount and plod on foot, with Napoleon leading the way. On Christmas Day the Emperor was near Valladolid, in hourly expectation of catching the English between his own

Napoleon crosses the Guadarrama

forces and those of Soult. Sir John Moore, who was about to engage Soult, learned through the Marquis of Romana of Napoleon's rapid advance and prudently fell back. The road to Coruña was encumbered by the Spanish transports, and the British had to go by the way of Benevento toward Astorga, blowing up the bridge over the Ezla.

Fight of Medina del Rio Seco General Lefebvre, with an advance guard of cavalry at Medina del Rio Seco, was so eager to catch up that he swam his squadron across the river. There they were met by Lord Paget's rearguard of cavalry and were put to the sword. Lefebvre himself was made a prisoner while struggling in the water. Napoleon pursued the British until the end of the year, amid wretched weather and over muddy roads. When he reached Astorga, he saw

Napoleon gives up pursuit that he was no longer able to prevent Moore from embarking at Coruña. Abruptly he turned the command over to Soult and Ney, and returned to Valladolid. In one of his letters of that period, Napoleon stated that he did so because further pursuit would have carried him twenty days' distance from Paris.

In Paris, the intrigues of Fouché and Talleyrand made him uneasy, and the continued military prepa-

French home affairs rations of Austria made war with Germany appear imminent. The finances of France were once more in such a shape that only a successful war could help them.

The effects of the tremendous struggle between Great Britain and Napoleon were felt even at the other end of the world, in China. Fearful of a French attack on the Portuguese trading station at Macao, a squadron of the East India Company landed marines at Wampoa. Thereupon, the mandarin Vu, the governor of Canton, addressed a "chop" or proclamation to Commodore Craig on the "Elphinstone." It read in this wise: "I, the Mandarin Vu, by favor of the son of heaven, Tsonto, of the province of Quangtong and Quangsi, member of the tribunal of war and of the Tsungli-yamen, warn you, that, being certain that your bad kingdom is situated in the islands of the sea, and that you originally employed yourselves in making **Chinese manifesto** watches to enable you to pay your taxes, afterward by the especial and profound goodness of our great Emperor, who was desirous of benefiting you, he granted you permission to come to this empire to trade. If you do not cease your disturbances our innumerable soldiers shall arrive, who will destroy and burn you, even if you are as hard as stone or jasper. In order that you may heed this I direct this chop to you in the thirteenth year of the Emperor Kia King, on the seventeenth day of the tenth moon" (December 3, 1808).

The British reply to this note was no less quaint: "May it please your excellency, we the undersigned **British admiral's reply** - commanders of the Honorable East India Company at Wampoa, for ourselves, our officers and our men, have the exalted honor to acknowledge the receipt of your excellency's most gracious letter delivered to us by the two mandarins whom, we are informed, it was your descending pleasure to send for that purpose. Our object in visiting this country is purely commercial, to continue in the same manner that friendly and useful intercourse which has existed for many years, and is now become from its magnitude of the very first importance to both our vast empires. We understand that our admiral, who is an officer of high rank, at the request of the Portuguese landed some troops at Macao to help them defend it against the French. This wicked nation, ever since they murdered their sovereign, have waged war upon all nations within their reach, and we understand are now marching by land to make war upon the Celestial Empire, as the British navy prevents them by sea. We, of course, wish to have no concern with any disturbance in the Celestial Empire, and we most humbly implore your excellency to order trade to be reopened, that we may thereby find employment in the quiet habits of industry."

Efforts to implicate France

This reply did not satisfy the ruler of China, and trade was suspended for the nonce. Great Britain had too much at stake in other quarters of the world to pick a quarrel with China, and so British traders had to be content to bide their time in the East.

1809

ON the first of January, Sir John Moore's rearguard quit Astorga. On the same day Napoleon confessed himself beaten in this final order to Marshal Soult, transmitted to him through Berthier: "The Emperor, foreseeing the embarkation of the British, commands that when the English shall have embarked you shall march on Oporto." Next day Napoleon, having received new despatches from Paris, in his turn left Astorga and hastened back to Valladolid, en route for Paris. Marshal Lannes, who had just caught up with him, having been summoned from a sick-bed, was placed in charge of the second siege of Saragossa. Immediately after his departure, the British cavalry beat off their pursuers in a sharp skirmish at Calcabeles. At Prieros a Spanish division laid down their arms. By January 6, the British rearguard, having thrice checked the French pursuit, rejoined the main body at Lugo. For two days the exhausted British troops lay at rest there in battle order. They needed a rest badly. When they crossed the snow-covered mountain ridge between Villafranca and Lugo their provisions had failed them. Then the men had to live by pillage; horses were slaughtered for food, and stores of all kinds had to be

Napoleon's anticipations in Spain

French victory at Calcabeles

thrown away by the exhausted soldiers. Thousands of stragglers were left to freeze to death or fall a prey to the French. By the time Lugo was reached the whole army, excepting the rearguard, was in a state of dissolution. Marshal Soult neglected to press his advantage by a pitched battle at Lugo, and the English slipped out of their position during the night of the second day. The night march from Lugo to Batanzas cost the British in stragglers more than double the number of men lost in all preceding operations. The troops got to Batanzas on the 10th of January. By a forced march next day they reached Coruña. In nine days of marching they had covered 150 miles. Napoleon, during the early part of his pursuit, had covered 164 miles over worse roads in seven days.

At Coruña the British to their dismay found no sign of their fleet. Nothing remained for Moore but to prepare for a last stand. With their backs to the sea, the British soldiers were lined up for battle. Happily for them the French were slow in coming up. At last, on January 14, the British squadron hove in sight off Coruña. Then Marshal Soult woke up and made a determined effort to prevent the British from embarking. All day long, on the 16th of January, the battle raged, but the English held all their positions. Their two commanding generals, Moore and Baird, were struck down in battle. Moore, while in the midst of the fight, received a cannon ball in his breast. The wound was so gaping that the

Margin notes:
British halt at Lugo

The retreat to the coast

Battle of Coruna

hilt of his sword got entangled in it. When an officer tried to remove it Moore stopped him, saying: "It is well as it is. I would rather have my sword to go out of the field together with me." Sir John Moore died in the knowledge that his men were saved. With his eyes on the transports, he expired in the arms of his friend, Colonel Anderson, murmuring, "You know that I always wished to die thus—I hope the English people will be content." That night the whole British army embarked to the last man. Next morning they put to sea.

Death of
Sir John
Moore

The end of the first English expedition to Spain was followed by a burst of feeling in England. As it happened, a terrible storm off Coruña scattered the transports. Many ships were wrecked, and the others driving up the Channel were glad to put in wherever they could. The soldiers were thrown on shore from Land's End to Dover in a pitiable state. Their tales of the sufferings they had undergone were harrowing. A Parliamentary inquiry was called for, and severe strictures were passed on the conduct of the campaign. Moore's character was vindicated even by his enemies. His immediate foe, Marshal Soult, said: "Sir John Moore took every advantage that the country afforded to oppose an active and vigorous resistance. He finished by dying in a combat that must do credit to his memory." Napoleon, in later years, both at Elba and St. Helena, affirmed that Moore's talents and firmness alone had saved the English army from destruction.

Miserable
end of the
expedition

General
Moore
vindicated

The most famous tribute to the memory of Sir John Moore was Charles Wolfe's poem on his burial, which has become a classic:

Not a drum-beat was heard nor a funeral note,
   As his corse to the rampart we hurried;
Not a soldier discharged his farewell shot
   O'er the grave where our hero lay buried.

We buried him darkly at dead of night,
   The sod with our bayonets turning,
By the struggling moonbeams' misty light
   And the lantern dimly burning.

No useless coffin inclosed his breast,
   Nor in sheet, nor in shroud we bound him;
But he lay like a warrior taking his rest
   With his martial cloak around him.

Few and short were the prayers we said,
   And we spoke not a word of sorrow;
But we steadfastly gazed on the face of the dead,
   And we bitterly thought of the morrow.

We thought, when we hollowed his narrow bed,
   And smoothed down his lonely pillow,
That the foe and the stranger would tread o'er
     his head,
   And we far away on the billow.

Lightly they talk of the spirit that's gone,
   And o'er his cold ashes upbraid him—
But little he recks, so they let him sleep on,
   In the grave where a Briton has laid him.

But half of our heavy task was done
   When the bugle blew for retiring,
And we knew by the distant random gun
   That the foe was sullenly firing.

Slowly and sadly we laid him down
   From the field of his fame, fresh and gory;
We carved not a line, we raised not a stone—
   But we left him alone in his glory.

During the acrid Parliamentary discussions that
followed the unfortunate campaign in Spain, an
opportunity was afforded to clear the reputation of
Sir Arthur Wellesley for the part he bore in ratify-
ing the Convention of Cintra. The inquiry into the
causes of this sore disappointment resulted in an
official vindication for the generals concerned in it British
general
with this qualification: "Considering the extraor- exonerated
dinary circumstances under which two new commanding generals arrived and joined the army (the
one during and the other immediately after the battle of Vilmeiro—and these successively superseding
both each other and the original commander within
a space of twenty-four hours), it is perhaps not surprising that the army was not carried forward."
Sir Arthur, who strongly condemned the inaction
of his superior officers after the battle, agreed with
them that when the enemy had once been permitted
to escape, the evacuation of Portugal was the best
result the English could obtain. Accordingly the
King of England, while approving the verdict of
the board of inquiry, formally announced his dis-
approval of the convention itself. By way of con-
solation for Sir Arthur's enforced inactivity during
these proceedings, Parliament gave him a vote of Wellington
gets an-
thanks, and he was promptly appointed to another other command
command in Spain. The wrath of the people
turned against the Duke of York, the commander-
in-chief of the British army, who was found to
have carried on a corrupt traffic in military commissions through the medium of his mistress, one Duke of
York dis-
Mrs. Clarke. At the end of the sensational trial graced

the matter was so plain that the Duke of York had to resign.

Across the Channel, at the same time, equally high functionaries of the French Empire found themselves in trouble. Napoleon had left Valladolid on January 17, without waiting to learn the outcome of Soult's operations against the English. He contented himself with leaving instructions to reoccupy Portugal, to send the best masterpieces of Spanish art to the Louvre, and to hang a score or so of Spanish malcontents in Madrid. From Valladolid he sent a warlike circular note to the princes of the Germanic Federation, bidding them beware of Austria. He announced to them that he was ready to move into the valley of the Inn with 150,000 men without withdrawing a single soldier from Spain. From Valladolid to Paris Napoleon travelled at such speed that all his suite were left behind at various stages of the journey. In the first five hours he rode eighty-five miles, by means of saddle horses posted along the route in relays of nine horses for every ten miles. At Bayonne he took a coach and travelled thence to Paris by equally rapid relays of post horses. On the 23d of January he arrived in Paris. Marshal Berthier was despatched at once to Germany to assemble the French forces of the Danube. From the scenes that followed in the Tuileries it was clear that the Emperor had returned to his court in a very ill humor. Acting on the reports of his spies, who informed him of the recent reconciliation of Talleyrand and Fouché, and of their alleged plans to make

Napoleon's parting measures

A flying trip to France

Preparations for another war

Murat Napoleon's successor, he summoned each in turn before him. Unable to prove the truth of these allegations he took occasion to overwhelm Fouché with public censure at the first meeting of the Imperial Council. Talleyrand was called to account for some of his reported comments on Napoleon's dealings with the Bourbons, in particular those with the princes of Spain and the Duke of Enghien. The Emperor became very violent during the interview, and once or twice threatened to strike Talleyrand with his fist. Talleyrand received his master's reproaches in silence. When all was ended he made a low bow and retired. Next day he attended the Sunday levee at court as usual. Napoleon pretended not to see him. He deprived Talleyrand of his dignities as Grand Chamberlain at the imperial court. One of Talleyrand's royalist friends, Madame de Chevreuse, for her refusal to act as lady-in-waiting to the deposed Queen of Spain, was banished from Paris. Murat, at Naples, was informed that his presumption in bestowing Sicilian orders on some of his friends was "supremely ridiculous." Louis of Holland was sharply reprimanded for his benign toleration of the smuggling trade that flourished between England and Holland. The social atmosphere of Josephine's imperial court, never too free from apprehension, was full of gloomy forebodings. Several former favorites were exiled from court. Josephine's friend, the Duchess of Gesvres, an old lady of eighty, was to be punished similarly, but Josephine succeeded in saving her from the imperial wrath. Since the

Fouche and Talleyrand disgraced

Louis Bonaparte reprimanded

day that Talleyrand had broached the subject of a possible divorce for Napoleon at Erfurt, the position of Josephine had been precarious. At the Elysées, the new palace, which the Emperor had taken over from Murat, Napoleon did not hesitate to vaunt his latest love affairs before Josephine.

Josephine
Bonaparte
slighted

While at the Elysées the Emperor was informed of the progress of the second siege of Saragossa. This city, though still unfortified, put up a more gallant defence even than during its first siege. At this period the city had a population of barely 50,000, together with the remnants of the Spanish army that had been scattered at Dudela. As before, Palafox was in command. He had taken an oath to bury himself beneath the ruins of the city rather than surrender to the French. Gibbets were raised in the market-place for those who should dare to speak of capitulation. The siege was begun on December 20, 1808, when Mortier's and Moncy's divisions arrived before Saragossa. Next day the French assaulted the place. Monte Torrero was stormed and the city was entered through the canal sluices. The French were beaten off with a loss of 400 men. Then engineering tactics came into play under the direction of Chief Engineer Lacoste. By the end of December the French were ready for a general assault from their earthworks, which now completely encircled the city. A summons to surrender was sent, in which the recent example of Madrid was cited. Palafox replied: "If Madrid has surrendered, Madrid has been sold. Saragossa shall neither be sold nor surrendered." The French

Second
siege of
Saragossa

attacked at three points at once, but were beaten off again with heavy losses on both sides. Moncy's place was now taken by Junot. An epidemic of cholera, together with famine, rendered the suffer- ings of those within almost intolerable. Yet they harassed the French by sallies almost every day. On January 10, the city was bombarded by thirty-two siege guns, and the convent of St. Joseph was battered to pieces. Next day the French stormed the convent, and a few days after succeeded in seizing all the bridge works in front of Santa Engracia. Strong batteries of fifty guns, reaching the bridge over the Ebro, cut off the city from all intercourse with the suburbs. Withal, the condition of the French army was unenviable, for its ranks, too, were wasted by famine and fever. From the rear, the French were worried by various bodies of Spanish insurgents eager to relieve Saragossa. On January 22, Marshal Lannes arrived and the siege was pressed with more vigor. The Spaniards, too, became more aggressive as their situation became more desperate. In one sortie Mariano Galindo succeeded in penetrating through the French lines and in spiking a mortar battery behind the second parallel trench. In the hand-to-hand fight he was cut down with all his followers. January 29, the French attacked at four points, and three chosen columns leaped upon the ruined walls of Saragossa. They did not get further than the first large cross-street. Some of the stone houses along this street had to be stormed no less than three times by successive bodies of Frenchmen. Finally the French

Cholera and famine

Saragossa cut off

Desperate resistance of Spaniards

lodged themselves within the city walls, and street fighting became general. During the first day's onslaught 600 Frenchmen and nearly that number of Spaniards were killed. Chief Engineer Lacoste was killed during the fight, and so was San Genio, one of the foremost Spanish colonels. From then on, fighting grew so fierce that every house had to be assaulted in turn, while mines were laid under it as if it were a fort. General Brandt in his memoirs has given a glimpse of the horror of those days: "The more we advanced the more desperate grew their resistance. One by one we had to take each house, transformed into a redoubt. Death lurked for us everywhere, from the cellar, between the doors and from behind shutters. If you entered a house, you had to inspect and search it from cellar to attic. Often, as you entered a room, you would be shot at from the room above through holes drilled in the flooring. The stairways, galleries and queer turns of those old Spanish houses were admirably adapted for such warfare." On the last day of January the convents of Santa Monica and Santa Engracia were blown up by the French sappers, but the Spaniards fought on in their ruins. Whenever the French succeeded in taking a house, the Spaniards, having previously saturated it with oil, would set it on fire. In this manner the fight was carried on from street to street until February 7, when the French got a firm lodging all along the Cosso. Under that great thoroughfare they dug six galleries and made mines to be exploded simultaneously with those under the university. By this time the siege had lasted fifty

Death of Lacoste

Brandt's description

The Cosso taken

days. Half of the fighters on both sides had succumbed to sword and fire, or to sickness from pestilence and hunger. Those that were left carried on
the struggle underground among the heaps of the
dead and dying. On February 18, having completed all preparations, Lannes ordered a general
assault. Three thousand pounds of powder were
sprung under the University of Saragossa, and the *University of Sara-gossa blown up*
walls of the ancient edifice fell in a heap. Even in
the ruins the French were beaten off, but finally got
a foothold. A score of similar explosions all around
the city made the French masters of the remaining
fortifications between the Convent of St. Augustine
and the Ebro. The concentrated fire of fifty cannon
opened a breach in the Convent of St. Lazarus, and
Baron Versarge with nearly a thousand of his fol-
lowers were put to the sword. Three hundred beat *French penetrate into inner city*
their way into the inner city across a burning
bridge. This success for the French was followed
on the 19th by another attack on the right bank
of the Ebro, where a whole row of buildings was
blown up by a series of mines. At last Palafox,
who lay sick in his bomb-proof, sued for terms.
Most of the other leaders of the siege lay dead, *Heroes of the siege*
among them the famous Tios Jorge and Marino,
the curate of St. Giles and the indomitable lemon-
ade seller of the Corso. The simultaneous explosion of 45,000 pounds of gunpowder together with
the bombardment of 16,000 bombshells had shaken
the city to its foundations. Thousands of dead
bodies lay about the streets and in the vaults.
Throughout the last month the daily deaths among

the besieged had been five hundred, and the living were too weak to bury the dead. Yet the people of Saragossa wanted to kill Palafox when they learned of his offer to surrender. Only by abandoning the citadel to the French could the Spanish generals make the populace come to terms. According to French writers, Saragossa surrendered at discretion; but, judging from Brandt's memoirs and the Spanish records, the garrison was permitted to march out with all the honors of war, while the peasants were returned to their homes, and the property of the citizens and church was guaranteed against the French plunderers. The Supreme Junta of Spain pronounced the funeral oration over Saragossa in the following pronunciamiento:

"Spaniards, the only boon which Saragossa begged of our unfortunate monarch at Vittoria was that she might be the first city to sacrifice herself in his defence. That sacrifice has been consummated. More than two months the murderous siege continued; almost all the houses were destroyed, those which were still standing had been undermined; provisions were nearly exhausted, ammunition all consumed; 16,000 sick were struggling with a mortal contagion, which every day hurried hundreds to the grave; the garrison was reduced to less than a sixth part; the general dying of the pestilence; O'Neille, the second in command, dead; St. Marc, upon whom the command then devolved, prostrated by the fever. So much was required, Spaniards, to make Saragossa yield to the rigor of fate, and suffer herself to be occupied by the enemy. The surrender was made upon such terms as the French have granted to other towns, and those terms have been observed as usual by the perfidious enemy. Thus only were they able to take possession of those glorious precincts, filled only with demolished houses and temples, and peopled only with the dead and the dying; where every street, every ruin, every wall, every stone, seemed mutely to say to the beholder, Go, tell my king that Saragossa, faithful to her word, hath joyfully sacrificed herself to maintain her honor!"

The story of the twofold siege of Saragossa, together with the three sieges of Gerona, has justly taken foremost rank among the most famous sieges of history. Among the notable achievements of the Peninsular War, the defence of Saragossa stands forth as one of the proudest traditions of Spain. Even Napoleon, who had watched the siege from afar, as soon as he learned of the capitulation, gave orders to have a special work prepared giving a full record of this siege, "to serve as a model for all cases where an open city is attacked, and the inhabitants wish to defend themselves." *Proudest tradition of Spain*

In Catalonia, during the same winter, the French were likewise beset with difficulties, but were victorious in the main. Gerona had to be besieged again and so had Rosas, but these annoyances were offset by St. Cyr's victories over the Catalonians at Cardadeu, Molino Del Rey, Capelladaes and Valls. The last battle, fought on February 25, finished the regular campaign in Catalonia for a time. Coming so closely after the fall of Saragossa, the defeat of *Battle of Valls*

Valls spread dismay far and wide in Spain. It looked as if the backbone of the war had been broken. Yet St. Cyr's campaign, though costing great efforts on the part of all troops concerned in it, remained without corresponding advantages. St. Cyr attributed this to the wretched condition of his soldiers, "destitute and neglected because the Emperor disliked their chief and therefore wished their ruin." In this St. Cyr was prejudiced.

St. Cyr dis-satisfied

Napoleon, indeed, had been watching the operations of his scattered divisions in Spain with constant anxiety. This is attested by the great number of records containing his military instructions to his various generals. After the fall of Saragossa, with the dispersal of the Catalonians, and after Marshal Soult's second invasion of Portugal had been successfully accomplished, Napoleon breathed more freely. Cuesta's defeat at Medellin, on March 28, settled it. Now he could turn his attention to another point. He did so with that singleness of view which his secretaries, Bourrienne and Méné-val, have characterized as one of the most striking features of his genius.

Battle of Medellin

There was enough to distract the attention of a statesman. In England it looked as if the government were falling to pieces. The old king, nearly blind, and mentally unbalanced, was in no condition to bear the scandal of his son's disgraceful resignation from the command of the army; nor did the Prince of Wales stand in better repute. In the Ministry, Canning was arrayed against Castlereagh, the new Secretary of War, and each took pleasure

Affairs in England

in foiling the other's projects. Regular commerce
was upset by the conditions brought about by the
continental blockade and the American embargo. Low ebb
of British
English credit stood at a low ebb. The public credit
funds were shaken by the constant drain of money
for the British expeditions and financial subsidies
to Spain. In the absence of specie, discounts at
long date became the rule, and doubtful joint-stock
speculations were rampant. At the close of 1808,
gold coin had risen at one leap from the prevailing
rate of 103 to a steep premium of 113. A finan- General
financial
cial crash seemed close at hand. In Holland and depression
France, public finances, if possible, were in a worse
condition.

Such was the state of affairs in Europe when
Thomas Jefferson relinquished control in America.
Reviled by his political opponents, and beset by
private creditors, he passed out in gloom. His
debts amounted to $20,000. This practically ruined Exit of
Thomas
him as a grand seigneur of Virginia. He returned Jefferson
to Monticello alone on horseback, as he had come
to Washington. To a deputation of his townsfolk
welcoming him home, he said: "Of you, my own
neighbors, I may ask in the face of the world,
Whose ox have I taken or whom have I defrauded?
Whom have I oppressed, or from whose hands have
I received a bribe to blind mine eyes therewith?
On your verdict will I rest."

On March 4, Madison was inaugurated as Presi- James
Madison
dent. George Clinton of New York went in as inaugurated
Vice-President. Most of the former members of
the Cabinet held over. They were Robert Smith

of Maryland, Secretary of State; Albert Gallatin of Pennsylvania, Treasury; William Eustis of Massachusetts, War; Paul Hamilton of South Carolina, Navy; Gideon Granger of Connecticut, Postmaster, and Cæsar A. Rodney of Delaware, Attorney-General. Immediately after the change of administration had been accomplished, both America and England took mutual steps to remove the embargo so harmful to both nations. On March 6, Parliament entered into a debate of this subject, and the British press voiced the public discontent. The London "Times" went so far as to say: "If America will withdraw her Embargo and Non-Importation Acts, so far as they relate to England, provided we rescind the Order-in-Council, we cannot consider this as a disgraceful concession on our part." On March 15, the American Cabinet agreed to remove the Embargo, but commercial intercourse between England and the United States was still prohibited. On April 7, Canning sent instructions to the British Minister at Washington, Erskine, to settle up the "Chesapeake" affair and the commercial relations between the two countries at one stroke. The attack upon the "Chesapeake" was disavowed, and some impressed American sailors were returned. Admiral Berkeley was to be recalled. The American demand for a court-martial of the British Admiral was not entertained. President Madison accordingly withdrew the demand, but added that he was "none the less persuaded that to grant the American demand would best comport with what is due from his Britannic Majesty to his own honor."

English conciliatory measures

"Chesapeake" affair disavowed

It was an unfortunate sentence destined to breed Erskine's premature promise trouble. Erskine further offered the withdrawal of the late British Orders-in-Council if the President would issue a proclamation renewing trade intercourse with Great Britain. Within two days President Madison's proclamation to this effect was published in the "National Intelligencer." Erskine in a few lines declared that he was authorized to state that "His Majesty's Orders-in-Council of January and November, 1807, shall have been withdrawn, as respecting the United States, on the 1t0h of June next." The American people hailed this outcome with delight. Without waiting for June, the merchants along the sea-coast began to hurry ships and American trade with England resumed merchandise to British ports. For the time being everything seemed plain sailing in America.

Not so in Europe. In Sweden the people were so aroused by the disastrous consequences of the King's antagonism to Napoleon, the reverses of the army in Norway and the loss of Finland, Stralsund and Rügen, that they rose against their king. Young Gustavus Adolphus IV. drew his Revolution in Sweden sword on the deputation that came to protest against a further continuance of the war. One of his nobles disarmed him, saying: "Sire, your sword was given to you to use against the enemies of the country, not to be drawn on your own subjects. We desire nothing but your happiness and the prosperity of Sweden." The King was confined under guard, and his uncle, the Duke of Soedermanland, assumed the regency. Within ten days Gustavus Adolphus abdicates Gustavus Adolphus abdicated, to be succeeded by his uncle as King Christian XIII. Napoleon congratulated Sweden on having got rid of "the supremacy of a fool." An armistice was granted by Bernadotte, but the war with Russia went on.

The aged General Klercker commanded a Finnish army at Tavastehus, where Klingspor arrived with his royal orders, which were for retreat and evacuation of the country. The troops were deprived of their hopes of a battle and forced to make a retreat of nearly 600 miles, suffering from cold and hunger. The retreat continued without interruption for two months, until the army in April found itself between Brahestad and Uleoborg. A battle was fought at Siikajoki, April 18, the sub-commander, General Adlercreutz, receiving instructions to make a stand against the enemy until the safety of the army supplies could be insured. After five hours of fighting, the Finns won a glorious victory over the Russians, but royal orders for a continued retreat arrived. Siikajoki and Sveaborg, the Gibraltar of the North, were treacherously surrendered to the Russians.

Battle of Siikajoki

The German people in Austria and Prussia were likewise seething. In Prussia secret patriotic organizations, like the Tugendbund and Father Jahn's Deutsche Turner, were preparing young Prussia for the inevitable conflict, while in the army such men as Scharnhorst, Blücher and Schill had their hearts set on another trial of strength with France.

Prussia in a ferment

In Austria, the preparations for war were quite open. Since the Austrian Emperor had been left out of the Conference of Princes at Erfurt, the at-

Austria prepares for war

titude of his government had grown almost defiant.
Count Stadion, Prime Minister since the Peace of
Pressburg, had become convinced by the proceedings in Italy and Spain that Napoleon had designs
on all the thrones of Europe. Special suspicions
were excited concerning the French and Russian
intentions as to Turkey and the Balkans. Stadion
accordingly encouraged Archduke Charles in bringing the army to a greater strength and efficiency
than ever before. By the beginning of March, 1809,
Austria had 260,000 men ready. Prince Schwarzenberg was sent to St. Petersburg to try to win over
Russia. Alexander, with his mind set on Turkey,
thought that he had more to fear from Austria
than from France, and therefore held fast to Na-
poleon. So strong were the hopes of a general na- Russia sides with France
tional rising in Prussia and other parts of Germany,
however, that the Austrian generals based the plans
for their campaign on such an event. The original
intention was to take the offensive against the French
in central Germany, where they were weakest. With Austrian plan of campaign
this plan in view, the troops were massed in Bo-
hemia. Early in the spring, Count O'Donnell, the
Austrian Finance Minister, found that the resources
of the Empire no longer sufficed for a continued
maintenance of the army on a war footing.

France, too, was bleeding to death. By a new
levy of 180,000 men from the conscript class of
1810, Napoleon had forced up the French deficit
to nearly one hundred million francs. No relief
was in sight from any internal fiscal measures. In
brief, the strain for both nations was growing un-

Urgent reasons for war bearable, yet neither could afford to disarm. War had become only a question of time.

On March 2, Metternich, the Austrian Ambassador at Paris, complained to Champagny that the measures adopted by Napoleon had forced Austria to place Germany on a footing of war. A few weeks later, Metternich coolly answered Napoleon's question: "Why does your Emperor want so large Diplomatic friction an army?" with the remark, "To make his ambassador respected by you." Henceforward it was merely a race in the completion of mutual military preparations before actual hostilities should commence. Marshal Berthier, at Strasburg, received urgent orders to draw together all remaining French plan of campaign ing French garrisons at Regensburg. Davoust was to advance a corps from Wuerzburg to Regensburg. Lannes was despatched to Germany to concentrate an army corps at Augsburg. In Italy, Murat was ordered to fall upon Rome with the speed of lightning, to seize the papal dominions and replace the French troops hurried northward. Nothing restrained the French from taking the offensive but the Czar's conditional agreement with Napoleon to aid him against Austria only in case France should be first attacked. Had Austria struck then and there, the advantage Austrian plans upset might have been on her side. Unluckily for her, Archduke Charles at the last moment upset the excellent plan of a quick advance into North Germany, and, instead of that, marched his troops down to the Danube to safeguard Vienna.

Early in April, things were brought to a point by mutual acts of aggression. A French diplomatic courier between Vienna and Munich was arrested on International dis-courtesies Austrian ground and despoiled of his despatches. A day or so later, Davoust's outposts violated the territory of the Austrian Empire. On April 10, Metternich demanded his passport. On the same day, the peasants of the Tyrol from one end of the Rising of the Tyrol mountain ranges to the other rose to shake off the yoke of Bavaria. In anticipation of probable hostilities by the middle of the month, Napoleon had fixed April 15 as the day when he would join his armies on the Danube. On the night of April 12 he received a transmitted semaphore message that Archduke Charles had crossed the Inn, and that his troops were even then marching on Munich. The War begun in earnest next morning, on April 13, Napoleon left the Elysée, and driving night and day reached his headquarters at Donauwoerth on the fifth day. At Ludwigsburg and Dillingen he stopped for a few hours of the night to meet the kings of Bavaria and Wurtemberg.

As the Emperor stepped out of his carriage at Donauwoerth, on April 17, he learned that the Austrians, turning to the right, were slowly marching on Regensburg. "That's a lost army," was his first Napoleon on the Danube remark. Napoleon then learned for the first time that Berthier had failed to carry out his instructions to combine the French armies. Davoust was still north of the Danube, cut off from the French main army. The ruin of Davoust's corps appeared imminent. Napoleon on the instant changed his plans and hastened to Eggmuehl with three corps to intercept the inevitable advance of the enemy against

Davoust. For Berthier he left this sharp note:
"What you have done appears so strange that, if I
were not aware of your friendship, I should think
you were betraying me. Davoust is at this moment
more completely at the disposal of the Archduke
than of myself." To Masséna, at Augsburg, he
wrote: "Descend toward the Danube at once.
Leave all your sick and stragglers behind. Never
have I had more need of your devoted zeal, activity
and speed!" To Davoust he sent a despatch rider
with this order: "Quit Regensburg at once, leaving
one regiment behind! Break down the bridge there
so that it cannot be repaired! Manœuvre carefully
between the river and the Austrians! Beware of
running any risk of an engagement before joining
me near Abendsberg!" These various manœuvres,
by which Napoleon concentrated his army in the
face of threatening disaster, have ever been considered a remarkable demonstration of the very
highest skill in war.

The forces which Napoleon had at his command
were thus given by Chauvent: In Poland, 18,000
commanded by Bernadotte; in Saxony, 12,000 under Gratien; in Westphalia, 15,000 under King
Jerome. The main army consisted of the division of Lannes 25,000, that of Davoust 45,000, that
of Masséna 30,000, Lefebvre's 30,000, and 30,000
more under Vandamme. The Confederation of the
Rhine furnished 12,000 men besides those serving
in Spain. Prince Eugene Beauharnais, Vice-roy
of Italy, had 45,000 at his disposal. Marmont had
15,000 in Dalmatia. Altogether there were 287,000

men under arms with 560 guns, besides the 200,000
still in Spain. Under the immediate eye of Napoleon, 150,000 Frenchmen were now arrayed against
the enemy, numbering about 200,000, in ten army Disposal of Austrian forces
corps. One corps under Archduke Ferdinand oc-
cupied Warsaw. Another corps under Archduke
John covered northern Italy and the Tyrol. Two
army corps marched from Bohemia straight for Regensburg. One remained at Linz for the protection
of the capital, while the main body, comprising
seven corps, zigzagged between Linz and Regensburg, so as to effect a junction with either at short
notice. As one of Napoleon's most ardent biog-
raphers has said: "The mind that could grasp
such interests and guide such enormous combinations must have been one of extraordinary
mold."

While the allied troops on the Danube were skirmishing on all sides, Napoleon issued this address:
"Soldiers, I was surrounded by your bayonets when
the Emperor of Austria arrived at my bivouac at Napoleon's address to his army
Austerlitz. You heard him implore my clemency
and swear me eternal friendship. Conquerors in
three wars, we granted everything to Austria in our
generosity. Three times has she perjured herself.
Our former victories are our guarantee for future
triumphs. Onward, men, and let the enemy see
the faces of his conquerors!"

In the Tyrol, meanwhile, the peasants had chased
the Bavarian garrisons from their mountain seats, Peasants capture Insbruck
and seized the capital, Innsbruck. A French de-
tachment under Brisson, marching for Innsbruck

from Italy, was caught unawares and had to surrender. The captives numbered two generals, ten
staff officers, 100 field officers and 1,000 men. In

Pordenone
and Sacile Italy, Archduke John defeated the French at Pordenone and again at Sacile.

By April 18, Napoleon, while urging Masséna to
do his utmost to reach Pfaffenhofen on the next
night, gave this precis of the situation on the Dan-

French
prepare
for battle ube: "One word will explain to you the urgency
of affairs. Archduke Charles, with 80,000 men,
debouched yesterday from Landshut on Regensburg. The Bavarians skirmished all day with his
advance guard. To-morrow (April 19) all the
troops that can be mustered at Pfaffenhofen with
the Wurtembergers and our cuirassiers, should be
in condition to fall upon the rear of Prince Charles.
A single glance must show you that never was there
more pressing need for diligence than now. I consider Prince Charles ruined without resource if
Oudinot and your three divisions are on his rear
before daybreak on the 19th. On the 18th, 19th
and 20th the whole affair of Germany will be
decided."

On the night of April 19, after the Austrians
had been outmanœuvred in a sanguinary encoun-

Abends-
berg ter at Abendsberg, Napoleon learned of the safe
arrival of Davoust at Neustadt. In great elation
he mounted his horse and galloped along the entire
line of his bivouac fires. Next morning he pushed
his main army between the Austrian forces under
Archduke John and Hiller. The French divisions
of Lefebvre and Masséna, operating together, over-

threw Hiller's corps and drove the Austrians back
to Landshut. Davoust cleverly extricated his de- ^{Davoust} tached army from the immediate vicinity of the
Danube, and joined Napoleon's main body on the
left. On the 22d, Archduke Charles made a rapid
advance southward, hoping to overwhelm Davoust.
Instead of that, he came upon Napoleon's main army
united to Davoust's strong division at Eggmuehl. Eggmuehl

The battle that followed was waged in modern
style, that is, by different bodies of troops, extended over a large area, manœuvring against
different positions. The Austrian centre under
Rosenberg was overthrown by Vandamme's division. The hottest fighting, that on the left, fell to
Davoust's men. The most decisive part of the
complicated battle was Lannes's successful flanking Austrians
movement toward Regensburg. Napoleon made his
headquarters on a rise in the ground, and there received a constant stream of aides-de-camp, bringing
the bulletins from the various corps commandants.
One officer, while pointing out the position of his
command to Napoleon, had his arm torn off by a
cannon shot. Not long afterward, General Cervoni,
while in the act of opening a map before Napoleon,
was killed by a shell. The officers of the Old Guard
tried to drag the Emperor away, but he waved them
off impatiently: "What is the use? I must see how
matters are going."

Late in the afternoon, when the belated Austrian
cavalry rode into battle line, the Emperor had re-
course to one of those magnificent cavalry charges
which were carried so far in the Napoleonic cam-

A Napo-
leonic
cavalry
charge
paigns. At sundown he ordered the imperial cavalry, which had been held in reserve all day, to
charge the massed squadrons of Austrian cavalry
riding into the firing-line. As the cuirassiers of
Bessiéres, incased in glittering breastplates, and
helmets surmounted by plumes, cantered to the
crest of the slope, a mighty shout arose from
the French infantry below. The soldiers felt sure
that a blow was now to be struck that would prove
decisive. With a wild battle cry of "Vive L'Empereur," the imperial cavalry charged into the
plain. The Austrian cuirassier squadrons, led by
Prince Lichtenstein, galloped forth to meet them.

Austrian
troopers
out-
matched
With sabres flashing the contending hosts of horsemen fell upon each other and fought it out in plain
sight of the infantry, until darkness spread over the
battlefield. In the hand-to-hand struggle, the Austrian horsemen, though better mounted, were no
match for the French cuirassiers, since they were
armed only with breastplates, while the French
cuirass incased the body all around. Whenever
an Austrian trooper was caught in the rear, he
was doomed, and even in face-to-face fencing the
French swordsmen soon learned to rely on side
thrusts. At length the Austrian squadrons, having lost nearly two-thirds in killed and dismounted,
wheeled in dismay and rode for life. Napoleon's
imperial guards followed in mad pursuit. The
French infantry heard the shout of their conquer-
ing comrades and charged the wavering enemy with
the bayonet. The Austrians fell back in the dark-

Retreat to
Regens-
burg
ness and retreated during the night to Regensburg.

Next morning, April 23, the Austrians at Regensburg recrossed the Danube by two pontoon bridges. The French did not force their way into the town until nearly all the Austrians had crossed. A small portion of the rearguard was captured. The fighting of the last five days—at Thann, Abendsberg, Landshut, Eggmuehl and Regensburg —had changed the doubtful backward movement of French victorious all along the line the French into a victorious advance. Never had strategic difficulties of such an extremely awkward character been solved with greater coherence or despatch. Napoleon's severest critic, Lanfrey, even, has felt compelled in this instance to give the great captain his due. He says: "The opening of this campaign is a model of scientific warfare; a masterpiece alike of boldness and of prudence worthy in Lanfrey's critical approbation all its points of the first campaign in Italy, and also above criticism, but for the falsehoods contained in Napoleon's bulletins." This is an allusion to Napoleon's claim that the whole Austrian army of 300,000 men had been crushed, and that they had lost one archduke, twenty generals, and upward of 30,000 prisoners. So far as can be judged from the widely conflicting estimates, the Austrian casualties probably amounted to less than one-third of that number. At St. Helena, Napoleon said of this campaign: "The greatest military manœuvres I ever made, and those for which I give myself most credit, were executed at Eggmuehl. They were Napoleon's own estimate infinitely superior to those at Marengo, or to any other of my actions."

As the French were advancing on Regensburg,

The
Emperor
wounded

Napoleon was wounded in the foot by the bullet of a Tyrolese sharpshooter. The news that the Emperor had been shot spread through the French ranks. It caused such a commotion that Napoleon remounted his horse and rode along the lines until loss of blood made him faint. In its effects the wound proved trifling, and the Emperor continued in active com-

Austrians
retreat
down the
Danube

mand at Regensburg. The Austrians retreated down the Danube. Archduke Charles marched for Bohemia, hoping to threaten the French advance on Vienna from their flank and rear. Hiller tried to cover the capital by recrossing the Inn, but had to deviate from his march at Linz, when he found that Masséna's pursuers were outflanking him. At

General
Hiller out-
flanked

the river Traun he made a stand in the little stronghold of Ebelsberg. Had the French possessed themselves with patience, Marshal Lannes could have made the enemy's position on the Traun untenable, by flanking the Austrians at Steyer. As it happened, General Coehorn, a Corsican hot-head, commanding the so-called "infernal legion" of Corsicans and Bersaglieri, arriving prematurely, wildly dashed his men against the overwhelming forces of the Austrians. A wooden bridge, some 600 feet long and protected at each end by bastions, sur-

Charge of
the "infer-
nal legion"

mounted by a citadel with 100 pieces of cannon, was stormed by the frenzied Italians. Colonel Clapareda, in the face of fearful losses, led his men to the assault again and again, and at last succeeded in breaking down the city gate. Other French troops entered into the fight, and a detachment of Legrand's division got a foothold in the little town. At last Masséna brought up his whole division, yet the Austrians held firm until after nightfall, and then evacuated the place in good order. Napoleon, who arrived next day, was dismayed to find that nearly 5,000 of his men had fallen before Ebelsberg, and that Clapareda's brigade was practically wiped out. Masséna was censured for countenancing a frontal attack, when flanking manœuvres were possible, but the Corsican leader Coehorn was patted on the back as "a man of great worth." The pursuit of the Austrians was kept up with vigor. Neither Hiller's division nor Archduke John's forces were able to get a foothold in front of Vienna. By the middle of May they barely succeeded in joining forces at Krems on the other side of the Danube many miles beyond Vienna.

The fight at Ebelsberg

Vienna now lay open to the French columns. On the way there the Emperor's staff rode by the ruins of Dierstein, the dungeon of Richard Cœur de Lion. Napoleon turned to his companions, Berthier and Lannes, and said: "He, too, fought in Syria, and he had better luck than we had at St. Jean d'Acre. Still the lion-hearted was no more valiant than you, my brave Lannes. Those were barbarous times, which they now have the folly to represent to us as so heroic."

Vienna left exposed

On May 10, the French appeared before Vienna. The old part of the city, containing some hundred thousand inhabitants, was still encircled by the ancient walls that had once kept out the Turks. In the city, Archduke Maximilian had 15,000 regulars with 10,000 militia. He sacrificed the suburbs with their population of nearly 200,000, and tried to defend the city from behind the old ramparts.

Captain Marbot, bearing Napoleon's summons to surrender, was struck down in the street. Next day Old Vienna was bombarded. For thirty-six hours

3,000 shells were dropped into the city. Toward evening a flag-of-truce bearer from the Archduke begged Napoleon to spare the imperial palace, where the Princess Marie Louise had been left behind on account of illness. She was Napoleon's future bride. As one historian has said of the incident: "It was by the thunders of artillery and the flaming light of bombs across the sky that Napoleon's first addresses to the Archduchess Marie Louise were made." Archduke Maximilian after the second day gave up the struggle, and burning the great bridge of Tabor behind him crossed the

Danube. His successor in command capitulated within a short time. Napoleon entered the city just one month after he had left the Elysée. General Andreossy was appointed governor of Vienna.

Two days after his entry into Vienna, Napoleon issued the famous decree deposing the Pope. In his proclamation he said: "Since the time of Charlemagne, the union of spiritual and temporal power has been and still is a source of dissension. The Popes have but too frequently availed themselves of the one to support their pretensions to the other."

All the papal dominions were united with the French Empire. Rome was declared a free imperial city. The Vatican was reserved for the use of the Pope without restrictions, and a pension of 2,000,000 francs was accorded him. Pope Pius VII. **Napoleon excommunicated** launched his long-threatened bull of excommunication against Napoleon. After that the Pope's fate was but a question of time.

During these days Joseph Haydn, "the favorite of the Austrian people," lay dying. During the siege a French bomb burst near his house in the Kleine Steingasse (now Haydn Strasse), where the great composer lay. After the occupation a French officer, a passionate admirer of Haydn's music, visited the old composer and played to him a selection from his "In tempore Belli." The dying maestro was deeply affected and embraced his caller at parting. On May 26, he called his family around him, and having himself carried to the piano, solemnly played his great national anthem, "Gott erhalte unseren Kaiser." A short time after this he **Death of Joseph Haydn** died. Mozart's requiem was performed in his memory, and his funeral was attended by many French officers and a French guard of honor. In Paris a sacred cantata by Cherubini, written on a previous false report of his death, was given in his honor.

Haydn's rank in the history of music is of the first importance. The foremost among his contemporaries, such as Mozart and Beethoven, called him Father Haydn. All his works, multitudinous as they were, are characterized by lucidity, perfect form and rich development. To him the world **Haydn's contributions to music** owes the evolution of the two finest phases of the sonata form, the orchestral symphony and the quartet. Chamber music was brought by him to its greatest perfection. "It was from Haydn," said Mozart, "that I first learned the true way to compose quartets." Haydn's masses and offertories to this day are among the favorite pieces played on the church organs of Austria and Germany. His celebrated oratorios have remained unsurpassed. Haydn may be said to have stood in direct line of succession from Sebastian Bach, the great protagonist of modern music. Bach said of Haydn that he alone fully understood his music, and knew how to build on it. His worldly success dated from the time that Prince Anton Esterhazy engaged him as a second leader of his private orchestra in Hungary. There Haydn met Gluck, the great composer. After the death of Prince Anton, his successor, Prince Nicolaus, made him first leader of the orchestra. Nicolaus Esterhazy was a typical Hungarian magnate, very rich and an enthusiastic patron of the arts. Haydn himself said: "The Prince was always satisfied with my work. Not only had I the encouragement of his constant approval, but as a conductor of his orchestra I could make experiments, observe what produced an effect and what weakened it, and was thus in a position to improve, alter, make additions or omissions, and be as bold as I pleased. I was cut off from the world; there was no one to confuse or torment me, and I was forced to become original." When the castle of Esterhazy burned down in 1779, Haydn got up his famous "Farewell Symphony," in which one musician after another arises and leaves his

Influence of Sebastian Bach

Encouragement of the Esterhazys

Haydn's appreciation of their help

place in the orchestra, until only the leader is left.
"If all go," said the Prince, "we may as well go
too," and so the company was dispersed, until Castle
Esterhazy was rebuilt.   In the new theatre Haydn   *Inspiration*
performed Gluck's operas, and there he also met the   *for notable*
Czarina of Russia, wife of Paul, to whom he dedi-   *compositions*
cated his famous Russian songs and quartet com-
posed in 1802.   For the Russian Princess he also
wrote the opera, "Orlando Paladino," the most frequently performed of all his operas.   About this
time Mozart dedicated his first six quartets to
Haydn in terms of filial affection.   Haydn said
to Mozart's father: "I declare to you on my honor   *Friendship*
that I consider your son the greatest composer   *of Mozart*
I have ever heard."   After the death of Prince   *and Haydn*
Nicolaus, Salomon of London hastened to Vienna
and induced Haydn to come to London.   He did
this regardless of the protests of the King of Naples,
then in Vienna, who wished Haydn to come to Italy
with him.   Mozart saw Haydn off and promised to
follow him to London, but before he could do so he   *Haydn*
died.   In London Haydn was lionized by the musi-   *goes to*
cal set.   The University of Oxford made him a   *England*
doctor of music.   One of Haydn's quartets was performed at the royal palace, with the Prince of Wales
playing the bass violin, the Duke of York the viol,
and the Princess of Wales at the piano.   In London
Haydn was visited by J. B. Cramer, then twenty
years old, and by Clementi, the boy violinist, for
whose benefit Haydn performed his new "Seven
Words."   He also aided in the Händel commemora-
tion at Westminster Abbey.   When the Hallelujah

chorus swept through the nave, Haydn wept, and said with a choking voice, "He is the master of us all." His symphonies written at this period, known
The Salomon Symphonies as the Salomon Symphonies, are accounted his greatest orchestral works. When he returned to Germany next year he met Beethoven at Bonn, and passed judgment on a new cantata of that rising composer. Beethoven followed him to Vienna and became his
Beethoven meets Haydn pupil. In later years Haydn was again summoned to London to write six more symphonies. He returned to Vienna with a competence sufficient for the rest of his days. During the last decade of his life Haydn wrote his greatest works, "The Four
The "Creation" Seasons," and his stupendous "Creation," inspired by Milton's "Paradise Lost." His last composition was the vocal quartet, "Hin ist alle meine Kraft"— "My strength is gone; old and weak am I." His last public appearance was at the performance of his "Creation" at the University of Vienna in 1808. He was taken to the hall in an armchair, and was
Haydn's last appearance so overcome by his own music that he had to be carried away. As he was leaving, the ladies of the court thronged around him, and Beethoven, rushing forward, embraced and kissed him. Among the pupils left behind by Haydn besides Beethoven must be mentioned Ignace Pleyel, Edward Von Weber, the Countess Thun, Streck, Neucomm and Lessel.

At the time that Haydn died, Napoleon had already removed his headquarters from Schoenbrunn to the island of Lobau, where the Danube branches below Vienna. There the French established them-

selves with a view to crossing the river to give
. battle to the Austrians on the northern shore. The
strength of Austria's remaining forces, and the
threatening situation elsewhere, made a decisive
battle a political necessity for Napoleon.

The British fleet under Lord Cochrae, on April
11, had destroyed a French squadron in the roads French
fleet de-
of Aix. Four French warships were blown up and stroyed at
Aix
seven were driven ashore. In the south the second
French occupation of Portugal, after the successful
seizure of Oporto, ended in failure; when Craddock,
commanding the weak British forces there, had been
superseded by Sir Arthur Wellesley, the fortunes
of war turned against the victor Soult. The British
crossed the Douro in spite of French resistance, and
drove the enemy back to Vallonga. Soult was so Wellington
crosses the
hard pressed that he had to burn his wagons, stores Douro
and ammunition. By May 19, he finally got his
army out of Portugal, having lost 6,000 men and
all his guns. Still the retreat was conducted in
so masterly a manner that Soult's reputation as a
general was undiminished.

In Italy there was similar sharp fighting between
the Austrians under the Archduke John, and Prince
Eugene Beauharnais. On the part of the French,
the opening of the Italian campaign was badly mis- Eugene
Beauhar-
managed by Prince Eugene. His reverses did not nais's
blunders
cease until Napoleon ordered General Macdonald
to supplement Beauharnais's faulty strategy with his
more experienced counsels. With his help Eugene
won his first point against Archduke John at Cal- Battle of
Caldiero
diero, near Verona, and passing the Piave inflicted

a severe defeat on the Austrians. Trieste was occupied by the French. The headquarters of the French army of Italy were established at Villach, with advanced posts as far as Klagenfurt. In the Tyrol an expedition under Lefebvre gained some headway against the rebellious peasants, and re-captured their capital of Innsbruck. In the interval 700 Frenchmen and 1,800 Bavarians had been massacred in the mountain fastnesses of the Tyrol.

French regain the Tyrol

In northern Europe likewise public affairs bore a threatening aspect. The Czar of Russia, after his easy victories over the Swedes, displayed marked hesitation about living up to his part as the ally of Napoleon. Only when the French came out as victors, and the Austrian offensive had been seen to fail at every point, did Russia at last declare war on Austria and move an army corps into Poland.

Russia's lukewarm alliance

In Prussia, the failure of the Austrian generals to throw the campaign north of the Danube caused deep chagrin to those patriots who had counted on arousing Northern Germany. Some of the hot-heads still persevered in their plans. The leaders of this military conspiracy were the Duke of Brunswick, Baron Dörnberg, an officer in the service of King Jerome, Major Von Schill, a Prussian cavalry officer who had distinguished himself in the defence of Colberg, and Lieutenant Katt at Magdeburg. It had been agreed between them that Dörnberg should raise the Hessian standard in Westphalia, and turn Jerome's own army against him. Schill at the same time was to march from Berlin with whatever troops he could collect, and try to arouse the

Anti-French conspiracy in Prussia

people by proclaiming war against the French in defiance of the government. At the last moment, Dörnberg was transferred from his own regiment to the command of other troops on whom he could not rely. He placed himself at the head of a band of peasants, and raised the standard of insurrection. King Jerome's household troops dispersed the rioters with a volley, and Dörnberg had to flee for his life. He took refuge with the Duke of Brunswick. The revolt in Hessia was ended. In the meanwhile, Schill blindly did his part. On April 28, he led his battalion out of their barracks in Berlin and marched his men out of the city, as if for some routine exercise. Outside of the city he was joined by a small detachment of cavalry raiders who had been let into the secret. He addressed his troops and offered to lead them against the French. The proposition was received by the soldiers with shouts of approval. The march to Westphalia was begun. On the way, many volunteers joined the movement. The Elbe was crossed and Schill prepared to fall on the communications maintained by the French with their forces operating on the Danube. On reaching Halle, Schill learned of Napoleon's victories near Regensburg, and of the failure of Dörnberg's coup d'état in Westphalia. Henceforth his raid became hopeless. The only chance for Schill and his compromised troops was to escape either to Bohemia, where they might effect an ultimate junction with the retreating Austrians, or to fight their way to the sea in the hope of rescue from British cruisers. After many purposeless marches, Schill

[marginal notes:] Hessian revolt foiled

Dornberg's flight to Brunswick

Major Schill's raid

chose the latter course. On May 5, he was over-

taken by a detachment of Westphalian troops from Magdeburg, and successfully fought his way clear of them. A price was set on his head. Late in May, the raiders fell in with 3,000 Poles and Meck-lenburgers, commanded by the French governor of the province. Schill's 1,800 men fought their way through the French brigade, and suddenly appeared before Stralsund, just as the French gun-ners on the ramparts were firing a salute in honor of Napoleon's entry into Vienna. The garrison was

surprised, and a short hand-to-hand fight put Schill in possession of the town with all its stores. Until the arrival of an English fleet, Schill hoped to make a second Saragossa of Stralsund. But, on the last day of May, 8,000 Danes and Frenchmen moved on the town. Capitulation was out of the question for the rebels. In overwhelming numbers the French stormed the town. Fighting in the streets, Schill split open the head of Carcaret, the Dutch general.

He was himself killed by a cannon ball. With him fell one-third of his men. Five hundred of his followers under Lieutenant Brunow cut their way out and escaped. Of the prisoners taken, all officers were shot at Wesel, and fourteen subalterns at Brunswick, while the common soldiers, about 500

in number, were sent to the galleys at Tunol. Only 120 survived the treatment there. Schill's head was cut off and sent to the library of Leyden.

Less tragic, if no less unfortunate, was the young Duke of Brunswick's raid. Of his duchy nothing was left but the family seat of Oels. To avenge his father's death he raised 2,000 volunteers. His followers, known as the Black Brunswickers, on account of their coal-black uniform with a silver death's-head on the helmet, beat off several detachments of Westphalian troops, and finally fought their way through a strong force under General Ochs. At the mouth of the Weser they were picked up by British cruisers, and were finally enrolled as an auxiliary brigade under Wellington in Spain.

Failure of Brunswick's raid

Such were the threatening diversions which prompted Napoleon to risk a decisive blow. His secretary, Méneval, who was attached to his headquarters at the time, recorded this memorandum: "If the ill-arranged enterprises of Dörnberg, Schill and the Duke of Brunswick had taken place somewhat earlier and simultaneously, French domination in the North would have been seriously jeopardized." On the night of May 20, Napoleon's light cavalry under Count Lasalle crossed the Danube.

Napoleon crosses the Danube

They were followed next day by the divisions of Masséna, Lannes and the Imperial Guard, 40,000 strong. Next night the same troops laid pontoons and crossed the second branch of the Danube to the north bank. Early in the morning the villages of Aspern and Esslingen were occupied by the French. The Austrian army encamped within easy striking distance. At noon a number of heavy rafts and river barges loaded with stones were suddenly cast loose by the Austrians above Lobau, and came sweeping down the river headed for the French pontoon bridge between Lobau and Oberstof. At

French pontoon bridge broken

the same time the whole Austrian army advanced
upon the French from Bisamberg. Fighting began
at once and soon grew hot. From their fresh intrenchments at Aspern and Esslingen, the French
repulsed all the first onslaughts. The bridges were
repaired in a hurry, and the French reserves of
heavy cavalry and artillery had a chance to get
over the river. By nightfall the French, who had
been holding out against the Austrians all the afternoon, were almost as strong as their enemy. For
Napoleon, much depended on the timely arrival of
Davoust's division in Oberstof. That marshal was
ordered to cross over to Esslingen from the Island
of Lobau, to support Lannes's division in his attack
on the Austrian centre, while Masséna engaged the
enemy at Aspern. By noon next day Napoleon
had word of Davoust's arrival. His reserves could
be counted on for the afternoon. In the meanwhile
the river had swollen, and the Austrians took advantage of this to launch whole barns, boathouses
and burning mills to be swept down against the
French bridges by the flood. Lannes received orders to advance forthwith from Esslingen. He did
so with his two veteran divisions of grenadiers,
supplemented by the Young Guard and thirty-two
squadrons of horse under General Lasalle, one of
the most brilliant of French cavalry leaders. The
Austrian centre was pushed back, so that the Archduke's battle line became almost concave, but his
regiments held their own manfully. The officers
encouraged their men by personal example. The
Archduke himself snatched a flag from one of his

French re-
serves
cross the
river

Battle of
Aspern

Esslingen

Zach grenadiers and led the regiment forward.
Suddenly the French attack slackened. Lannes,
who perceived himself unsupported, gave orders to
fall back. In the ranks the news spread that the
great pontoon bridge had again given way before
the flood, and had been rent asunder by the floating French
retreat
rams of the Austrians. This cut off the French cut off
from all further aid or from a safe retreat. Lannes's
soldiers were alarmed. During the retreat General
Espagne was killed and St. Hilaire was mortally
wounded. The backward movement was covered
with cavalry attacks by General Lasalle. The
whole French cavalry was ordered to advance.
The combined cuirassier regiments galloped forward with sabres and breastplates flashing. The
Austrian dragoons could not sustain the shock.
Together with their horse artillery, they were
driven back between the Austrian infantry massing in squares. The French cuirassiers swept The Cavalry at
down upon these in solid squadrons. The Aus- Aspern
trian musketeers and gunners held their fire until
the heavy cavalry men were nearly upon them.
When the white of the horses' eyes could be seen,
the gunners fired at pointblank range with grape
and canister, while the squares volleyed. The foremost horsemen went down in whole platoons, while
those that followed wheeled in panic, so as to make
the French battle line revolve upon itself. At all
points the attack had been repulsed. Prince Lich- Napoleon
repulsed
tenstein's dragoons pursued the fleeing cuirassiers,
and the French line of infantry was made to waver.
Napoleon himself, who had ridden out of Aspern

to watch the success of the cavalry charge, had to take refuge within a square of his guards. Members of his suite and the chief equerry of the Empress Josephine were taken captive. The Austrian infantry renewed its attack on the village of Aspern, and at Esslingen the struggle became desperate. Marshal Lannes, while conducting the retreat across the Marchfeld, was struck by a cannon ball which carried away both his legs. When Napoleon heard of this, he left his post of observation, and hurried to the litter of the dying general. There he threw himself on his knees, and with a choking voice said: "Lannes, do you know me? It is your friend, Bonaparte." The dying marshal languidly raised his head and murmured incoherent

Death of
Marshal
Lannes

words. According to Cadet Gassicourt, who attended the fallen hero, Lannes said: "I am dying for you, like so many others. You will not mourn my loss any more than the rest. Make peace before it is your turn." General Petit, on the other hand, has recorded that Lannes's words were these: "I am dying for you and for my country. Do not mourn my loss. May you live and save the army." Whatever may have passed between the two, Napoleon did mourn the loss of Lannes most keenly. When he was told that the Marshal was dead, the Emperor sat for a long time staring dumbly before him, then he buried his face in his hands. To Masséna, who was fighting the battle of his life at the time, he said: "Nothing but so terrible a stroke could have coaxed me from headquarters at that time." To Josephine Napoleon wrote: "The loss

of the Duke of Montebello deeply afflicts me.
Thus all things end. If you can contribute to
the comfort of his poor wife do so." In later
years Napoleon wrote at St. Helena: "At the
period of his death, Lannes had reached the highest point in his profession. He was a most able Napoleon's
commander. I found him a dwarf, but I lost him estimate of
a giant."

Masséna had a hard time in covering the French
retreat over an emergency bridge across the Danube.
The Austrians made assault after assault on the two
intrenched river towns, and with the help of incessant artillery fire succeeded in setting fire to both.
The French were driven from Esslingen into a narrow peninsula where they brought up at the brink
of the river.

At last, at the personal request of Napoleon,
General Mouton headed his famous fusilier guard
in a bayonet charge against the Austrians, and
pushed them back to the further end of Esslingen. Mouton
For this exploit the Emperor gave to Mouton the saves the
new title, Count of Lobau. Long after nightfall day
the last French detachment returned safely over
the improvised bridge to Lobau. As soon as they
had marched over the bridge, the pontoons were
cast loose. Meanwhile the Emperor sat on the
river bank angrily switching his boot with a riding-
whip. "Are you satisfied, little corporal?" cried
one of the wounded guards, as they marched by him.
Later in the night Napoleon was ferried across the
river in a small boat. With him were an aide-
de-camp and Lieutenant Field-Marshal Von Weber

of the Austrian army, a mortally wounded prisoner. "How is it with you, General?" asked Napoleon, as he heard the wounded man groaning. "It is well," said the dying hero, "Have I not seen you tremble." Napoleon said no more. On the other shore the Emperor held a council of war. Masséna, Davoust, Bessières, and Berthier joined him. Savary, who was present, has recorded that all the Marshals advised further retreat across the other branch of the Danube and thence to Vienna. Napoleon would not have it. "If we retreat it will not be a retreat to Vienna, but to Strasburg. Our allies, dismayed and made treacherous in their weakness, would turn against us. The good fortune of the Empire would be at an end and the grandeur of France destroyed. You, Masséna and Davoust can save the army. Come! show yourself worthy of your own past." Napoleon had his way. It was decided to remain on the island of Lobau, and to intrench it against all attacks.

The drawn battle of Aspern and Esslingen was found to be one of the most bloody affairs of the century. In its fearful losses and lack of result to both sides it can only be compared to the battle of Eylau. On the French side, the casualties were four general officers, five hundred other officers and at least 18,000 soldiers. The Austrians reckoned their losses at 16,000 killed and 42,000 wounded. Both sides claimed a victory, but Napoleon got his couriers out first, and so, producing the first impression, weakened the effect of the Archduke's bulletins. He claimed but 1,100 dead

French marshals advise retreat

Napoleon stands firm

French claim the victory

and 3,000 wounded. Only "General Danube," he avowed, prevented him from profiting by his victory.

While holding the Austrian main army in check on the Danube, Napoleon and his generals made the most of their breathing space. The Island of Lobau was made impregnable. The Tyrolese revolt was put down without mercy. General Wrede commanding the Bavarians succeeded in driving the Austrians out of Salzburg. The greater part of the Tyrolese occupying the valley of Strub, having quit fighting on Ascension Day to go to church, were overpowered and butchered. The stronghold of the Scharnitz was taken, and the Bavarians under Arco penetrated into the country from that side. The news of Napoleon's defeat at Aspern spurred the Tyrolese to new activity. The Austrian Emperor encouraged them with this statement: "My faithful county of Tyrol shall henceforward ever remain incorporated with the Austrian Empire. I will agree to no treaty of peace save one forever uniting the Tyrol with my monarchy." The Tyrolese besieged General Deroy in Innsbruck. Hofer, Eisenstecken and the brave Speckbacher assembled their peasants on the mountain of Isel. The fighting lasted three days. In the forefront of the battleline could be seen Hofer's little boy Anderl, who brought the men their ammunition, and Haspinger, a red-bearded monk who led his parishioners gun in hand. The Count of Stachelburg from Meran, who fought as a volunteer among the peasants, fell on this occasion. The fortress of Kuffstein was

Tyrolese revolt quelled

Emperor Francis' promise

Battle of Innsbruck

likewise besieged by a detachment under Speckbacher. Finally, General Lefebvre led a strong column of 30,000 Frenchmen, Bavarians and Saxons
into the Tyrol and ended the revolt, amid general
bloodshed.

General Macdonald commanding the right wing
of the French army of Italy compelled 4,000 Aus-
Surrender
of Laybach trians under General Meerfelt to surrender at Laybach, in Carinthia, shortly after the battle of Aspern. On May 25, Prince Beauharnais, by a series
of successful manœuvres, pushed his main army
through to Loeben in Steiermark, and overcame
the major portion of Jellalich's Austrian corps.
Goerz, Klagenfurt and Trieste opened their gates
to the French. Next day the advance outposts of
the French army of Italy came in touch with those
French
join forces of the grand army at Bruck, south of Vienna.
This event had been anxiously awaited by Napoleon, who sent his aide-de-camp Lauriston to
cut his way through to the viceroy. As soon as
the French joined forces, Archduke John had to
fall back into Hungary. The French occupied the
whole of Tyrol and the region of Salzburg, Vorarl-
berg, Carinthia, Frioul and Istria. General Marmont, marching up from Dalmatia, penetrated
Austrians
retreat
into Hun- through Croatia as far as Fiume. Prince Beau-
gary harnais presented himself at Napoleon's headquarters on the Danube by the end of May.

In the north, Napoleon's Russian allies made so
threatening a demonstration against Poland, that
Archduke Ferdinand felt constrained to withdraw
his Austrian forces from Warsaw and to commence

his retreat southward. On the other side, Russia was relieved of embarrassment by the conciliatory attitude of the new King of Sweden, Charles XIII., who, having failed to drive the Russians from west Bothnia, speedily reversed his nephew's warlike measures.

Austrians retreat from Poland

Napoleon's star was once more in the ascendant. It was at this moment that Pope Pius VII. incensed by the French occupation of Rome, launched his bull of excommunication against Bonaparte: "Let the Sovereigns of the world learn once more that they are subject by the law of Jesus Christ to our throne and our commands. For we too hold sovereignty, and a sovereignty far more noble; for it shall not be said that spirit must yield to flesh, nor the things of heaven to those of the earth." Napoleon did not suffer himself to be distracted by such things. He simply issued orders to Murat to have the Pope seized in person to be sent as a prisoner to Savona. This done, he devoted himself to the completion of his military campaign with accustomed ardor. The pursuit of Archduke John's forces by the army of Italy carried them well beyond the borders of Hungary to the banks of the Danube. At Raab, Archduke John tried to join forces with the Archduke Palatine. Beauharnais attacked him and was aided in his advance by General Grenier. General Macdonald with the right and General Lauriston with a detachment of the grand army came up toward the end of the day. Together they defeated the Austrians with great loss. The town Raab was invested.

Napoleon excommunicated

Pope Pius VII. made a prisoner

French victory at Raab

Within a day or so of this success, it so happened that General Suchet at Belchite in Spain utterly routed a Spanish army under General Blake. The Spaniards, though largely outnumbering the French, ran away without firing a shot, and threw down their arms. Their own general denounced them as cowards. Wellington wrote to his brother, the Marquis of Wellesley: "I am of the opinion that an effort should be made immediately for clothing the Spanish troops in a national uniform. This would put a stop to the custom, which I am sorry to say so generally prevails, of their throwing down their arms and accoutrements and betaking themselves to flight on pretence of their being not soldiers but simply peasants."

A few days after this the stronghold of Raab in Hungary capitulated to General Lauriston. This threw Hungary open to the French. Napoleon called upon the Hungarians to secede from Austria; but no one responded. Then he ordered the advance on Pressburg. When the news of these various victories had been spread far and wide, Napoleon thought the time was right to try for another decisive blow on the Danube. In response to his brother Jerome's clamors for help in Westphalia he wrote a reassuring letter: "Take things quietly. You have nothing to dread. The English are not to be feared. All their troops are in Spain and Portugal. They can do nothing in Germany. Even so, it will be time enough when they come. I always wait until an affair is ripe and I understand it well. Then I act."

Side notes:
Spaniards routed at Belchite

Wellington's explanation

Hungary remains loyal

In three weeks' time the island of Lobau had
been transformed into a bristling fort. Material
had been amassed for crossing the river at short
notice. Under Napoleon's directions General Bertrand had constructed two bridges on spiles, 800
yards long. Both were protected against floating
rafts and fire-ships by a breakwater and stockades. The
bridges of
Marines in boats guarded the waterway day and Lobau
night. The big bridge was wide enough for three
artillery trains to pass abreast. The other, but
eight feet wide, was intended for the infantry. Napoleon grandiloquently compared his work to that
of Cæsar. "Cæsar's bridge over the Rhine," he
said, "was thrown across in eight days, to be sure,
but no carriage could pass over it."

On July 2, Napoleon issued his orders for the
crossing of the Danube. Everything was regulated down to the most minute details, and the
exact time was fixed for every man to act. That
same night a feint movement was made on Mill
Island, where the first crossing had been made.
On the night of July 4, during a heavy rainfall,
a flying bridge was floated from Alexander's Island
and was swung in place. At the same time, six
pontoon bridges were strung across the Danube,
while a flotilla of ferryboats made incessant trips French re-
cross the
to and fro laden with troops. A sham attack at Danube
Aspern and Esslingen diverted the Kleinau grenadiers, who guarded the Austrian position on the
water-front. The first French detachments, as they
got over immediately deployed in skirmish order
and engaged the Austrians in regular battle at

Essendorf, five leagues from Vienna. The rest of
the army crossed the Danube during the night,
marching as if on a solid road. The Austrians
knew something was under foot, but did not realize the extent of the movement. The Emperor of
Austria in his anxiety sought out his brother
Charles, where he stood on the river-bank looking out into the darkness. The Archduke reckoned
that twenty-four hours at least would be needed

Archduke
Charles's
mistake

to effect a crossing in force. "The French vanguard has indeed crossed the Danube," he admitted to his brother, "and I am letting some of
the rest come across." "Very good," said Emperor Francis, "but don't let too many of them
come over." This remark subsequently became
a byword in the army.

Before daylight, 200,000 French soldiers—infantry, cavalry and artillery—had crossed the
Danube. At sunrise the whole army was ranged
in battle line. Oudinot commanded the centre,
Masséna the left, Davoust the right. In the second line were the forces of Beauharnais, Bernadotte,
and Marmont, with the Bavarian corps. They were
supported by the Guards, and the heavy cavalry
and artillery.

Archduke Charles was caught at a woful dis-

The Aus-
trians
over-
matched

advantage. Of his available forces 20,000 were
in Hungary, 12,000 were at Vienna under Prince
Roess, 6,000 at Nussdorf, and as many more before
Krems. This left him weaker than the French by
40,000 men. The result could only be a foregone
conclusion.

Painted by Horace Vernet

NAPOLEON AT WAGRAM

From Carbon Print by Braun, Clement & Co., N. Y.

XIXth Cent., Vol. One

It was a magnificent sight when Napoleon's
army moved to the advance. The slanting rays
of the morning sun shone on the serried lines of
warriors clad in all manner of colors and equip-
ments, as befitted their cosmopolitan commands.
Frenchmen, Germans, Italians, Dutchmen, Poles
and Dalmatians, marching under their respective
colors and standards, surged forward against the
white clad lines of the German Austrians, Mag-
yars, Roumanians, Czechs and Slavonians. The
French Emperor on a white charger galloped along
the front of his battle line, and repeated his last
instructions to his marshals. The artillery opened
the battle from the heights. The Austrians received the French advance with a hail of grape
shot and musketry. The first attack of Masséna's Battle of
corps was repulsed. The whole left wing of the Wagram
French army was outflanked at Süssenbrunn and
pressed back toward Wagram and the Danube. On
the French right wing, on the other hand, Davoust
outflanked the Austrians at Markgraf-Neufchatel.
It was the greatest flanking manœuvre of all the
Napoleonic campaigns. The Austrian corps of Rosenberg was overthrown, and Montbrun's squadrons
of chasseurs-à-cheval were sent out to intercept a
possible support from Archduke John. The Austrian centre swerved over to the rescue of Rosenberg's left wing. In the meanwhile, Masséna's men,
fighting stubbornly, had been forced back as far as
the bridge of Aspern. Several officers of his staff
were cut down at his side. Masséna himself suffered severely from a fall with his horse. In

desperation he despatched his aide-de-camp, the
Margrave of Baden, to the Emperor. The young
prince galloped to the very centre of the square
of guardsmen, where Napoleon was crouching on
the ground sticking pins into his map of battle.
He reported that Masséna could no longer hold
his lines, and held the battle for lost. Napoleon
looked up and said: "What time is it, Berthier?"
That marshal, resplendent in the yellow uniform of
his ducal bodyguard of Neufchatel, looked at his
watch and said: "Twelve o'clock, sire." "Tell the
Prince of Rivoli," replied Napoleon, "that the battle is won. It is noon and Archduke John has
not yet come." Dumfounded, the young prince
rode off.

A Napole-
onic effect

Napoleon gave instant orders to Beauharnais to
advance his strong corps on Wagram with those
of Marmont and Grenier, while Oudinot was to
advance between Wagram and Neufchatel. The
Emperor's guards swung in behind the central
advance. Napoleon himself mounted his white
charger and galloped over to the left wing, followed by all the reserve cavalry and artillery.
He arrived in time to encounter the regiments
of Bernadotte's shattered divisions retreating from
Aderklaa. Masséna was found sitting in a field
wagon desperately holding his own. Napoleon
climbed into the wagon beside him. Here he
gave orders for an unprecedented manœuvre: the
junction of three entire divisions under Macdonald,
Gerra and Wrede with Beauharnais's army in one
solid column. While these four corps were welded

Berna-
dotte's ill
success

A gigantic
manœuvre

into one irresistible whole, their movements were masked by an impetuous cavalry attack led by General Lasalle. He had not ridden a hundred yards before he was killed by a cannon ball. His squadron wheeled before the murderous fire of the Austrians and came streaming back upon the French infantry. Bessières was ordered to charge with all the cavalry reserves, so as to pierce the Austrian centre. Riding through a tempest of grape and chain shot, Bessières led his cuirassiers into the thick of the fight. Suddenly he was seen to pitch headlong to the ground, where he lay as dead. A wail went up from the Old Guard. The Emperor averted his eyes, and, spurring his horse onward, shouted: "Let us go! I have no time to weep." Bessières, who had only been grazed by a passing cannon ball, revived and clambered into the saddle again. The Emperor sent Savary after him. When next he saw him, he said: "The ball which struck you down, my dear Bessières, drew tears from all my Guard. It ought to be very dear to you." By this time Lauriston had brought up the reserve artillery and had unlimbered his batteries close to the Austrians. Macdonald had advanced his infantry far into the wedge opened by the French cavalry. Over three miles of ground his corps advanced, fighting steadily. Then it got wedged under a murderous cross-fire from the Austrians. His men were mowed down by whole companies. Of his sixteen thousand soldiers he lost nearly ten thousand. Napoleon, watching Macdonald, grew anxious. Several times he ex-

General Lasalle killed

Bessières goes down

Macdonald's famous advance

claimed, "Brave homme!" The death gaps in
Macdonald's corps were filled by men from the
divisions of Wrede and Beauharnais. At last the
artillery of Davoust was seen to pass the tower of
Neufchatel, where one wing of the Austrian army
was cut off by Macdonald. Napoleon's face lighted
up. "The battle is gained!" he exclaimed. The
French cavalry was ordered to wheel around and
charge into the right wing of the Austrians. Under
the combined shock of the threefold attack, the
Austrian line wavered and broke. Beauharnais's

French storm Wagram

and Marmont's columns stormed Wagram. Masséna burst his bonds at Aspern and threw his ad-
versaries back to Süssenbrunn. At three in the
afternoon, Archduke Charles ordered a general retreat. Emperor Francis, watching the course of
the battle from a high tower in Wolkersdorf,
mounted his horse and sought the protection of
his retreating columns. Not till then did Arch-

Archduke John arrives too late

duke John's vanguard come up to the main army.
His corps had to be withdrawn without a chance
to strike a blow. While the battle was still raging
in the distance, Napoleon, burning with fever, had
his Mameluke orderly spread a bearskin on the
ground and went to sleep on the battlefield under
a pyramid of bayonets. The Austrians withdrew

Napoleon goes to sleep

in good order. The rearguard fought off the
French pursuers, and their retreat was covered by
a well-directed artillery fire. The French cavalry,
though ordered to harry the retreating Austrians,
for some unexplained reason did so but languidly.
During the pursuit, Oudinot's brother, who had just

been promoted to a generalship by Napoleon, was shot dead. Masséna, Davoust, Friant, Mortier and brave Gudin were wounded. Late in the evening Napoleon rode over the battlefield. Over a distance of nine miles the ground was covered with the bodies of the dead and wounded. The advance of Macdonald's corps in particular could be traced by the heaps of his slain. Presently the Emperor met Macdonald. A coldness had existed between Bonaparte and the Scotch Jacobite since the Emperor's persecution of Moreau, the hero of Hohenlinden. After that Macdonald refused all preferments from Napoleon. Now the Emperor offered his hand and said: "Accept it, Macdonald! Let there be no more ill will between us. From this day we must be friends. I will send you as a pledge your marshal's staff, which you have so gloriously earned." Macdonald gave in. Oudinot and Marmont were likewise made marshals.

Reconciliation of Macdonald

It proved a dearly won battle. The French had 27,000 killed and wounded, while the Austrians lost 25,000. Three general officers fell on either side. The disparity in casualties was due to the fact that the French had been forced to advance in compact formation under a long-sustained artillery fire. Both sides lost heavily in prisoners, guns and standards. Oudinot's corps alone, according to that marshal's report, lost 8,946 men, while Gerot's division suffered so severely that it had to be disbanded. Bernadotte's beaten corps was likewise disbanded, and their commander was sent back to France in disgrace. In later years, Napoleon told Admi-

The losses of Wagram

ral Cockburn, while on his way to St. Helena, that it was the biggest battle of his entire career. After the battle, the Austrians went to pieces. The French under General Marmont pursued so impetuously that by July 10 they suddenly found themselves in the midst of the enemy at Znaim, twenty-six leagues from Wagram. There was no available support. Davoust and Masséna were full two marches away. Perceiving his danger, Marmont showed a bold front and ordered a mad attack on Znaim, as if confident of support. The Austrians contented themselves with a mere repulse of his forlorn attack and suffered him to hold his own until nightfall. Thus the Archduke lost a splendid chance to avenge his defeat by the destruction of one of Napoleon's finest divisions. On the following day Masséna came to the rescue. Fighting had recommenced when Prince Lichtenstein presented himself with powers to conclude a general armistice. This put a stop to hostilities.

Marmont's predicament at Znaim

The Emperor of Austria at first refused to ratify the armistice, but after five days he gave in. Until the final conclusion of peace the French occupied Vienna, and Napoleon established himself at Schoenbrunn. For fifteen long days the ambulances rattled through the streets of Vienna. Twenty-three hospitals had to attend to them. Without waiting for further pourparlers, Napoleon called for a war indemnity of 237,860,000 francs.

Armistice of Znaim

On the day that the armistice went into effect, the English seized the French colony of San Domingo with the help of the Spanish colonists. Martinique,

Loss of French colonies

and Senegal in Africa, also fell into the hands of
the English. The time had come for the British to
strike nearer home. In the Peninsula, Sir Arthur
Wellesley, after his return from the pursuit of Marshal Soult, had remained long inactive in the vicinity of Lisbon. At last a plan for combined action
was agreed upon between him and the Spanish generals, particularly Don Cuesta. Both began from
different points to march on Madrid. A junction
of their armies was effected on July 20. The main
body marched toward Ollala, where the French were
encamped under Marshal Victor. Within a week Allies ad-
vance on
Madrid
the advance skirmishers were engaged near Tor-
rijos. Both sides prepared for a general battle.
General Wellesley, by virtue of his greater aptitude,
took command. He had 19,000 British and Brunswickers with thirty guns. Cuesta had 33,000 Spaniards with seventy guns. Against this combined
army the French could oppose not quite 50,000
veterans with eighty guns.

The position taken up by Wellesley's troops at
Talavera extended over two miles. The right
wing of the allied army was held by Cuesta's
Spaniards, immediately in front of Talavera down
to the Tagus. The ground was very rough and Battle of
Talavera.
covered with olive trees. On July 27, the French
attacked and drove General Mackenzie's vanguard
back on the allies. The attack was covered by
heavy artillery fire. At night the French were
driven back in a bayonet charge, and were likewise
repulsed on their right wing. A famous cavalry
charge was made by the Twenty-third Light Dra-

goons over a sunken chasm, in which two-thirds went down before reaching the enemy. The rest
A disastrous cavalry charge
were killed off by Victor's Polish Lancers. The German hussars, only, escaped. On the 28th, the British attacked in force, and the French gave way all along the line. Their losses were twenty cannon and 10,000 in casualties. Among them were General Lapisse and a brigadier-general. The British lost nearly 6,000 men. Among their killed were Generals Mackenzie, Langworth and Becket. The Spanish troops, having been but partially engaged, lost only 1,200. The victory was not completed, owing to the oppressive heat and the great fatigue of the British soldiers, who had covered sixty-two miles in twenty-four hours. The Spaniards, when called upon to press the defeat home, did not respond. For the victories
Wellington rewarded
of Oporto and Talavera, Sir Arthur Wellesley was raised to the peerage with the title Baron Douro of Wellesley and Viscount Wellington of Talavera. The title was chosen by his brother William, then in the Ministry, to minimize the change of name. Napoleon, when he heard of Victor's defeat at Talavera, remarked: "Il parait que c'est un homme, ce Wellesley."

The British joy of victory was of short duration. In the first days of August, word was received that Soult, Ney, and Mortier, having joined forces, were advancing through Estremadura to fall on the rear of the British. In Wellington's own words "the allied army could only be saved by great celerity of movement." Wellington and Cuesta separated their

forces so as to present a front either way. By
August 2, the French, 30,000 strong, had pushed
in between the British and the bridge of Almarez.
The allies moved off in haste. The British crossed
the Tagus on August 4, at Arzo Bispo, and retreated toward Deleytosa and Badajos. The Spaniards under Cuesta followed in the same direction,
leaving all the British wounded behind. This circumstance, in connection with the fact that the
British retreated in advance of the Spaniards, became the subject of caustic comment. The "Moniteur" in Paris said: "The post of honor is that
which is nearest the enemy, but Lord Wellington,
having it in his option to give the post of honor either
to the English or to those Spaniards of whom he
speaks so ill, determined in favor of the Spanish troops." In England, a parliamentary vote of
thanks to Lord Wellington only went through after
much opposition. The retreat of the allied army
was pressed so hard by the French that the English
were forced far up the course of the Tagus. The
Spaniards, thus isolated, were surprised at Arzo
Bispo and lost all their artillery. Cuesta was replaced by General Eguia as generalissimo. At the
same time, a strong Spanish army under General
Venegas was routed by General Sebastiani at Almancid in Old Castile. Shortly afterward the same
forces under General Ariezaga were routed again at
Ocaña on the side of New Castile. The Spaniards
lost 4,000 killed and wounded with 10,000 prisoners. The defeat of Ocaña was quickly followed by
the reduction of Cordova and Seville. In Catalonia

Retreat of the allies

British wounded abandoned

Spanish defeats at Arzo Bispo, Almancid and Ocaña

the event of the year was the third heroic siege sustained by the little town of Gerona with a garrison of scarcely 2,800 men. The siege lasted from midsummer to the end of the year. As during the preceding sieges, priests, monks and women fought on the ramparts with the peasants and soldiers. To utter the word capitulation meant death. While the garrison defended itself behind its wretched earthworks, General Blake with a force of Spanish regulars made numerous diversions from without. The frequent repulses of the French so displeased Napoleon that St. Cyr and Verdier, the two commanding generals, were recalled, and Marshal Augereau appointed in their place. Not until Alvarez, the Spanish commander, went mad under the long strain, did the Geronese give in. Finally they surrendered with all the honors of war. Alvarez died in an ambulance while on the way to France. Some idea of the desultory character of the military operations in the Peninsula this year may be gathered from this estimate of the situation, given by Lord Wellington to his brother in 1809: He calculated the disposable forces of the French in Spain as 122,000 men, well provided with cavalry and artillery, without including the troops in Pampeluna, Barcelona and other garrisons. There was the Catalonian corps under St. Cyr and Suchet amounting to 32,000 men. The other 90,000 were distributed in Castile and Estremadura. Of the aggregate forces, 70,000 men were actually in the field, namely the divisions of Victor, Soult, Ney, Mortier and Sebastiani. The rest were distributed

Third siege of Gerona

Forces in the Peninsula

in Madrid, the Escurial, Avila, Valladolid, Toledo
and other convenient centres. To these forces the
Spaniards could only oppose two corps under
Venegas and Eguia. Blake, in Catalonia, had about
6,000 men. The Marquis of Romana had 15,000,
but having neither artillery nor cavalry, he had to
keep to the mountains of Gallicia. There was also
a stationary Spanish garrison of 9,000 at Ciudad
Rodrigo. The English numbered from 20,000 to
25,000 in Portugal. Toward the end of the year
all the Spanish fortresses had fallen into the
hands of the French and most of the patriot
armies had been practically dispersed.

In other quarters, British military operations were
carried on against Napoleon. In early summer, Sir
John Stewart, who commanded the British army in
Sicily, embarked with 15,000 troops to capture
Naples and Calabria. The expedition was joined British attempt on Naples
by a body of Sicilian troops. On June 6, the
French garrisons of Procida and Ischia surrendered to the British. By this stroke 1,500 regular troops, one hundred guns and forty gunboats
fell into British hands. After considerable fighting
for the possession of the castle of Scylla, which was
taken and retaken several times, the British were
forced to abandon the slight footing they had
obtained.

Another British expedition of a more formidable nature was intended to create a diversion
in favor of Austria by invading Holland. Toward Simultaneous attempt in Holland
the end of July, troops were collected to the num-
ber of 40,000, with 150 siege guns, supported by

forty ships of the line, thirty-six frigates and a fleet of gunboats and transports. The whole expedition numbered about 100,000 sailors and soldiers. The fleet was commanded by Sir Richard Strachan, while the Earl of Chatham led the land forces. The departure of the expedition at the end of July was a great event. On the arrival of the troops at Walcheren and South Beveland, it was found that the French had evacuated their position, to concentrate at Antwerp. The French squadron likewise took refuge in the harbor of Antwerp. Resistance was encountered only at Flushing. By the middle of August, Flushing was bombarded for thirty-six hours. The next day General Mounet surrendered with his garrison of 6,000 men. Napoleon was incensed at the news, and had Mounet court-martialled and condemned to death while still a prisoner in British hands. Instead of pushing straight on to Antwerp, the British lay a long time idle at Flushing. They were quartered in a marshy region, which was so notoriously unhealthy that Napoleon had forbidden any French troops to be garrisoned there. Thousands of the soldiers fell ill with malignant fever. All idea of pushing up the Scheldt to destroy the arsenal and dockyards of the French at Antwerp and Terneuse was abandoned. At last, by the middle of September, Lord Chatham returned to England with the greater portion of the troops. Only the island of Walcheren was retained by a British force to maintain a blockade on the Scheldt.

The ignominious failure of this expedition

[Margin notes: The Walcheren expedition; Malaria at Flushing; Lord Chatham returns]

stirred up bad blood in England. The Ministry
was rent by factions. Percival, Castlereagh and
Canning were at cross-purposes. For some time
the Duke of Portland and Castlereagh had been at
odds—ever since Canning had privately stipulated
that he would not remain in the Cabinet unless
Castlereagh were removed from the War Office. The
unfortunate Walcheren expedition, a pet project of
Castlereagh, brought matters to a head. The Marquis of Wellesley had wished the troops to be sent
to Portugal, where his brother was fighting. Canning supported him in this, but said nothing to
Castlereagh. When Castlereagh was finally brought
to resign, and Wellesley was selected for his place,
Castlereagh charged Canning with double dealing.
On September 22, they fought a duel on Putney
Heath. Canning was shot in the thigh. The Duke Canning's
of Portland resigned from the Ministry, and a few reagh
duel with
Castle-
days afterward he died. Thus ended the first part
of Canning's ministerial career. Walter Scott, who
had interested Canning in the founding of the
"Quarterly Review," advised him to take his own Review"
"Quarterly
started
ground in Parliament and hoist his own standard.
This Canning did.

Canning's conduct of the Foreign Office had given
much umbrage. This was especially true of America.
All the rejoicing over the termination of the hurtful
embargo was turned to wormwood when Canning
disavowed the promises and negotiations entered
into by his Minister, Erskine. Upon Erskine's American
Canning's
policy
remonstrances Canning wrote: "I must signify to
you the displeasure which his Majesty feels that

any Minister of his Majesty should have shown himself so far insensible of what is due to the dignity of his sovereign as to have consented to receive and transmit a note in which such expressions were contained." To others, Canning justified his

Erskine re-pudiated

repudiation of the compact with America by the single reason that the United States government could not be trusted long enough to prove its good faith. For Erskine's place, Canning selected Jackson, whose conduct at Copenhagen had made him notorious. The London "Morning Chronicle" published this comment: "The appointment has excited general surprise owing to the character of the individual." Pinckney, from the American Legation in London, sent this warning to President Madison: "It is rather a prevailing notion here that this gentleman's conduct will not and cannot be what we wish." Jackson himself complained that Canning

Jackson's doubtful mission

had sent him on an errand which he knew to be impossible to perform. On July 1, Jackson received his instructions. Their wording showed them to be conceived in the spirit of arrogant intolerance, which did so much to arouse the United States to war with Great Britain. Erskine's compact was repudiated with a charge of bad faith against President Madison, founded on the "publicity so unwarrantably given by the American government."

The news of Canning's disavowal did not reach America until July 21, after three months of un-

Consternation in America

restricted trade with England. The first effect was general bewilderment. "The late conduct of the

British Ministry," commented the "National Intelligencer" of July 26, "has capped the climax of
atrocity toward this country." President Madison
was away from Washington on his Virginia plantation. Gallatin, in temporary charge of affairs, realized at once that a crisis was at hand and advised
the President to return. "I will only observe," he
wrote in his letter, "that we are not so well prepared for resistance as we were a year ago. . . .
We have wasted our resources without any national
utility, and, our treasury being exhausted, we must
now prepare for resistance with considerable and
therefore unpopular loans." Madison wrote to Jefferson: "I find myself under a mortifying necessity
of setting out for Washington to-morrow (August 4).
The intricate state of our affair with England, produced by the mixture of fraud and folly in her conduct, . . . requires that I should join my Cabinet."
Upon his arrival in Washington, without waiting
for the authorization of Congress, Madison issued
a proclamation, reviving the non-intercourse act
against Great Britain. Madison saw no reason
why he should remain in Washington to receive
the British Minister upon his arrival, the more so
since he agreed with Gallatin that Jackson's dis-
claimer was likely to be neither operative nor agree-
able. When the President returned at last, in early
autumn, he received the British Minister in frock-
coat, "as one gentleman another, in strong contrast," wrote Jackson, "to the audiences I have
had with most of the sovereigns of Europe."
When Jackson failed to make any oral proposi-

*Premo-
nition of
war*

*Madison
receives
Jackson*

tions to the Secretary of State, the President requested

Immediate diplomatic friction

him to submit proposals in writing. Jackson wrote a letter of remonstrance, beginning with the assertion, "there does not exist, in the annals of diplomacy, a precedent for stopping verbal communication within so few days after the delivery of credentials."

Madison replied *in extenso*, reminding him at the outset that only in the previous year Canning had put an end to oral communications after two interviews with Pinckney on the subject now under consideration. The rest of the letter drove the awkward position of the British Minister home to him. Jackson wrote to Canning: "Madison is now as obstinate as a mule. Until he gets the absolute surrender of the Orders in Council, he will not even accept satisfaction for the affair of the 'Chesapeake,' which has now for the third time been offered to him in vain." A few days after this, Jackson received a third note, requesting him to show his full powers, as an indispensable preliminary to further negotiations. In reply to Jackson's insinuation that the American government had connived with Erskine, when the latter exceeded his instructions, Madison wrote sternly: "The view which you have presented on the subject makes it my duty to ap-

Jackson called to account

prise you that such insinuations are inadmissible in the intercourse of a foreign Minister with a government that understands what it owes to itself." This communication placed Jackson in a difficult position. Unable to defend himself against the charge, he asserted that it was based on fact.

The President's reply to this note came on No-

vember 8. It was short and to the point: "Sir—
Finding that, in your reply of the 4th inst., you
have used a language which cannot be understood
but as reiterating and even aggravating the same
gross insinuations, it only remains for me, in order
to preclude opportunities which are thus abused, to
inform you that no further communications will
be received from you."

The British envoy dismissed

On Napoleon's foreign policy, the effects of America's dealings with England were various. Napoleon was in Vienna, preparing for the battle of
Wagram, when the news reached him that America
and England had settled their commercial disputes.
Fearful of forcing the United States into the coalition
against France, he sent to Champigny the draught
of a new commercial decree. It declared that since
the United States, by their firm resistance to the
arbitrary measures of England, were no longer
obliged to pay imports to the British government,
the Milan decree of December 17, 1807, should not
longer be applied to the United States, and neutral
commerce with America should be restored. Before this change of policy could be effected, the
battle of Wagram was won. At the same time,
Canning repudiated the new American arrangement, and the United States and Great Britain
were once more at odds. These events were followed by a corresponding change in the tone of the
French Emperor. On August 22, Champigny informed the American Minister that France would
not revoke her retaliatory decrees on commerce
until England should raise her blockades.

Napoleon's American policy

A French change of tone

While residing at Schoenbrunn, Napoleon was beset with other problems beyond the remote vexation of commercial non-intercourse with America. The peace negotiations with Austria were dragging, and in the meanwhile the Tyrolese insurgents refused to be pacified. The rebellion, secretly fomented by the Austrian government throughout the armistice, had to be put down with fire and sword. A thousand Saxons were massacred in the valley of the Eisach, and the Bavarians lost 1,200 men in the Pusterthal. The peasant leaders caught were shot. Speckbacher escaped to Vienna after great suffering. Andreas Hofer, the soul of the Tyrolese insurrection, was betrayed by an unfrocked priest. He was dragged off to Mantua to be tried by drumhead court-martial. It was at this time that Staaps, a young German student from Erfurt, tried to kill Napoleon. He approached the Emperor, during a military review at Schoenbrunn, with a paper in his hand; but General Rapp stopped him, and finding his answers suspicious, had him arrested. On his person was found a large kitchen knife. Later, Napoleon had Staaps called into the drawing-room, where he was receiving his marshals. The young man declared that he wished to free Germany in freeing Europe. He added that he was neither ill nor mad. In the face of the Emperor, Staaps expressed regret that he had not succeeded in his attempt. "But," said Napoleon, "you have a family whose ruin you will cause. You will fill with despair the heart of the young girl who loves you. If I grant you your life, will you be grateful?"—"I

The Tyrol unpacified

Attempted assassination of Napoleon

will kill you none the less," said Staaps. Napoleon
had him removed in the hope that the young man
would express repentance. Staaps remained three
days without eating; then he walked to the place of
his execution, crying: "Long live Germany! Death
to the tyrant!"

Execution of Staaps

Peace between France and Austria was at last
concluded on October 14, 1809, a few days after
Napoleon had called for a new levy of troops in
France. Count Stadion resigned from the Ministry, and Metternich took his place. The treaty of
Vienna, the last which Napoleon signed as a conqueror, took from the Austrian Empire 50,000
square miles of territory and nearly five million
inhabitants. Austria, which at the beginning of
the Napoleonic wars possessed territory from the
Danube to the Rhine, with the greater part of Italy,
now found herself cut off from Germany and from
the sea. The dominion of Napoleon extended without a break from the North Sea to the borders of
Turkey. Bavaria and Saxony were increased at
the expense of their once powerful neighbor. Salzburg and upper Austria, in addition to the Tyrol,
were ceded to Bavaria. Austrian Poland was transferred to the Grandduchy of Warsaw, under the
control of the King of Saxony. This was a direct
slight to the Czar, intended as a punishment for
Russia's lukewarm conduct as an ally. Part of
Carinthia, and the whole of the country lying between the Adriatic and the Save, as far as Bosnia,
were annexed to the French Empire as the Illyrian
provinces. Napoleon appeared to have gathered

Peace concluded at Vienna

Extent of French empire

richer spoils than ever before, but in truth his position had grown worse rather than better. The continued revolts in Spain and the Tyrol held out a hope to northern Europe, while the estrangement with Russia involved new dangers from that quarter. The maritime war with England, with the resulting stoppage of foreign trade in France and Holland, had stricken a hidden wound which weakened the internal resources of the French Empire. Yet Napoleon was confident of ultimate victory. At

American decree of Vienna

Vienna, he wrote another decree revoking his conciliatory attitude toward American trade. It called for confiscation of American merchandise, in retaliation for penalties imposed on French ships for violating the American embargo. Furthermore, Napoleon declared that American merchandise was English property in disguise, and should be treated as such. Peace was finally concluded between France and Denmark as well as Sweden. In return for a promise to close all Swedish harbors against English ships, Pomerania was returned to Sweden. In the treaty between Sweden and Russia, signed at

Sweden makes peace

Fredericshamm, on September 17, Sweden had to cede Finland, the archipelago of Aland and a part of Swedish Bothnia. So it came that the great national singer of Finland, John Ludvig Runeberg, who was to become the greatest poet that ever wrote in the Swedish language, was born a Russian subject.

Immediately after signing peace, Napoleon left Schoenbrunn. As a parting measure, he gave orders to raze the Vienna fortifications to the ground.

After a short visit to the Bavarian court at Nymph-
enburg, he arrived at Fontainebleau, on October *Napoleon returns to Paris*
29, without having been announced.   Empress
Josephine was not there to receive him.   Napoleon
made this a pretext for a violent scene.   It served
to foreshadow the divorce which had long been
arranged by Fouché.   At the imperial palace, the
doors were closed between the apartments of Napoleon and those of Josephine.   Méneval, who
witnessed these scenes, wrote in his memoirs:

"So cruelly was Josephine troubled that she was
constantly appealing to me.   My part became embarrassing, and, in order to escape from the unhappy princess and her questions, I had to avoid her.
When by hazard she was able to keep the Emperor
with her for a moment, she did not dare to touch on
this question for fear that the fatal sentence should
fall from his lips. . . .   At last the Emperor was *Open break with Josephine*
unable to bear it any longer, and one evening, after
the most silent and sorrowful of meals, he broke
the ice. . . .   From that day, Josephine was seen
no more at court."

It was on December 16 that a *senatus consultum*
announced the dissolution of the marriage of Napoleon Bonaparte with Josephine Tascher de la
Pagerie, mother of Prince Eugene Beauharnais,
Viceroy of Italy, etc.   The act read as follows:

"Article I.—The marriage contracted between
Emperor Napoleon and Empress Josephine is dissolved.

"Article II.—Empress Josephine will retain the *Napoleon's divorce*
titles and rank of a crowned Empress.

"Article III.—All arrangements which may be
made by the Emperor in favor of Empress Joseph-

ine, on the funds of the civil list, must be observed by his successors."

After the decree was entered, Napoleon gave orders to conduct Josephine to Malmaison, and went to say farewell. Méneval, who was present, thus describes the scene: "When it was announced that the carriages were ready, Napoleon took his hat and said, 'Méneval, come with me!' I followed him up the little winding staircase from his study to the Empress's apartments. Josephine was alone, and appeared wrapped in the most painful reflection. The noise we made in entering aroused her. Springing up, she threw herself on the Emperor's neck, sobbing and crying. He pressed her to his bosom, kissing her again and again; but in the excess of her emotion she had fainted."

Joseph-
ine's
farewell

Napoleon left Josephine with Méneval, who finally followed alone. That gentleman, as he put it, "felt very miserable, and could not help deploring that the rigorous exactions of politics should violently break the bonds of an affection which had stood the test of time, to impose another union full of uncertainty."

The rest of the month, until the close of the year, was spent by Napoleon in solitude, at Trianon. By an odd coincidence, it was at this same time that the King of Prussia and Queen Louise made their joyful entry into the old royal palace at Berlin, after an absence of three years.

King and
Queen of
Prussia
return to
Berlin

1810

N APOLEON had reached a point in his career when he was more bent on holding fast what he had already acquired than on making new conquests. The war with England, in his mind, had resolved itself into a test of endurance. He was satisfied, therefore, to leave the active prosecution of the war in Spain to his marshals, while he trusted to the effects of his continental blockade to bring England to time. The retroactive effect of commercial stagnation on the Continent itself was not yet realized by Napoleon. Yet the French peasants had to extract sugar from beet root, and substituted chicory for coffee. In Germany and the Netherlands, smokers had to forego their tobacco and took to canaster. But for a flourishing smuggling trade, Holland would have been ruined. In Scandinavia, likewise, the inclusion of Sweden and Denmark in the continental union made smugglers out of the hardy seamen of the North. In Russia, where there was no such outlet, the ruin of trade was complete, and public finances went from bad to worse. All this was lost on Napoleon. For the present he was bent on securing his empire as a dynasty by a personal alliance with one of the oldest reigning families in

Effects of Continental blockade

Financial ruin of Russia

Europe. Having failed in one of his matrimonial
advances on the side of Russia, he turned to Aus-
Napoleon's
matri-
monial
advances
tria. The fact that marriage with the Corsican
usurper could not even be classed as a morganatic
alliance, for a princess of the ancient House of
Hapsburg, was not permitted to interfere with the
plans of so calculating a Prime Minister as Prince
Metternich. Before Napoleon divorced Josephine,
Prince Metternich had already been sounded on
the subject by Napoleon's emissary, Alexandre
Laborde. Metternich wrote to Prince Schwarzenberg, the Austrian Ambassador in Paris: "His
Majesty, the Emperor [Francis], to whom nothing
is repugnant which can contribute to assure the well-
being and tranquillity of the state, far from reject-
Overtures
to Austria
ing this idea, authorizes you, Sir, to follow it up,
and to refuse no overtures which may be made on
the subject. . . . You will also try to determine,
so far as possible, the advantages that France will
offer to Austria in case of the conclusion of a family
alliance."

On New Year's day Princess Metternich, who had
remained in Paris, was presented to Napoleon at the
Tuileries. The next day the Princess was bidden
to Malmaison to meet the ex-Empress. Josephine
herself broached the subject of the projected marriage of Napoleon to Marie-Louise. She said: "It
must be represented to the Emperor of Austria that
his ruin and that of his country is certain, if he does
not consent. It is perhaps the only means of preventing the Emperor from making a schism with
the Holy See."

Metternich replied to his wife:

"I regard this affair as the greatest which could, at this moment, occupy Europe. . . . This consideration led me from the first moment I was informed of the probability of a divorce, to turn to the Princess, who might be called to take this part. The Archduchess is ignorant, as is only right, of the views concerning her . . . but our princesses are little accustomed to choose their husbands from affection, and the respect due to the wish of a father from a child so good and well brought up as the archduchess makes me hope that there will be no obstacle on her part."

Metternich's private views of the prospects of such a union may be gathered from this observation in his letter to Schwarzenberg on the same subject: *Metternich disposes of Marie-Louise*

"If the deepest feeling arise in the heart of any father against the mere notion of an alliance with Napoleon, how much must these feelings be increased when the father finds himself the sovereign of a great empire."

Definite arrangements for the marriage were concluded on February 7. When the news was made public in Vienna, stocks fell at the bourse. Metternich wrote to Schwarzenberg: *Effects of the news in Vienna*

"At a distance it would be difficult to judge of the sensation generally produced here by the news of the marriage. The first effect on the exchange was such that the rate to-day would have been at three hundred, and even less, but that the Government had interest to hold it higher. It was only by buying a million of guldens in specie within the limit of two days that we were able to fix it at three hundred and seventy. Count Shuvalov [the Russian Ambassador] was terrified at the news."

Metternich forthwith set out for Paris to add to the splendor of the imperial wedding. The celebration was set for April, and was to be modelled closely after the ceremonial used when Marie Antoinette was married to Louis XVI.

While Metternich was thus employed in serving his imperial master according to his lights, another faithful servant of the Austrian emperor was abandoned to his fate. Andreas Hofer, the leader of the Tyrolese peasants, who had been betrayed into **Execution of Hofer** French hands after the abandonment of the Tyrol by Austria, was court-martialled as a bandit. Some of the judges stood out for acquittal, but a peremptory order arrived from Napoleon by the heliograph from Milan, fixing Hofer's execution within twenty-four hours. He was shot on the morning of February 20, on the bastion of Mantua. His last words were: "Good-by, wretched world, this death is easy!"

Scarcely a fortnight after Hofer's execution came the death of Lord Henry Cavendish in England, one **Death of Cavendish** of the greatest scientists of the time. With Watt, Black and Priestley in England, and with Laplace, De Luc and Lavoisier in France, Cavendish had conducted a series of experiments in chemistry which determined the true character of air. He was the first who by purely inductive experiments converted hydrogen into water and who established that water consists of two gases. This discovery, announced by Cavendish in his "Experiments on Air," published in 1780, provoked a greater amount of discussion and angry polemics than any other discovery in the history of chemistry. Arago went so far as to charge Cavendish with deceit and plagiarism, in a formal charge brought before the French Academy of Sciences. Cavendish's observations on the action of light, and on specific and latent heat, prepared the way for the more important scientific discoveries in these subjects later in the century. Cavendish also anticipated several of those great facts in common electricity that were subsequently made known to the scientific world through the investigation of Coulomb. It was Cavendish that first computed the density of the earth at 5.45. He did this by means of but seventeen experiments. The approximate accuracy of Cavendish's observation was shown by the fact that the German scientist, Reich, after fifty-seven experiments, came to the conclusion that the density of the earth was 5.44. Lord Cavendish died, in his eightieth year, alone. Though a peer of the realm, and very rich, he had spent almost all his long life in solitude. He avoided all intercourse with women and scarcely ever spoke to any one. Visitors were not received at his house, and his dealings with the few servants who attended to his wants were carried on by means of notes which he left on the hall table. Lord Brougham, who saw him at one or two meetings of the Royal Society, has recorded "the shrill cry of the old philosopher as he shuffled from room to room, seeming to be annoyed if looked at, but

His analysis of water

Computation of earth's density

sometimes timidly approaching to hear what was
passing among others. On all points which had no
scientific bearing, Cavendish was coldly indifferent;
but when the discovery of a new truth in science
was announced, he seemed to glow all over.''

At the time of Cavendish's death, public opinion
in England was wrought up by the parliamentary
storms raging over the Walcheren fiasco, and the
questions that arose out of them relative to the
privileges of the House of Commons and the liberty of the press. Mr. Percival, who had become
Prime Minister after the death of the Duke of Portland, first tried to weaken the opposition by drawing Lord Grey and Lord Grenville over to his
side. Failing in this, he formed a cabinet, with
the Marquis of Wellesley as Secretary of State for
Foreign Affairs, the Earl of Liverpool Secretary of
War, and Mr. Ryder for Home Secretary. On the
meeting of Parliament, late in January, the opposition, headed by Canning, Grenville and Grey, immediately called for a censure of the government for
its conduct of foreign affairs, involving the military
expeditions to Holland and Spain. Lord Chatham
had to resign his master generalship of ordnance.
The Ministry yet prevailed by a majority of ninety-
six, and finally obtained a parliamentary vote of
thanks for Lord Wellington and his army in the
Peninsula. During the parliamentary debates over
the course of the war, all gazetteers were excluded
from the house. Sheridan objected to this in a
great speech on the liberty of the press, and was
supported by Cobden, but their motion was de-

Change in
British
Ministry

Conduct
of war
criticised

feated. This outcome was severely censured by a London debating club called the "British Forum." For this insult to Parliament, John Gail Jones, the president of the society, was haled before the House and was committed to Newgate jail. The editor of the "Morning Chronicle," who pleaded his own case, and likewise his printer, were let off. Sir Francis Burdette objected to such summary measures as an infringement of the right of all Englishmen to jury trial, as secured by Magna Charta. His motion to liberate Jones was overwhelmingly defeated. Sir Francis Burdette repeated his arguments in an open letter to his constituents, in which he denounced the action of Parliament. For this infringement of parliamentary privilege Burdette was committed to the Tower by a vote of 190 against 152 of his colleagues. Burdette's house was surrounded by a mob, and the warrant for his arrest had to be executed by a large force of constabulary and soldiers. Riots occurred around the Tower and in Piccadilly. In the street fighting that followed a number of persons were killed. Remonstrances and petitions about the matter were sent to Parliament from all over England. Sir Francis Burdette brought an action in law against the Speaker of the House and the sergeant-of-arms, but lost his case. When he was finally released at the prorogation of Parliament, his supporters in great numbers paraded London with placards bearing such inscriptions as "Magna Charta," "Trial by Jury," etc. At night all the lower districts of London were illuminated. The episode served to

Agitation over liberty of the press

Francis Burdette imprisoned

establish the custom of newspaper reports of parliamentary debates as a public privilege. The "British Register" of that year commented on this as follows: "When the House of Commons first connived at the introduction of booksellers, or their reporters in the gallery, they were little aware of the consequences that were to follow this indulgence. A breed of satellites have now fastened themselves on Parliament, whom it is irksome and grievous to endure, yet whom it would be dangerous in different respects altogether to exclude."

Reporters' privileges in Parliament

While the mistakes of the British Ministry were thrashed out in Parliament the Spanish situation became ever more complicated. The national struggle for independence in Spain had produced a political revolution there unforeseen by Spaniards, Frenchmen, or Englishmen. The threatening attitude of the various provincial juntas, and of the old royal councils, induced the Supreme Junta, itself an irregular and revolutionary body, to convoke the Cortes or National Parliament for March 1, 1810. According to old Spanish usage, there were three chambers in which three estates were entitled to representation; to wit, the clergy, nobility and the people. The Spanish Liberals now demanded a single chamber for all three estates, while the Junta, headed by Jovellanos, declared for a double chamber, with an Upper House for the clergy and nobles, and a House of Commons for the representatives of the people. Writs of election had already been issued when the advance of the French drove the Junta from Seville to Cadiz. Here the Junta found

Cortes convoked in Spain

itself divided among its own members, and fell into such execration that by the end of January, 1810, it resigned its powers into the hands of a fivefold regency. On January 20 and 21, the French forced their way over the Sierra Morena, and marched on Beylen, Cordova, and Seville. Soult sent a division under Sebastiani against Granada. The French defeated ten thousand Spaniards under Ariesaga and Frere, and captured all the artillery. Granada opened her gates to the French, and a battalion of Swiss who had deserted to the British eagerly returned to French allegiance. Sebastiani left a strong garrison at the Alhambra and pushed on to Malaga. There he defeated a large body of insurgents. On the battlefield some fifteen hundred dead bodies were found, among them many peasants, priests and monks. The capture of Malaga was of great importance to the French, since it cut off communications between the maritime provinces of Spain on the east coast and the region of Cadiz and Gibraltar. The whole peninsula was cut in two parts by a military cord stretching from Bayonne through Burgos and Valladolid to Madrid, and thence by Toledo, Andujar and Jaen to the Gulf of Malaga. In Portugal, Wellington prepared for another French invasion by establishing a cordon of his own along the line of the mountain ridges, running from the Tagus to the sea. While the English army wintered near Almeida, Wellington, with the help of thousands of Portuguese, turned this mountain tract into an impregnable barrier by a double serried line of fortifica-

French successes in Peninsula

Wellington's preparations

tions. No rumor of the work was allowed to reach the French or even the babbling newspapers at home.

On the first day of February, Seville surrendered to Marshal Victor. The Supreme Junta, on the approach of the French army to the Guadalquivir, fled to the Isle of Leon. Of the eighty-six members of **Flight of junta** the Junta, most betook themselves to Cadiz, some went over to the French, while others fled to England and America. Thus Count Tilly found means to reach Philadelphia with a round sum of three million dollars. By the middle of February, Cadiz was invested by the French, with King Joseph acting as commander-in-chief. The French forces before Cadiz were about fifty thousand, while the Spaniards, Portuguese and English, numbered twenty thousand, with a fleet of eight sail-of-the-line and a dozen smaller ships. In anticipation of the siege, the South American loyalists sent large contributions of money; and flour in great abundance was brought from the United States. The siege went on but slowly. About the middle of March a terrific storm wrecked half of the Spanish fleet and drove the ships ashore. Later, a party **Siege of Cadiz** of two thousand French prisoners succeeded in escaping from the bay of Cadiz on board of their prison ship. It was a notable exploit. During this interminable siege, as at Saragossa and Gerona, Spanish women figured in the fighting on the ramparts. The French during this same time made attempts at Valencia and Hostalrich. From Valencia they were beaten back with great loss. At Hostalrich, the Spanish column under O'Donnell tried to relieve the garrison, but was beaten back after a desperate battle at Vich, in which thirty-five hundred Spaniards were taken prisoners, with almost as many killed and wounded. General Souham, commanding the French forces, had an eye shot out. On the night of May 12, the garrison of Hostalrich made a desperate attempt to escape from the city, but they were caught in the act and slain almost to a man. General Suchet captured Lerida with all its stores by refusing to let the women and children escape, and he also took Mequineza, the key of the Ebro. Valencia and Tortoza were invested in turn. Ney's corps settled down to besiege Ciudad Rodrigo.

Battle of Vich

Fall of Hostalrich

French siege of Ciudad Rodrigo

While matters stood at such low ebb in Spain, the tide of revolutionary spirit rose in South America. Early in the year the Junta at Sevilla granted direct representation to the South American colonists, proclaiming them to be an integral part of the Spanish nation. "At last you are raised to the dignity of free men," declared the Junta. "The times are already past in which, under an unsupportable yoke, you were the victims of absolutism, ambition and ignorance. Bear in mind that in electing your representative to the Cortes, your destiny will no longer depend on kings, ministers or governors, but is in your own hands." The regency at Cadiz, while confirming this measure, granted to the South American colonists but one deputy for every million inhabitants. Spain had one representative for every hundred thousand, re-

South American affairs

gardless of the fact that the greater part of the peninsula was under French dominion. At the same time French commissioners arrived in South America to demand the oath of fidelity to King Joseph. The arrival of the hateful "afrancesados," as they were called, was like a spark in a powder mill. All South America was ripe for revolution, and as of one accord the colonists rose in the north, south, east and west to throw off the yoke of Europe. The movemer' had already started in Mexico, when the viceroy, Don José de Iturrigaray, was deposed by the people and superseded by a marshal of the army. After a few months of his rule, the central Junta in Spain ordered him superseded by the archbishop in Mexico. He was replaced in turn by the regency of Cadiz, who appointed General Vinegas as viceroy. In these rapid changes of rule the people discovered how easy it was to overturn a government. The doctrine, that on the disappearance of a monarch his sovereignty reverted to the people, found an enthusiastic advocate in Hidalgo, a Mexican curate, who had already been disciplined by the Inquisition for maintaining dangerous opinions. In Venezuela, there was Don Simon Bolivar, who had sworn to free his country years ago on the Monte Sacro of Rome, after he saw Napoleon place the iron crown of Lombardy on his own head. Bolivar had just returned to his country after a personal study of republican institutions in the United States. On April 18, Wednesday of Holy Week, the Spanish commission arrived in Caracas, and demanded adhesion to the Regency

Marginal notes:

Mexican viceroy deposed

Hidalgo

Bolivar

in Cadiz. Bolivar spoke the word which set South
America aflame. "This power," he said, "which
fluctuates in such a manner in Spain and does not
secure itself, invites us to establish a Junta of
our own and to govern ourselves." The next
day the Municipal Council of Caracas invited Emperan, the Spanish governor of the colony, to attend their session, with the intention of offering
him the presidency of the Junta. José Cortez Ma-
dariga, a Chilian, rushed into the council room and
exclaimed: "Beware what you do. You are blind
if you put yourselves at the mercy of the representative of Spain." Emperan fled to the balcony and
addressed the crowd below: "Are you content with
me?" he asked. "No," shouted the crowd, "we Revolution
don't want you!" "Then I don't want you!" re- of Caracas
torted Emperan, and gave up his governorship.
That day the Junta of Caracas was proclaimed. It
refused to recognize the regency of Cadiz, and
banished the former governor to the United States.
The revolution had been accomplished without a
gunshot.

Previous to this there had been similar revolts,
the first of which was instigated by Miranda in 1806.
In 1809 the colonial authorities of Quito were over-
turned and a governing Junta was set up with a
proclamation that "law has assumed its authority
under the Equator." In the same year the Creoles Other
of Peru rose in Chuquisaca and La Paz, and set up revolts
an independent government composed exclusively
of Americans. Both these revolts were put down
and the leaders were hanged or shot. The success

of the revolution of Caracas inspired the other colonists to follow Bolivar's example. The viceroy of Nueva Granada was exiled to Cartagena. In Buenos Ayres an assembly of six hundred natives rose against Portugal, and deprived the viceroy, Balthazar de Cisneros, of power. The Portuguese soldiers were beaten and retreated to Montevideo, but here, too, as in all other provinces of upper Peru, the revolution prevailed, and an independent Junta was established. In lower Peru the colonial government of Lima was able to hold the revolutionists in check. Chile likewise rose in 1810 and succeeded in throwing off the Spanish yoke, though the Creoles, who fought for independence, had nothing but the most primitive arms. In Mexico the new viceroy Vinegas's demand of money for the support of the Spanish cause was met by Hidalgo's Grito de Dolores, "The Cry of Wrongs." It was taken up by a couple of hundred insurgents. They succeeded in seizing the stronghold of Guanuajato. Driven from there, Hidalgo established an independent government on Guadalajara, where he maintained himself for the rest of the year. In western Florida, filibusters from the United States assaulted the Spanish fort at Baton Rouge. Louis Grand Pré, the commandant, died as its sole defender. Western Florida was turned over to the United States. Even Cuba became uneasy.

The divorce of the American colonies from Spain and Portugal was effected at a turn in their career when further union was only hurtful to all concerned. When these revolutions

Margin notes: Buenos Ayres / Montevideo / Chile / Mexico / Baton Rouge

broke out in 1810, there was but one other re
public in the world—the United States of North
America. Switzerland had long since become a
dependency of the French empire. It was confidently asserted by European statesmen that South
America would have to revert either to France or
to England as soon as one of these two great con-
testants should prevail over the ciner. Otherwise
nothing but barbarism was expected. That South
America did not fall into British hands at this
time can be ascribed only to the forbidding attitude of the United States. Already an English
fleet but a few years before had seized Buenos
Ayres and Montevideo, only to be ousted again
by the native settlers. Both ports then had to
sustain a long and formidable blockade on the British
part of British cruisers. During the course of the seizures
year 1810, the British also seized the French colonies of Guadeloupe and Isle de Bourbon. Finally
Java and Isle de France fell into the hands of the
British, who thus were made absolute masters of
the sea.

Napoleon's new Prime Minister, Fouché, conceived a fantastic plan to offset this loss of French
prestige beyond the seas. Early in the year he sent
a secret agent named Fagan to suggest that if Great
Britain would yield Spain, France would join in
creating out of the Spanish-American colonies an
empire for Ferdinand VI. of Spain. From Louisiana it was suggested a monarchy might be created Plans of
Fouché
for the French Bourbons. Fouché was instigated to and
Aaron Burr
this in a measure by Aaron Burr, who had betaken

himself to Paris and there presented a memoir to the French Government, showing that the destruction of the United States could be accomplished by a combined attack of French troops from Canada and from Louisiana. Fouché's proposals were contemptuously dismissed by the British Ministry. Napoleon learned of Fouché's secret correspondence by an accident, as he was about to set out with his new empress on their wedding journey to Holland.

Fouché dismissed

"Fouché," said the Emperor, "is always thrusting his ugly foot into other people's shoes." The overzealous Minister was dismissed and was exiled to Italy as Governor of Rome.

The marriage between Napoleon and Marie Louise had been first solemnized at Vienna, on March 11, without Napoleon. On this occasion he felt called upon to write an autograph letter to Emperor

Napoleon's betrothal

Francis as his prospective father-in-law. Hitherto, owing to the fact that Napoleon could not write legibly, all his letters had been written by secretaries.

"What a terrible business it was for him," wrote his secretary, Méneval. "At last, having taken infinite pains, he succeeded in writing a letter which was fairly legible. He told me to rectify the badly formed letters in such a way that my corrections would not be noticeable. I did my work as best I could, and sent it off to 'His Majesty, Sir, my Brother.' Of course Emperor Francis never knew what trouble it had caused the writer."

When Marie Louise left Vienna, the people rioted on the streets. She was conveyed in triumph

through southern Germany and through France.
It was arranged that she was to meet her husband
for the first time at the Chateau of Compiègne, in
the presence of all his court. To save her from
embarrassment, Napoleon set out from Compiègne
with no other escort but Murat. He entered her
carriage and embraced her cordially. Marie Louise,
who was then but eighteen years old, was agreeably
surprised by his youthful appearance. "Your portrait, Sire," she said, "has not done you justice."
Later she confessed that she had looked forward
to her union with Napoleon in terror. How Napoleon was regarded in the imperial household in
Vienna may be gathered from the fact that the
young princes used to burn him in effigy, a game
which they called "roasting the monster." The re-
petition of the marriage ceremony in France, though
a mere formality, was made a state occasion. Napoleon gave a dowry of 725 francs to each of six
thousand young girls who on the day of his French
nuptials should marry a soldier of his army. On
April 2, the Emperor and Empress, seated in the
coronation carriage of glass and gold, with a train
of a hundred equipages following behind them, entered Paris by the Arc de Triomphe. Three hundred thousand persons thronged the Champs Elysées.
Hand in hand Napoleon and Marie Louise passed
into the Tuileries through the long gallery of magnificent paintings which connects it with the Louvre. In the evening, amid brilliant illuminations,
they received the nuptial blessing. From her retreat at Navarre, Josephine wrote: "Your Majesty

Wedding with Marie Louise

shall never be troubled in your happiness by any expression of my grief." Napoleon said to his friends: "Josephine is indeed the best woman in France." At St. Helena Napoleon freely recognized that his divorce was a mistake. He then said: "A son by Josephine would have completed my happiness, not only from a political point of view, but as a source of domestic happiness. As a political result it would have secured to me the possession of the throne. The French people would have been as much attached to the son of Josephine as they were to the King of Rome, and I should not have set my foot in an abyss covered with flowers."

Napoleon's retrospect

From Paris Napoleon set out on his wedding journey to Holland. Napoleon's brother, there, King Louis, had come under extreme disfavor by his lenient attitude toward his Dutch subjects, who carried on their commerce in spite of the continental blockade. To help out the French deficit of fifty millions, much to the disgust of Louis, Napoleon gave orders to seize all American ships that should enter Dutch ports in violation of his Milan decree. To the Prussian government, Napoleon wrote at the same time: "Let the American ships enter your ports! Seize them afterward! You shall deliver the cargoes to me, and I will take them in part payment of Prussia's war debt." To the American Minister, Napoleon thus explained his attitude: "If American ships have been sequestered in French ports, France only imitates the example given her by the American government. The American act

Louis Bonaparte's troubles

American ships seized

of Congress of March 1, 1809, which orders in certain cases the sequestration and confiscation of French ships, that are excluded from American ports, practically interdicts France to Americans. In the ports of Holland, of Spain, of Italy and of France, American vessels have been seized because the Americans have seized French vessels." Napoleon's official orders in that sense, known as the decree of Rambouillet, were issued in March. The total amount of the American seizures was then estimated by Napoleon at six million dollars. The American consul at Paris reported that between April, 1809, and April, 1810, fifty-one American ships had been seized in France, forty-four in Spain, twenty-eight in Naples, and eleven in Holland. Had Louis carried out his brother's orders, the seizures in Dutch ports would have been far more numerous. Louis was summoned to France, and by way of punishment was compelled to sign the Dutch treaty of March 16, in which he ceded the provinces of Brabant, Zeeland and a part of Guelders to France. All Dutch commerce with the outside world was to be suppressed. When Louis returned to Holland, he could not bring himself to carry out these humiliating pledges. He tried to evade the surrender of the American ships to France, and objected to the invasion of his kingdom by French troops. During riotous public proceedings in Amsterdam, Louis publicly expressed his sympathy with the cause of the Dutch people against his brother. Napoleon wrote to Louis: "They who do not love France, do not love me.

Decree of Rambouillet

Treaty of Holland

Your Majesty will find in me a brother, if I find in you a Frenchman. But should you be unmindful of the sentiments which attach you to our common country, you must not take it amiss if I disregard those which nature formed between us." In private, Napoleon said angrily: "Louis has been spoiled by reading the works of Rousseau." A French army of occupation was sent into Holland. The Exchange at Rotterdam was turned into a stable for French cavalry. About the middle of June, a French column of 20,000 moved on Amsterdam. At this, Louis left his capital and abdicated the throne of Holland. In a farewell address to the Dutch people he said: "I have the cruel satisfaction, yet now the only one that is left me, that I have fulfilled my obligations to Holland. . . . I should be much to blame if I consented to retain the title of King, being no longer anything but an instrument, no longer commanding in my own capital, and perhaps soon not even in my own palace. By doing so I should betray my conscience, my people and my royal duty," etc. Louis went to Toeplitz in Bohemia without a single attendant. To his wife, Hortense, then living in Paris, he wrote a letter forbidding her to accept anything from Napoleon. Napoleon was more than vexed. Savary relates that when Napoleon received the news of his brother's flight and abdication, he sat silent for several minutes. After that momentary stupor, he became greatly agitated. "It cannot be denied," adds Savary, "that his brother's conduct seriously affected the Emperor's cause in public

Invasion of Netherlands

Louis Bonaparte resigns

opinion." Napoleon made matters worse by first refusing to recognize Louis's abdication as not authorized by him, and next by his annexation of all the Netherlands, "as a mere affluvium of the rivers of France." Amsterdam was made the third city of the Empire. Of the effect of these measures, Napoleon said in after years at St. Helena: "My annexation of Holland produced a most unfavorable impression throughout Europe, and contributed greatly to lay the foundation of our misfortunes." While Louis Bonaparte went into voluntary exile to Bohemia, Lucien· Napoleon's other refractory brother, prepared to ship his family to America. The vessel was intercepted by British cruisers on the way, and Lucien was taken to England, where he remained in like voluntary exile.

In England, Napoleon's continental system wrought havoc in all commercial enterprises. Financial failures became alarmingly frequent as the common people fell into pauperism. Many eminent merchants committed suicide, among them Francis Baring and Abraham Goldschmid. Paul Benfield, the East-Indian millionnaire, died in extreme poverty. Napoleon, observing these effects, gave another turn to the screw. He issued a decree that all English manufactures found in France, Holland or the German states, should be burned. Another blow for England was the absolute accession of Sweden to the continental system. Late in spring, the Crown Prince of Sweden had died suddenly. During a parade of troops at Qvidinge he suddenly dropped dead from his horse. Reports

of attempts to poison him had been in circulation
before his death. A post-mortem examination by
the celebrated chemist Berzelius, favored this sup-
position. The people became greatly excited. At
the funeral of the prince in Stockholm, the mob
killed Count Furzen, marshal of the realm, who was
suspected of complicity in the death of the prince.
Sweden was once more without an heir-apparent
to the throne. Those in power were anxious to
see a good soldier put in charge, who could recapture Finland. Count Otto Moerner, who had been
a prisoner in Jutland when Marshal Bernadotte
commanded that province, conceived the original
scheme of placing him on the throne. Bernadotte
consented in a guarded manner, and so did Napoleon, though privately he declared himself averse
Bernadotte to the project. Count Moerner's act was disavowed
called to
Sweden by the Swedish Mi...try, but Moerner carried on
his agitation with so much success that the Swedish Riksdag selected Bernadotte. Thus Bernadotte,
though by no means among the most brilliant of the
military adventurers produced by the French Revolution, found himself at the goal of all, on as high a
plane as the Bonapartes and their immediate relatives, Murat and Eugene Beauharnais.

Jean Baptiste Jules Bernadotte, at the outbreak
of the French Revolution, was a common soldier
in the Royal Marine corps. After ten years' ser-
His
previous vice he had been promoted only to a sergeantcy.
career
The disorders of the Revolution gave him his
chance. On the flight of his superior officers, he
was made captain of his company. General Kleber

took him unaer his patronage and made him a
colonel. After Kleber's victory at Fleurus, Bernadotte was given command of a brigade. He
served with Napoleon throughout the first Italian
campaign. Having opposed the latter, at the time
of his coup d'état, on the 18th of Brumaire, he
found means of making peace with him through his
marriage with the sister-in-law of Joseph Bonaparte,
one Mademoiselle Clairy, the daughter of a grocer
in Marseilles. Though thus related to Napoleon by
marriage, the two never got on well together. His
career as a general was attended by varying success.
Altogether he saw so much service, that by dint of
experience alone he was bound to learn the art of
war. Thus he distinguished himself at the crossing
of the Rhine at Neuwied, and in the battle of Austerlitz. At other times his lack of success exasperated Napoleon. This was notably the case during
the early part of the last Austrian war, and again
at the battle of Wagram, when he was sent home
in disgrace. As military governor of Jutland and
Pomerania, he showed himself an able administrator, and his treatment of the Swedish captives,
who were then under his charge, was so humane
that he endeared himself to them forever. It was
to this that he owed his elevation to the Swedish throne. The last obstacle was overcome when
Napoleon lent him a million francs. Bernadotte
joined the Lutheran Church at Elsinor. As he
landed in Sweden, on October 10, 1810, he was declared heir-apparent as Prince Charles, or Charles
Johann, as he called himself henceforward. By

Marginal notes:
Family connection with Bonaparte

Military fortunes

Bernadotte made Prince of Sweden

his politic conduct and diplomatic manners, he
soon gained such an ascendency that the throne
of Sweden fell to him as by right.

Those Swedish politicians, who had thought by
their selection of Bernadotte to please Napoleon
and gain a strong point with him, were mistaken.
Napoleon revealed his true motives in consenting
to their choice in a private conversation with
Metternich.   To him he said: "For my part I

Napoleon's comment am delighted to be rid of him, I ask nothing
better than his removal from France.   He is
one of those old Jacobins with his head in the
wrong place. . . . Yet a French marshal on the
throne of Gustavus Adolphus is one of the best
tricks that could be played on England."

Other measures to hurt England were not neglected.   Throughout this time, the war in Spain and
Portugal had been carried on with obstinate vigor.

French capture Ciudad Rodrigo On the day after the French flag was hoisted over
Amsterdam, Ciudad Rodrigo, at the end of a long
siege, was compelled to surrender to Marshal Ney.
His troops were about to storm the last breach.
Half a year had ∙passed since the French had resumed the offensive in Spain.   Battle on battle
had been won, and stronghold after stronghold
had fallen.   Portugal alone remained unsubdued.
To hold Portugal, Lord Wellington called for reinforcements to bring the British fighting force up
to 30,000 men.   He also asked for a financial subsidy of several million pounds sterling, wherewith

Welling- ton in Portugal to keep 60,000 soldiers on their feet.   The British
Ministry, though startled at these figures, granted

Wellington's demand, and undertook to pay an annual subsidy, £1,000,000, to Portugal. Wellington had himself made marshal-general of Portugal, independent of the Portuguese Regency. By virtue of this authority he revived the ancient military laws of the kingdom, by which he brought 56,000 Portuguese to the colors, and forced them to devastate their own country along the entire line of the invasion, four hundred miles long. The French forces available for the invasion numbered over 80,000. The famous triple line of defence of the The Torres Vedras was Wellington's own idea. Between the lines lay a wasted country in which no invader could maintain himself for any length of time. The innermost line of intrenchments was thrown up in case disaster should make sudden embarkation imperative. For the same purpose, an English fleet was held in readiness wherein to embark the army at short notice. As the ravages Heavy English subsidies of the war increased, all Portugal had to be fed by England.

During the siege of Ciudad Rodrigo, the English lines of outpost under General Craufurd were gradually forced back on the banks of the Agueda. Wellington felt himself too weak to succor Ciudad Rodrigo, and had to see the place fall, though within easy striking distance. On July 24, General Craufurd, having kept on the other side of the Coa against Wellington's express orders, was British outposts overwhelmed by Ney's whole army. His forces thrown back were thrown across the river in great confusion. At the bridge of Castillo Boin, the British made a stand, and successfully held up the advancing columns of the French. A thousand Frenchmen fell in trying to force the passage. Ciudad Rodrigo furnished the French with a good base of supplies, and Wellington's situation soon became embarrassing. The corps of Ney and Reynier were too strong to be attacked by the British, and on the other side Masséna was approaching with the Spanish army. The Spanish generals, discontented with Wellington's abandonment of Ciudad Rodrigo, grew restive, and undertook operations on their own responsibility. Romana and Ballesteros, in a joint action at Benveneda, were routed by Mortier. Their defeat was a serious matter for the defence of Portugal. It might have proved disastrous, had an English expedition landing at Moguer not drawn Mortier's forces rearward. Still more serious for Wellington was the fall of Almeida and the accidental explosion of the British powder-magazine at Albuquerque, which killed four hundred men. In September, Masséna's forces at last invaded Portugal for the third time. Masséna, now grown cold with age and honor, was in complete ignorance concerning the strength of the lines of Torres Vedras. Even the English officers and soldiers generally believed that their unpropitious campaign, like that of Sir John Moore, would end with embarkation for England. Indeed, the British Ministry was prepared for such an event. Lord Liverpool, writing to a friend in Lisbon about this time, opened his letter thus: "As it is probable, the army will embark in September." Deceived by imperfect reconnoissance,

Marginal notes:

Stand at Castillo Boin

Spanish defeat of Benveneda

Fall of Almeida

Painted by Sir Thomas Lawrence

WELLINGTON

Masséna threw the main column of his army, numbering 61,000 men, on the worst road in Portugal, on the right bank of the Mondego. The British and Portuguese retreated all along the line. They concentrated their forces in a formidable position on the Sierra Busaca in front of Coimbra. Masséna's slow approach gave Wellington a chance to rally his retreating troops. Before daybreak, on September 29, the columns of Ney and Reynier stormed the heights. They were driven from the crest again by the countercharge of British reserves. Thenceforward the fight was for the possession of the hilltops. During this battle occurred the famous incident of the Portuguese girl, who drove an ass laden with baskets straight through the contending lines of both armies, apparently unmindful of the fact that she was in the thick of a bloody battle. By nightfall the French gave up the attempt to gain the Sierra. They had lost two generals and forty-five hundred men, while the British and Portuguese lost thirteen hundred. Though Wellington won his battle, he had been compelled to fight it at too great a risk. He himself in later years characterized it as a political battle and therefore a mistake. On the part of Masséna it was a still worse mistake, as his army was not in a condition to fight. Napoleon, while commenting on this battle, said of Masséna that his dispositions for battle were always bad.

The French reached Coimbra on the first day of October, just as their fortnight's supply of bread was exhausted. Three days afterward, Masséna

Battle of Sierra Busaca

A mistake on both sides

pushed on. The next day Colonel Trant, operating with a detached column in the neighborhood, galloped into Coimbra with several squadrons of yeomanry, and seized the French stores and hospitals in Masséna's rear. Nearly five thousand prisoners fell into the hands of a small British force. The brilliance of the exploit was tarnished by acts of barbarous atrocity.

Masséna did not let this deter him from pushing on. By the middle of October he came up to the line of the Torres Vedras. The first line stretched from the Alhandra on the Tagus to the mouth of the Zizandro on the sea-coast, twenty-nine miles away. The next line, about ten miles further back, extended from Quintello on the Tagus to the mouth of the St. Lorenzo, twenty-four miles away. An innermost short line, intended to cover the possible embarkation, ran from the Passo d'Arcos on the Tagus to the Tower of Junquena, a distance of three miles. Altogether the three lines included fifty miles of fortifications, a hundred and fifty separate forts, with six hundred mounted guns, commanding good ranges. Here the combined British and Portuguese armies were reinforced by Romana's force of six thousand Spaniards. In all, 120,000 fighting men were stationed between the lines behind ramparts of stone walls and crossed trees twenty feet in thickness. As Napier, the great historian of the Peninsular war, has remarked: "Not even the Romans ever reared greater works in their time."

Masséna, when he realized the strength of the

Torres Vedras, sat down with his army at Santarem. The war thenceforth was reduced to a blockade. For the Portuguese this proved a severe trial of endurance, and 10,000 men of their line deserted before the end of the year. The generals on either side were loth to risk a battle without distinct advantage, and therefore preferred to wait for reinforcements. Thus the war in the Peninsula dragged itself out with the French besieging Cadiz on one side, and Wellington holding them in check before the Torres Vedras on the other. Late in November, the French forces in the north had to fall back on their base, and Wellington descended from the Torres Vedras to harass their retreat.

Peninsular war at standstill

In England there was great reluctance to reinforce Wellington, largely on account of the King's incapacity for public affairs. The spell of insanity from which he had suffered in 1788, and intermittently since that time, returned during the continued illness of his youngest daughter, Amalie. When she died in the autumn the old king grew unmanageable. Parliament appointed a commission of inquiry preparatory to appointing the Prince of Wales regent of the kingdom. During this period of political depression, the arts and sciences flourished in an unusual degree. The end of this year was made signal in literary annals by the first appearance of Shelley's early lyrics, and by the simultaneous publication of Southey's "Curse of Kahama" and Walter Scott's "Lady of the Lake."

George III. incapacitated

Rise of English letters

From a political-economical point of view, gloom at this time seemed to hang over a large part of

Europe. Austria passed through a financial crisis, worse than ever before, aggravated as it was by an

issue of spurious government bonds that had been printed by Napoleon before the conclusion of the peace of Schœnbrunn. An affliction fell on the royal

house and people of Prussia by the death of Queen Louise, the idol of her country. This sad event in a measure spoiled the popular rejoicings over the

long-deferred foundation of the University of Berlin, which began its academic career under the leadership of Wilhelm von Humboldt. From the start this university, like the older universities of Germany, became a hotbed of patriotic agitation against Napoleon and the aggressions of the French. By the students of the universities, Napoleon's high-

handed annexation of the three Hanseatic cities, Hamburg, Bremen and Lubeck, at this time, was openly resented as a national affront.

In the south of Europe great preparations were made during this period, by King Joachim Murat of Naples, for an invasion of Sicily. To this end 37,000 troops and a flotilla were collected. Early in the summer, Murat had declared he would be in Palermo by the middle of August. The people of Sicily were called upon to throw off the British yoke. Sir John Stuart gathered together a Sicilian army and his own fifteen hundred troops, and encamped them along the coast from the Straits

of Messina to the Faro Pont. A strong British squadron cruised up and down the coast of Sicily. A debarkation of 3,500 Neapolitan and Corsican troops was effected only by September 18. After a sharp encounter they were driven back to their boats with a loss of eight hundred prisoners. On October 3, Murat gave up the attempt with a proclamation to his soldiers that the expedition had been adjourned.

In spite of the armistice supposed to exist in the Balkans, the Russian troops there continued their encroachments against the Turks. When the Sultan refused to countenance their aggressions the war recommenced. The Russians conquered nearly all the forces on the Danube, but were defeated in Bulgaria by the Grand Vizier. The Russians took Vidin, Custov, Georgioi, but their progress was arrested at Rustshuk, Shumla and Varna, with heavy losses on both sides. Field-Marshal Kemenski reconquered Bulgaria as far as the Balkans and gained a brilliant victory at Batyma. The Servians, too, were successful in almost all their operations against the Turks. Pressed as the Sultan was by these troubles in the Balkans, he was able to send troops into Syria to suppress the rebellion of the Wachabites, and he also sent a fleet into the Black Sea, as a demonstration against the Crimea. At last the imminence of a rupture with France forced the Czar to withdraw several divisions of his army from the Danube.

War in the Balkans

Withdrawal of Russian troops

The estrangement between Alexander and Napoleon was gradually becoming more acute. Napoleon vented his discontent at the lukewarm support of Russia during his war with Austria, by favoring the growth of the Duchy of Warsaw, and by his abrupt abandonment of the project of his marriage with a Russian princess. It was at this time that

Lésur published the famous book entitled: "The Progress of the Russian Power," in which we meet for the first time with the apochryphal "Will of Peter the Great," enjoining upon his descendants never to lose sight of Constantinople. To the personal bitterness of feeling between Alexander and Napoleon, was added the increasing rivalry of the two nations on the Danube, and the commercial distress occasioned in Russia by Na-

poleon's continental blockade. The ruble, which was worth sixty-seven kopeks in 1807, was worth not more than twenty-five kopeks in 1811. When Napoleon, emboldened by his easy annexation of the Canton of Vallis, in Switzerland, without further warning announced the annexation of the

Duchy of Oldenburg in the north, the patience of Alexander was exhausted. First he issued a formal protest against this spoliation of his kinsman, the Duke of Oldenburg. He followed this up by an imperial decree breaking up the continental blockade as far as Russian ports were concerned. All colonial produce was to be admitted to Russia, while, on the other hand, he forbade

the importation of articles of luxury, to wit: silks, ribbons, embroideries, bronzes, porcelain and wine —in fine, all the chief products of France. After the pattern of Napoleon's latest measure, all contraband goods were ordered to be burned. This struck France in a tender spot. Napoleon, enraged, said to the Russian Ambassador: "I would rather have received a blow on the cheek."

1811

AT THE opening of the year 1811 in England the question of the insanity of King
George III. came up for final settlement.
The Prince of Wales was appointed regent pending The English regency
the king's indisposition. That he, too, regarded this
as a mere temporary measure was made plain by the
fact that he continued his father's ministers in office, although personally out of accord with them.
Furthermore, he refused to open Parliament in person, nor would he accept a special grant for his household pending the regency. The Crown's opening address to Parliament, accordingly, was written by the
ministers of the mad king, as heretofore. The most
important point of the speech was a pledge to continue the war in the Peninsula.

The campaign in Portugal had by this time taken
a turn distinctly favorable to the English. Masséna,
with his French army, lay in a devastated country
remote from all sources of supply, whereas Wellington was among a friendly people, with Lisbon for a
base of supplies and a harbor accessible to all the
vessels that the power and wealth of England could
freight. For a while brisk fighting continued. Dur- Fall of Tortosa
ing the month of January, Marshal Suchet took
Tortosa and Santo Filipe de Balagnier in Cata-

lonia. The important stronghold of Olivenza likewise fell into French hands after a short siege.
Soult now marched on Badajos. The untimely

Death of Romaña

death of the Marquis of Romaña, who commanded the Spanish forces in that region, proved
a great loss to the allies. He was succeeded by
General Mendozabal, who imprudently shut himself up in Badajos with six thousand men. The
siege of the French was enlivened by constant sallies and skirmishes beyond the works. On February 19, Marshal Soult crossed the Gebora and
beset Mendozabal's fortress with such fury that
the Spaniards were routed early in the forenoon.
The Spanish general escaped with difficulty. Nearly
eight hundred Spaniards were taken with all their
stores. The rest got into Badajos. Near Cadiz, in
the meanwhile, the English landed reinforcements
and marched on Victor's forces at Barosa. The
French attacked first and routed the Spanish auxiliaries under General La Peña. The British, under

Battle of Barosa

Graham, made a counter-attack, and in a brief but
hard-fought action overcame the French. Generals Ruffin and Chaudron-Rousseau, commanding the
French grenadiers, were both killed. The French
lost 2,500 men, two general officers, six guns and
one eagle. The British casualties were 1,200 soldiers and five officers. General Graham, who won
this battle, was so imbittered by the attempt of La
Peña to claim the victory as his own, that he fought
a duel about the matter, and then relinquished his
command, to join Wellington's army in Portugal.
Then Imas, the new Spanish commandant of Bada-

jos, misled by false reports of the French numbers, weakly surrendered the town to Soult. When the place fell, Mortier marched against Campo Major, and Latour-Maubourg seized Albuquerque and Valencia d'Alcantara. Great as were the successes of Soult, he was compelled to fall back into Andalusia when he heard of Masséna's retreat from Sant' Arem. Masséna claimed that Soult's delay before Badajos, instead of coming down the Tagus, was the chief cause of his failure. The more obvious reason lay in the inability of the French to maintain communications. The arrival of British reinforcements early in March, before the promised reinforcements from France could reach Masséna, compelled the latter to fall back. The French retreat was conducted in a masterly manner. A full week passed before the English got into touch with the French rearguard under Ney. In a brilliant rear action, at Redinha, Ney foiled his pursuers. At this point Masséna could have seized Coimbra, but a demonstration of British cavalry in his rear scared the French into a belief that British reinforcements had come by sea to the Mondego. Thereafter the retreat of the French became ever more hurried. At Fontecoberta, Masséna, having lingered too long, only escaped himself by plucking the feathers off his hat and making a dash for life through the lines of pursuing cavalry. At Castelnova, Marshal Ney was nearly captured by the Fifty-second British Infantry, which, advancing through a mist, found itself detached in the midst of the French rearguard. By a general

French capture Badajos

Masséna's retreat

Battle of Castelnova

engagement only did Wellington succeed in extricating this regiment from its dangerous predicament. In the face of heavy losses, Ney held the entire British line until the end of the day, and thus saved Masséna's retreat. During this retreat, all the resting-places of the French were burned down by the Spanish peasantry, and the country was ravaged for miles around. Colonel Napier, who was an eye-witness of some of the miseries of those days, has thus summed up the general impressions: "Every horror making war hideous attended this dreadful retreat. Distress, conflagration, death in all modes—from wound, from fatigue, from water, from the flames, from starvation; on every side unlimited ferocity. Even the body of John I. of Spain was wantonly exhumed from its tomb in the convent of Batalza and was pulled to pieces by British officers."

Ravages of war

British vandalism

When Masséna opened communication with the town of Almeida, his retreat was practically at an end. To retrieve his fallen fortunes, he determined to countermarch through Sabougal, thence to resume communications with Soult across the Tagus, and, by the valley of the Tagus, with Joseph. At this point long-standing quarrels between him and his marshals broke out afresh. Ney refused to march his division to Coimbra and was deprived of his command. The absence of so able a fighter as Ney was felt by the French at Belmonte, where a sharp action drove them back on Sabougal. Here the premature attack of a solitary British brigade brought on a general action. The brigade led by Beckwith took the nearest hill and held it against 15,000 Frenchmen. Around the hill the fight raged Battle of Sabougal for hours. The crest was stormed several times by both sides, and several notable exploits were performed. When the French were finally driven down the slope, three hundred dead bodies were found heaped up around a howitzer that stood on the top of the hill. It was no exaggeration for Wellington to report—"This was one of the most glorious actions British troops were ever engaged in."

The defeat at Sabougal spoiled Masséna's plans. He felt compelled to continue his retreat to Ciudad Rodrigo and Salamanca. On April 5, accordingly, the French crossed the frontier of Portugal and re- French evacuate Portugal entered Spain—a beaten army. The third invasion of Portugal had cost them 30,000 men. Wellington once more invested Almeida and Badajos.

Another brilliant two days' battle was fought at Fuentes Onoro on May 5 and 6, during which a Fuentes Onoro British battery of horse artillery cut its way out of a squadron of French dragoons. After the battle, a French soldier named Tillet dashed singly Tillet's exploit through the British lines to Almeida and brought them orders to evacuate that city. Bernier de Morano, the French commandant, destroyed all his guns and most of his fortifications, and then, with his garrison of 1,500 men, broke through the investing lines of the British, numbering 45,000. Stung Wellington foiled by this event, Wellington issued a severe rebuke to his officers.

The French reverses in Portugal were a serious

matter for Napoleon. Already he had determined
to bring matters to a point with Russia. For a
successful invasion of Russia, as he well knew, he
would need all the military resources of his empire.
Further reinforcements to Spain, therefore, were out
of the question. It became desirable, on the contrary, to withdraw some of the best French troops
from the Peninsula. As Metternich wrote in one of
his résumés of the situation for Emperor Francis:

"The Spanish war has recently taken a turn
which leaves France little hope of a favorable termination. The latest information speaks of the
very serious situation of Masséna's army. . . .
Further defeats in Spain might be the signal for
fresh disturbances in other directions. . . .
France is very far from being happy. Under
an iron rule, an unexampled finance, a tremendous load of taxes, an entire destruction of commerce, the idea of their internal condition would
be intolerable to the French were it not softened
by what appears like a calm after prolonged storms,
in comparison with other nations and their heavier
burdens. By his marriage with your Majesty's
daughter, Napoleon has found in his sense the
guarantee for peace which he formerly intended to
find in the overthrow of the Austrian throne. Yet
your Majesty will deign to observe that the following all-decisive question is now presented to us:
Can Austria prevent the outbreak of a fresh continental war with Russia? To this question, from
my innermost conviction, I give a decided 'no'."

Metternich knew whereof he wrote. But a short
time before, Napoleon had proposed to him the
terms of a defensive and offensive alliance against

Russia, and had in conversation with him fore-shadowed his plan of campaign for the forthcom-ing invasion of Russia.

During this interval an event had occurred which appeared to some a more substantial guarantee of peace than any other. On March 20, Marie Louise was delivered of a son. Napoleon presented the in-fant to the marshals of his empire, saying: "Here is the king of Rome!" Elaborate preparations had been made for the event. If it should prove to be a son a salute of one hundred and one guns was to be fired. Only twenty-one shots were destined for a princess. All France awaited the issue with sus-pense. In Paris the vast crowd collected before the Tuileries remained in deep silence until the twenty-first shot had been fired. When the twenty-second boomed forth the crowd went wild. Napo-leon himself said after the birth, which had proved very laborious for the mother, that he "would have preferred being present at a battle." Dr. Dubois told Napoleon that a second confinement would result in the death of the mother—a diag-nosis which was confuted eight years later. All the poets of France were invited to write some-thing on the occasion. Excepting Chateaubriand, most of them responded promptly. Among the best productions were those of Casimir Delavigne, and Pierre Lebrun. Gerard painted a charming half-length portrait of the baby, and Prud'hon portrayed the imperial child asleep in the shrub--bery.

Among those who came to congratulate Napo-

Birth of the King of Rome

leon in person were Prince Poniatovski of Poland
and King Joseph of Spain. Both had more serious matters to bring to the attention of the Emperor. Joseph told Napoleon that if the military

Relief for
Spain

government of Spain and the annexation of several
of its provinces were not repudiated, he would feel
constrained to abdicate. Napoleon was induced
thereby to promise relief. Joseph was advised to
convoke the Cortes. Poniatovski came to enter into
a full discussion of Napoleon's plans for the coming
invasion of Russia through Poland and the part that
was to be played in the affair by the Poles. With
Poland, Napoleon, so far, had played a double
game. He had promised Alexander not to favor
any enterprise which might tend to the re-estab-

The hopes
of Poland

lishment of Poland. On the other hand, he won
Poniatovski by his plans for the reconstruction of
Poland to serve as a buffer state against Russia.
The loss of Galicia to Austria was to be made up
by the restitution of the Illyrian provinces, while
the King of Saxony was to be consoled in some
other way for the loss of Warsaw.

Friction
with
Russia

By autumn, 1811, it was plain to most men that
war with Russia was on the cards. Shortly after
Napoleon's seizure of Oldenburg the Czar had remarked to Caulaincourt, the French ambassador at
St. Petersburg: "Tell your Emperor that the earth
here trembles beneath my feet. Tell him that here
in my own empire he has rendered my position
intolerable by his violation of treaties. Transmit
to him from me this candid and final declaration:
If once the war be fairly entered upon, either he,

Napoleon, or I, Alexander, must lose our crown."
Napoleon thus commented on these preliminary Alex-
pourparlers in later life: "Alexander and I were prophecy
in the condition of two boasters, who without wishing to fight were trying hard to frighten each other.
I should most willingly have maintained peace, Napoleon's
surrounded and overwhelmed as I was by unfavorable circumstances. All I have since learned con-
vinces me that Alexander was even less desirous
of war than myself." Financially considered, the
war was the worst thing that could happen to both
countries, yet neither sovereign could bring himself
to back down.

"Toward the end of the year 1811," says the
Duke Gaeta, at that time acting finance minister
of France, "I availed myself of the liberty which
the Emperor had always granted me in our private Situation
conversations to express to him my solicitude. 'A of France
new war,' I said, 'conducted at the distance of eight
hundred leagues, will impose upon us a great expense, of which but a small portion can be defrayed
by that distant country, which offers no resources.
What, then, must become of the present state of
our finances, particularly should the events of the
war prove disastrous?'

"'You speak thus,' answered Napoleon, 'because you do not fully comprehend our true political situation. I have strong reason to believe that
Austria, who will now march with us, soon will
march against us. . . . I cannot refrain from preparing for war without at the same time neglect-
ing to adopt measures to keep its ravages at a
distance. Thus I am driven to obey a necessity
which my position unhappily exacts, that I should
be now the fox, and now the lion.'"

With two world powers thus inevitably drifting into war, nothing remained for the other nations but to take sides quickly and fall into line. The various States of Lower and Middle Germany had long ago thrown in their lot with Napoleon. For Austria, Metternich struck a bargain that she was to aid France only as an independent ally, on Napoleon's promise that the Illyrian provinces should be restored to her. Prussia wavered for a while between Russia and France, but Russia had little use for a foreign alliance, since it was intended from the start to fight a purely defensive campaign on Russian soil. Napoleon, on the other hand, was in no mood to bargain for something which he could obtain by force. Late in 1811 he moved an army from the Rhine toward the Prussian frontier, and at the same time he raised the strength of the French garrisons on the Oder. With Prussia thus at his mercy, Napoleon dictated the terms of his proposed alliance, which meant, in short, unqualified submission, and the despatch of an auxiliary force of 20,000 Prussians to be incorporated in the French army. As Fyffe has expressed it in his "History of Modern Europe":

Napoleon's allies

Coercion of Prussia

"The sovereign who was about to be attacked by Napoleon and the sovereigns who sent their troops to Napoleon's support perfectly understood one another's position. The Prussian corps, watched and outnumbered by the French, might have to fight the Russians because they could not help it: the Austrians, directed by their own commanders, would do no serious harm to the Russians as long as the Russians did no harm to them. Should the Czar succeed

Spirit of the alliance

in giving a good account of his adversary, he would have no difficulty in coming to a settlement with his adversary's forced allies.''

When it was suggested to Bernadotte that he should furnish a quota of eight thousand Swedish soldiers to Napoleon, the temper of the new-made king was early shown. "Sweden, not being a member of the Rhenish confederation," he replied, "is under no obligation to furnish a quota of troops. Sweden maintains no more soldiers than are necessary for her own security."

Bernadotte defiant

Napoleon forthwith moved an army corps northward to threaten Scandinavia. While western Europe was thus once more drifting into a general war, an extraordinary act was perpetrated in the East. The threatening growth of power of the Mamelukes in Egypt was broken by a high-handed measure similar to that whereby Peter the Great broke the backbone of his notorious bodyguard, the Strelitzi. The reigning Khedive of Egypt, Mohammed Ali, some time previous to this had made his peace with the Mamelukes on the stipulation that the whole corps should serve as his household cavalry at his palace in Cairo. The greater part of them did so, but nevertheless they connived with the Pasha of Acre to overthrow Mohammed Ali should he fail in his war with the Wachabites. The plot was discovered by the Khedive and was foiled in a manner characteristic of the Orient. The Mamelukes were bidden to attend a solemn festival on the day when the Khedive's son was invested with the command of the expedi-

Troubles in Egypt

tion against the Wachabites. The Mamelukes were placed between the vanguard of Turkish infantry and a rearguard of household cavalry. At the instant when the infantry had entered the citadel, and the Mamelukes were passing between the inner and outer ramparts, the gates were suddenly closed. The Turkish troops fired on the helpless horsemen until most were slain. Those that surrendered were beheaded. Thus the flower of the Egyptian cavalry was destroyed, and Mohammed rested more secure on his viceregal throne.

In America, during those days, a new spirit was abroad. Two men had come to South America to help the patriot cause. One was Francisco Miranda, the old conspirator who had served with Lafayette under Washington, and had commanded a regiment under Dumouriez in the campaigns of Valmy and Jemappes. He soon made common cause with Bolivar in Venezuela. The other was San Martin, an Argentinian, who had likewise learned the trade of war in Europe, and who has been styled by the foremost South American historian as the "greatest of the Creoles of the New World." When San Martin returned to Argentina in 1811, he had some reputation as a soldier. Eight days after his arrival he was intrusted with the task of raising a squadron of cavalry. This was the origin of the famous South American regiment of mounted grenadiers, which fought in so many battles of the South American war of independence, and which gave to America nineteen generals and more than two hundred officers. San Martin and

(marginal notes)
Massacre of the Mamelukes

South America restive

Miranda

San Martin

His mounted grenadiers

his friend **Alvear** founded the secret society of
the Revolution known as the Lautaro Lodge.

In Caracas, similarly, Bolivar was the leading Bolivar
spirit of a patriotic society, which, like the Jacobin
Club of France, practically controlled the destinies
of the revolution. The society held its first meeting
on July 4, 1811. In a fiery speech, Bolivar called
upon them to lay the foundation stone of South
American liberty. The next day the Congress of
Caracas adopted Bolivar's resolution and Venezuela
was declared a republic. The declaration of inde- Indepen-
pendence was modelled on that of the United States Venezuela
of North America. It was declared that "the
united provinces of Venezuela are and ought to
be by act and right, free, sovereign and independent States, and they are absolved from any submission and dependence to the throne of Spain."
On the same day the Congress adopted the tricolor
flag of Miranda as the emblem of new liberty.

About the same time that Venezuela was declared
a republic, a new British commissioner, Mr. Foster,
arrived in Washington to settle up the "Chesapeake" affair and enter a formal protest against the Protests
American seizure of west Florida—"as an attempt seizure
contrary to every principle of public justice, faith
and national honor." His remonstrances were received in a Pickwickian sense. On July 5, Foster
wrote to Wellesley: "It was with real pain, my
lord, that I was forced to listen to arguments of
the most profligate nature; to wit, that other nations were not so scrupulous, that the United
States showed sufficient forbearance in not assist-

ing the insurgents of South America, and looking to their own interests in the present situation of the country."

Unfortunately for any settlement of the "Chesapeake" affair, another similar outrage had just occurred on the high seas, in which the Americans were the aggressors. On May 16, Commodore Rodgers of the American frigate "President," carrying forty-four guns, overhauled the British corvette-of-war, "Little Belt," carrying twenty guns. She was believed to be the "Guerriere," and was approached for the purpose of ascertaining whether an American sailor named Digio was on board. At nightfall the two ships came within hail, with the American coming to, close to windward, a manœuvre which British captains were disposed to resent. After an ineffectual hail, both ships fired upon one another, each claiming afterward that the other had fired first. A series of broadsides from the "President" disabled the British corvette. Captain Bingham of the "Little Belt" reported afterward: "I was obliged to desist from firing, as, the ship falling off, no gun would bear. Not a brace nor a bowline left, upper works all shot away; starboard pump also. I have to lament the loss of thirty-two men killed and wounded, among whom was the master." The "President's" loss was one boy wounded, and some damage to the rigging.

So it came that Foster found himself compelled to demand redress for the "Little Belt" affair, rather than to offer such for the "Chesapeake" outrage. President Madison showed himself little inclined

Marginal notes: "Little Belt" affair · Damages done

to enter into a discussion of either, unless the British restrictions on American shipping were withdrawn. The more Napoleon played fast and loose with his own promises to suspend operations of the continental blockade in favor of the United States, the firmer was the stand of the American government toward England. At last when Napoleon issued a decree admitting American ships to French ports, though holding to the American seizures already made, President Madison and his new Secretary of State, Monroe, turned completely against England. As in former times a petty fight against Indians, far in the American wilderness, began a convulsion which was to end in full-fledged war. It was a favorite saying of General Harrison, Governor of the Indian Territory of those days, that "the conduct of the Indians was a sure thermometer for the chances of war or peace between Englishmen and Americans."

Napoleon's American policy

Attitude of the Indians

William Henry Harrison had been appointed Governor of the "Indian Territory" in 1800. It then consisted of two tracts, one on the Ohio and the other at Vincennes on the Wabash, and between these there was a hundred miles of wilderness. The population grew from twenty-five hundred in 1800 to as many thousand in 1811. Westward and northwestward stretched the Indian country to the lakes and the Mississippi, broken only by military posts at Fort Wayne and Chicago, over which roamed 5,000 Indians.

Tecumseh, the great one-eyed leader of the Indians, gathered his warriors about him at Green-

Tecumseh

ville, Ohio. He aimed to build up an Indian confederacy which should assume joint ownership of all Indian lands. With his brothers he established himself on the Tippecanoe Creek where it joins the Wabash. From this point they could by water reach Vincennes, Fort Dearborn (Chicago), Fort Wayne and Detroit, and the waters of the Ohio and Mississippi.

Harrison

Harrison's various transactions exasperated the Indians, and they turned to the British for help. Alarming reports concerning the Indians reached Vincennes. Harrison saw that an Indian war was inevitable, and that his safety lay in crushing the Indians before the British could come to their aid. On August 12 Tecumseh, at Harrison's request, came to Vincennes for a conference. Tecumseh said: "You are constantly driving the red people, and at last you will drive them into the great lake, where they cannot either stand or walk."

Conference of Vincennes

Later in 1811 Tecumseh, with 200 warriors, came to Vincennes for another interview, and spent two days expostulating with Harrison. A few days afterward Tecumseh passed down the Wabash on his diplomatic errand with the Indian tribes in the south. Immediate action before his return was urged on Harrison, and he spent the next week raising troops. In September Harrison sent his force, consisting of 300 of the Fourth Regulars and six or seven hundred volunteers, to a point in the new purchase, sixty-five miles above Vincennes, where he built a small wooden fort, called after his name. His outposts were fired on and the war was begun.

Fort Harrison

On October 28 Harrison broke camp and marched up the river, fifty miles from Tippecanoe to the mouth of the Vermilion, within one and one-half miles of the Indian town. There the soldiers encamped. Early the next morning a shot was heard from the sentinel at the farthest angle of the camp. In an instant came the Indian yell, and the soldiers were shot down by their camp fires. The Americans received the attack in good form. At the broken angle the Indians had not strength to follow up their advantage, and the Americans at daybreak drove them into the swamp. The fight lasted two hours. Harrison's total loss was 188, of whom 61 were killed, and the bodies of 38 Indians remained on the field. The number of Indians in the battle was probably not more than 400. Tecumseh, when he learned of it, deplored the en counter. The battle of Tippecanoe gave great satisfaction throughout the West. Harrison received the official thanks of Kentucky, Illinois, and Indiana, but in New England the aggressions against the Indians were deprecated.

Battle of Tippecanoe

When a deputation of eighty Indians with Tecumseh visited Harrison at Vincennes, and asked leave to go to Washington, permission was readily granted, but Tecumseh's Indian braves could not be held in check. Hostilities broke out all along the border, settlers were shot at Fort Dearborn, at Fort Madison on the Mississippi, at Vincennes, and within a few miles of the Ohio. Harrison reported: "Most of the citizens of the country have abandoned their farms and taken refuge in temporary forts." Yet

Premature Indian war

the American Government was slow to act. Tecumseh, on the other hand, waited for the inevitable outbreak of hostilities with Great Britain to throw his lot in with the Englishmen. In winter the war fever of 1811 was at its height. Madison, Monroe and Gallatin were generally supposed to be aiming for some diplomatic makeshift rather than open rupture. The active leaders in Congress were young men. Clay, Calhoun, Lowndes, Williams, Grundy, Porter and Johnson were all under forty. They were bent on "creating a nation," as they expressed it, by carrying the American flag up to Canada and down to Key West. Calhoun's speech of December 12 was, perhaps, the best made in the long debate on war. A famous sentence was: "Protection (of the citizen) and patriotism are reciprocal. This is the road all great nations have trod." Finally a resolution authorizing naval vessels to arm was adopted by 97 against 22 votes.

American war fever

About this time, Herman von Kleist, one of Germany's most brilliant poets, put an end to his career. Had he waited but a little while longer, the poet might have lived to see the fulfilment of his dearest patriotic hopes. Born at Frankfurt on the Oder, Kleist served as an officer in the Prussian campaigns on the Rhine. In 1803 he brought out the romantic tragedy "The Schroffensteins," followed presently by a mystic version of Plautus and Molière's "Amphitryon." While in Switzerland he began his classic, "The Broken Pitcher," one of the best comedies in German verse written dur-

Kleist

His works

ing the nineteenth century. In Koenigsberg, Kleist
wrote his famous short story, "Michael Kohlhaas,"
a stirring psychological study of the effects of
wrong on a deeply emotional character. During
the war of 1806, Kleist returned to the colors and
fell into the hands of the French as a prisoner of Kleist's career
war. On his liberation, in 1808, he published the
play "Kaethchen von Heilbronn," which in operatic
form was destined to achieve a great success some
seventy-five years later. Kleist's patriotic poems
against the French soon got him into trouble. The
production of a suggestive drama on the fight of
the ancient Germans against the Romans was forbidden in Germany, as was his Prussian soldier-
play, "The Prince of Homburg." On the revolt
of Austria against Napoleon, the poet tried once
more to plunge into the whirl of war, but he arrived on the field of Aspern only after that battle
had turned against the Austrians. For a while he
seemed to cherish a wild project of assassinating
Napoleon, but at last he returned to Prussia an
imbittered man. An unhappy love affair sickened Commits suicide
him of life. On November 21, Kleist shot himself
on the shore of the Wansee near Potsdam. But
for Tieck's efforts the literary remains of this greatest of Prussia's early poets would not have been
preserved.

1812

WHILE the prospect of war between the United States and Great Britain held public attention in America, the minds of most Englishmen were fixed on Spain and the war with France. The French armies of Marmont and Soult, 67,000 strong, lay within touch of each other, barring Wellington's entrance into Spain. The allied forces under Wellington numbered 35,000, badly wasted from sickness and insufficient supplies. In this extremity Wellington was meditating a leap upon the great frontier fortress of Ciudad Rodrigo, the French base of supplies in the province of Salamanca. Siege guns were collected for the ostensible purpose of fortifying Almeida, but the guns were secretly transshipped and brought to the mouth of the Douro. Early in January, when the French had been lulled into security, Wellington, to use Napier's expressive phrase, "instantly jumped with both feet upon Ciudad Rodrigo."

Situation in the Peninsula

Wellington's advance

The siege began on January 8 in bitter cold weather. The British had to encamp on the side of the Agueda furthest from the city. On the first night, Colonel Colborne, afterward Lord Seton, led the three light divisions against the redoubt that

crowned the Great Teson. The accidental discharge of a French hand-grenade burst the gate
open, and the attacking party swept through it. Siege of Ciudad Rodrigo
The fight lasted only twenty minutes, but at the
end of it every Frenchman within the redoubt was
killed, wounded or a captive. For ten days a
desperate artillery duel was kept up. The French
brought fifty of their guns to bear on the English
lines, and thus held them off amid wintry weather
until Marmont, with his relieving forces, came within four marches of the besieged city. On the eve
of January 20 Wellington issued the general order:
"Ciudad Rodrigo must be stormed this evening." General assault ordered
The third division, under General Mackinnon, was
to attack the chief breach with a forlorn hope led
by Ensign Mackie. The smaller breach was a gap
twenty feet wide, to the left of the larger one. This
was to be attacked by the light division, under Crau-
ford, its smaller party of twenty-five men, being led The storm-ing parties
by Gurwood, and its storming party by George Na-
pier, the brother of the historian. General Pack,
with a Portuguese brigade, was to make a feint
on the eastern part, while another attack was made
on the south front by more Portuguese troops and a
picked company of the Eighty-third regiment of the
line. In the storming party were the Earl of March,
afterward Duke of Richmond, the Prince of Orange
and Lord Somerset, afterward Lord Raglan, all volunteers unknown to the Commander-in-Chief.

Shortly after seven in the evening, the fortress was
assaulted from all four sides at once. As Napier has
described it:

"The men were walking on fire! Yet the attack
could not be denied. The Frenchmen—shooting,
stabbing, yelling—were driven behind their intrenchments. There the fire of the houses commanding the breach came to their help, and they
made a gallant stand. None would go back on
either side, and yet the British could not get forward. Men and officers falling in heaps choked
up the passage, which from minute to minute was
raked with grape from two guns flanking the top of
the breach at the distance of a few yards. Thus
striving, and trampling alike upon the dead and
the wounded, these brave men maintained the
combat."

Crauford, with whom Napier's brother was a
favorite, gave to that officer the command of the
assault on the lesser breach. Wellington himself
came to the trench and showed Napier and Colborne, through the gloom of the early night, the
exact position of the breach. A staff officer, looking on, said, "Your men have not loaded. Why
don't you make them load?" Napier replied, "If
we don't do the business with the bayonet we shall
not do it at all." "Let him alone," said Wellington; "let him go his own way!" Picton had
adopted the same grim policy with the third division. As each regiment passed him, filing into
the trenches, his injunction was, "No powder!
We'll do the thing with the *could* iron."

Half way up, Napier's right arm was smashed by
a grape shot. As he lay bleeding, he shouted:
"Push on, my men, and give them the bayonet!"
Crauford, the famous leader of the light division,

was killed, and so was Mackinnon, the leader of
the Highland brigade that stormed the great breach. Death of
Crauford
With them fell seven hundred officers and men. At and Mackinnon
last, near midnight, Ciudad Rodrigo was won, when
the French commandant had to hand his sword to
the beardless British subaltern, who, bleeding from
a staggering wound, had brought his forlorn hope Fall of
Ciudad
Rodrigo
into the heart of the citadel. In all, the capture of
Ciudad Rodrigo had cost Wellington twelve hundred men.

Allison has said in his "History of Modern Europe" that "with the fall of Ciudad Rodrigo began
the fall of the French empire." As a matter of
fact it was the first of that swift following
series of strokes which drove the French eagles
out of Spain, while Napoleon was facing disaster
in Russia. From the capture of Ciudad Rodrigo, Advance of
the English
Wellington pushed on to Badajos, the rocky fortress standing on the last spur of the Toledo range,
which twice already had been assailed in vain by
the English. It was now held by a resolute garrison of five thousand men under General Phillip-
son, a Scotch Jacobite, with a genius for defence.
Even without such defenders, Badajos was an all
but impregnable stronghold. The river Guadiana,
five hundred yards wide, served as a natural moat
on the north, with the river Rivilla on the west.
On their banks towered five great fortified outposts
—Christobal, Saint Roque, Picarina, Pardeleras and
a fortified bridge-head across the Guadiana. Wellington brought up 18,000 men for the siege. Most
of them were veterans led by young officers. The

siege was begun in March, and lasted three weeks.
It was waged in the stormiest weather, with the
rivers steadily rising, and under a continuous cannonade from the ramparts. The losses on the British side averaged 250 men for each day. On the
eighth night of the siege, Wellington ordered a
night attack on the Picarina.

Napier tells how "the axmen of the light division, compassing the fort like prowling wolves," discovered the gate at the rear, and so broke into the
fort. The engineer officer who led the attack declared that the place would never have been taken
had it not been for the coolness of these men in
absolutely walking round the fort to its rear, discovering the gate, and hewing it down under a
tempest of bullets. The assault lasted an hour,

and in that period, out of the five hundred men
who attacked, no less than three hundred, with
nineteen officers, were killed or wounded!

Then followed two weeks of furious trench fighting, during which the British lost almost as heavily
as in the actual assaults. Of these days Captain
MacCarthy, of the Fiftieth British Infantry, has left
a curious monograph, full of tragi-comic incidents.
On the night of April 6, Wellington, who had a
fondness for night attacks, ordered a general as-

sault from seven sides. On the extreme right, Picton, with the third division, had to cross the Rivilla
and scale the high walls of the citadel. On the side
of Badajos, the fifth division, under Leith, was to
attack on the strong bastion of St. Vincente, where
the glacis was mined, the ditch deep and the scarp

thirty feet high.   At ten o'clock the assault began.
MacCarthy says we can only picture the scene by ^{Mac-} Carthy's description
"supposing that all the stars, planets, and meteors
of the firmament, with innumerable moons emitting
smaller ones in their course, were descending on
the heads of the besiegers."   MacCarthy himself,
it is reported, addressed his commander with the
exultant remark, "'Tis a glorious night, sir—a glorious night!" and, rushing forward to the head of
the stormers, shouted, "Up with the ladders!"
The five ladders were raised, the troops swarmed
up, an officer leading; but the first files were at
once overwhelmed by cannon fire, and the ladders
slipped into the angle of the abutments.   "Dreadful their fall," records MacCarthy of the slaughtered stormers, "and appalling their appearance at
daylight."

With but one ladder left standing, the British The citadel scaled
scaled the battlements of the citadel, one by one,
in a hand-to-hand fight against heavy odds.

On the other side of the city, the French garrison
succeeded in beating off their assailants from the
open breaches.   Every time the British renewed
the attacks their ranks were mowed down by hundreds.   The baffled British soldiers became so stubborn that they would not obey the bugle call from
the reserve line, blowing to the retreat, and they
struck their own buglers who tried to repeat it.   At
last the sullen soldiers discovered a likely spot in
the ramparts, and by a couple of ladders swept into
the bastion.   Swarming through the streets they
met the men of Picton's division descending from

the citadel. Caught between two fires, the French
Capture of poured from the ramparts and were carried through
Badajos
the rear gates. In the wild night assault more than
five thousand men fell on both sides—but Badajos
was won.

Even more sullen, though unrelieved by such
brilliant exploits as marked the dash of Badajos,
was the siege of San Sebastian, the fall of which
finally cleared the way for Wellington's famous
Fall of San
Sebastian march through Spain. Spurred on by this victory, the British army crossed the Agueda and
marched for Salamanca three days before Napoleon crossed the Niemen on his way to Moscow.

Assassi-   In England, during this time, the assassination
nation of
Perceval of Perceval by a maniac named Bellingham, in the
House of Commons, had brought about a change
of Ministry, though not of parties. Another
Tory Ministry was returned under the guidance
of the Earl of Liverpool, a leader of uncertain
strength, but well qualified to hold discordant colleagues together. Thanks to their continued sup-
Ministry of port, Wellington and his army in Spain were soon
Liverpool
enabled to reap the fruits of their dear-bought
victories. As Green has said in his "History of
the English People:"

"The death of Perceval marked more than a
mere change of Ministry. From that moment, the
development of English life began to take its natural course again. The increase of wealth was indeed
enormous. In spite of the serious blow which commerce received from the quarrel with America, English exports had grown to be nearly double what

they were at the outbreak of the war. Manufacturers profited by the great discoveries of Watt and
Arkwright, and the consumption of raw cotton in
the mills of Lancashire rose during the same period
from fifty to a hundred millions of pounds. . . .
So long as Perceval lived, efforts at reform had
been vain, but under Lord Liverpool, the advancing strength of a more liberal sentiment in the nation was brought to a head by Canning. Catholic
emancipation became an open question in the Cabinet itself, and was adopted in 1812 by a triumphant
majority in the House of Commons.''

All questions of home politics, however, were
soon thrown into the background by the more
absorbing interests of war.

The extension of privateering rights to American merchant vessels practically had the effect of
a declaration of war with England. Adventurous American privateering
captains of privateering vessels on both sides were
not slow in taking advantage of the situation.
Early in the spring, four British barges in Hampton Roads were taken as prizes with all their
crews by the American cutter "Jefferson," supported by the United States frigate "Constitution." A few weeks later, on April 25, Captain
Cotthell, of the privateer schooner "Surprise,"
captured the British brig "Kutous," 12 guns, and
brought her into port. Next, Captain David Porter, of the United States ship "Essex," sailed off
on a cruise against the British with a flag bearing Prelimi-naries of war
the motto, "Free Trade and Sailors' Rights." On
April 10, Castlereagh's note defining Great Britain's measures of retaliation was received. Presi-

dent Madison immediately convened his Cabinet
and recommended open war. On June 1 he sent
his recommendation to Congress. In it he charged
that British cruisers had been "in the continued
practice of violating the American flag on the
great highway of nations, and seizing persons
sailing under it; that British cruisers also violated the process of the courts, and harrowed entering and departing cruisers; that British coer-
cive measures, consisting of pretended blockade
without the presence of an adequate force, were
mere means by which our commerce had been
plundered on every sea; and this had culminated
in the fourth grievance, the sweeping system of
blockades known as the Orders in Council." On

June 18, after a fortnight's secret discussion,
the American Senate passed the bill declaring
war, the House accepted it, the President signed
it, and war was begun. Naval encounters occurred almost forthwith. Land operations were a
long time getting under way. This was owing on
one hand to a lack of adequate preparation in
America, and on the other hand to British reluctance to enter seriously into what could at most
be regarded as but a side issue.

On June 22, but four days after the American
declaration of war, Napoleon opened war on Russia—the second "Polish war," as he designedly
called it in a curious declaration ending with the
phrase, "Russia is swept downward by her destinies; her fate must be fulfilled."

Since the days of Xerxes no invasion of war

had been prepared on so gigantic a scale. Napoleon's grand army alone numbered 610,058 men, La grande armée with them lumbered 1,300 pieces of artillery and 20,000 commissary wagons.

Of the soldiers, 200,000 were Frenchmen, the rest were Germans, Italians, Poles, Swiss, Prussians, Austrians and Bavarians.

These troops, at the commencement of the campaign, were divided into five great masses. The first, 220,000 strong, was under the immediate orders of the Emperor; the second, 75,000 strong, was commanded by his brother Jerome; the third, under the Viceroy Eugene, numbered, also, 75,000; the right wing, under Schwarzenberg, consisted of 30,000 men, and the left, under Macdonald, also of 30,000. Seventy thousand more followed Distribution of French forces the corps, ready to support any division. Among the marshals were Victor, Murat, Davoust, Ney, Oudinot, Reynier, St. Cyr, Vandamme, Schwarzenberg, and Poniatovsky.

The Russian forces actually in the field at the commencement of hostilities, did not exceed 215,000 men; of whom 127,000 were commanded by Barclay de Tolly, 48,000 by Prince Bagration, and 40,000 by Tormasov. In addition to these, 35,000 men were assembled in the interior provinces, and 50,000 were in Moldavia, all of whom eventually aided in the war, and raised the total strength Russia's forces brought into action during the campaign, though never all collected together at one time, to 300,000 men.

On the 23d of June, Napoleon approached the

Niemen, and the numerous columns of the grand army converged toward Kovno. This town at the extreme point of a salient angle where Prussia projected into Russian territory, seemed a favorable spot for commencing operations. As Napoleon rode along the banks of the river, his horse stumbled and threw him upon the sand. Some one exclaimed, "It is a bad omen: a Roman would retire."

A bad omen

Characteristic of the whole subsequent campaign was the final banquet which Napoleon gave to his marshals just before the outbreak of hostilities. In contrast to other similar functions all the generals sat grim and silent. At last Napoleon exclaimed angrily: "What, my brave men, you don't seem to enjoy the prospect of more glory?" "How can we," answered one of them, "since we have everything to lose and nothing to gain?"

Napoleon crosses the Niemen

During the next few days the Niemen was crossed by the whole army marching in three parallel columns. As Napoleon's army advanced, the inferior Russian forces fell back, leaving a ravaged country devoid of food and fodder. The resulting distress to the marching columns of the French was aggravated by the sultry summer heat followed by drenching rainstorms, which spoiled the supplies. The horses fell by thousands and the raw recruits straggled from the ranks until a mass of 30,000 marauders in the rear gave almost as much trouble as the Russian Cossacks swarming in front. When the French army had been on Russian soil but six days, and before the first general engagement had

Early troubles

been fought, more than 25,000 men were invalided in the field hospitals at Vilna.

The first action was fought between retreating Cossacks on one side and the extreme vanguard of Murat's cavalry. On June 26, Murat brought his Polish Lancers and ten picked regiments of the French cavalry to bear on Count Ostermann's extended division of Cossacks, and there was fighting all along the line. In the main, the various actions were desultory and undecisive, serving no other purpose than to give each side a chance to bring up their main columns. On the eve of June 29, Napoleon had brought forward 180,000 of his men, ready to fall upon Barclay's army of 82,000 drawn in at Vitepsk.

The first fight

Preparations for battle

As Napoleon retired into his tent, his last words to Murat were: "To-morrow at five, the sun of Austerlitz!" The next morning the Russians were gone. Nothing had been left behind but their smoldering watch-fires. Murat's skirmishers, riding far in advance, could not determine whether the Russian army had taken the road to Moscow or that to St. Petersburg. Baffled in their hopes of a decisive conflict, the French marshals fell to quarrelling among themselves, while their various commands became an unwieldy mass, as difficult to move as to keep on its feet. The transport service fell into confusion, and the suffering of the soldiers grew in proportion. Among the allied Germans and Austrians the officers and men alike showed such apathy that they could scarcely be reckoned upon for the prompt execution of any

Napoleon disappointed

French sufferings increase

movement. While Napoleon's army was thus coiled up at Vitepsk, the Russians executed their retreat to Smolensk without molestation.

At last Emperor Alexander had been induced to leave his army, where the memories of Austerlitz counted against him, and hastened to Moscow to arouse his nobles there. On July 27, they were all summoned to a banquet at the Imperial palace, and, toasting their Emperor unanimously, voted to raise and equip at their own expense a levy of every tenth man in the population. The merchants contributed two million roubles on the spot. Amid the burst of enthusiasm that followed the proposal, Alexander swore on his sword that he would "exhaust the last resources of the crown rather than give in." Thus the *opoltchenye*, a powerful reserve of bearded peasants, was created in sixteen interior provinces of the vast empire, while the Russian army at the front, falling back step by step, was steadily drawing the invaders further away from their supplies.

Wise as this policy proved in the event, the continued retreat of Barclay exasperated most Russians at home and many of the young hot heads serving in the army. The feeling among his officers grew so that Barclay at last detached Wittgenstein with 25,000 men to make an offensive movement on the Doina, while Tormasov, on the other flank, was permitted to demonstrate against the Austrians and Germans under Schwarzenberg and Reynier. Kutusov, commanding Wittgenstein's vanguard, got into action with Oudinot's corps on

Interior Russia aroused

Dissatisfaction with Barclay

the last day of July. In spite of heavy losses he held out until heavily reinforced and then suc- Battle of the Drissa ceeded in throwing Oudinot back over the river Drissa. Four thousand Frenchmen fell in the fight. At the same time Tormasov, finding Schwarzenberg unwilling to do anything serious, fell upon the Saxon corps stationed at Kobrien and captured Tormasov's victory a whole brigade of Reynier's best troops. This double disaster so weakened Napoleon's ends that he had to deprive himself of his reserves to strengthen his flanks. Yet Barclay continued to draw in his front and fell steadily back until he succeeded in effecting a junction with Bagration's Russian generals join forces corps of 40,000 men at Smolensk. Here the Russians resolved to make a stand. On August 8, a determined attack was made on the French right wing under Murat, but only a drawn fight ensued. Napoleon responded in force. Within a week, he suddenly pushed 200,000 of his men over the Dniepr and thus entered the soil of Old Russia. Napoleon crosses the Dniepr The Russians promptly fell back on Smolensk. The French vanguard under Murat and Ney overtook the Russian rearguard under General Neverovskoi. Murat sent eighteen cavalry regiments to detach and capture the slow moving column of Russian infantry, but though outmatched three to one, the Russians, marching in square formation, withstood Neverovskoi's famous retreat assault after assault and fought their way through to Korytnia. This fight is cherished as one of the proudest traditions of the Russian army. It lasted all day, and during its course forty distinct cavalry attacks were launched against the column by Murat.

Neverovskoi lost 1,100 men and five guns, more than one-fifth of his force, but he reached Korytnia with unbroken ranks, and the next day joined forces with 12,000 men under Raeffskoi and so succeeded in gaining Smolensk. The two generals threw themselves into the old town, resolved to hold it until the last extremity. The next day Napoleon drew up before the city with the main body of the army. Marshal Ney, leading the first corps, tried to take the place by assault, but was repulsed with great loss. While the fight was on, the Russian main column under Barclay arrived and regained Smolensk from the rear. Napoleon now felt sure of his prey and ordered a general assault on the morrow.

Russian stand at Smolensk

Barclay, realizing the weakness of his position and the danger of being cut off entirely from his rear, ordered Bagration and the main army to quit the city under cover of the night, while he remained with a rearguard of 25,000 to hold the enemy in check. The next day Napoleon, as yet unaware that he had been foiled once more, assailed Smolensk with his whole army, but the Russians fought so well that the fight lasted all day. At seven in the evening Napoleon at last gave up the attempt for that day, having lost 15,000 men. Of the Russians nearly 10,000 had fallen. Too weak to face another day of such frightful losses, Barclay during the night set fire to the ancient city and retired in safety from the flaming citadel with all his wounded and the town refugees. When Davoust with his vanguard scaled the smoking ramparts at three

Smolensk evacuated

in the morning they found all the magazines and stores destroyed, the bridges over the Dniepr broken down, with nothing of value left behind save the brass cannons mounted on the outer fortifications.

Napoleon, bound to bring his elusive enemy to bay, drove his army headlong in quick pursuit. During the same day Ney's cavalry overtook Barclay with his rearguard at Valentina. Undismayed by his strong position, Ney attacked the enemy along the whole fighting line. The losses of the French were fearful, but they kept up the fight until their main body came up and the engagement became general. The Russians, thanks to reinforcements from Bagration's main column, stood their ground, and thus effectually covered their comrades' retreat. During the night they once more made good their own retreat. When Napoleon advanced to renew the attack next morning he found nothing but a desolate battlefield strewn with 15,000 dead and dying men from both armies. In front of Politsk, during these same days, another Russian corps under Wittgenstein fought two similar rearguard engagements against Oudinot's corps and a division of Bavarians, after which Wittgenstein, too, retreated further into the interior. *Battle of Valentina* *Russian retreat made secure*

Adam, the military artist, who accompanied the French general staff into Russia, has left a series of drawings which give a vivid idea of the depressing character of this campaign. The country was ravaged, the harvests trampled down, the wretched isbas of the moujiks in ashes. The carcasses of *Miseries of the campaign* thousands of dead horses and half-buried bodies of men infected the air, and broken-down wagons and caissons obstructed the roads. Typhus fever

and dysentery raged among the men and turned the military hospitals at Vilna and Vitepsk into vast charnel houses. Already the war, barren of glory as it was, had cost the army one-third of its original number. The total results of a week's protracted fighting since the middle of August, were 21,000 corpses and the smoking ruins of a deserted city.

Napoleon, though face to face with disaster, yet trusted to some conclusive masterstroke:

"The condition of the army," said he, "is frightful; I know it. At Vilna, one-half were stragglers; now, they amount to two-thirds: there is not a moment to lose: we must grasp at peace, and it can be found only at Moscow. Besides, the state of the army is such as to render a halt impossible; constant advance alone keeps it together; you may lead it forward, but you cannot arrest its movement. We have advanced too far to retreat. If I had only military glory in view, I should have nothing to do but return to Smolensko, and extend my wings on either side, so as to crush Wittgenstein and Tormasoff. These operations would be brilliant: they would form a glorious termination to the campaign; but they would not conclude the war. Peace is before us; we have to march only eight days to obtain it: when we are so near our object, it is impossible to deliberate. Let us advance to Moscow."

On August 22, Napoleon set out from Smolensk on his march to Moscow. At St. Petersburg the

feeling of dismay at the enemy's steady approach
on the sacred city had reached such a pitch that
Stein, Emperor Alexander's best counsellor during
these gloomy days, found himself unable to maintain Barclay de Tolly in chief command. Of for- General
eign extraction, like Stein himself, the crafty Scotch relieved
general was execrated by the Slav party at court
and in the army. He had to give way to Kutusov, the septuagenarian soldier, notorious for his
pronounced Muscovite traits.

Kutusov took charge at Gyatsk and soon bid a Kutusov
halt to the general retreat at Borodino. This was charge
on the second day of September. Redoubts and
trenches were thrown up and everything prepared
for a strong stand. The Russians mustered 121,-
000 men, many of whom were Opoltchenye militia
or raw recruits that had never been under fire.
Within four days the French column came up.
Murat's vanguard immediately threw themselves
upon the first line of Russian redoubts, the Che-
varadino, held by twelve thousand under Gort- Russian
shakoff. After severe fighting the redoubt was stand at
carried at nightfall and the Russians fell back on Borodino
their second line of defences, the Raevsky battery
between the Red Mount and the village of Borodino. Deep silence reigned in the Russian camp
on the eve of battle; religious fervor and patriotic
fury inflamed all hearts; they passed the night confessing and communing; they put on white shirts
as if for a wedding. In the morning 100,000 were
blessed on their knees and sprinkled with holy
water by their priests. The eikon of the Virgin

of St. Vladimir, rescued from Smolensk, was carried around among the troops.

Napoleon next morning was elated to find the Russians still drawn up in the line of battle. The French officers and soldiers shared his enthusiasm; and even to the wearied allies the prospect of battle appeared to bring relief. At sunrise Napoleon, appealing for the last time to his "sun of Austerlitz," ordered all the bugles and drums along the French battle front to sound for the charge. The French artillery posted on an eminence behind the vanguard, opened fire. Under cover of this, the French right under Davoust charged into the Russian left, where three little redoubts were held by Bagration. Davoust went down with his horse at the first shock. Generals Rapp and Campans were likewise struck down. When Rapp, wounded for the twenty-second time, was carried past Napoleon, the Emperor said impatiently: "Always Rapp!" After a hot hand to hand fight, the French, with superb dash, succeeded in taking the second line of redoubts, but were almost immediately dislodged by the Russian reserves brought up by Bagration. Ney now threw himself into the fight with his entire corps and retook the redoubt, but Kutusov, seeing his left wing shaken, threw Baggovud's corps over from his right, and thus once more made himself master of the position. Ney returned to the attack again and again, but after a most stubborn fight of several hours, found himself constrained to send for help to the Emperor's headquarters. The officers of the Old Guard clamored to be sent, but the Emperor re-

Battle of Borodino

fused them: "Eight hundred leagues from France
I will not risk my last reserve." Instead he ordered up the Young Guard. A column of three
full army corps thus combined advanced to the
attack led by Ney and Davoust. The Russian
batteries concentrated their fire on this mass.
The French ranks were mowed down in platoons.
When they still persevered, Bagration, staking all
on this end of the battle, ordered his entire left
wing out of the trenches and charged them into
the French flank. He himself led the charge, and
fell, mortally wounded, at the head of his troops. Death of Bagration
For more than an hour the battle was carried on
with the utmost fury until nearly 80,000 troops on
both sides were engaged in it. Only when the
Russian centre under Barclay began to give way
at Borodino and on the Red Mount, under repeated charges of the cuirassiers and a final bayonet charge of the Old Guard, did the Russians
yield the battle. Fighting still, they withdrew
slowly to a strong position behind the ravine of
Semenevskoy at Psarevo. There they resolutely
held their ground. "Napoleon," says General Brandt's description
Brandt, in his memoirs, "had succeeded, but at
what a price! The great redoubt and its surroundings offered a spectacle which surpassed the
worst horrors that could be dreamed of. The
ditches, the fosses, the very interior of the out-
works had disappeared beneath a hill of dead
and dying, six or eight men deep heaped one
upon another."

In this terrible battle the total casualties aggre-

gated nearly one hundred thousand. In the
French bulletins it was designated as the battle
of the Moscova. The Russians know it as the
battle of Borodino. There, in Tolstoi's pregnant
phrase, "the beast was wounded to the death."
The French lost 12,000 killed and 38,000 wounded.
Among the killed was one of the Caulaincourts who
led the cuirassier charge, and Montbrun, while Davoust, Rapp, and Campans were severely wounded.
The Russians lost 15,000 killed, 30,000 wounded
and 2,000 prisoners. Among the dead were Kou-
taisov and the two Tutshkovs. The loss of brave
Bagration was felt the most.

In the face of such frightful losses Kutusov,
heeding the counsels of Barclay, resumed the retreat toward Moscow, nor did he bid a halt until
half a league in front of that city. On September
15, the Russian generals held a council of war on
the hill of Fily, which overhangs Moscow, and determined in the end to abandon the ancient city to
its fate. Bennigsen, Ostermann, and Prince Eugene
of Wurtemberg were in favor of a last battle, but
Barclay declared that after all Moscow was "only a
city like any other." Kutusov, after listening to
all, said: "Here my head, be it good or bad, must
decide. We will retreat." In justification of this
tragic measure Kutusov wrote to the Czar that "it
was indispensable to preserve the army until the
new levies could be brought up, and, moreover,
that it would *lead the enemy into a snare where his
destruction would be inevitable.*"

The next day the Russian army defiled sorrow-

Apalling losses

Russian retreat resumed

Moscow abandoned

fully through the streets of Moscow, and marched
for Kolomna, followed by an endless train of 300,-
000 refugees from the city. During the forenoon of
the same day the advance columns of the French
came within sight of the sacred city. As they be- Arrival of
held the rays of the sun glinting from the golden the French
dome of the Kremlin and descried the many mina-
rets of the old Russian metropolis, the soldiers
broke into a jubilant shout: "Moscow!" Napoleon himself drew rein on an eminence to exclaim:
"Here is the famous city at last!" But he added
immediately: "It was high time."

When the French entered the city they marched
through silent streets and found deserted quarters.
No one appeared to present the keys of the city,
and Napoleon asked impatiently, "Where are the
Boyars?" On the great red staircase of the Imperial Kremlin palace he waited until late in the
evening before Mortier's provost guards succeeded
in getting together a deputation of nondescripts to
present their submission. The next day, September 15, when the bulk of the French army had ●
been quartered in the city, fire broke out in different parts of Moscow. No fire pumps were to Incendiary
be found. Many incendiaries were caught red- fires
handed and were shot by the soldiers. No less
than four hundred were court-martialed. At midnight the windows of the Kremlin were lighted up
by flames leaping from the roof of the Governor's
palace. Prince Rastopshin, a true Muscovite, com- Rastop-
bining the polish of a European with the savagery shin's part
of a Tartar, had the torch put to his own palace.

At the same time he ordered Voronenko to set fire
to the public stores of vodka and oil. Withal he
took pains to spread the report that the fire was the
work of the foreign invaders. As he grimly put
it in his curious memoir, "The Truth About the
Burning of Moscow": "It was an event which I
had prepared, but I contented myself with inflam-
ing the spirits of men." On the iron door of his
splendid country seat at Vorovono, Prince Rastopshin wrote: "For eight years I have lived happy
here with my family. Frenchmen, at your approach, I set fire to my house, lest it be polluted
by your presence. I have also given you my two
houses in Moscow worth half a million of rubles.
You will find nothing but ashes."

A veering wind spread the conflagration in Moscow. By the next morning the Tartar quarter, the
"white town" and parts of the suburbs or "land
town," were a sea of fire. Napoleon's guards
worked hard to save the Kremlin, but at last the
danger became too imminent and the Emperor had
to abandon the palace. With some difficulty he
made his way through the burning city to the
Czar's summer palace at Petrovski. For four
days the fire raged unabated, until by September
20 only one-tenth of the city's houses were left
untouched.

The news of the burning of the sacred city
aroused the mass of Russian peasants to a state
of blind fury against the French invaders. The
moujiks fell on foraging parties or single marauders and killed them with pitchforks. In the

"The truth about the burning of Moscow"

Fire becomes general

The peasants infuriated

single district of Porovsk 3,500 soldiers were thus slain. Guerilla war broke out wherever the French pitched their camps. The Czar, in St. Petersburg, exclaimed: "Now we shall make war in earnest." As if in token of these words the Russian com- Russians take the offensive manders at Kolomna, wheeling their divisions around the French outposts, assumed an offensive position at Tarutino—a masterly move which served to secure them reinforcements and supplies from the richest provinces of the empire, while at the same time it threatened the enemy's communications. Hordes of Cossacks skirmished in close vicinity of Moscow. At a loss what to do next, Napoleon bivouacked his army on the barren ground of what was left of Moscow, and waited for the Russians to give some sign of surrender. While he thus lost time his fate was accomplished in other quarters of the world.

The burden cast upon England by the maritime war with America, which had already cost the British navy some of her best cruisers, made the new Ministry the more anxious to profit by Napoleon's troubles in Russia. After Wellington had taken the last French stronghold on the Portuguese frontier, Marmont, cut off from Soult's forces in Andalusia, found his position very precarious. In response to his appeals, Napoleon wrote from the French retreat into Spain north: "You grumble about distances and the lack of food. I have in Russia very different distances to go over, and very different difficulties to overcome to feed my soldiers. Eh bien, we must do as we can." Marmont was forced back from the

Tagus after General Hill with 15,000 men had taken the bridge of Almarez. Unable to resist Wellington's march on Salamanca, Marmont withdrew first beyond the Tormes and then to the Douro. On June 28, Wellington, after a hot fight, stormed Salamanca. An Anglo-Sicilian army worried Marshal Suchet in Catalonia, and an English squadron, cruising on the Bay of Biscay, threatened the provinces of the north with a disembarkation. The siege of Cadiz had to be raised by the French, and Andalusia was evacuated. Marmont resolved to make a bold stroke. He crossed the Douro and met the steady advance of the British by a counter advance upon Salamanca. After a series of well-fought skirmishes on July 22, Marmont took up a strong position opposite the hills of Arapilez, one league from Salamanca. The battle had barely begun when Marmont, perceiving weakness at the British right end, detached his left wing to outflank the enemy. Wellington, from the height of Arapilez, caught sight of the widening gap between Marmont's centre and his left, and exclaimed joyfully to the Duke of Alava: "Behold, I have them: Marmont is lost." The whole of the British main column was driven like a wedge into the gap and the French army was cut in two. General Maucune, commanding the French left, turned columns and bravely fought his way back to the village of Arapilez, but the French centre succumbed to the shock. While trying to save the day Marmont was wounded, and so was Bennet, his successor in command. Young General Clausel,

Marginal notes:
Salamanca stormed

Siege of Cadiz raised

Battle of Salamanca

who next took charge, found the odds too heavy against him and ordered a retreat. The loss of the French had been 14,000, whereas the allies lost 5,600 men. Returning in good order, Clausel led his troops over the Douro, and fell back on Burgos. He was joined there by King Joseph and 13,000 men. It was too late. The campaign was over— lost to France.

At the continued approach of the British, King Joseph retreated first to the capital. Even Madrid had to be given up to retire to Valencia. Welling- French evacuate Madrid ton triumphantly entered Madrid on August 12. Only after Soult and Jourdan had joined forces with Joseph and Marmont were the French able to regain control of Madrid, but so acute was the dis- cord between the French commanders, that they failed to bring their united columns to bear, either on Wellington's main army, operating before Bur- gos, or on Hill's detached corps, which might have been cut off. The concentration of the three great French armies in Spain remained without result.

Great Britain's war with America, during the interval, had grown to serious proportions. The American navy, when the war of 1812 broke out, The Ameri- can war was but poorly prepared for service. The "Con- stitution," "Chesapeake" and "John Adams" were not ready for sea service. The only vessels avail- able were placed under the command of Com- modore Rodgers. They were the "President," "United States," "Commodore Decatur," "Con- gress," "Constellation" and "Argus." The Brit- ish ships stationed on the North Atlantic coast were neither many nor formidable. Their squadron in all numbered eight sail-o'-the-line and frigates bearing a total armament of 312 guns, not counting those mounted on the smaller corvettes and sloops-o'-war. Yet they were sufficient to render hopeless any naval attempt at Canada or the British West Indies. The war on sea, as it turned out, was fought as a series of single naval encounters—ship against ship—where all depended on individual seamanship and straight shooting.

Three days after the declaration of war Commodore Rodgers sailed out of New York harbor with his squadron. He reached Jamaica on June 23. Soon a sail was discovered, which proved to be the English "Blandina" with thirty-six guns. Rodgers himself fired the first gun. The first three shots were seen to do much damage. Then a gun on the "President's" main deck blew up, killing and wounding sixteen Americans, among them Commodore Rodgers. The "President" now bore up and fired her first broadside, but only injured the "Blandina's" rigging while sustaining a galling fire. Twice after that the "President" repeated these tactics, but the "Blandina" succeeded in wearing away and by midnight had run beyond danger. The chase took the "President" far out of her course, and so it came that the American squadron turned up at the Newfoundland banks early in July, cruising thence eastward nearly to the English Channel. Thence they returned to Boston. They had made seven prizes and succeeded in retaking one American vessel.

On July 23, the "Essex," Captain David Porter, insufficiently armed, set sail from New York. On July 11 she fell in with the "Minerva," then acting as a convoy to seven transports with 1,400 troops bound for Quebec. The "Essex" ran in and took one transport with 200 soldiers, but the captain of the "Minerva," by skilful manœuvring, kept in close touch with his other transports. Among the youngest midshipmen on the "Essex" was D. G. Farragut, then thirteen years old. He wrote in a letter home that the crew of the "Essex" had been so thoroughly trained as boarders that every man was prepared for such an exploit, with cutlasses ground to razor edge, boarding pistols, and dirks made out of files. On August 13, the "Essex" fell in with the British ship "Alert." Captain Porter handled the "Essex" in such a manner that the enemy was led to believe that he was trying to escape. Passing under the stern of the "Essex," the "Alert" sent in a broadside, doing no damage. Thereupon Captain Porter opened with all his guns. In less than ten minutes the "Alert" struck her colors, was boarded, and had her crew disarmed. On September 7, the "Essex" returned to New York, having made ten prizes.

The British frigate "Blandina," on escaping from Rodgers, carried the news of the war to Halifax. On July 5, Vice-Admiral Savage despatched a British squadron on a cruise for American vessels. It was commanded by Captain Broke of the "Shannon" with thirty-eight guns, and included the "Belvidera," thirty-six, the "Africa," thirty-

Exploits of the "Essex"

Capture of the "Alert"

four, and the "Æolus," thirty-two guns. After
capturing the "Nautilus" on July 16, when the
fleet was four leagues off Barnegat, they discovered
the frigate "Constitution," Captain Hull commanding. She had four hundred and fifty men who were
all new to the service. At 7.30 P.M., the "Constitution," having sighted the five sail of the enemy,
beat to action and signals were exchanged for an
hour with the "Guerrière." Early next morning
the captain of the "Guerrière," sighting the "Belvidera" and other British ships in the offing, came
to the conclusion that they were Commodore Rodgers' squadron and stood away from the "Constitution" before discovering his mistake. At five in
the morning the "Constitution" had on her lee
quarter two of the enemy's ships with three more
astern. The sea was calm and both the American
and British ships were towing. The "Shannon"
gained, but, thanks to the handling of Hull, the
American frigate glided away. Shortly after nine
in the morning Hull cleared for action. About
this time the "Guerrière," recognizing her enemies, opened fire, but her shots fell short. At
two in the afternoon Captain Byron on the "Belvidera" got near enough to the "Constitution" to
exchange shots with her. Hull expected to be
overtaken and had prepared to disable the first
frigate before her consorts should close with him.
All through the afternoon and evening the nearest
British frigate kept on towing barely out of gunshot. Next morning early, the "Belvidera," forg-
ing ahead off the "Constitution's" lee, tacked to

the eastward, compelling the "Constitution" to do likewise. By this time the five British frigates were all on the eastward tack with all canvas out. At noon Hull had dropped his pursuers from two to five miles behind. Near sundown Hull, taking advantage of a threatening rainstorm, bore away, and thus made good his escape from an overwhelming force after an exciting three days' chase. It was a bloodless encounter, but the honors for superior seamanship, so highly prized by British sailors, fell to America. A sailing contest

On August 2, the "Constitution" stood out of Boston Harbor again and headed for Cape Race. Having turned southward, Captain Hull, on August 19, made out a large sail which proved to be the "Guerrière." The English ship opened fire. For a full hour the two big ships exchanged broadsides. By six o'clock they came within half pistol shot and raked one another's decks with a furious cannonade. After twenty minutes of this murderous fire the "Guerrière's" mizzen mast came down. Then the ships got foul of each other and the Americans attempted to board. Captain Dacres of the "Guerrière" was severely wounded. At last the "Guerrière" got clear, but the loss of her mainmast and foremast left her a defenceless hulk. At seven in the evening the English ship struck her colors. Out of the crew of 272 men, the "Guerrière" lost 23 killed and 56 wounded. The ship itself was sinking and had to be blown up by Captain Hull, who forthwith returned to Boston to repair his badly battered ship. "Constitution" sinks the "Guerrière"

The career of the "Wasp," an American sloop of eighteen guns, commanded by Captain Jack Jones, was brief and brilliant. Her first opponent was the "Frolic," a sloop-o'-war of one hundred feet. They ran parallel, sixty yards apart, for fifteen minutes. Drawing closer, they at last ran foul. The "Wasp" crossed the "Frolic's" bow. Her crew then clambered over the bowsprit of the "Frolic" and found only twenty survivors aboard her. Of the "Wasp's" crew but ten had fallen. The fight was won by superior marksmanship. Before the smoke of the guns had cleared away, the British ship "Poictiers," of seventy-four guns, came up, and, capturing both, took them as prizes to Bermuda.

Rodgers and Decatur sailed from Boston on October 8 with the frigates "President," "United States," "Congress" and "Argus." Rodgers, with two of these vessels, cruised far and wide. The "Argus" in particular made valuable prizes and escaped from a British squadron by excellent manœuvring. Decatur in the "United States" sailed eastward, and when near the Azores sighted a sail. It turned out to be the British man-o'-war "Macedonian," with thirty-eight guns. The Englishman came too close and was badly handled by a raking fire that cut her rigging to pieces. After a number of her guns had been dismounted she surrendered. Decatur apologized for the length of time spent in forcing the surrender, "by reason of a rough sea and the enemy's reluctance to come to closer quarters." The "Macedonian" was the

only British man-o'-war brought in as a prize to
an American port.

Before the year closed the "Constitution" took
another cruise. She sailed October 25, with Bainbridge in command, in company with the "Hornet." By the middle of November she went into
port at San Salvador. There she left the "Hornet," and soon after sighted the British frigate
"Jena," of the same tonnage as the "Guerrière,"
with a crew of 426 men. Early in the afternoon
the "Constitution" came within pistol shot, and
ten minutes later the two ships were foul. Thereafter the conflict was a slaughter. In fifteen
minutes the "Jena's" rigging was cut to pieces.
At four in the afternoon she ceased firing. Her
captain was mortally wounded, 48 of her men lay
dead and 102 were wounded. The "Constitution"
lost only 12 men with 22 wounded.

"Constitu-
tion" de-
feats the
"Jena"

Thus ended the first year of the naval war between the United States and England. The commerce of the United States had suffered almost
total destruction. The contest so far hung not so
much on the losses which were inflicted on England, as on those which the people of the United
States could sustain. On land the American operations contrasted dismally with the brilliant exploits
won at sea.

Results of
naval war

One week after the declaration of war the American army was fixed at twenty-five regiments of
infantry, four of artillery and two of dragoons—
making 36,700 men. The actual force was only
10,000, of whom nearly half were recruits.

Detroit claimed early attention. It was within gunshot of British territory and was surrounded by hostile Indians. William Hull, the Governor of Michigan, advised an increase of the naval force on Lake Erie. General Dearborn, of Boston, was given a command on the Ontario and St. Lawrence. Hull set out in the spring of 1812, having no understanding with Dearborn or the Secretary of War. The force destined for Detroit consisted of 1,500 men, and they were joined in June by 1,000 more men. Hull took command. Detroit was two hundred miles away, and the little army had to cut its way through wild forests and over unbridged rivers. Late in June, when he had advanced seventy-five miles, Hull received a despatch from Secretary Eustis urging haste, and he left his camp equipage behind and hurried to the Maumee River, thirty-five miles away. There he despatched his personal effects, including his papers, in a schooner, and within twenty-four hours received a despatch announcing the declaration of war. On the same day the schooner was seized by the British. Hull reached Detroit on July 5. The fort was a square inclosure of two acres, but did not command the river. The people of the territory numbered about 5,000, while the town itself contained 800 souls. On July 9, Hull received orders to invade Canada, and on the 12th he crossed the river.

Meanwhile Dearborn at Albany and Boston wasted time with details for two months. On June 22, he received news of the declaration of war. On July 9, he received orders to engage the

Land operations

Hull invades Canada

enemy on Lake Champlain, at the same time that Hull's army crossed into Canada and challenged the British forces on the lakes. On July 19 and 24, American detachments were driven in by the British. Then came news that Mackinaw had sur- American reverses rendered, and that the Indians were gathering to fall on Detroit.

Upper Canada from Detroit to Ottawa contained 80,000 people. The political capital was York (now Toronto) on Lake Ontario. The British civil and military commander was Brock. He was a man of unusual power and of military training. During the winter vessels had been armed on Lake Erie, giving him command of the inland waters to Detroit. Hull's passage of the Detroit, on July 12, showed Brock where the first blow was to be struck. Brock's energy at once burst forth; he sent to Amherstburg all the force possible, and he ordered the seizure of Mack- British activity inaw. On August 5, he left for Lake Erie. Secure at Niagara, he took 300 picked men and coasted up to Detroit River. Early in August, Hull awoke to the dangers of the situation. He made arrangements to send 1,000 men to the relief of Niagara. Alliance with Indians On August 15, Brock held a council at which there were 1,000 Indians.

"Among them," he said, "I found some extraordinary characters. He who attracted most my attention was a Shawnee chief, Tecumseh, brother to the prophet who the last two years had carried on an active warfare, contrary to our remonstrances, against the United States. A more sagacious and active man does not, I believe, exist."

At noon on August 15, Hull was summoned to
surrender and refused. Brock instantly ordered
two armed vessels to move up the river, while
a battery opened fire from the Canadian shore.
During the night Tecumseh, with 600 Indians,
crossed the river two miles below and cut off
communication between the fort and McArthur
and Cass. Brock crossed before daybreak. He
came to close quarters within three-quarters of
a mile of the American 24-pounders. Nothing
but the boldness of the enterprise rendered success possible. Brock formed his column for assault. The ships were firing into the fort. On
the American side two companies of Michigan
men deserted, and Hull sent a flag to surrender. The capitulation included McArthur and
Cass. "The treachery and cowardice of Hull,
like that of Arnold, cannot be a matter of
blame to our government," wrote Jefferson to
Lewis Cass on learning the story. At the same
time Fort Dearborn in Chicago was in flames.
Hull had ordered it evacuated, and on August
15, the garrison was attacked and murdered by
a large body of Indians. With it went the last
vestige of American authority on the lakes.

Capitula-
tion of
Detroit

Massacre
at Fort
Dearborn

Lake Erie was lost to the Americans; but on
Lake Ontario new supplies and troops were gathered, the ships were moved to Sackett's Harbor
and became the nucleus of a fleet. On the night
of October 8, Lieutenant Elliott of the navy, with
one hundred men, cut out two British vessels under
the guns of Fort Erie. Van Rensselaer formed a

plan for a double attack, a part of which was to
land boats in the rear of Fort George. He was Fight at Fort George
successful. Captain Wood with a few hundred
men climbed up an obscure path and found themselves thirty yards in the rear of a battery, from
which Brock was watching the contest below.
While leading the subsequent attack Wood was
killed. Lieutenant-Colonel Winfield Scott volun-
teered to take command of Wood's forlorn hope.
At two o'clock a scarlet line of British was seen
advancing from Fort George, with a thousand
Indians against the six hundred Americans on
the heights. The Americans were cut up. Gen- Death of Brock
eral Brock was killed in the action. Several hundred surrendered; the rest were scalped. Scott and
his followers were pushed down to the river. Scott
saved his life only by fighting his way through the
Indians into the British lines.

The burden of defending the border between the
Ohio and the lakes fell on Ohio, with its quarter of
a million of people, and Kentucky, with its four
hundred thousand. Harrison's ambition drew him
to lead a new crusade for the recovery of Detroit. Harrison's army of the North-west
Under the immediate advice of Henry Clay and
others, he was given command and proceeded to
organize a campaign. The news of Hull's surrender
reached him at Frankfort. He was swept on far
beyond where he thought it prudent to go by the
current of Western enthusiasm. The President and
Cabinet decided to give him the command of the
Army of the Northwest with ten thousand men.

On September 27, he announced his plan of cam-

paign, which was to concentrate at Maumee Rapids
and to have 2,000 Kentucky militia destroy the Indian settlements. But he found himself unable
either to advance or to retreat. He passed weeks
searching in vain over two hundred miles of dry
ridges. Throughout October and November his
army stood still. Late in 1812, Harrison wrote to
Monroe that Malden, rather than Detroit, should
be the point of attack. An ill-conceived raid into
Canada, led by General Dearbórn, turned out an
utter fiasco. The American troops fired into each
other, and then beat a precipitate retreat. The
Army of the North went into winter quarters;
thus bringing to a close the American land
campaign for that year.

Dearborn's invasion of Canada

Napoleon, in Moscow, for some time nursed the
illusion that the fall of the ancient Russian capital
would be followed by a speedy peace. In his extremity he did not hesitate to make the first overtures. On September 20 he wrote to the Czar:

Napoleon in Moscow

"MY BROTHER: Having learned that the brother of
your Imperial Majesty's Minister was at Moscow, I
sent for him and had some conversation with him.
I requested him to wait upon your Majesty and
acquaint you with my sentiments. The handsome
and superb city of Moscow no longer exists. Ros-
topchin has had it burned. Four hundred incendiaries were taken in the act; and having all
declared that they had lighted the fire by order
of that governor and the director of police,
they were shot. The fire at last seems to have
ceased. Three-fourths of the houses are burned,

His overtures for peace

and one-fourth remain. Such conduct is **atro-**
cious, and serves no purpose. It is the procedure followed since Smolensko, and it has reduced
600,000 families to beggary. Humanity, the interests of your Majesty and this great city, demanded that it should have been intrusted to my
keeping, since it was deserted by the Russian army.
They ought to have left administrations, magistrates,
and civil guards. That is what was done at Vienna
twice, at Berlin and Madrid; and what we have
ourselves done at Milan, when Souvarov entered.
If I thought such things were done by your Majesty's orders, I should not write you this letter;
but I consider it impossible that, with your principles, heart, and sense of justice, you have authorized such excesses, unworthy of a great sovereign and a great nation.

"I made war upon your Majesty without ani-
mosity. A letter from you before or after the
last battle would have stopped my march, and I
should have been ready to forego the advantage
of entering Moscow. If your Majesty still retains
aught of your former sentiments, you will take
this letter in good part. In any case, you must
feel indebted to me for giving an account of what
is taking place in Moscow."

By the advice of Stein, Emperor Alexander sent
no reply to this letter. Romantzov, who represented the peace party in the Czar's councils, was
dismissed and Nesselrode took his place. Stein
wrote to Bernadotte, who, by this time, unreserv-
edly cast the lot of Sweden with that of Russia:
"After the wound of Moscow all our previous reverses are but mere scratches. Now, more than
ever, shall we fight it out to the bitter end. Rather

Napoleon's letter un-answered

Stein's comment

be buried under the ruins of the empire than come
to terms with this new Attila!"

After waiting several weeks in ill-concealed anxiety, Napoleon despatched Lauriston to Kutusov's
headquarters.   Lauriston's obvious errand was to
arrange for the exchange of prisoners.   Inciden-
tally he was to bring up the topic of a possible
peace, and thus smooth the way for it.   Succeeding in this, he was authorized to ask for passports
to St. Petersburg, there to conclude the final peace
negotiation.   Kutusov craftly detained Lauriston
until he could get word to St. Petersburg.   In
the meanwhile he replied that the word "peace"
figured nowise in his instructions, nor did he feel
free to conclude even an armistice.   By way of em-
phasizing this determination, Prince Kurakin captured the French convoys on the way to Smolensk,
while Dorokhov, with his Cossacks, took the French
stores at Vereiya by assault.   Altogether the Cossacks, forever hovering about the French outposts,
made no less than 15,000 prisoners.   The most serious Russian move during this period was the junction of the Army of the Danube under Admiral
Tchitchakov, with Tormasov's corps on the Styr,
and the accession to the Russian ranks of Platov's
twenty-one fresh Cossack regiments, recruited from
the Don.   At last Prince Volkonsky arrived at
Kutusov's headquarters with this answer from
Alexander:

"All the advices which you have received from
me, all the determinations expressed in the orders
addressed to you by me—everything ought to con-

Marginal notes:
Lauris-
ton's peace
errand

Activity
of the
Cossacks

vince you that my resolution is immovable.   At the present moment no proposal of the enemy can make me think of ending the war.   I shall not fail in the sacred duty of avenging our outraged country."

Before this defiance could be communicated to the French Emperor in Moscow Napoleon had already realized that the game was up.   On October 13, came the first snowfall.   To Napoleon and his veterans it recalled the horrors of their first winter campaign in Poland.   Within an hour Napoleon gave his orders for the evacuation of Moscow.   The advance columns had scarcely got to the valley of Vinkovo when they were attacked by the Cossacks, supported by Bennigsen's infantry.   They came within an ace of being surrounded and cut off from the main army.   Only the splendid dash of Murat and Poniatovski's Polish lancers saved the French from this disaster.   As it was, they lost 1,500 men, 3,000 horses and 38 guns.   The leader of the Russian attack, General Baggovud, was killed in the first onslaught.   Within two days after this misfortune Napoleon left Moscow with 107,000 men, 15,000 horses and 605 guns, ostensibly "for the pursuit of the enemy."   The bitterness of his resentment found expression in these final orders to Mortier, the Governor of Moscow:

"The Duke of Trevisa will put on march, to-morrow at daybreak, all the tired and lame soldiers of the corps of Prince Eckmühl and the viceroy, of the foot cavalry, and the Young Guard, and to direct the whole upon Mojaisk.   On the 22d or 23d, at two o'clock in the morning, he will set fire to the

[side notes] Alexander bent on war

French evacuate Moscow

Battle of Vinkovo

Death of Baggovud

Napoleon's resentment

brandy storehouse, the barracks, and the public
buildings, except the Foundling Hospital. He
will have the palace of the Kremlin set on fire.
He will take care that all the guns are broken
into pieces, that powder is placed under the towers of the Kremlin, that all the gun-carriages are
broken, as well as the wagon wheels.

"When these orders are attended to, and the
Kremlin is on fire in several places, the duke will
leave the Kremlin, and advance on the Mojaisk

Destruc-
tion of
Kremlin
palace

road. At four o'clock, the officer of artillery appointed to that duty will blow up the Kremlin, according to instructions.

"On the march he will burn all carriages left behind, use every endeavor to bury all the dead, and
burn all the muskets he can find. On reaching the
Gallitzin Palace, he will take the Spanish and Bavarians stationed there, and put fire to the ammunition wagons, and everything which cannot be removed. He will collect all the commanders of
posts, and order the garrisons to fall back.

"He will be particular to remain in Moscow till
he has himself seen the Kremlin blown up; and he
will also set fire to the Governor's two houses and
to that of Rasomovsky."

French
demon-
stration
against
Kuluga

Napoleon, with his main column, advanced toward Kuluga, hoping to defeat Kutusov there and
thus gain access to the rich inner provinces of
Russia. Kutusov anticipated him by breaking up
his cantonments to meet the French half way.

Battle of
the Lugea

Prince Eugene's advance division penetrated as
far as the Malo-Jaroslavetz on the Lugea, when
they encountered the Russian vanguard. General
Dorochov charged into the French and fell in the
mêlée. A fierce all-day fight followed. Six times

the town was stormed and lost again by the French,
until at nightfall they finally remained victorious.
They had lost nearly 10,000 men and seven generals. The Russian losses, too, were very heavy.
When Napoleon arrived he was shocked at the
heaps of the fallen soldiers around the ruins of
the town. As he was reconnoitring along the
banks of the Lugea, that evening, there was a sudden cry of "Here come the Cossacks," and the next
moment he and his followers were swept into the
river, with hand-to-hand fighting all around them. *Napoleon's narrow escape*
General Rapp barely managed to extricate the Emperor. That evening Napoleon held a council of
war amid the charred ruins of the village Gorodino. Murat, Berthier and Bessières attended.
In the face of their heavy losses, and the growing lack of horses, the three generals objected
strongly to another battle, and advised the abandonment of Kaluga. After they had their say,
the Emperor, with his head in his hands, sat mute
for more than an hour staring vacantly at a map
spread over his knees. Then he sighed deeply and
dismissed his marshals without announcing his intentions. Late in the night he issued orders for a *Retreat from Moscow*
retreat to Moschaisk. This meant a march over the
same barren stretch along which the French army
had advanced to Moscow. The greater part of the
stores forwarded from Moscow had been used up in
the demonstration against Kaluga. As a result the
retreat, from its very start, was attended by unusual
hardships. Horses fell right and left and hundreds
of ammunition wagons had to be blown up. In the

wake of the army, along the stretch of forty-eight
miles from Gorodino to Smolensk, Russian peasants
found no less than 208 pieces of abandoned artillery.
On October 27, the retreating army, now thoroughly
discouraged once more, came within view of the battlefield of Borodino. There the troops were demoralized by the ghastly spectacle of 30,000 dead bodies
rotting on the ground. The marching soldiers had
to turn deaf ears to the heartbreaking plaints of their
wounded comrades bedded on the stone floors of the
Monastery of Kolotsov near by. Already the nights
were bitterly cold. The Russian prisoners were
stripped of their clothing and afterward murdered
by the fierce hordes of stragglers. These, in turn,
fell into the hands of the pursuing Cossacks, or were
butchered by the enraged peasants if they ventured
beyond the protection of the marching columns.
Alternating snowfalls and thaws made the roads
impassable. On November 3, the rearguard under
Davoust, having reached Viazma one day behind
the main column, was attacked by Platov's Cossacks, and was all but cut off by a flank attack
from Miloradovich's column. Davoust and his
staff officers were driven headlong through the
streets of the town by the levelled spears of
the Cossacks. Six thousand Frenchmen fell in
the fight. Previous to this the constant skirmishing on the rear had cost Davoust 10,000
men. Only the reluctance of the Russians to
follow in force on the hunger-stricken route of
the French army had saved the rearguard from
early annihilation. Now Napoleon answered Da-

Horrors of
the retreat

Trials
of the
rearguard

Davoust
relieved

voust's despairing appeals for succor by relieving
him of command and putting Ney in his place. It
proved the severest task ever imposed on that hero
of a hundred battles. On November 6, the Russian
winter set in with a howling snowstorm. It be- Ney's rear
command
came frightfully cold. Shoes and blankets were
scarce, and there was nothing to eat but horse-
flesh. The soldiers perished by thousands from
hunger and cold. All the bonds of discipline
were relaxed. "Au diable avec les officiers! Il
n'y a que les malheureux!" was heard on all sides.
As one eye-witness put it: "To see men die before
your eyes in this triumphal March of Death made
no more impression than a drunken man at a Polish country fair." Henceforth the retreat became
a rout. Other no less telling scenes of this famous
tragedy of history can be gleaned from the con-
temporaneous accounts of eye-witnesses who have
given us glimpses of the disastrous march from Moscow, through Moschaisk, Gyaatsk, Viazma, and Smolensk, from the Lugea to the Dniepr and Beresina
and thence to Vilna and the Niemen. When the Losses
during the
retreat
Emperor reached Smolensk, only his cherished Old
Guard had preserved its entity. Of the 100,000 men
who set out from Moscow, but 40,000 men remained
under arms, with only 5,000 mounted men. There
were 30,000 stragglers, and 350 field guns had been
abandoned. Worse disaster awaited Napoleon at
Smolensk. The stores had been pillaged, and nothing was left wherewith to feed the starving soldiers.
The long-awaited reinforcements of the Ninth Corps,
which Victor had been bringing from Germany, were

summoned away to support Oudinot and St. Cyr's corps, which were threatened on three sides by three Russian corps under Wittgenstein, Tchitchakov and the auxiliaries from Finland. Napoleon's Austrian allies, under Prince Schwarzenberg, as usual, showed themselves averse to serious hostilities, and Napoleon had to detach Prince Eugene to protect Vitepsk. In spite of all heroic attempts to reach there in time, the viceroy found the place already in the hands of the Russians. Wittgenstein had established himself in force. General Hilliers, who advanced along the Jelnia road, was surprised by the Russians, and lost 2,000 men. Already the Russians were threatening the French base of supplies at Minsk and Warsaw. Worse than that, they were preparing to effect a junction between their armies at the passage of the Beresina, so as to bar the French from their only safe return to Poland.

Austrian allies unreliable

French lose Vitepsk

Hilliers' column ambushed

Napoleon saw that there was not a moment to lose, and, leaving Smolensk, he marched at once for Vilna. His marshals were to follow with their respective corps in extended columns. Ney, who had been fighting incessantly since he took command of the rearguard, received orders to blow up what was left of the ramparts of Smolensk, and to bury the remaining guns. By this time the French had only 1,800 horses left, all of which were intrusted to Latour-Maubourg, the leader of the cavalry. Napoleon and his staff marched on foot. When they reached Krasnoe they found the vanguard under Sebastiani, in a church, beleaguered by

Smolensk evacuated

the enemy. Broussier's division had been all but annihilated. The village of Kutkovo had to be Battle of Kutkovo taken in the face of severe artillery fire, and there the fight was stubbornly maintained while Napoleon hurried up the other columns lagging behind. At last, finding himself more and more hemmed in, Napoleon was constrained to cut his way through without regard for the fate of Ney and his rear- Ney's rearguard abandoned guard. Luckless Davoust was ordered to do the impossible—to wit, keep in touch with Mortier's retreating columns and at the same time wait for Ney to come up. With the Cossacks closing in upon him, Davoust was finally compelled to fight his way along with Mortier's 5,000 men. Thus the remnants of the French army, under constant fire, advanced to Liady and Orsha.

When the French rearguard was cut off, Tormasov and General Wilson, who had been sent to Russia by the British Government, urged Kutusov Kutusov hangs back to drive his whole column of 50,000 men into the French flank, but they could not move the old general. "You think the old man a fool," he said. "You are young and do not understand. Napoleon is still terrible. If he turns back we shall all regret it. Let him proceed to the Beresina, ruined and without an army, and I shall be satisfied."

Marshal Ney, in his extremity, proved himself Ney's unpleasant surprise the resourceful soldier he was known to be. Without warning of his danger—for all despatch riders had been intercepted by the enemy—he came face to face with Kutusov's main army before Krasnoe at nightfall. A crushing repulse of his first at-

tempt to fight his way through showed him how
thoroughly he was cut off. Undismayed, he resolved to swerve his column sidewise toward the
Dniepr, and to cross that river, so as to regain
the main army by the right bank. "But if the
Dniepr is not frozen, what shall we do?" said
some of his officers. "It will be frozen," retorted
the marshal. "Besides, frozen or not, we shall do
as we can. But we shall cross." For an hour
Ney drew his men back toward Smolensk. Then
turning abruptly to the north he marched at double
quick for the Dniepr with a flying column of one
thousand picked men. At the village of Syrokenci,
his vanguard picked up a peasant who pointed out
His brill- a place for crossing the frozen river in safety.
iant escape Under cover of the night Ney succeeded in moving
eight hundred of his men over the ice, without
horses or artillery. He even gave his stragglers
three hours time to come up, while he wrapped
himself in his cloak and slept till the last man was
over the river. Breaking the ice behind him, he
made straight for Orsha. The remainder of his
corps, 11,000 men in all, fell into the hands of the
Rest of Russians. Altogether the Russians captured 26,000
rearguard
taken French soldiers, 300 officers, and 28 guns. Ten
thousand Frenchmen were killed. The total loss
of the Russians barely exceeded 2,000 men.

At Orsha, Napoleon mustered his waning forces.
There remained but 6,000 effective men of the
Napoleon's 35,000 Imperial Guards; Eugene had saved 1,800
waning
forces out of 43,000; Davoust 4,000 out of 70,000, and
Ney 750 out of 40,000. The situation was critical

Painted by E. Meissonier

THE RETREAT FROM MOSCOW

From Carbon Print by Braun, Clement & Co., N. Y.

XIXth Cent., *Vol. One*

in the extreme. Tchitchakov, with 33,000 Russians, lay in front guarding the approach to the Beresina, Wittgenstein's corps occupied an impregnable position on the right, while Kutusov's main army was coming upon the left. Napoleon, after cleverly joining forces with Victor and Oudinot's corps as well as with Dombrovsky's Poles, formed his troops into one strong column and demonstrated against the lower Beresina as if to join forces with Schwarzenberg. Tchitchakov speedily took alarm, and, drawing in his long-extended line on the other side of the river, counter-demonstrated against the apparent point of attack. In the meanwhile Napoleon sent all his engineers to the upper Beresina with orders to construct two bridges at any cost. On the night that they began work, as it happened, Tschaplitz's division, guarding that point of the river, was ordered to join Tchitchakov's main army on the lower Beresina. The next morning, thanks to this stroke of fortune, the French engineers, under General Eblè, finished the first bridge, and a French brigade, passing over, established itself in the deserted bivouacs of the Russians. Another bridge for artillery and wagons was soon completed. Then Napoleon drew his columns together at that point, leaving but one division on the lower Beresina to further hoodwink the enemy. That same day the Russians, made aware of what was going on, attacked the French on both sides of the river. Wittgenstein opened the affair by intercepting the forlorn Partouneaux division which had been left below to fight it out alone. After

Further retreat cut off

Passage of the Beresina

Partouneaux's division abandoned

standing his ground for twelve hours, General Partouneaux and eight thousand men laid down their
arms. Tschaplitz's efforts to regain his lost position only brought him great loss. The next morning Tschaplitz renewed his attack, but during the
night Ney's corps had crossed with the Imperial
Guards and would have routed Tschaplitz's division if the whole of Tchitchakov's corps had not
come up to his support. More than 10,000 men on

Battle of the Beresina both sides fell in the fight. During the same day
Wittgenstein, on the other side of the river, sig-
nally defeated Victor's corps and drove it down
the slopes to the river's edge. While the men were
struggling to get across the bridges, the Russian
batteries from the heights concentrated their force
on this point. The artillery bridge broke down
and the horses and guns with their gunners fell
through in an inextricable mass. Artillery, wagons, horsemen and foot soldiers all commingled now
rushed over the other bridge, and hundreds were
crushed to death or pushed over the sides. Marshal Victor and his rearguard had to fight their
way through the struggling hordes of their own
comrades at the point of the bayonet. A desperate
throng of stragglers hung back on the shores of the
river, wavering between the fears of capture and
all but certain death in the frightful crush. These

Horrors of the flight horrors continued throughout the night. When
day broke at last, and the Russian Cossacks were
seen charging down the hillside, Marshal Victor
abandoned all those that had stayed behind to
their fate, and burned the bridge down before the

eyes of the wailing multitude. Sixteen thousand prisoners fell into the hands of the Russians. The loss of life during the passage of the Beresina was later estimated at 12,000. Twenty-five pieces of artillery had to be abandoned. Losses at the Beresina

On December 5, Napoleon, dragging himself along with his ragged bodyguard of officers, the so-called "Sacred Squadron," reached Smorgoni. There he received tidings of what was to him the most alarm- Alarming news from Paris ing thing of all. A conspiracy in Paris, working on a false report of his death, had shaken the foundations of his throne. Gathering his marshals around him, the emperor explained the need of his immediate presence in Paris and bade them all farewell. Then he dictated a final summary of the situation, the famous Twenty-eighth Bulletin of the Grand Army, in which he strove to explain The 28th bulletin to the world the causes of the terrible tragedy that had overwhelmed him. It ran in this wise:

"The army was in good condition on the 6th November, and till then the weather had been perfect. The cold began on the 7th, and from that time we lost every night several hundred horses, which died during bivouac. Soon 30,000 had succumbed, and our cavalry were all on foot. On the 14th we were almost without cavalry, artillery, and transports. Without cavalry we could gain no information beyond a quarter of a league. Without artillery we could not fight a battle, nor keep positions steadily. It was necessary to march, to avoid a battle, which the want of supplies made undesirable. It was necessary to occupy a certain space, to avoid being taken in flank, and that without cavalry to gain information and unite the columns. This difficulty, together with the excessive and sudden cold, rendered our position dangerous.

"The enemy, seeing on the roads traces of the frightful calamity which struck the French army, tried to take advantage of it. Our columns were all surrounded by Cossacks, who, like Arabs in the desert, carried off the trains and carriages which had separated from the army. That despicable cavalry, which comes silently, and could not repulse a company of light-horse soldiers, became formidable under those circumstances.

"The Cossacks took a number of isolated men, engineers and wounded officers who exposed themselves imprudently. Many also lost their baggage through the Cossacks in ambush. Some, not sufficiently steeled against adversity, lost their spirits and dreamed of misfortune. The brave were ever cheerful.

"Throughout all those operations the Emperor has always marched in the midst of his guard; the cavalry under the Duke of Istria, and the infantry under the Duke of Dantzic. Our cavalry was deprived of horses to such an extent that the officers who were still mounted had to be collected, to form four companies of one hundred and fifty men each. Their generals acted as captains; the colonels as under-officers. This sacred squadron, commanded by General Grouchy, and under the orders of the King of Naples, did not lose sight of the Emperor in all his movements. The health of his Majesty has never been better."

Napoleon's flight to France

Napoleon never admitted the full extent of his losses in Russia. As he was flying homeward in a solitary sleigh a few days afterward, General St. Cyr, his companion, remarked: "We left 300,-

000 men in Russia." "No, no!" replied Napoleon, "not so many as that." Then, after a moment's reflection, "Ah! 30,000 at the Moskova; 7,000 here, 10,000 there; and all those who strayed on the marches and have not returned. Possibly you are not far wrong. But then there were so many Germans!" Losses of the campaign

The Germans did not forget it! In one of the public squares of Munich stands a tall obelisk made from the bronze of cannon captured in France. On it are inscribed the words: "To the 30,000 Bavari- ans who perished in Russia." German resentment

On Napoleon's departure the conduct of the retreat was intrusted to Murat. He brought the wretched army as far as Vilna. Then he, too, found that important matters in Naples demanded his presence there. Platov's Cossacks made prolonged stay in Vilna impossible. In the flight from Vilna to Kovno even the French army funds, regimental eagles and the flags taken from the enemy were abandoned by the roadside. Marshal Ney and old General Lefebvre were the only commanders resolute enough to hold the Cossacks in check while the others fled onward. On December 12, the panic-stricken soldiers arrived at Kovno on the Niemen. As the covering force under Ney entered the gate of the city it was seen that the remnant of the Imperial Guard consisted of but three hundred men. The next morning the approach of the Russians drove the French out of Kovno. Pell-mell they crossed the bridge across the Niemen and thus quitted the soil of Russia. Murat's flight to Naples French driven out of Russia

Before abandoning Kovno, Ney seized a musket, and, with a corporal's guard, held the bridge-head against the forerunners of the Cossack vanguard. When the last French column had retired in safety, Ney threw his musket into the Niemen and left **Ney's last stand** the ramparts. He was the last combatant soldier of the Grand Army who left Russia. The next morning he walked into the last French outpost in the Prussian village of Gumbinnen, empty-handed, ragged and unkempt. To the challenge of the sentry he replied: "Here comes the rearguard of the Grand Army!" At Koenigsberg, the Russians, assisted by the friendly attitude of General York and his corps of Prussians, inflicted a last defeat **Russians invade Prussia** on their fallen foe. This brought the total losses of the French army up to 552,048 men, 167,000 horses, 12,000 guns, and 12,000,000 francs in money. When Emperor Alexander arrived in Vilna on December 21, 15,000 dead bodies still littered the ice of the Niemen. "What frightful horrors!" exclaimed Von Arndt. "This is not the work of Kutusov or of Wittgenstein. It is the finger of God," said the Czar. But the Russians, too, had suffered almost corresponding losses. The long-drawn pursuit cost Kutusov's corps 62,000 men, of whom 48,000 lay in hospital. The total Russian losses were later estimated at 300,000 men.

In all it is safe to state that the wars of 1812, in- **A million lives sacrificed** cluding the Peninsular campaign, and the American war, cost the lives of over a million men. But greater hecatombs were still to be demanded.

When Napoleon arrived in Paris his mere pres-

ence quelled the commotion caused by the disas-
trous news from Russia, and the all but successful New French levies
coup-d'état of Malet. The Emperor's first measure
was to call for a new levy of 350,000 conscripts.
Next he stamped out the last dying embers of the
conspiracy aimed at his throne. Malet and the
fourteen prisoners taken with him were condemned
to death and executed. What alarmed Napoleon
the most in the whole affair was that in the crisis Malet's cospiracy
of the attempted *coup-d'état* his son seemed to have
been overlooked by common consent. Every one
took for granted that the Emperor's death, as falsely
reported, would render a new election indispensable. "What!" exclaimed Napoleon, again and
again, "did nobody think of my son, my wife, or
the constitution of the empire?" He took instant
measures to secure his throne by additional decrees of the Senate with provisions for all contin-
gencies. This done he threw himself heart and The fifth coalition
soul into preparations for the inevitable war of the
coming year. Already the fifth coalition against
him was forming.

1813

THE first ally lost to Napoleon was Prussia. From the first the Prussian force of auxiliaries under General York of Wartenburg had been a source of misgiving to the French. When York succeeded Gravert in command, he insisted on being treated as an independent commander by Marshal Macdonald. As such the Prussian general distinguished himself in two actions against heavy Russian odds at Eckau and at Bauske. When the tide turned against the French the attitude of the Prussians became a matter of solicitude to both sides. Napoleon acknowledged York's independent rank, and allowed Macdonald to offer the Prussian commander a marshalship, with a gratuity of 20,000 francs. On the Russian side, General Essen, Count Pelucci and Prince Repnin, each in turn, made personal efforts to induce York to throw his Prussian corps into the balance against Napoleon. In December, when the ruin of the French cause was plain, the position of the Prussian auxiliaries was precarious, and York began to waver. In a despatch to the King of Prussia he explained matters in detail, and asked the king's permission to break off his allegiance to the French. At the same time, as the king well knew, Russian confi-

York of
Wartenburg

dential envoys in Vienna were doing their utmost
to induce Emperor Francis and Metternich to cut
loose from France.   Accordingly, York received
word to accommodate himself to circumstances
until the political atmosphere had cleared, and,
above all, not to kick over the traces ("Nach den
Umständen handeln, aber nicht über die Schnur
hauen").   For York this was not so easy.   When
Macdonald with his corps fell back on Dantzig late
in December, York and his Prussians brought up
the rear.   By a well-fought action before Tilsit the *Prussians cornered*
Russians succeeded in cutting off York's rearguard
from Macdonald's main body.   The Russian commander, General Dibitch, asked for an interview
between the lines.   York was informed of the
general Russian orders to avoid active hostilities
against Prussia, and was asked to enter into an
arrangement for full neutrality.   The next morning Count Pelucci, the Governor of Riga, appeared
with a personal letter of the Czar, in which Alexander promised to fight for the deliverance of Prussia
as well as of Russia, if the Prussian troops fought
on his side.   A last reconnoissance convinced York
that his corps was utterly cut off and surrounded.
After a moment of reflection York said quietly:
"You have got me.   To-morrow I shall enter your
lines."   York's officers and men received the news
with wild joy.   Next morning, York and Dibitch *Convention of Tauroggen*
met at the mill of Tauroggen, and signed a con-
vention whereby neutrality was declared between
Prussia and Russia.   The Russians were privileged
to move their troops through Prussia.   In case of

repudiation of the contract, York and his officers
were paroled not to serve against Russia for a
period of three months. In January, York's troops,
escorted by Russian Cossacks, entered Tilsit, and
effected a junction with a detached body of Prussians, under Massenbad. This practically delivered Koenigsberg over to the Russians. The
German revolt against Napoleon had begun.

First Prus-
sian defec-
tion

York thus reported his act to the King of
Prussia: "I lay my head at the feet of your
majesty. If I have erred, I should gladly die,
in the consciousness that I have not sinned either
as a faithful subject or a true Prussian. Now or
never is the time when your Majesty can tear loose
from the haughty demands of an ally whose intentions in regard to Prussia have ever been a matter
of serious concern. These considerations governed
my conduct. God grant it be for the good of the
Fatherland." King Frederick William of Prussia,
surrounded as he was by French troops quartered
in Berlin, repudiated York. He declared the convention of neutrality null and void. York was
summoned before a court-martial. Thanks to
the vigilance of the Russian outposts, the king's
couriers bearing these orders were not permitted
to reach the Prussian general. Failing to receive
any answer, York could only surmise his predicament. As a soldier of the old school, who had
once before been cashiered for criticising a superior officer, York took it hard. "With bleeding
heart," he wrote, "I burst the bonds of obedience,
and carry on the war upon my own responsibility.

York
repudiated

The army desires war with France; the nation desires it; the king himself desires it, but his will is not free. The army must make his will free."

Stein, Moritz, von Arndt, and other Prussian patriots, returning from exile to Russia, hastened to Koenigsberg to strengthen York's resolution. Stein bore a commission from the Czar to assume the government of the Prussian province occupied by Russian troops, and raised a Prussian army for the war with France. Stein's powers were to continue until the Czar could come to some arrangement with the King of Prussia. Stein's return

Armed with this commission, Stein appeared in Koenigsberg and boldly convoked an assembly of the people to take proper measures for the Fatherland independent of their king. York, though declining to act as chairman, was induced to give some countenance to the movement. On the promise of Stein's abstention from further Russian interference, he entered the house and spoke a few words. York's undisguised declaration of war was received with unbounded enthusiasm. Forty thousand Prussians flocked to arms from the province of East Prussia alone. Recruits began to arrive *Germans aroused* from all other parts of Germany. This unprecedented spectacle of the people working out their salvation without help from the crown, decided the timid Prussian king and his councillor, Hardenberg. Moreover, the Russians were advancing toward the Oder. On January 25, the royal family removed from Berlin to Breslau. This put the king beyond the power of the French troops at Berlin, and brought him so much nearer to Alexander. York's defection was condoned. Warlike preparations began at once. Swarms of Prussian volunteers bound for East Prussia passed through Berlin, shaking their fists at the French soldiers. On February 3, appeared a royal edict calling for volunteers. A week later all the Prussian men between the ages of seventeen and fifty were called to arms. Onefourth of the entire population responded to the call. General Knesebeck was sent to the headquarters of the Czar to arrange for military co-operation. The Czar sent Stein to Breslau with a Russian plenipotentiary to conclude the terms.

Treaty of Kalisch

On February 27, the treaty of Kalisch was signed. Russia undertook not to lay down her arms until the Prussian state should be restored to the same strength of area and population which it had before 1806. Russia reserved to herself the lost provinces of Prussian Poland, on a promise that Prussia should indemnify herself by an equal amount of territory taken from western Germany. This arrangement, though deplored by the foremost Prussian statesmen of the time, contained the germ of Prussia's coming leadership in German affairs.

Prussia's formal declaration of war was still withheld until her feverish military preparations could be perfected. The Russians, on the other hand,

War preparations

sure of popular support throughout Prussia, carried the war into Germany with undiminished vigor. The French rearguard under Eugene Beauharnais had to abandon the strong line of the Oder and fall back to Berlin and the Elbe. On February

20, the first Russian Cossacks appeared before Berlin and fought in the outskirts. Within a week the French had to quit the capital, closely pursued by the Russian vanguard. Some days later, Wittgenstein, who took command after the expiration of aged Kutusov at Bautzen, entered Berlin with the Russian infantry. On March 17, York and his Prussian corps made their appearance. They were received with tumultuous joy. On the same day came the king's long deferred declaration of war. It was the famous appeal "To my People," which stirred the Germans of those days to their depths:

York in Berlin

"For my faithful people, as for all Germans, there is no need of justification for the war which now begins. The causes for war are clear to the unblinded eyes of Europe.

"We succumbed to the overwhelming numbers of France. A peace which deprived me of half my subjects brought us no blessings. It inflicted wounds deeper than those of war. The marrow of the land was sucked out by our invaders. The strongholds of the country were held by the enemy. Agriculture and the arts were laid low. The freedom of commerce ceased and the sources of trade and prosperity were dried up. The country became a prey to robbers.

Frederick William's appeal

"By a strict fulfilment of my pledges I hoped to make things easier for my people and to convince the French emperor that it was to his own advantage to leave to Prussia her independence. My honest intentions were frustrated through his pride and faithlessness. It was plain that the emperor's treaties, worse still than his wars, aimed at our sure perdition. The moment has come when we can no longer be deceived about our condition.

"Men of Brandenburg, of Prussia, Silesia, Pomerania and Lithuania! You know what you have suffered for nearly seven years. You know what your sorry lot will be if you do not wage this war with honor. Remember your forefathers! Remember the great Elector, and Frederick the Great! Recall your blessed privileges for which our ancestors paid with their blood, freedom of conscience, honor, independence, commerce, art and science. Behold the great example of our powerful allies, the Russians! Behold the men of Spain, of Portugal! Lesser peoples than we have striven for the same ends against mightier foes and they have won. Remember the heroes of Switzerland and the Netherlands!

"It is the last decisive fight that we make for our existence, our independence and our property. There is no alternative but peace with honor or glorious defeat. Even this can be endured so it be in honor, for without honor life is nothing for a Prussian and a German. Yet we can trust to the future. God and our strong will must bring victory to our just cause. After victory we shall have glorious peace and the return of happy times.
                                            "FREDERICK WILLIAM."

Military reserves

On the same day that Frederick William issued his proclamation to the people, he decreed the formation of the great military reserves known as the Landwehr and the Landsturm. As the result of these measures and Scharnhorst's farsighted military preparations, 100,000 men were joined to Prussia's standing army of 45,000. Scharnhorst, against the advice of York and others, gave to Blücher the chief command. A general feeling of enthusiasm swept through the country like unto that which created the armies of the French Revolution. Beardless youths and gray haired men flocked to the colors. Clergymen, professors, and the students of the universities shouldered muskets. Even women found their way into the ranks. Prussia in arms Other women contributed their jewelry and trinkets, receiving in turn delicately wrought ornaments of iron, with the inscription: "I gave gold for iron; 1813." The king instituted the order of the Iron Cross, to be awarded for acts of bravery in battle. Thus a fresh impulse was given to the wrought-iron industry of Berlin, which has since been carried so far. Already the peasantry was rising against its French oppressors, and flying detachments of volunteers under Dornberg and Lützow carried raids into the French districts. The poet Koerner, himself a soldier, appealed to the Patriotic literature people in strains of patriotic ardor that have lived to the present day. His song

> "The people rise,
> The storm breaks loose,"

or the stirring lines on "Lützow's Raid," were sung from one end of Germany to the other.

"What is the German Fatherland?" wrote Arndt, the people's poet from Rügen:

> "Where'er resounds the German tongue, Arndt's song
> Where'er its hymns to God are sung!
>> That land is the land,
> Brave German, that, thy Fatherland!

> "That is the German Fatherland!
> Where scorn shall foreign triflers brand,
> Where all are foes whose deeds offend,
> Where every noble soul's a friend:
>> Be this the land,
> All Germany shall be the land!"

Other German poets joined in the chorus with the exception of Goethe, who said: "Well, well, shake your chains! That man Napoleon is too strong for you. You will not break them."

Napoleon, in Paris, faced the gathering storm with a bold front. In reply to a letter of warning from Davoust he wrote: "Pah! Germans never can become Spaniards." Yet he lost no time in gathering his new army of 350,000 conscripts and 27,000 fresh horses. Money was raised by floating paper currency. To allay the growing resentment arising among the French peasantry, he went to conciliate the Pope in his prison palace at Avignon, and greeted him by the name of Father. Pius VII. was set at liberty in Savona, and Napoleon consented to come to an agreement with him in which both parties yielded some of their long contested points. On February 13, Napoleon opened the Corps Legislatif with this characteristic speech:

"GENTLEMEN—The war again begun in the north of Europe presented to the English a favorable opportunity for their plans; but all their hopes have fallen to the ground. Their army failed before the citadel of Burgos, and after suffering great losses was obliged to evacuate the territory of all the Spains. I myself entered Russia. Everywhere our eagles triumphed.

"But the excessive and premature rigor of the winter subjected my army to a frightful calamity. In a few nights I saw everything changed, and I suffered great losses. They would have broken my heart if, at such an important time, I had been accessible to other sentiments than the interest, the glory, and the future of my peoples.

"In view of the evils which have weighed upon us, the joy of England has been great and her hopes unbounded. She offered our fairest provinces as a reward for treason; she laid down as a condition of peace the dismemberment of this beautiful empire. It was, in other words, a proclamation of perpetual warfare.

"The agents of England are propagating among all our neighbors the spirit of revolt against the sovereigns. England wishes to see the whole continent a prey to civil war and all the terrors of anarchy; but Providence has marked herself to be the first victim of anarchy and civil war.

"I have myself personally drawn up with the Pope a Concordat which puts a stop to all the difficulties which had unfortunately arisen in the Church. The French dynasty reigns and will reign in Spain. The Russians will go back to their frightful climate.

"I wish for peace; it is necessary for the world. Four times since the rupture which followed the Treaty of Amiens I have offered it in a formal manner. I shall never make any peace except an honorable one—one suited to the interests and greatness of my empire. So long as this murderous war continues, my peoples ought to be ready for sacrifices of every kind; for a bad peace would cause us to lose everything, even hope itself; and everything would be compromised, even the prosperity of our grandchildren."

To Emperor Francis of Austria, Napoleon wrote:

"I shall take no steps toward peace, because the last circumstances having turned to the advantage of Russia, it belongs to her Cabinet to take steps, if they understand the position of affairs. Nevertheless, I shall not object to those made by your Majesty."

Austrian mediation invited

It was too late. Austria was already being irresistibly drawn into the new coalition against France, for which England as heretofore had to furnish the money. In addition, the British Ministry agreed to furnish 30,000 troops. For the nonce Austria remained neutral, but the hasty return of Schwarzenberg's corps and the mobilization of Austria's remaining troops revealed to Napoleon that nothing but a victorious campaign could keep his newly acquired father-in-law off his heels.

The fifth
coalition

Blücher's new Prussian corps had not yet formed a junction with Wittgenstein when Napoleon returned to the fray at the head of 160,000 men. He advanced over the familiar country of Erfurt and Merseburg, headed straight for Saxony; for the fate of Saxony hung in the balance. Already Blücher had entered Dresden at the heels of a retreating French garrison, and Wittgenstein, pushing forward to Magdeburg, had repulsed 40,000 Frenchmen at Möckern. Now Napoleon threw his 160,000 men into the path of the 80,000 allies and marched on Leipzig. On the first day of May Marshal Ney, with 40,000 men, overwhelmed Winzingerode's Russian vanguard at Weissenfels and forced him back. Marshal Bessières, the famous French cavalry chieftain, lost his life in this fight. Wittgenstein brought the Russian column up and fell on Ney's flank at Gross-Görschen. The fight lasted nearly all day, and gave the raw Prussian recruits a chance to measure their strength against the equally youthful new conscripts of France. Unfortunately for the Russians, the affair was dragged out by Wittgen-

Battle of
Möckern

Weissen-
fels

Gross-
Gorshen

stein, who ordered up one brigade after another in-
stead of massing their attack at Lützen. Blücher's ^{Lutzen}
slowness in bringing up his Prussians, owing to the
negligence of a despatch rider, gave Napoleon a
chance to swing his long lines around the enemy's
ends. The Russians would have been encircled had
Blücher not arrived in time to interpose his Prussian reserves. Firing incessantly until after dark,
the allies finally retired in good order. On the
evening of the bloody engagement of May 2, the
Prussian Hussars under Ziethen, supported by a
Cossack brigade, tried to pierce the French centre
with a fierce night attack, but were repulsed by
Napoleon's well-concentrated artillery fire. They ^{Death of}
captured some guns, but suffered irreparable loss ^{Scharn-horst}
in the death of Scharnhorst. Further away a Prus-
sian division, during this same time, stormed Halle,
but had to fall back after the main army, lest it
be cut off. After a sharp rear action at Koldiz, the ^{Koldiz}
allies gained Dresden and made a stand at Bautzen.
An attempted French diversion against Berlin was
frustrated by Barclay de Tolly and York at Koe- ^{Koenigs-warte}
nigswarte and Weissig, and both armies drew in
their reserves for the coming battle. The accession ^{Weissig}
of two Bavarian and Saxon corps brought Napo-
leon's fighting force up to 150,000, whereas the
allies had 90,000 men. On May 19, Napoleon advanced on Bautzen and delivered a determined
attack on Blücher's right wing. It resulted in a
drawn fight with heavy losses on both sides. The
next morning the engagement became general.
During the battle the French crossed the river

Spree under fire and made a combined attack on
the centre. The fight was kept up as long as the
French infantry could see to shoot, until Napoleon
had accomplished his object of making the enemy
strengthen his centre at the expense of his right
wing. Under cover of darkness, Ney's corps made
a long night march to get around Blücher's right
end. Early the next morning, Napoleon made a
sharp attack on the Russian left under Milarado-
vitch, and, meeting with determined resistance there,
followed it up by throwing Macdonald's and Oudinot's divisions against the Russian centre, where
Alexander and his suite had their headquarters.

Battle of
Bautzen

While the battle was on, Napoleon listened anxiously for the sound of Ney's cannon on the extreme right. Ney's instructions had been to work
around the enemy's flank and to attack in force no
later than noon. At the early hour of ten, the distant roar of artillery on the enemy's right flank and
rear announced to Napoleon that Ney had carried
out his difficult manœuvre. The Emperor immediately despatched a courier to Paris with a pencilled
note to Marie Louise proclaiming a sure victory.
Then he galloped over to his left to press home
Ney's success. Ney had Blücher surrounded on
three sides, and beset the Prussians so fiercely that
Blücher had to call for reinforcements wherewith
to protect his retreat. As soon as these manœuvres
had the desired effect of weakening the Russian
centre, Napoleon hurled his whole mass of 75,000
men into the centre of the enemy's line. The result was an almost instantaneous retreat all along

the line. The Russians fell back on Hochkirch and
Lobau, while the Prussians fought their way back
to Wurschen and Weissenburg, holding that position through the night. The next morning the allies, in the face of Napoleon's continued advance,
fell back steadily into Silesia behind the strong line
of the fortress Schweidnitz and the ridges of the
Riesengebirge, where they could readily join hands
with the Austrian forces massed on the frontier of
Bohemia. Napoleon entered Breslau. The continued fighting of the last five days had cost him
25,000 men. The hospitals of Dresden were filled
with 18,000 wounded men. Generals Bruyères and
Kirchner were among the dead, and Marshal Duroc
was killed close to the Emperor's side. They were
buried without religious honors. "I will have no
priest!" said Napoleon. When the pursuit came
to an end, the Emperor exclaimed angrily to his
surviving marshals: "Quoi? No result after such
a massacre? No prisoners, no guns, nor standards?
They leave me not even a nail!"

Barren vic-
tories

The threatening presence of the Austrian troops
caused Napoleon anxiety to ascertain the precise
intentions of Austria before exposing his flank and
long-drawn communications to an attack from that
quarter. An armistice was proposed and gladly
entered into by both sides. The convention was
signed at Pleswitz, on June 4, and all hostilities
were suspended for six weeks. The struggle shifted
instantly from the battlefield to the diplomatic chan-
celleries at Vienna. To win the support of Austria
was alike the endeavor of Napoleon and of the al-

Truce of
Pleswitz

lies. Even the British Ministry awoke to the exigencies of the situation. Shortly after the conclusion of the armistice, Sir Charles Stewart and the Earl of Cathcart appeared at the allied headquarters. A formal agreement was reached by the convention of Reichenbach on the 14th of June. In this treaty Great Britain agreed to furnish to Prussia £666,000, on King Frederick William's promise to restore the *status quo* in Hanover. Russia obtained a subsidy of £1,333,000 and the continued maintenance free of cost of her fleet locked up in English harbors since the convention of Cintra, on the Czar's formal permission to keep 160,000 men in the field against Napoleon. Besides this, the British Government guaranteed fifty per cent of an issue of Prussian war bonds amounting to £5,000,-000. In fine, England, Russia, Prussia and Sweden bound themselves not to conclude any truce, peace or convention whatsoever otherwise than by mutual consent. Napoleon, on the other hand, entered into an offensive and defensive alliance with Denmark, thereby securing a valuable hold on the mouth of the Elbe, where Davoust held Hamburg, besides the acquisition of 20,000 troops in that quarter. At Vienna, during the first three weeks of the armistice, all negotiations hung fire. Prince Metternich, rather than compromise himself with either party, chose the rôle of mediator. To the French ambassador he suggested a "suspension of last year's treaty of alliance between France and Austria." As Maret insisted that this was equivalent to a dissolution of the alliance, Metternich himself finally

Margin notes:
Convention of Reichenbach

British subsidies

Denmark with France

Austria in balance

repaired to Dresden to have a personal interview with Napoleon. The two men met on the night of June 28. Both have recorded their recollection of the interview. "You are welcome, Metternich," said Napoleon, "but why do you come so late? We have lost nearly a month in coming together, *Napoleon meets Metternich* and your mediation has assumed almost a hostile aspect. . . . Is it because you conceive yourself in a position to dictate terms, that you pay me this visit?" Metternich soon came to the point, demanding not only the return of Illyria, but the evacuation of Germany, Italy, Holland, Poland and Spain. Napoleon flew into a rage. "How much has England given you?" he demanded. At the same time the Emperor dropped his hat. When Metternich made no movement to raise it, Napoleon turned pale, and, after striding past it several times, at length kicked it away.

"You are not a soldier, sir," he exclaimed. "You have not, like me, a soldier's soul. You have not lived in camps. You have not learned to despise the life of another man, and your own, when need be. What care I for 200,000 men?"

Metternich turned on him with unwonted emotion. "Let us open the doors, sire!" he exclaimed. "And if the doors are not sufficient, open the windows! that the whole of Europe may hear you."

When he at last left the Emperor's room he *Metternich's comment* remarked to Marshal Berthier, "I declare to you solemnly, that your master is out of his mind." The final upshot was that both Metternich and Napoleon agreed to postpone the settlement of

terms to a Peace Congress to sit at Prague dur-
Prague
Peace
Congress
ing the first week of July, while the armistice
was to be prolonged until August 10.

While the delegates to this congress were convening, tidings came from Spain which quite offset
the moral effect of Napoleon's latest victories. It
was the news of Wellington's victory of Vittoria.
Its immediate effect was to give England such an
ascendency in the impending negotiations that Austria ceased to waver. From that moment the sittings of the Peace Congress served no other purpose
but to give either party more time wherein to rush
the last reinforcements to the front.

In Vittoria   The battle of Vittoria was the result of half a
year's patient waiting and planning on the part
of Wellington. After the campaign of Salamanca
large reinforcements reached Wellington in Portugal. He made a hurried visit to Cadiz, and the
Cortes invested him with the supreme command
of the nation's forces in Spain. He set to work
at once to restore the disorganized Spanish army
to a state of efficiency. In this he was left comparatively unhampered by the Spanish Government
—all engrossed as it was at that time by the dissensions that followed the government's suppression
of the Inquisition. By the beginning of April the
total forces arrayed against the French in Spain
aggregated 185,000 men, 75,000 of whom were under Wellington's immediate direction. The French
mustered altogether 230,000 men, of whom 100,000
Shrapnel's
invention
lay in Central Spain. It was at this time that Major
Shrapnel's new invention of explosive shells filled

with small bullets came into use. The campaign
began on April 11, when Suchet, with a corps of
68,000 men, was foiled in an attack on Sir John
Murray and Elio's allied forces numbering 36,000
men at Castilla. Suchet retired in good order with
a total loss of 2,000 men. A fortnight later a concentric movement on Madrid was begun by the
army of reserves in Andalusia, followed by the
Duke del Pargne's march into La Mancha, and
Wellington's southward advance from Portugal.
As the British forces crossed the frontier stream, Wellington
Wellington rose in his stirrups and waving his Spain
re-enters
hand exclaimed: "Farewell, Portugal!" Thanks
to the demonstration in New Castile, the French
failed to oppose Wellington in force, and he was
thus enabled to drive them from Valladolid, and
from the southern banks of the Douro and Carrier.
On June 14, King Joseph abandoned Burgos. The
ramparts of the stronghold had to be blown up in
such a hurry that 300 Frenchmen were killed in the
explosion. From Burgos the king with all his court
and army retreated to Vittoria. Their flight was King
Joseph's
flight
encumbered by an endless file of wagons and carriages loaded down with the accumulated spoils
of five years. Rather than lose all this loot, the
French army, on July 19, faced about in front of
Vittoria. Wellington came up, on June 20, with
78,000 Englishmen, Portuguese and Spanish, supported by 90 guns. The next morning Wellington
advanced all along the line. The Spanish division
under Murillo led the attack, but after Murillo had
been wounded, a regiment of British infantry and

a battalion of Highlanders had to go to their support. The colonel of the Highlanders was killed at the decisive moment when the French lines were swept back.

In the centre, meanwhile, Wellington had broken through into the plain of Vittoria; but the battle was not won until Graham, after a long fight on the left, drove the French from their strong position on the Heights of Ariega. When the French gave way they left behind them 7,000 killed and wounded, and 151 guns, 451 caissons of ammunition, and a wagon train containing immense spoils, among them Jourdan's marshal's bâton, Joseph's private carriage, the military chest with twenty-two million francs and private loot beyond estimation. More than that, the victory of Vittoria meant the immediate expulsion of the French from all the northwestern provinces of Spain. It was the most brilliant achievement of the Peninsular war. At its close, to quote Napier's clarion sentences: "The English general, emerging from the chaos of the Peninsular struggle, stood on the summit of the Pyrenees, a recognized conqueror. From these lofty pinnacles the clangor of his trumpets pealed clear and loud, and the splendor of his genius appeared as a flaming beacon to the warring nations."

The victory not only freed Spain from its invaders, and prepared the way for an early invasion of France, but it restored the spirit of England, sorely tried by the unsatisfactory progress of the war with the United States.

In America, the campaign on land this year had

(margin note: Battle of Vittoria)

(margin note: American war)

opened with a British reverse at Frenchtown, offset by the successful capture of General Winchester French-town and his force of 800 Americans. The Indians afterward massacred 260 wounded Americans. A week later, fortune again favored the American cause when Captain Forsyth, with 200 volunteers, succeeded in surprising the British at Elizabeth and Elizabeth took 68 prisoners. Then came the famous exploit when the American sloop-of-war "Hornet," commanded by Captain Lawrence, attacked and sunk Hornet sinks Peacock the "Peacock," a British sloop-of-war of superior cock armament. This put an end to the oft-repeated boast of Englishmen that British sloops could lay alongside of American frigates and whip them. Next the "Hazard," an American privateer schooner, captured the British frigate "Albion" and her convoy, the cutter "Caledonia." In de- Hazard takes Albion fiance of the blockade of Chesapeake Bay by a British squadron under Admiral Warren, the American privateer schooner "Adeline," on March 10, attacked and sunk a British schooner in that same bay. Shortly afterward, another naval action was fought out on the waters of the Chesapeake between four American vessels and seventeen British barges. An American ship was lost in the fight. The British blockade was now extended all along the Atlantic coast, and British men-of-war cruised outside of Boston. The captain of one of them, the frigate "Shannon," challenged Captain Lawrence, of "Peacock" fame, to come out with his new frig- Shannon challenges Chesapeake ate, the "Chesapeake," and fight him. Stung by peake the challenge, Lawrence prematurely put out to

sea and made for the "Shannon." The fight was
watched by multitudes on the high shores. After
a repeated exchange of broadsides, the "Chesapeake" fouled with the "Shannon," and became unmanageable. As the British boarders were
swarming over the side, Lawrence was shot through
the body. He fell shouting: "Don't give up the
ship! Fight her till she sinks!" The carnage on
the two ships was dreadful. In thirteen minutes
252 men were killed. The first officer of the
"Shannon" was killed by his own men, for mis-
takenly hoisting up the Union Jack under the Stars
and Stripes. Captain Broke of the "Shannon" had
a narrow escape. As he stood alone for a moment on the breach of the forecastle, three American seamen leaped upon him. He was felled to the
ground with the butt of a musket and was slashed
in the head with a cutlass. As he lay on the deck
grappling with his antagonist, a British marine ran
up, and, taking him for an American, raised his
bayonet for a final thrust. "Pooh, pooh, you
fool!" said Broke as he lay pinioned down by his
foe, "don't you know your captain?" whereupon
the marine changed the direction of his thrust and
slew the captain's assailant.

On the same day with this encounter in Massachusetts Bay a British squadron chased Decatur
into New London, with the "United States," the
"Hornet," and the prize "Macedonia." None of
these ships got to sea again while the war lasted.
Decatur claimed that his movements were signalled
to the enemy by means of blue lights. Hence the

"Don't give up the ship!"

Broke's narrow escape

opprobrious term "Blue Lights" applied to the Federalists of New England. The news of Broke's The Boston Blue Lights victory was announced in the House of Commons, on July 7, just as Lord Cochrane was concluding a fierce denunciation of the Admiralty for the repeated naval defeats inflicted by the Americans. By way of defence, the Secretary of the Admiralty read aloud the report of Broke's victory. Amid Broke's reward wild cheers, the Crown, then and there, created Broke a baronet and a Knight of the Bath.

In Europe, the end of Napoleon's armistice had been postponed to August 10. Within a few days of that date, the Congress at Prague was still sitting, while both sides were preparing for the resumption of immediate hostilities. From Italy, from France, from the provinces of Germany, from Denmark, Sweden, and from Russia, reinforcements were hurrying to the theatre of war. Even from America, still warring with England, the allies derived some unexpected help. General Moreau, the victor of Hohenlinden, who had lived in exile at New York, since his trial and condemnation by Napoleon in 1804, was induced by the Czar to pit his military genius against that of his former Moreau's reappearance commander-in-chief. The old general consented to come only on condition that France should be maintained within the limits she had acquired under the Republic, and that the French people should be suffered to choose their own government. As soon as he received the Czar's reassurance on this score, Moreau embarked from New York on board the American ship "Hannibal," and, eluding British cruisers, landed at Gothenburg late in July. In the company of Bernadotte and Jomini, the great theoretical strategist, he journeyed from Stralsund to Prague. They arrived at the Czar's headquarters in time for Moreau to put a final touch to the plan of campaign which was adopted by the allies.

Other defections

On August 7, Metternich transmitted to Napoleon the ultimatum of the Austrian Cabinet. Metternich promised to procure peace if France would restore the provinces taken from Austria in 1809, the North German districts and free cities annexed in 1810, and the Polish territory wrested from Prussia and Russia during the last war. Independence was to be re-established in Italy, in the papal dominions, in Holland and in Spain. Napoleon was ill disposed to grant any of Metternich's demands. A new French army from Italy was marching straight for Austria. The appearance of these troops on the Austrian frontier, according to his calculations, would put the most effective stop to the warlike attitude of Austria. It was a game of intimidation, but, unfortunately for Napoleon, he was seriously misinformed concerning the strength of Austria's armaments. Maret's spies in Vienna had led him to believe that the whole force of Austria was but 100,000, whereas, in truth, more than 200,000 men were assembled on the frontier.

Austria's ultimatum

Disparity of forces

At the time that Napoleon received Metternich's ultimatum, his armies in Germany had grown to a total strength of more than half a million men. Of these, 235,000 were under his immediate command in Saxony; Oudinot had 80,000 at Torgau facing Bernadotte; 50,000 Frenchmen and Bavarians lay in upper Bavaria threatening the Austrian frontier, while some 150,000 men held the northern strongholds from Hamburg to Dantzig and along the Elbe and Oder. The available forces of the allies aggregated 400,000 men, of whom 220,000 threatened the French flank and rear from Bohemia. Two more armies of 80,000 and 90,000 respectively pressed on Napoleon from the east and from the north. Behind them 200,000 reserves were on the march.

Strength of allies

On August 10, twelve hours after the receipt of Austria's ultimatum, Napoleon returned a partial answer. He conceded some of the demands, but refused peremptorily to restore either Trieste or the middle German provinces. His terms were unacceptable—moreover, they did not reach Prague until August 11. By that time the armistice had terminated and the Peace Congress was dissolved. Before dawn of the next morning, the soldiers bivouacked in Silesia beheld the blaze of innumerable beacon-fires along the ridges of the Riesengebirge. It was the signal that hostilities would resume and that Austria had declared war on France.

End of truce

Napoleon's plan was to descend first on the enemy's rear, from the heights of the Koenigstein, and to push him toward Dresden, to be caught between his armies on the Elbe under St. Cyr. This done he meant to make a dash for Prague. Berlin was to be taken by a concentric movement of the strong armies of Davoust, Girard and Oudinot, ad-

Napoleon's plan

vancing from Saxony, Magdeburg and Hamburg.
Moreau's counter plan The plan of the allies was to let their main column of 128,000 Austrians and 70,000 Russians, un-
der Schwarzenberg, push through the Erzgebirge
to take Napoleon in the rear. The first engagement of importance was that of August 21, between
Wallmoden and Davoust at Wellahn. It was in the
skirmishing that followed this fight that Theodore
Koerner lost his life. He was struck by a stray
Death of Koerner bullet at Gadebusch. One hour before, he had composed his famous sword song. On August 23, Oudi-
not, near Berlin, came in contact with his old com-
rade Bernadotte, at Blankenfeld. A general en-
Gross-beeren gagement followed at Grossbeeren. Without the
aid of the Swedes, whom Bernadotte held back,
the Prussians routed the French. They captured
2,400 prisoners. Girard's division of 8,000 advancing from Magdeburg was turned back after a sharp
encounter with the Prussian Landwehr, under
Hirschfeld. At the same time, Napoleon, to free
himself from the Prussians in Silesia, made a dash
into Bohemia, and in a series of well-fought engage-
Battle of the Katzbach ments forced Blücher back to the Katzbach River.
The last fight cost Blücher 2,000 men. With Na-
poleon thus engaged, Moreau advised Schwarzenberg to make an immediate advance on Breslau.
Napoleon had to abandon all further pursuit of
the Prussians. Wheeling his columns in haste
he countermarched for Dresden, while Vandamme,
with his 40,000 men, was ordered to cut off the
allies' retreat at the Koenigstein and Pirna. Had
Schwarzenberg been alive to the situation the allies

could have captured Dresden with comparative ease. As it was, the Austrians moved with accustomed slowness. Dresden was not attacked until the 25th of August. Then the city was heavily bombarded and St. Cyr's outposts were driven into the suburbs. On the morrow the wellnigh frantic citizens of Dresden were overjoyed to see Napoleon ride into the city from the other side, followed by his strong army. He was received by the King of Saxony and King Murat, who had come from Naples at last to throw in his lot with the Emperor. The combined attack of the allied forces on that day was met with a murderous repulse. During the night, Napoleon made all his dispositions for a masterstroke. At daybreak, the French columns poured out of the city and attacked in turn. The Austrian left wing was drawn off into the valley of Plauen by Murat and Victor, and there succumbed to their combined attack. Vandamme, advancing from Koenigstein, drove the Prince of Würtemberg into Pirna. Napoleon himself, with the bulk of his artillery, pierced the centre of the allies. Emperor Alexander's suite at Racknitz came under a heavy fire. General Moreau at his side had just remarked, "It is rather warm here," when a cannon shot laid him low. "That Bonaparte is always lucky," remarked the dying hero as they dragged him from under his horse. His legs had to be amputated where he lay, and he died soon afterward. It needed no Moreau to tell that the battle was lost to the allies. In great disorder they fell back into Bohemia. The French took thousands of prisoners.

Attack on Dresden

Allies repulsed

Death of Moreau

So signal a victory might have brought more decisive results for Napoleon, had Vandamme succeeded in intercepting the retreat of the allies. He was foiled in this by the gallant stand of the Russian rearguard under Ostermann. Though overmatched as four to one, the Russians held back the French for a whole day at Kulm, until the first corps of their army came up. Ostermann's 8,000 men had been reduced to 2,000, and he himself lost an arm during the fight; but those who survived had the satisfaction of seeing Vandamme's division overwhelmed in turn by superior numbers. The French tried to escape through the mountains, but there fell into the hands of Kleist's Prussian corps retreating from Dresden. Vandamme and the bulk of his corps were taken prisoners. The victory of Dresden was further offset by a severe reverse of the same day inflicted on the French by Blücher in Silesia. After having drawn Macdonald's wide extended lines from the banks of the Bober across the Katzbach and foaming Neisse, Blücher suddenly turned about and shattered the French centre by a fierce attack with his whole column. Under a heavy thunder-shower the French were driven into the swollen rivers. When the wet firelocks of the Prussians put an end to their volleys, Blücher drew his sword shouting "Vorwärts!" and led a bayonet charge against the French over the ancient battlefield of Wahlstadt. The French were utterly routed. A part of their retreating troops under General Puthod fell into the hands of the Russians. In all, the allies captured 18,000 prisoners and 103

Russian stand at Kulm

Battle of Wahlstadt

guns. Blücher lost but one thousand of his men. For this action he was created Prince of Wahlstadt, but his soldiers surnamed him Marshal Vorwärts. Macdonald returned to Dresden almost unattended and broke the melancholy news to Napoleon: "*Votre armée du Bobre n'existe plus!*" Blucher's reward

Oudinot reported a similar distressing disaster. Napoleon despatched Ney to take his place, but even that undaunted leader sent back discouraging reports. "It is my duty," he wrote from Wurtzen, "to declare to your Majesty that with the present organization of the Fourth, Seventh and Twelfth army corps no good results can be expected from them. Both generals and officers are demoralized. . . . Your Majesty should be informed that the foreign troops of all nationalities show a very bad disposition, and that it is doubtful whether the cavalry which I have with me be not more hurtful than useful." On September 6, Ney risked a general engagement at Dennewitz and met with a crushing reverse. The Prussians under Von Buelow and Tauenzien, supported by two inactive corps of Russians and Swedes, utterly routed the French army and nearly annihilated their rearguard of Würtembergers. The Bavarian corps under Raglowich, which had remained almost inactive during the battle, retired in another direction, firing on their French allies whenever the fugitives came too near them. Ney lost 8,000 men, eighty guns and three eagles. The loss of the allies was but 6,000, of whom nearly 5,000 were Prussians. Ney's report of the disaster of Dennewitz was sufficient-

Ney relieves Oudinot

Dennewitz

ly ominous: "I have been totally defeated, and do not know yet whether my army has reassembled. The spirit of the generals and officers is shattered. To command in such condition is but half to command. I had rather be a common grenadier." Napoleon tried to offset these reverses by another dash on the Prussians in Silesia, but Blücher, after a

series of exhausting marches and countermarches amid torrents of rain, skilfully evaded him. "These creatures have learned something!" exclaimed Napoleon bitterly as he returned to Dresden to ward off another attack from that city. While the time consumed in these constant fights meant so many more marches for Bennigsen's reserves hurrying down from Russia, it meant nothing for Napoleon but an increasing consumption of men and stores. For the French army the situation became serious. Already orders had been sent to strengthen the Rhine fortresses along the line of retreat. The French Minister of War in transmitting Napoleon's orders wrote:

"Our army is still large and in good condition, but the generals and officers, wearied with the war, have no longer that action which formerly led them to great exploits; the theatre is too extended. The Emperor is victorious whenever he can be on the spot; but he cannot be everywhere, and the generals who command in his absence seldom answer to his expectations. You are aware of what happened to General Vandamme; the Duke of Tarento has met with reverses in Silesia, and the Prince of the Moskova has just been beaten in marching upon Berlin. I present you with this picture in order that you may know all, and take steps accordingly."

While Napoleon lay at Dresden a series of minor defeats were inflicted on his outlying marshals. As Davoust was retiring to Hamburg in the middle of September, his rearguard was cut off by Wallmoden Russian victories on the Gorde. During the last days of September Platov's Cossacks captured 8,000 Frenchmen at Zeitz, and then descended upon Cassel and drove King Jerome flees King Jerome from his dominions. Thieleman, a Saxon soldier of fortune now serving on the Prussian side, intercepted the French convoys at Leip- Weissenfels zig, capturing 1,200 prisoners at Weissenfels and 2,000 more at Merseburg. Lefebvre's division was Merseburg badly handled at Altenburg. On this occasion the Altenburg French auxiliaries from Baden fired on their allies and helped to disperse them. Napoleon, while manœuvring incessantly around Dresden, felt the ground shaking under him. On October 7, he left Dresden, to demonstrate against Blücher's corps which had crossed the Elbe. The next day came Defection of Bavaria the defection of the Bavarians. Wrede, an old-time favorite of the Emperor, united his forces to the Austrians and laid himself across the line of Napoleon's retreat. The King of Bavaria justified this change of front in an official note recalling the fact that he had been compelled to sacrifice 30,000 of his subjects in Russia "under punishment of felony." Napoleon spent the next four or five days in painful irresolution. Meanwhile, the allies were concentrating on Leipzig. At last Napoleon executed a few rapid manœuvres to overwhelm Schwarzenberg's main column advancing from Bohemia, but it was already too late. On October 14, the flower of

Wachau

the French cavalry under Murat was engaged by Blücher's and Wittgenstein's cavalry at Wachau. The contest, which was the most important cavalry engagement of the campaign, lasted all day and resulted in a drawn fight. The next day a hurricane swept through the French camp, carrying away roofs and tents and drenching the soldiers.

At midnight two rockets were fired from Schwarzenberg's headquarters, on the south of Leipzig. They were immediately answered by blue and red lights from Blücher's camp on the north. These signals told the allies that all was in readiness. On the morning of October 16, while Napoleon was riding forward to direct the attack on Schwarzenberg, the French were unexpectedly attacked by

Battle of Pleisse

the Austrians on the right bank of the Pleisse. The attack was repulsed. Latour-Maubourg carried the French cavalry so far into the enemy's lines that the Russian Czar and King of Prussia had difficulty in escaping. Only the fall of Latour-Maubourg's horse saved them from capture. Napoleon joyfully exclaimed: "Le monde tourne pour nous!" and sent off couriers to Dresden and Paris announcing his victory. Unfortunately for him, a simultaneous attack from Neerveldt's division of Austrians across the Pleisse kept the French engaged until Blücher with the Prussians could throw himself upon the corps of Marmont at

Mockern

Möckern, and compelled him to retire with the loss of 6,000 men and forty guns. One single Prussian brigade in this fight lost all but one of its officers. On the other side Napoleon succeeded in repulsing

the troublesome Austrians. Neerveldt himself was
taken prisoner. This was the same officer who had
on former occasions come a suppliant to solicit the
armistice of Loeben, who had represented the Emperor of Austria in the negotiations of Campo
Formio, and who, on the night following Austerlitz, bore the proposals for the famous campfire conference of the two emperors. Napoleon summoned
him to his headquarters and engaged him in conversation. "This struggle is growing very serious," he
said. "Should we not put a stop to it?"—"That
is all we are fighting for," replied Neerveldt.—"Let
England restore me my colonies," rejoined the Emperor, "and I will give her back Hanover." Then
he spoke of the possibility of an armistice.—"The
allies want no armistice," said Neerveldt; "they
reckon to go to the Rhine this autumn."—"To the
Rhine!" exclaimed Napoleon. "Before they can
get there, I must lose a battle!" Then he dis- Neer-
missed Neerveldt on parole to repeat what he had veldt's
mission
told him. "Au revoir, general," he called after
him; "when you speak to the two emperors you
may recall some of our recollections of the past."

Neerveldt's report only strengthened the allies in
their determination, the more so since Bernadotte's
reserves and Bennigsen's reinforcements were expected hourly. Napoleon was weak enough to hold
his army in leash throughout a whole day awaiting
the results of Neerveldt's mission. When no answer came by nightfall, he reluctantly made his
dispositions for a retreat through Leipzig. After
a night spent in going over the whole ground,

Napoleon returned to his bivouac at Probstheyda at daybreak just in time to see three columns of the enemy advancing on his reformed lines of bat-tle. From all sides the French, now numbering barely 190,000 men, were attacked by the united forces of the allies mustering 300,000 men. "Mes enfants," said General Maison, "this is the last battle of France, and we must all be dead be-fore night." Everywhere, throughout the French ranks, like despondency reigned. When Marshal Augereau rode up to the Emperor's headquarters, Napoleon chid him: "You are long in coming, my old Augereau. You are no longer the Augereau of Castiglione." "I shall be the same old Augereau," replied the marshal, "so soon as you can give me back the soldiers of Italy." The Emperor himself was deeply discouraged. While the first cannon balls were striking into the French lines he still pondered over the map spread out at his feet. "What an intricate problem it all is," he sighed. "No one but myself can get me through it. But for luck, I, too, may find it too hard a task." The arrival of Bennigsen's reinforcements really turned the day against him. It swelled the army of the allies to nearly double the number of Napoleon's forces. All day long the great battle of the na-tions raged. As the German historian, Menzel, has admirably summarized the action:

The Austrians, stationed on the left wing of the allied army, were opposed by Oudinot, Augereau, and Poniatovsky; the Prussians, stationed on the right wing, by Marmont and Ney; the Russians

Marginal notes:
Probs-theyda

Arrival of Bennigsen

and Swedes in the centre, by Murat and Regnier. In the hottest of the battle, a Saxon cavalry regiment, with two brigades of Saxon infantry, went over to Blücher with bugles blowing, and General Normann, when about to be charged at Taucha by the Prussian cavalry under Bülow, also deserted to him with two Würtemberg cavalry regiments. The whole of the Saxon infantry, with thirty-eight guns, under Regnier, shortly afterward went over to the Swedes, five hundred men and General Zeschau alone remaining true to Napoleon. The Saxons stationed themselves behind the lines of the allies, but their guns were instantly turned upon the French.

Battle of the Nations

In the evening of this terrible day, the French were driven back close upon the walls of Leipzig. Their losses were 40,000. On the certainty of victory the three monarchs, who had watched the progress of the battle, so it is reported, knelt on the open field and returned thanks to God. Napoleon, before nightfall, gave orders for full retreat. But next morning he returned to the fight with a part of his army to save the retreat of the rest. At the last bridge remaining across the Elster, the scenes of the Beresina were re-enacted. The allies overwhelmed the fugitives with grape-shot. Under cover of the artillery, Blücher's cavalry charged into the French masses thronging through the streets of the suburb Halle. A French corporal of engineers, under orders to blow up the bridge at the approach of the enemy, deemed the moment come and exploded the mine. The bridge collapsed with 20,000 fugitives still on the wrong side. A cry of horror arose. While the rearguard rallied for a last stand against the enemy, thousands of fugitives threw themselves into the water. Marshal Macdonald swam his horse across the river. Prince Poniatovsky, who tried to follow him, was drowned **Ponia-** with his horse. Generals Reynier and Lauriston **tovsky** and a score of other generals, as well as the King **drowned** of Saxony, were made prisoners with nearly 23,000 men. Thus ended the battle of Leipzig.

Napoleon with barely 100,000 men fell back precipitately to Erfurt and thence to Mentz. While passing through Weimar, he sent a farewell message to Goethe. On the march, nearly half of his raw recruits gave out under the strain. At Hanau, Napoleon found his retreat barred by an Austrian-Bavarian corps under Wrede. By this time he could count on barely 20,000 men wherewith to oppose nearly 60,000 fresh troops. Napoleon was undaunted. As he surveyed the position of the Ba- **Bavarians** varians he exclaimed disdainfully: "Poor Wrede! **routed at** I made him a count, but I could not make him a **Hanau** general." Then he hurled his main column into the Bavarian flanks like a thunderbolt and utterly dispersed them. Wrede, while trying to save the day, was severely wounded. The French troops regained Mentz, after one more reverse at Hochheim. The allies occupied Frankfort. As Napoleon crossed the Bavarian frontier, he said significantly: "The King of Bavaria and I will meet again. He was a little prince whom I made great. Now he is a great prince whom I shall make little."

Germany as far as the Rhine was now completely freed from the French. St. Cyr, with his corps of 35,000 men at Dresden, was tricked into capitulation. In November, 140,000 Frenchmen and 790 captured guns were in the hands of the allies. Next the French garrison at Dantzig surrendered with fourteen generals, among them Napoleon's aide-de-camp, Rapp. The allies, too, lost heavily. The Austrian casualties alone aggregated 80,000.

St. Cyr's capitulation

Surrender of Dantzig

The French were no sooner driven across the Rhine than the whole of the Rhenish Confederation declared for the German cause. After King Jerome's ignominious flight from Westphalia, the exiled princes of Hesse, Brunswick and Oldenburg returned to their domains. Switzerland, Holland and Italy revolted against French rule. Even Murat went over to the enemy. Before the end of the year Trieste and the greater part of Dalmatia surrendered to the Austrian troops. Almost simultaneously with the events around Leipzig, Wellington drove Soult's forces across the Pyrenees and invaded France. The French garrison of Pampeluna, cut off in the rear, had to surrender.

Collapse of Napoleon's empire

President Madison, in America, during this interval, had become profoundly discouraged by the disheartening progress of the war with England. The unsuccessful siege of Fort Meigs had cost the Americans nearly one thousand men. At last, in the autumn, two events occurred which served to hearten the American President and his Cabinet. On September 5, the American ship "Enterprise," 16 guns, Captain Barro, sighted the British brig

The war in America

"Boxer," 14 guns, off the coast of Maine. The two vessels promptly came into action and exchanged broadsides. Early in the fight both captains fell. The "Boxer" finally struck her colors and was towed into Portland as a prize.

On September 9, Barclay with a British squadron started on his cruise for the American fleet under Commodore Perry, then at anchor off Put-in-bay. The British fleet consisted of six vessels: the "Detroit," of 490 tons, carrying 19 guns and Commander Barclay; the "Queen Charlotte," 17 guns; the "Lady Prevost," 13 guns; the "Hunter," 10 guns; the "Little Belt," 3 guns, and a small sloop with one gun, numbering in all 63 guns and 450 men. Perry's squadron consisted of nine vessels: the "Lawrence," Perry's own brig, carrying 20 guns; the "Niagara" of the same armament; the "Caledonia" of 3 guns, and the schooners "Ariel," "Scorpion," "Somers," "Proserpina" and "Tigress," carrying ten guns altogether, and a one gun sloop, in all bearing 54 guns and 532 men. The American broadsides threw at close range 950 pounds, against 450 of the British. At long range the British ships could throw 195, against 288 of the Americans. In tonnage, the Americans overmatched the English as eight to seven.

At daylight on September 10, Perry bore down, striking the British fleet obliquely near its head. He was anxious to fight at close range. The battle began in earnest about noon. The British fire was very destructive. Perry's flagship, the "Lawrence," within canister shot, sustained the action for two hours, until every gun was useless and the greater part of the crew was killed or wounded. The "Niagara" then came into action, and Perry went on board of her. "At quarter to three in the afternoon," wrote Perry, "signal was made for close action. The 'Niagara' as yet but little injured, I determined to pass through the enemy's line; bore up and passed ahead of their two ships and a brig, giving them a raking fire from our starboard guns. Our small vessels, under command of Captain Elliot, by this time got their grape and canister to bear, and the two British ships, two brigs and a schooner, surrendered." More than any other battle throughout the American war, the victory was won by the courage and obstinacy of one man. The losses of the British amounted to nearly one in three. On September 12, General Harrison received Perry's famous despatch: "We have met the enemy and they are ours. Two ships, two brigs, one schooner and one sloop."

Perry's despatch

Harrison's force at this time was less than three thousand. Richard M. Johnson, who gathered a thousand Kentuckians and Tennesseeans armed with guns and bowie-knives, had joined Harrison during the summer. While his mounted men went by road, Harrison's main force embarked in boats and were conveyed, 4,500 in number, to the vicinity of Fort Malden, reaching there toward the end of September. The British withdrew to the north bank of the Thames. To the left of the road was a river, to the right a forest. Harrison followed and formed in line of battle early in the afternoon.

Johnson led half of his men up against the six-pound guns of the British, while the other half wheeled to the left across a swamp to attack twice their number of Indians. The battle was over in less than half an hour. Tecumseh was among the slain.

Thus ended the troublesome war with the Creeks. Its cost to the United States had been nearly 20,000 men and $5,000,000 in money. Thereafter the British ceased to be formidable in the Northwest. Tecumseh's confederation of Indian tribes was broken up.

When Napoleon arrived in Paris, Soult was preparing for a stand on the banks of La Nivelle. On November 9, he was overthrown and the British colors were planted on the French fortress. Soult was forced back to Bayonne. Still, Napoleon declined to accept the terms of peace offered to him by the allies at Frankfort. He levied new war contributions in France. Failing to obtain immediate funds, he ordered Soult to provision his troops at the expense of the country. As a result, hundreds of French peasants flocked to the English lines, where they received hand money for their provisions. "The English general's policy, and the good discipline he maintains," wrote Soult, "does us more harm than ten battles. Every peasant longs to be under his protection." During the second week of December, Wellington made a determined assault on Bayonne, and drove the French into the inner city. Napoleon realized that Spain was irretrievably lost to France. He offered to release the imprisoned Prince of Asturias and to restore him to his throne. When his brother Joseph talked of indemnities, Napoleon became impatient: "Joseph has lost Spain and will certainly never recover it. Let him consult the lowest of my generals. He will be told how impossible it is to retain a single village beyond the Pyrenees. The first condition of any peace with Europe is the restoration pure and simple of Spain to the Bourbons—happy if at that price I can rid myself of the English and bring back my armies of Spain to the Rhine! As for compensations elsewhere, where are they to be found?" New levies of troops were ordered from the classes of conscripts liable for service two years ahead. Frenchmen were struck with consternation. On December 19, the Emperor opened the Corps Legislatif:

Napoleon gives up Spain

"As a monarch and a father, I feel what peace adds to the security of thrones and of families. Negotiations have been begun with the allied powers. I have adhered to the preliminary bases proposed by them, and was therefore in hopes that before the opening of this session the Congress would have assembled at Mannheim; but new delays, for which France is not blamable, have deferred that event."

Frankfort peace proposals

The Frankfort proposals of peace were turned over to a commission of the Chambers. Their report, recommending peace on almost any basis, so enraged Napoleon that he determined to dissolve the legislative body. When the deputies appeared before him at the close of the year, he assailed them with these words:

Napoleon
rejects
peace

"Deputies of the Legislative Body, you can do much good, and you have done much harm. I summoned you to assist me, and you have come to say and do what is necessary to help the foreigner. Eleven-twelfths of you are good, the rest are factious, and you have been their dupes. Your commission has been inspired by the spirit of the Girondins. M. Laine, who drew up your report, is a worthless man. He is sold to England; I shall keep my eye on him. Two battles lost in Champagne would have done less harm than his report. M. Raynouard, who said that Marshal Masséna pillaged a citizen's country-house, is a liar. . . How can you blame me for my misfortunes? You say that adversity has given me good advice. Is it by reproaches that you propose to restore the glory of the throne? I am one of those men who can face death, but not disgrace. Besides, what is the throne? Four pieces of wood covered with a piece of velvet: everything depends upon him whose seat it is. The throne is in the desire of the nation, whom I represent; I cannot be attacked without attacking it. Four times have I been called by the nation; I had the votes of 5,000,000 of citizens. I have a title, and you have none. You are only deputies of the departments. Is this a time for remonstrance when 200,000 Cossacks are crossing our frontiers? . . . I am beyond reach of your declamations. In three months we shall have peace, or I shall be dead. Our enemies have never conquered us, nor will they now. They will be driven away more speedily than they came."

Corps
Legislatif
dissolved

Bent on carrying out his will alone, Napoleon signed the decree for the dissolution of the Corps Legislatif on the last day of the year.

THE BATTLE OF LAKE ERIE

Painted by J. O. Davidson

Copyright by C. Klackner
XIXth Cent., Vol. One

1814

O N THE first day of the new year, Blücher crossed the Rhine at Kaub. The invasion of France was begun. From all sides vast armies poured into France. Wellington advanced from the south; the Austrians, under Schwarzenberg, from Switzerland, and Bernadotte's corps from the Netherlands. To stem this tide, Napoleon made haste to send his latest levies to the Rhenish frontiers. There Macdonald, Marmont and Victor, with the remnants of their armies, stood ready to meet the first shock. Another French army was concentrated at Lyons to block the allies' advance from Switzerland and Savoy. The outstanding French troops in Spain were drawn in to strengthen Soult's opposition to Wellington. On January 25, Napoleon started for Chalons-sur-Marne. Marie Louise and Joseph Bonaparte were made Regents of the Empire, with a Council of State, including Cambacérès and Talleyrand. When Napoleon kissed Marie Louise for the last time he gave Talleyrand a hard look, and said significantly: "I am well aware that I have in Paris other enemies besides those I am going to fight." The care of raising an army of reserves at Paris was intrusted to old Marshal Kellermann. A picture of the French capital at that time is given in Guizot's Memoirs:

Invasion of France

Marie Louise's farewell

"I have still before my eyes the appearance of Paris—for example, the Rue de Rivoli, which was then only partly built. No workmen, no move-

ment, materials in heaps unused, deserted scaffold-ing, structures abandoned from want of money, hands, and confidence; new ruins. Everywhere the population seemed uneasy and restlessly idle, like people who are in want both of work and rest. On the highways, and in the towns and villages, there was the same appearance of inaction and agitation, the same visible impoverishment of the country, many more women and children than men; young conscripts, sadly on the march to join their corps; sick and wounded soldiers pouring back. Never was such public apathy seen in the midst of so much national anxiety, or malcontents refraining to such an extent from all action, or agents so eager to dis-avow their master while remaining so subservient to his purposes. It was a nation of harassed onlookers, who had lost all habit of taking any share themselves in their own lot, and knew not what determination they were to desire or to dread for the terrible drama in which their liberty and national existence were at stake."

Those that left Paris with Napoleon fully appre-hended what was in store for them: "We are about

to undertake a task, not only difficult, but very use-less," said the Duke of Vincenza. "Do what we may, the Napoleonic Era is drawing to a close and that of the Bourbons is recommencing." A Minis-ter of the Regency asked the departing Emperor for instructions in case communications should come to be intercepted between Paris, blockaded by the enemy, and the imperial headquarters. "My dear fellow," replied Napoleon, "if the enemy reach the gates of Paris there is no more empire."

When the Emperor reached Chalons-sur-Marne, the situation was the reverse of encouraging. The new conscripts received him with black looks, and from their ranks arose cries of "Down with war-taxes!" "Does your Majesty bring reinforcements?" was the pointed question of the marshals as they gathered around him. "No, there were none to bring," replied the Emperor. Of immediately available forces, there were but 60,000 men wherewith to oppose 220,000 allies.

Napoleon sent instant orders to treat for terms to Caulaincourt, his rejected peace commissioner, then detained at the advance outposts of the enemy's army. "We are waiting for Lord Castlereagh," was the reply transmitted from Metternich to Coulaincourt. Napoleon, finding himself thus put off, resolved to exact a better hearing at the point of the sword. It was at this downward turn of his career that Napoleon's military genius shone forth in new splendor.

Futile peace overtures

While the allied armies were moving cautiously forward in expectation of a speedy termination of hostilities by the new peace commissioners convening at Chatillon, Napoleon suddenly pounced on Blücher's Prussian corps at Brienne. Though overmatched in numbers, Napoleon manœuvred his forces so skilfully over this ground, familiar to him from the days of his early military schooling at

Blucher driven from Brienne

Brienne, that Blücher's army was separated in detachments and routed piecemeal. Blücher barely
escaped capture in the citadel of Brienne. The
Prussians fell back until they came in touch with
the South German corps under Wrede and the
Prince of Wurtemberg advancing from Belfort.

French
defeat at
Rothière

Thus reinforced they advanced again to La Rothière, and there engaged the French with such
superior forces that the Emperor had to give way
with heavy losses. Seventy-three of his guns were
left sticking in the mud. Counting on the co-operation of Schwarzenberg's main column, which lay
within striking distance, Blücher pushed forward
with utmost haste over widely distant roads. Napoleon profited by the scattered marches of his enemies to deliver one telling blow after another. First
he caught the Prussians far in advance of the other

Napoleon's
brilliant
rally

allies and threw them off their route in utter confusion. Then he fell upon the Russians under Olsu-
fiev at Champcaubert; next upon those under Sacken
at Montmirail; then upon the second Prussian corps
under York at Chateau Thierry, and finally returned
to the reunited columns of Blücher at Beauchamp.
All were overthrown in turn. Having achieved so
much by the middle of February, Napoleon swung
his waning forces about and inflicted a telling defeat
on Schwarzenberg's Austrians; then he repulsed the
Russians under Pahlen at Marmont, the Bavarians
under Wrede at Villeneuve-Lecomte and the Wurtembergers after a hard-fought two days' battle at
Montereaux. Marshal Augereau in the north, rid
for the moment of his most pressing enemies, im-

proved the lull by driving the Austrians under
Bubna into Switzerland.

At a council of war held at Troyes, Schwarzenberg advised a general retreat. Blücher alone would
have none of it. In defiance of the commander-in-
chief's directions he pushed his column, and uniting
with Buelow and Winzingerode on the Marne, attacked Napoleon's dwindling army at Laon. The
first day's engagement resulted in a drawn battle.
The French rested on the battlefield. After dark
York's division turned one of the enemy's flanks
and burst in upon the French with a wild night attack. Everything was turned topsy-turvy, and the
French bivouac was stampeded. An artillery park
of forty-six guns was captured. At the news of this
brilliant success Schwarzenberg stopped his retrograde manœuvres and advanced once more far into
the interior. Napoleon gathered his demoralized
forces for a supreme effort, and on March 20, made
a bold dash for the enemy's position at Arcis-sur-
Aube. Schwarzenberg, stronger as he was by his
overpowering numbers and superior artillery, stood
his ground with unwonted resolution. Five times
in succession the Prince of Wurtemberg led his
troops to the assault against Napoleon's centre, but
at nightfall neither side had gained much advantage.

While things stood thus in the field, the peace
plenipotentiaries were deliberating at Chatillon.
Metternich and Castlereagh, as the representatives
of Austria and England, which held the balance of
power, were the guiding spirits. Stein stood for a

Blucher alone steadfast

Night attack at Laon

Battle of Arcis

united Germany. Wilhelm von Humboldt spoke for Prussia. Rasumovski and the vengeful Corsican Pozzo di Borgo represented Russia, though the Czar was always near enough to make his presence felt at crucial moments. It was at this time that Southey wrote his famous ode:

Who counsels peace at this momentous hour,
When God hath given deliverance to the oppress'd,
And to the injured power?
Who counsels peace, when Vengeance like a flood
Rolls on, no longer now to be repress'd;
When innocent blood
From the four corners of the world cries out
For justice upon one accursed head;
When Freedom hath her holy banner spread
Over all nations, now in one just cause
United; when with one sublime accord
Europe throws off the yoke abhorr'd,
And Loyalty and Faith and Ancient Laws
Follow the avenging sword!

Woe, woe to England! woe and endless shame,
If this heroic land,
False to her feelings and unspotted fame,
Hold out the olive to the Tyrant's hand!
Woe to the world, if Bonaparte's throne
Be suffer'd still to stand!
For by what names shall Right and Wrong be known, . .
What new and courtly phrases must we feign
For Falsehood, Murder, and all monstrous crimes,
If that perfidious Corsican maintain
Still his detested reign,
And France, who yearns even now to break her chain,
Beneath his iron rule be left to groan?
No! by the innumerable dead
Whose blood hath for his lust of power been shed,
Death only can for his foul deeds atone;
That peace which Death and Judgment can bestow,
That peace be Bonaparte's . . that alone!

For sooner shall the Ethiop change his skin,
Or from the Leopard shall her spots depart,

Than this man change his old flagitious heart.
Have ye not seen him in the balance weighed,
And there found wanting?—On the stage of blood
Foremost the resolute adventurer stood;
    And when, by many a battle won,
    He placed upon his brow the crown,
Curbing delirious France beneath his sway,
    Then, like Octavius in old time,
    Fair name might he have handed down,
Effacing many a stain of former crime.
Fool! should he cast away that bright renown!
Fool! the redemption proffer'd should he lose!
When Heaven such grace vouchsafed him that the way
    To Good and Evil lay
    Before him, which to choose.

    But Evil was his Good,
For all too long in blood had he been nurst,
And ne'er was earth with verier tyrant curst.
    Bold man and bad,
Remorseless, godless, full of fraud and lies,
And black with murders and with perjuries,
    Himself in Hell's whole panoply he clad;
No law but his own headstrong will he knew,
    No counsellor but his own wicked heart.
From evil thus portentous strength he drew,
    And trampled under foot all human ties,
    All holy laws, all natural charities.

O France! beneath this fierce Barbarian's sway
Disgraced thou art to all succeeding times;
Rapine, and blood, and fire have mark'd thy way,
    All loathsome, all unutterable crimes.
A curse is on thee, France! from far and wide
It hath gone up to Heaven; all lands have cried
    For vengeance upon thy detested head;
All nations curse thee, France! for wheresoe'er
In peace or war thy banner hath been spread,
All forms of human woe have follow'd there:
    The living and the dead
Cry out alike against thee! They who bear,
Crouching beneath its weight, thine iron yoke,
    Join in the bitterness of secret prayer
    The voice of that innumerable throng
Whose slaughtered spirits day and night invoke

> The everlasting Judge of right and wrong,
> How long, O Lord! Holy and Just, how long!
>
> . . . .
>
> One man hath been for ten long wretched years
> The cause of all this blood and all these tears;
> One man in this most awful point of time
> Draws on thy danger, as he caused thy crime.
> Wait not too long the event,
> For now whole Europe comes against thee bent;
> His wiles and their own strength the nations know;
> Wise from past wrongs, on future peace intent,
> The People and the Princes, with one mind,
> From all parts move against the general foe:
> One act of justice, one atoning blow,
> One execrable head laid low,
> Even yet, O France! averts thy punishment:
> Open thine eyes! too long hast thou been blind;
> Take vengeance for thyself, and for mankind!

Southey need not have feared. Napoleon's representative, Caulaincourt, cut off as he was from quick communication with his master, was playing a losing game. From the heat of battle, the Emperor sent him contradictory or vague instructions **Napoleon's instructions** like this: "Metternich's proposals are absurd. He thinks he can lead Europe by the nose. Matters must be decided immediately. Accept the allies' terms if they are acceptable; in the contrary case, we run the risk of battle and even of the loss of Paris with all that may result therefrom. You ought to know how to decide."

Coulaincourt was scarcely the man to take such responsibility. The allies' terms grew more and more exacting as they penetrated further into France. Metternich was always pressing Coulain- **Coulain-court irresolute** court to yield now or lose all. Whenever Napoleon won a battle, on the other hand, he despatched couriers to Coulaincourt urging him to stand firm.

All Caulaincourt's remonstrances broke themselves against the fixed resolve of Alexander to wipe out the humiliation of Moscow by a triumphal entry into Paris. In this resolution the Czar was strengthened by the impetuous Blücher and the ardent aspirations of the Bourbon princes, now drawn to France as vultures are to carrion. In their behalf Talleyrand at Paris was turning the situation to account. He advised the Empress to await her fate in Paris. Napoleon, feeling the last supports of the throne fail him, sent an indignant protest to his brother Joseph:

"I write to you frankly; if Talleyrand gives such advice, it is an act of treason implying conspiracy. I repeat to you, have no trust in that man! For sixteen years I have had experience of him, and have even shown favor for him; but he is certainly the greatest enemy of our house now that fortune has for some time abandoned it. I see that fear is turning all the heads in Paris. As for my opinion, I should prefer that my son's throat be cut rather than ever see him brought up at Vienna as an Austrian prince; and my opinion of the Empress is so good that I believe she is also of the same way of thinking, as far as a wife and mother can be so. I never saw Andromache on the stage without pitying the lot of Astyanax." *Talleyrand to the front* *Napoleon at bay*

The dragging negotiations were brought to a decided turn on the first day of March at Chaumont, when the allies accepted Lord Castlereagh's draft of a treaty for mutual defence and offence. The four great powers, England, Austria, Russia and Prussia, bound themselves together for a period of

twenty years to come. England undertook to furnish each of the powers with a subsidy of fifty million francs, throughout the duration of the war.
Sixth
Coalition
Each power in turn promised to keep a contingent
of 150,000 men in the field. The propositions to
Napoleon calling for a reduction of his empire to the
original limits of France were to remain open for a
fortnight longer. If he refused them then, all negotiations with him were to be broken off, and Napoleon was to be proclaimed an outlaw of Europe.
Treaty of
Chaumont
The compact was sealed at a game of whist played
by Metternich, Castlereagh, Nesselrode and Hardenberg.

The Emperor in the field rejected the allies' propositions with contumely. To Joseph he sent the minutes of the plenipotentiaries, characterizing them as
"not a proposal but a capitulation, dishonorable to
France." To Cambacérès he wrote: "You will see
from what King Joseph communicates to you how
moderate these gentlemen are—just like their soldiers, who pillage, slaughter and burn everything
in France."

The "Great
Week"
Then came the "Great Week," as it has been
called, when Napoleon, outlawed and everywhere
outmatched by the advancing allies, stood at bay
against the world. Schwarzenberg and Blücher had
effected a junction of their armies. Winzingerode
was detached with a cavalry division of ten thousand picked horse to hang on Napoleon's flanks.
Wellington and Hill, who had driven Soult and
Clausel to Toulouse and Bordeaux, advanced from
the south and fomented royalist risings in that quar-

ter. The Duc d'Angoulême entered Bordeaux in triumph. The restoration of the Bourbons was proclaimed by the mayor of the town amid acclamations from the merchants and wine-growers of Bordeaux, who had been ruined by the Continental blockade. Having lighted such firebrands all around Napoleon, the allies, on March 25, began their joint advance on Paris.

Return of Bourbons

By noon on the first day they overtook the detached columns of Marmont and Mortier, covering the Paris road at Sommessons. Both commands were completely overwhelmed, and narrowly escaped capture. General Pacthod's corps of National Guards was cut to pieces. Napoleon, about the same time, was fighting between Troyes and Arcis. Winzingerode's Cossacks made a dash for Napoleon's headquarters. The Emperor's horse was shot under him, and his Polish lancers had to rally around him in a square. Ney was fighting a losing fight at Grand-Farcy, and General Friant in vain sacrificed the Imperial Guards. Caulaincourt, at this juncture, rejoined the Emperor, fresh from his futile peace negotiations.

Marshals routed at Sommessons

Further French defeats

"You did well to return," said Napoleon. "Death is preferable to what they offered. We are old enough soldiers to have no fear of death. But you shall see something worth while."

"Your Majesty has no doubt other resources that we are not aware of?" asked General Sebastiani.

Napoleon motioned toward the fight raging all around them and said: "Nothing more than is before your eyes."

"Then, why does your Majesty not think of a general rising?"

"Such ideas are purely chimerical, my dear Sebastiani," replied Napoleon. "Fine recollections of Spain and the French Revolution. A general rising, indeed, in a country where the Revolution destroyed the nobles and priests, and where I myself have destroyed the Revolution!"

The Emperor resolved on the desperate expedient of taking the enemy on the rear. He hoped to create so powerful a diversion as to draw the allies off from Paris. It was too late. By the time he realized that the forces operating around him were only detached cavalry the allies were already two marches ahead of him on their way to Paris. Blücher's vanguard skirmished at the very gates of the capital. Marmont and Mortier were gathering the National Guards for a last defence of Paris. There was no artillery, and half the National Guards were unarmed. Some one proposed to throw up barricades on the streets or to throw paving-stones from the windows. "Why, that is a revolutionary mode of defence!" objected General Savary. "I shall most certainly not do that. What would the Emperor say?" A detachment of 2,000 mounted National Guards were bidden to take the Empress and Prince Imperial to Rambouillet. The King of Rome clung to the curtains of his nursery, and Marie Louise wept as she entered her carriage.

From the north, south and east the allied forces, numbering 170,000 men, advanced to the attack. They were led by Blücher, the Prince of Wurtem-

Napoleon cut off

Flight of Marie Louise

berg, and Barclay de Tolly. Marmont and Mortier had 29,000 men, not quite 20,000 of whom were regular troops. Their resistance was to be confined to a pitched battle before the octroi wall. The heights of Montmartre and the Barrière du Trône, with the plateau of Romainville, were the points of attack. On the morning of March 30, the fight began in the suburbs. The plateau of Romainville was several times taken and retaken. The Prince of Wurtemberg carried the bridge of Charenton against the National Guards and the pupils of the Belfort School. Blücher's Prussians stormed the Montmartre. At the Barrière du Trône the students of the Polytechnic School held their ground under heavy artillery fire. Marshal Mortier was fighting, sword in hand, at Villette, when General Dejean, who had got through the enemy's lines, announced to him the Emperor's approach. At the same time an order arrived from Joseph's headquarters beyond Montmartre: "If M. le Maréchal Duc de Ragusa and M. le Maréchal Duc de Trevisa cannot hold their ground, they are hereby authorized to enter into pourparlers with the Prince of Schwarzenberg and the Emperor of Russia, now before the walls." Mortier sent a flag to request an armistice. The request was refused: "It depends on the marshals," said Schwarzenberg, "to put a stop to this butchery." Late in the afternoon the French forces all around Paris capitulated. They were permitted to withdraw with all their arms. "And what of Paris?" they asked of Marshal Marmont as he came out of his house on the Rue Paradis-Poissonière, his

Allies attack Paris

Marshals ordered to surrender

face blackened with gunpowder. "Paris is none of my business. I am only a corps commander, and I have saved my corps. I fall back on Fontainebleau and join the Emperor." Talleyrand alone remained to safeguard the interests of Paris. To the French aide-de-camp who sought out the allied monarchs at Chateau Bondy, the Czar said reassuringly: "It is not my intention to do the least harm to the town of Paris. It is not upon the French nation that we are waging war, but upon Napoleon." "And not upon himself, but upon his ambition," added the King of Prussia.

Paris evacuated

Early on Wednesday morning, March 31, the city was evacuated by the French regular soldiery. It was entered by 120,000 of the allied troops. The Prussian soldiers were found to be in too ragged a condition to share in the triumphal march. As the Cossacks rode through the Faubourg St. Germain a profusion of white lilies was showered upon them.

Napoleon, in the meanwhile, had come up in the rear of the allies as far as Villeneuve-l'Archevecque. When he learned of the defeat of his marshals at Fère-Champenoise his troops were driven onward in forced marches. Failing to catch up with his enemies at Villeneuve, the Emperor could no longer suppress his impatience, and threw himself into a

Napoleon arrives too late

carriage. He flew toward Paris. At Fromentain, about midnight, the postilion drew up his foaming horses at the approach of a troop of cavalry. "Who goes there?" called the Emperor. General Belliard rode to the carriage step. He has left this record of what passed between them:

"Where is the army?" asked Napoleon.

"Sire, it is coming behind."

"And the enemy?"

"At the gates of Paris."

"And who holds Paris?"

"Nobody, it is evacuated."

"What! evacuated? And my son, my wife, the government, where are they?"

"On the Loire, Sire."

"On the Loire! who sent them there?"

"Sire, it was said to be by your orders."

"My orders! Where is King Joseph, and Clarke, and Marmont, and Mortier?" *The news broken to Napoleon*

"Sire, we did not see King Joseph or the Duke of Feltre; the marshals did all that it was possible for men to do. A defence was made in every part, and the National Guards fought like soldiers. We had nothing, not even cannon! Ah! Sire, had you but been there!"

"I cannot be everywhere. Joseph lost Spain, and now he is losing me France! And Clarke, too; if I had believed that poor Rovigo, who always kept telling me that he was a coward and traitor! But we must go there at once! My carriage, Caulaincourt!"

The officers threw themselves before the Emperor, to stop him as he proceeded to walk along the road.

"It is impossible, Sire! It is too late! There is a capitulation! The infantry is behind us, and will presently reach us."

Some of the detachments were already coming in sight. Napoleon let himself fall by the roadside and hid his face. It was the end of his empire, and he felt himself once more reduced to the rank of an adventurer.

After the fall of Paris, Napoleon remained at Fontainebleau awaiting developments. The soldiers and officers of the line still stood ready to fight, but the marshals and general officers were utterly weary. They insisted on giving up the struggle. Even Ney turned from his master. Yielding to their pressure, Napoleon sent Caulaincourt to Paris with a formal abdication in favor of his infant son. Caulaincourt was informed that only an unconditional abdication would be accepted. The Emperor convened his marshals. They were obdurate. Marshal Marmont drew off his whole Sixth Army Corps. At length, on April 11, Napoleon signed an act surrendering the throne of France for himself and his heirs. He was permitted to retain the empty title of Emperor with an annuity of two million francs. Furthermore, he was allowed to retain a bodyguard of one thousand men wherewith to retire to Elba, one of the Tuscan islands in the Mediterranean Sea. Parma and Placentia were reserved as the dowry of Marie Louise and the King of Rome. Ex-Empress Josephine retained an annual income of one million francs. She only enjoyed it for a few weeks, as her death came within a month.

Napoleon's abdication exacted

Death of Josephine

Before leaving France, Napoleon tried to poison himself, but failed. Next day he took leave of the remaining members of his Old Guard, kissing their colonel and their flag. Then he departed, under a Russian escort, to embark for Elba on the British cruiser "Undaunted." On the way he had to disguise himself in an Austrian uniform to escape the insults of the populace. On May 30, he stepped ashore at Porto Ferrajo and received the homage of the island population of Elba.

Napoleon in Elba

With Napoleon out of the way the question arose what was to be done with France? The Austrian Emperor would have liked a Regency under Marie Louise. Bernadotte had high hopes of assuming charge. Alexander showed himself not averse to a return of republican rule. The proposed restoration of the Bourbons at first excited scant enthusiasm except among themselves. At the advent of the Count of Artois, some weeks previous, neither the Austrian nor the Russian commanding generals would give him official recognition. Wellington would not receive the Duc d'Angoulême at his headquarters. He wrote to Lord Bathurst: "The only opinion I can form is this: Twenty years have elapsed since the princes of the House of Bourbon left France. They are all but unknown here. In proposing a sovereign in place of Napoleon it matters little to Frenchmen whether he be a prince of Bourbon or of any other royal family."

Talleyrand was the man who most keenly recognized the expediency of recalling a prince of French blood to preside over the destinies of France. As he put it: "The Republic is an impossibility; the Regency or Bernadotte means nothing but perpetual intrigues. The Bourbons alone represent a principle."

Conflicting claims in France

Talleyrand was pre-eminently the man of the hour. As the only remaining officer of the Regency, and

an old aristocrat of France as well, he had the immediate entrée to the sessions of the allied sovereigns
and their councillors. Trained diplomat that he

Talleyrand to the fore was, he knew how to cope with the wiles of Metternich and Pozzo di Borgo, no less than with the more
blunt proposals of Castlereagh and Humboldt. In
his capacity as Vice-President of the French Senate,
Talleyrand convened some thirty remaining members of the Corps Legislatif. With their help he
hastily drafted a new constitution, which, as he
phrased it, "restored to France her rightful king—
Prince Louis Stanislaus Xavier de Bourbon." On
the fourth day of May the new king appeared in

Louis XVIII. Paris. He soon showed that he preferred to rest his
claim to the throne on the "divine right of kings,"
never relinquished by him or his house. He was
recognized by the royalists as Louis XVIII., King
of France and Navarre. Ten days later, Prince

Ferdinand VII. re-enters Spain Louis Ferdinand of Asturias re-entered Madrid in
triumph, and ascended the throne of Spain. On
May 20, Prince Victor Emmanuel of Savoy returned
to his capital, Turin. Bernadotte and Murat, the
two upstart rulers of Sweden and Naples, strove to
make sure of their doubtful thrones by absolute ad-

Berna-dotte's hold on Sweden hesion to the new order of things. Bernadotte had
improved the last interval by wresting Norway from
Denmark with the help of a Russian army corps.

On May 27, the draft of the new French constitution, known as the Charta, was submitted to Louis
XVIII. It was signed by him on compulsion only
of the Czar of Russia. Three days later the Treaty
of Paris was signed by the representatives of France

and of all the great powers. France got off very lightly, thanks to the generous spirit of Alexander and the ascendency over him gained by Talleyrand. In vain did old Blücher vent his wrath against the "quill drivers," as he called all diplomats. France was allowed to retain her limits of 1792, and got some slight additions of territory besides. Nearly all the French colonies, captured by Great Britain, *Changes in Europe* were restored to France. Alsace-Lorraine, wrested from Germany under Louis XIV., remained a province of France. No money indemnity whatever was exacted. Even the French prisoners still held in Germany had to be sent back to France at the expense of the German people. Of the rich spoils plundered from Italy, Spain and Germany, none were returned but the bronze horses taken from the Brandenburg Gate in Berlin and some priceless manuscripts of the Library of Vienna. By other clauses of the treaty the navigation on the Rhine was made free. Switzerland was declared independent. Holland was restored to the Prince of Orange. Italy and Germany, with the exception of the Austrian provinces in both countries, were rearranged as clusters of independent principalities.

This arrangement, while it satisfied the princes who profited by it, or such simple loyal people as the Tyrolese, deeply outraged the growing feeling for national unity, which had arisen in Germany *National* *sentiments* and Italy. Englishmen, and the lovers of freedom *outraged* throughout the world, took it hard to see the old sea-going republics of Venice and Genoa brought absolutely under Hapsburg rule. Poland and Finland had to bend their necks to the yoke of Russia. The Norwegians, much against their will, found themselves cut off from their ancient union with Denmark to have their political destinies linked to those of Sweden. At a Diet held at Eidsvold, the Norwegian people repudiated the arrangement. They drew up a constitution of their own and elected Prince Christian Frederick of Denmark King of Norway. When the Diet dissolved, all the members formed a ring, and locking hands, chanted in chorus: "United and true until Mount Dover falls." England promptly put the coast of Norway under blockade. Russia sent troops to the border. It was to adjust this and similar difficulties that the representatives of the great powers determined to convoke within the same year a great European congress at Vienna. To this congress the settlement of all vexed questions was to be committed.

Revolt of Norway

A period of universal rejoicing followed. After the festivities of Paris, Emperor Alexander and the King of Prussia visited England. Their stay there was clouded only by the gloom at court, arising from the continued insanity of the blind old king and from the open rupture between the Prince of Wales and his consort, Caroline of Brunswick. General Blücher was the lion of the occasion. When the University of Oxford conferred a doctor's degree on him, the old warrior remarked: "Why don't you make General Gneisenau apothecary? It was he who prepared my pills." About the same time that these visitors were honored in

Rejoicing in England

England, Lord Wellington was raised to a duke-
dom, and had his annuity increased by Parliament.
Robert Southey was made Poet Laureate—the best _{Southey, Poet Laureate}
of his kind since the laureateship of Ben Jonson in
Elizabethan times. He set himself to work at once
on an elaborate prose "History of the Peninsular
War." Of his work as poet laureate, little has out-
lived his day but the exquisite lines of his "Ode on
the Death of the Princess Charlotte."

The withdrawal of the British army from Spain
and France, and the collapse of the Continental
blockade, left England free to put more vigor into
her war with the United States. The blockade of
the Atlantic coast was made more stringent. Admiral Cockburn, by his relentless raids along the
shores from Long Island to Charleston, inspired ap- _{The war in America}
prehension and resentment in the hearts of all who
dwelt on the Atlantic seaboard. Fourteen thousand
veterans who had fought under Wellington were
sent into Canada. The American army, under General Wilkinson, lay idle until February 1, when
2,000 troops were sent to Sackett's Harbor and 4,000
to Plattsburgh. Wilkinson was retired in March and
Izard took his place. The British at that time had
control of Lake Erie. Early in May a British force _{British success at Oswego}
destroyed the American base of supplies near Os-
wego in northwestern New York.

In June, General Brown with a force of nearly
5,000 American troops marched to York in Canada.
Having seized Fort Erie, he hastened on to Chippewa, where he found a strong force of British.
General Riall, the British commander, drew up

in three columns on Chippewa Plain. Scott had ordered a general parade, "to keep the men in breath." When the presence of the enemy was reported to him he advanced his men across a bridge dividing the two forces, and formed them in columns on the other side. Thomson's battery of twelve-pounders on the right opened fire. The artillery fire was so well directed that the British columns were unable to withstand it. During the advance of the American infantry that followed the British columns broke and withdrew. Riall's losses were 515, while those of the Americans were 300.

On July 24, the American force under Brown in Canada encamped on the field of Chippewa. When the American forces marched to Lundy's Lane, a mile below Niagara Falls, the British followed. The two armies camped but three miles apart. Riall was joined by Drummond with 815 men. Scott advanced in the hope of meeting the British, and deployed in line of battle as soon as a hostile

Battle of Lundy's Lane

force was sighted. Lundy's Lane, at right angles with the river, ran close behind the British position. The American attack was delivered on the British left. An American battalion under Jessup opened a wedge and let Scott's main column through into the British rear. General Riall himself was taken captive. From seven until nine in the evening Scott's brigade clung to the British left and centre, and at last ceased firing when the ammunition was exhausted. The order was then given to Ripley's brigade to capture the British guns. Miller, the officer in command of the American vanguard, as the order was repeated to him, replied: "I'll try, sir." The 21st Regiment of American infantry silently advanced under cover of the darkness, and with a sudden rush carried the guns at the point of the bayonet. Behind the guns was massed a force of 2,600 British soldiers For twenty minutes a hand-to-hand fight was carried on, but at last the British fell back. Their guns were turned on them from the hilltops. The British reformed under this artillery fire for a night attack. The two lines were engaged along their whole length at close quarters. After half an hour of such fighting the British retreated again, but three times more were called upon to recapture their guns. The battle ceased late in the night from sheer exhaustion on both sides. The American losses were 853, those of the English 878. Both Generals Brown and Scott, on the American side, were severely wounded. Next day the Americans retired to Fort Erie, leaving the captured batteries behind them.

On August 13, Fort Erie, held by 2,000 Americans, was assaulted by a force of 3,400 British. The attack failed. The British casualties were 780, as against 84 of the garrison. A month later General Porter took the chief blockhouse by assault, and, spiking the guns, blew up the powder magazine. The first American battery remained untaken. General Drummond thereupon retired with the whole of the British forces. Thus ended the indecisive operations along the northern border.

In August, General Ross with 3,500 men, fresh from their victories against the French, arrived in

British assault Fort Erie

the Chesapeake. They were reinforced by 1,000 marines from Cockburn's squadron. Their obvious objective point was the city of Washington. The attack could have been anticipated, for Gallatin, writing from England two months before, had forewarned President Madison. Nothing, however, was done. Although General Winder, in command of the District, could marshal 5,000 men against the British column of 4,000, no determined resistance was offered. Instead of sending troops to protect the flotilla of gunboats lying at Marlboro, Commodore Barney was ordered to burn his ships and retreat.

After great confusion within the city of Washington a force of 2,500 men, with twelve field-pieces, was brought together by General Winder. He marched beyond the confines of the city. On information that the British were coming for Bladensburg the American column headed for that point. President Madison, Colonel Monroe, and General Armstrong, the Secretary of War, were with Winder's column at the first encounter with the British, at the bridge of Bladensburg, on August 24. The American infantry gave way at the first shock and scurried out of danger. Their total loss was one man killed. The only real fighting was done by the marines stationed at the bridge. They held the bridge for one hour in the face of repeated charges by the British. The losses of the enemy, here, were greater than the total number of American marines. They were surrounded at last by flanking parties that forded the river. Not until Com-

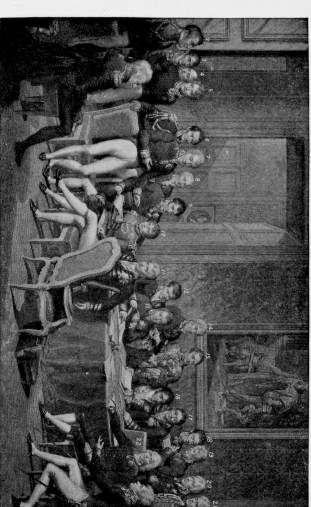

Painted by J. Isaney

1 **Hardenberg**, Germany
2 **Wellington**, England
8 **Lobo**, Portugal
4 **Saldana**, Portugal

5 Lowenhlelm, Switzerland
6 Noailles, France
7 Metternich, Austria
8 Dupin, France
9 Nesselrode

10 Palmella, Portugal
11 Castlereagh, England
12 Dalberg, France
13 Wessenberg, Austria
14 Rasoumovsky, Russia

15 Stewart, England
16 Labrador, Spain
17 Clancarty, England
18 Wacken, England
19 Gentz

20 Humboldt, Germany
21 Cathcart, England
22 **Talleyrand**, France
23 **Stackelberg**, Russia

CONGRESS OF VIENNA (TREATY OF PARIS)

XIXth Cent., Vol. One

modore Barney and Captain Miller, his second in command, had been shot did the marines surrender. The British pushed on to Washington after the retreating American army. "The Race of Bladensburg," as the battle was satirically called, and the undignified exploits of the President and his Cabinet, who took to the woods, were a bitter pill for the American patriots of those days. As Judge Cranch, an eye-witness of the invasion of Washington, wrote in a letter: "A wound has been inflicted which age will not cure; and a scar has been left which time will scarcely efface." _{Flight of President Madison}

Before abandoning Washington, the Secretary of the Navy, Jones, ordered the Government Navy Yard to be set on fire. The loss in ships and stores was enormous. The British on entering the town followed suit by burning the White House, the unfinished structure of the Capitol, with the books and archives of the Congressional Library. One of the traditions of the day is that Admiral Cockburn, bursting into the halls of Congress, leaped upon the Speaker's chair and shouted: "Shall this harbor of Yankee democracy be burned? All for it will say 'Ay.' The ays have it. Light up!" The building went up in flames. Two days afterward the British marched to Marlboro, twenty-five miles away. President Madison returned to the Capital on horseback, but finding the White House in ashes crossed the Potomac and joined his wife in the country. Driven by false alarms they took refuge in the woods. The adventures of Secretary Monroe were scarcely less mortifying. He had passed the night _{Capitol burned by British}

in seclusion in Maryland until he succeeded in joining the President. The British frigates came up the
Potomac River, and Fort Washington had to be
abandoned. The squadron then crossed to Alexandria and destroyed the government buildings and
stores.

Baltimore
threatened
Next, an attempt was made to attack Baltimore.
The British fleet bombarded Fort McHenry, while
the land forces were to move on the city. Both attacks were repulsed. During the bombardment,
Francis S. Key, who had gone to the British fleet
under a flag of truce to obtain the release of a friend,

Fort
McHenry
bombarded
could see the Stars and Stripes blowing over Fort
McHenry from the deck of the enemy's flagship.
The British commander boasted to Key that the
American garrison could not hold out all night, and
that Baltimore would surely be taken. At early
dawn Key was up to watch for a glimpse of the
American flag. When he beheld it still waving he
wrote the famous song which has become one of
America's national anthems.

Key's
stanzas
"Oh, say, can you see, by the dawn's early light,
    What so proudly we hailed at the twilight's last gleaming,
Whose broad stripes and bright stars, through the perilous fight,
    O'er the ramparts we watched were so gallantly streaming?
And the rocket's red glare, the bombs bursting in air,
    Gave proof through the night that our flag was still there;
    Oh, say, does that star-spangled banner yet wave
    O'er the land of the free and the home of the brave?"

After the failure of the attempt on Baltimore the
British re-embarked for Halifax. At this time the
British had 10,000 soldiers near Lake Champlain,
with a fleet of sixteen vessels, consisting of the

"Confiance," a 36-gun ship, two sloops with 10 guns each, and twelve gunboats. The American ships, under Macdonough, comprised the "Saratoga," with 240 men and 26 guns; the "Eagle," 20 guns; "Ticonderoga," 17 guns; "Preble," 7 guns, and ten gunboats, in all 86 guns against 90. Prevost, in command of the approaching British land forces, reached the Saranac River, and saw the ridges beyond surmounted with formidable works and the American flotilla at anchor.

On September 11, the British fleet hove in sight. Prevost ordered a general assault. The "Confiance," under Captain Downie, sailed in and tried to range alongside of the "Saratoga." The first British broadside disabled one-fifth of the "Saratoga's" crew. Captain Downie was killed. After a two hours' fight the American squadron was on the point of capture, but Macdonough wound ship and raked the "Confiance's" decks with one gun after another. The "Confiance" soon struck her colors, and three other British ships followed suit. Only the light draught gunboats escaped. The British attack by land was equally unsuccessful. The news of the defeat caused great mortification in England. Izard returned to Sackett's Harbor late in September, and in October went into winter quarters.

The American privateer "General Armstrong," commanded by Captain Samuel Reid, put into the harbor of Fayal in the Azores about the middle of September. Her armament consisted of eight 9-pounders and one long gun, with a crew of ninety men. A British squadron, bound for Jamaica to

Battle of Lake Champlain

join Admiral Sir Thomas Cochrane's naval expedition against New Orleans, halted at Fayal on September 25. The British squadron consisted of three
vessels: the flagship "Plantagenet," 74 guns, Captain Robert Floyd; the frigate "Rota," 38 guns,
Captain Philip Somerville, and the brig "Carnation," 18 guns, Captain George Bentham. These
vessels were manned by 2,000 men.

Affair of
Fayal On entering Fayal harbor, Captain Floyd sighted
the Yankee privateer and distributed his ships
around her so that escape was impossible. Though
he was in the waters of Portugal, a neutral power,
Captain Reid put his ship nearer shore, with springs
on her cables and boarding nets. At eight o'clock
a number of boats were lowered from the British
men-of-war, and filled with armed men. The accounts in regard to the boats are conflicting. An
English eye-witness of the affair has reported that
there were fourteen boats with about forty men each.
The "Carnation" came within shot of the privateer
to prevent escape. At midnight all the boats rowed
close for the attack. Three boats were sunk by the
American long gun as they approached. The
others lay alongside, and the boarding nets were
hacked to pieces. The British sailors clambered
over the bow and stern, shouting "No quarter."
They were cut down to a man. The English lieutenant who led the expedition was the first man
killed. Only two boats managed to get back with
Portuguese
protest a handful of men. Early next morning the Portuguese Governor sent a peremptory request to Cap-
tain Floyd to stop hostilities in the harbor. Captain

Floyd replied that he would do as he chose, and that
if he were hindered he would treat Fayal as a hostile
port. The American captain prepared for the worst.
Before close of day the British ships closed in on
the "General Armstrong" and poured their broadsides into her. The privateersmen replied in kind,
and soon disabled the "Carnation." Yet the fight
could have only one end. The British had three *A plucky fight*
vessels against one smaller than their smallest, one
hundred and fifty guns against nine, two thousand
men against ninety. Captain Reid, to avoid capture, scuttled his ship, and pulled for the shore.
By the time the British reached the "General Armstrong" she was beyond hope. So they set her afire
and she burned to the water's edge. Captain Reid
seized a stone fortress ashore and dared the British
to follow. They did not come. The "Carnation"
was damaged so badly, and all the British ships had
lost so many men, that the British squadron had to
put back to England to refit, delaying Sir Thomas
Cochrane's expedition. As a result, that admiral
arrived at New Orleans four days after Jackson
reached there.

The affair in the harbor of Fayal resulted in a
long diplomatic correspondence. President Madi- *Diplomatic recrimina-tions*
son took steps to compel Portugal to insist upon
the inviolability of her neutral ports. He also
claimed indemnity, and obtained the promise of an
award, but later Louis Napoleon, to whom the matter
was referred as arbiter, reversed the award. Great
Britain apologized to Portugal for the act of Captain
Floyd in attacking an enemy in a neutral port.

The stirring fight at Fayal inspired James Jef-
frey Roche to write the ballad, the opening lines of
which are:

> "Tell the story to your sons
>   Of the gallant days of yore,
> When the brig of seven guns
>   Fought the fleet of seven score.
> From the set of sun till morn,
>   Through the long September night—
> Ninety men against two thousand,
> And the ninety won the fight,—
>   In the harbor of Fayal in the Azores."

Military movements in the South attracted little
attention, though they were scarcely less important.
The hope of obtaining the Floridas had encouraged
the Southern States to enter into the war. The
President had expected Congress to approve the
seizure of Spanish Florida. Andrew Jackson, as
the most prominent military man in the South, was
appointed major-general of militia. He wrote: "If
the government so orders, I will rejoice at the opportunity of placing the American eagle on the ramparts of Mobile, Pensacola and St. Augustine."
While Madison and Monroe raised no objection to
seizing the territory of a friendly power, Congress
was reluctant to act. At last a bill was signed
authorizing the seizure of western Florida and the
occupation of Mobile. Pensacola was captured.
This was the only gain of territory made during
the war.

A particularly atrocious Indian massacre at Fort
Mims in southern Alabama was avenged by General
Jackson in the battle of Horseshoe Bend, in which
800 Creeks were slain. Not only the power of the

Creeks was broken at Horseshoe Bend, but the power of the red men east of the Mississippi. At Battle of Horseshoe Bend Tehapecathe the long struggle for the possession of the western world was ended by the surrender of Weathersford. It was plain even to the Indians that the continent had changed owners. Tecumseh and Weathersford were the last Indian chiefs who could style themselves spokesmen of a sovereign race.

Fort Jackson completed the line of forts which separated the Indians of northern Alabama from the hostile Indians and their British allies. Hundreds of the Indians fled to the swamps of Florida after Holy Ground was taken. Jackson returned to Ten- End of Indian war nessee after eight months, and announced the end of the Indian troubles. Peace reigned throughout Mississippi, hitherto uninhabitable to white men.

In the North, on the other hand, the presence of the British weighed heavily on the people of New England. A large part of Maine and the southern portion of Massachusetts was held by the British. The complete ruin of New England's shipping was felt even more severely. As a result the people of that section became more confirmed in their hostility to the war. From the outset they had refused to put their State troops at the disposal of the Federal government. Now there was talk of separating from the rest of the country. The Legislature of New England restive Massachusetts called for a convention of delegates from all the New England States at Hartford "to consider their public grievances." The story of John Henry, a former British spy, that plans were underfoot to restore New England to British rule found ready credence in Washington. Already the people of Nantucket had declared neutrality and placed themselves under British protection. President Madison and his Ministers grasped eagerly at the first overtures for peace coming from England.

While the American war was thus drawing to a dreary close, the brief war of Norway against Sweden came to an inglorious end. Before leaving Paris, the representatives of the great powers had granted Bernadotte's request to urge Norway to ac-

Scandina-
vian war

cept the supremacy of Sweden. The special envoys of the powers arrived in Christiania on June 30. They brought with them, besides their instructions, a letter from the Danish king to his son Christian Frederick, recently elected King of Norway, commanding him to abdicate and return to Denmark under pain of disinheritance. Prince Christian refused. A British squadron put the Norwegian coast under blockade. The Swedish fleet, under the personal command of Charles XIII., took up a position outside of Fredericksstad. Insufficiently defended, the fort, on August 4, was compelled to surrender. About the same time, the main Swedish army, under Charles John, crossed the frontier south of Frederickshald. One division of it laid siege to the for-

Norwegian
reverses

tress of Frederickssteen, which was stanchly defended by General Ohme. The Norwegian army was eager for a general action; but the king ordered a retreat across the Glommen River. North in Soloer, where Lieutenant-Colonel Krebs had the command, the Norwegian forces were more successful.

A Swedish force, under General Gahn, was defeated
by the Norwegians on August 2, at Lier. The Nor- Temporary successes
wegians, under Colonel Krebs, afterward attacked
the Swedes at Matrand and drove them back across
the frontier. The battle at Matrand was the most
formidable encounter during this war. General
Gahn's losses were 16 officers and 320 men. The
Norwegian loss was 140 officers and men. This
was the last important engagement of a compara-
tively bloodless war. At the Convention of Moss, Convention of Moss
on August 14, the rebellious Danish prince came to
terms. He convened the Storthing, or Norwegian
Parliament, to which he surrendered his claims to
the crown. This done, he sailed back to Denmark.
On October 20, the Storthing by a vote of 72 to 5
accepted the supremacy of Sweden, and elected the
King of Sweden for King of Norway. The Scandi-
navian union, as finally agreed on, made the person
of the king and his management of the foreign affairs Scandina- vian union
of the country the only common bond. Each coun-
try had its own constitution, diet, and cabinet. In
case of war, Norway reserved to its own diet the
right of refusing troops or financial support.

By the time the diplomats began to assemble for
the Congress of Vienna, much had happened to
efface the transformations of the last twenty years.

In England such important domestic problems as
the question of the Corn Laws came up for settlement. During the last years of the contest with
Napoleon, England by dint of her own agricultural
development had rendered herself independent of
foreign countries as regarded bread stuffs. Now

that grain could be imported again, and this at a
cheaper price than it was grown at home, the landed
proprietors and farmers, who had invested capital
and labor in this species of culture, felt threatened
in the means of their existence. The matter was
British corn agitation debated at great length in the Commons by Huskisson, Vansittart, Frankland Lewis, and Sir Henry
Parnell, in favor of the Corn Law, with Rose and
Canning in the opposition. A bill was finally passed
by large majorities in both Houses of Parliament,
establishing the sliding scale, to commence with a
duty on imported wheat of twenty-four shillings,
when the price should be sixty-three shillings the
The sliding scale quarter; and this duty was to decrease one shilling
for every shilling of rise in the market price of
grain.

In France, one of the first results of the restoration was that 14,000 of Napoleon's old army officers
were retired on half-pay. The common soldiers had
to substitute the white cockade of Bourbon for their
tricolor emblems of the Revolution. The head of
Napoleon was removed from the badge of the Legion
of Honor, and his statues were dismantled throughout the land. Such idols of the army as Masséna
and Davoust were exiled to their country seats as
"foreigners." General Dupont, known only for his
Restoration in France disgraceful capitulation at Baylen, was made Minister of War. Fouché and Chateaubriand returned
to Paris. Napoleon's great code of law was wisely
retained in its entirety. The provisions of his famous Concordat with the Church were repudiated.
The Society of Jesus was invited to return to

France. The government's efforts to prohibit all
buying and selling on religious holidays and Sun-
days precipitated a crisis of the Cabinet. Deep
offence was given by the Duke of Wellington, now
holding the new post of Ambassador to France,
by his thoughtless hunting excursions through the
wheat fields of the peasants. Everywhere in France
there were premonitions of that situation which Napoleon's malevolence foresaw when he said: "The
Bourbons may put France at peace with Europe;
but how will they put her at peace with themselves?"

In Spain, the first acts of Louis Ferdinand were
to dismiss the Cortes, to abolish the liberal constitution of 1812, and to re-establish the Inquisition. *Bourbon
rule in
Spain*
Prominent Liberals were placed under arrest, and
the censorship of the press was restored. In the
face of a financial crisis the clergy and their restored
monasteries and church lands were exempted from
taxation. The soldiers, left unpaid, degenerated
into banditti. With commerce and agriculture all
but extinct, the country rapidly relapsed to the
semi-barbarous condition of feudal times.

In certain parts of Germany similar changes went
into effect. The aged Prince of Hesse, notorious of
old for the way he had farmed out his subjects for
service in foreign wars, abolished all modern reforms
on the day after his return to Cassel. The Code
Napoleon was set aside, as was the decimal system.
The feudal burdens of the peasantry were revived. *Petty
German
despotism*
The former state lands were wrested from their pur-
chasers without recompense, and the iniquitous class

system of taxation was restored. Even pigtails and periwigs once more became the order in the army. In Hanover, torture was restored, and punishment of death by breaking on the wheel. In Wurtemberg, the peasants were once more reduced to serfdom.

When a part of Saxony was turned over to Prussia, and the Saxon troops in that district revolted, the whole corps was ordered to be decimated. General Borstel, the hero of Dennewitz, was cashiered for refusing to burn the Saxon colors. A characteristic incident occurred as the men were drawing lots to die. A drummer boy threw away the dice, exclaiming: "It was I that beat the summons for revolt. I will be the first to die." He was shot before the eyes of his comrades. In Switzerland, the various cantons fell to quarrelling among themselves on the score of old territorial claims, and the peasantry took to arms.

Prussian rule in Saxony

Discord in Saxony

Such were some of the aspects of the general situation in Europe when the delegates to the Congress of Vienna began to assemble in the Austrian capital. Gathered at the court of Emperor Francis were the Czar of Russia, the Kings of Prussia, Bavaria, Wurtemberg and Denmark, with nearly all the statesmen of eminence in Europe. By common consent Prince Metternich presided at the councils of the delegates. Among them were the Duke of Wellington, Viscount Castlereagh, Lord Stewart, Count Clancarty, and General Cathcart, representing Great Britain; Counts Nesselrode, Stackelberg, and Prince Rasumovski attached to the Czar of Russia; Har-

denberg, Wilhelm von Humboldt, and Stein with
the King of Prussia; Prince Talleyrand de Péri-
gord, the Duke of Dalberg, and Count Alexis de
Noailles, representing France; Count Loevenhielm
for Sweden, and a host of other titled personages,
sent by Spain, Portugal, and all the minor German
and Italian principalities. Of the recognized powers, only the Sultan of Turkey and the United States
were unrepresented. By way of background to this
brilliant picture, Napoleon's wife and infant son could
be seen walking in the Gardens of Schoenbrunn.

*Congress
of Vienna*

The first few weeks of the Congress were spent in
a succession of magnificent festivities. Notwithstanding the financial ruin of the country, the Austrian Exchequer diverted sums amounting to 25,000
guldens a day for this purpose. Among the long-
forgotten records of these faded pageantries one
chapter still stands forth with the lustre of immortal genius. Ludwig van Beethoven was in Vienna.
The Emperor placed the great assembly room of
his court at the disposal of the composer. Beethoven was privileged to send out invitations in his
own name to all of the sovereigns and grandees then
in Vienna. To Beethoven the homage and admirers
thus won came doubly welcome, since he had by
this time turned totally deaf, and had been left to
live in solitude. Among his compositions presented
to the world at this period was the descriptive piece
on the "Battle of Vittoria." He also assisted at the
great mass which Talleyrand arranged to solemnize
the anniversary of the execution of Louis XVI. of
France.

Beethoven

Talleyrand was the leading spirit of the whole Congress. This was but another proof of his high diplomatic talents, for in a secret clause of the treaty of Paris the allies had agreed to exclude France from participation in any of their territorial arrangements. Talleyrand, who was well aware of this, insisted that France, too, must now be reckoned as one of the allies, and in the end he carried his point. He also brought it about that the Congress met in open session and not behind closed doors, as first arranged by Metternich. Talleyrand used the question as to what was to be done with Saxony and the duchy of Warsaw as an instrument wherewith to break up the concert of the powers. Russia and Prussia had agreed, in the treaty of Kalisch, that Prussia should yield all of her Polish provinces to Russia and indemnify herself therefor by the annexation of Saxony. Already a Prussian military government was administering Saxony. To this aggrandizement of the Russian empire, Austria and England were opposed. The British statesmen wanted to see Poland restored to her former independence, while Austria dreaded to have Cracow and other Polish strongholds on the Austrian frontier pass into Russian hands. Talleyrand, accordingly, made the defence of the King of Saxony the keynote of his policy. In pursuance of this object he reared a fetich of legitimacy, which Metternich promptly seized upon as the best of means wherewith to hold together the patchwork fabric of the Austrian empire. The minor princes of Germany, who had in their day sided with France, like the

King of Saxony, and who had reason to fear the growing strength of Prussia, cordially agreed with Emperor Francis's sentiment: "It would be too bad to thrust an honest German prince from his throne."

Talleyrand's enthusiasm for legitimacy was regarded by the Englishmen in Vienna as one of the drolleries of the former Minister of the Directory. Talleyrand, in his letters to Louis XVIII., ascribed this British attitude to a consciousness of their own blood guilt toward Tippoo Sahib. Yet, when the two northern powers had been thoroughly isolated, and France offered to join her army to those of Austria and the southern German States, England fell into line. A rash threat of war by Hardenberg was followed by immediate armaments on the part of Austria, Hanover and Bavaria. The Czar sent instant orders for his soldiers, then returning to Russia, to halt in Poland. *Friction among the Powers*

With another European war in prospect, the British Ministry was glad to dispose of the troublesome war with America and its serious annoyances to British maritime commerce. The chief cause for dispute was removed by the withdrawal of the Orders in Council on the collapse of the Continental blockade. Since the time that Russia had offered to mediate, commissioners from both countries had been deliberating at Ghent for nearly five months. The American commissioners were John Quincy Adams, James A. Bayard, Henry Clay, Jonathan Russell and Albert Gallatin. Gambier, Gouldburn and William Adams represented Great Britain. The original instructions of President Madison were *British desire for peace* to insist on the abolition of forcib.e impressment at sea as a *sine qua non* of peace. The disquieting attitude of the New England States made the American government more tractable. By the time the notorious Convention of Hartford met, and the cry of disloyalty was raised, Madison's Secretary of State was ready for peace at any price. Colonel Monroe's last instruction to his commissioners was this: "Omit any stipulation on the subject of impressment, if found indispensably necessary to terminate the war." The American commissioners accordingly declared that, "the causes of the war having disappeared by the maritime pacification of Europe, the government of the United States does not desire to continue war in defence of abstract principles, which have for the present ceased to have any practical effect." Both commissions agreed in the end "that all questions between the two nations should be left essentially where they were when the war began." In fine, nothing had been accomplished by the war beyond the loss of lives and property. On the day before the treaty was ratified, Henry Clay still stood out, exclaiming: " 'Tis a damned bad treaty, and I don't know whether I will sign it or not." But on the morrow, —Christmas—the treaty was signed, and peace was held to be concluded.

Peace conference at Ghent

Return to status quo

1815

THOUGH a peace treaty had been duly signed by the commissioners of England and America, the news of this event did not reach the belligerents for several weeks. From England, reinforcements of 5,000 men had been sent some time previously to General Ross, with orders to "seize the whole province of Louisiana." The United States *American war drags on* had 2,378 soldiers at New Orleans. Andrew Jackson was in command. At that time the city of New Orleans contained 20,000 inhabitants, including the black slaves, who were greatly in the majority. On December 15, 1814, while Jackson was on a tour of inspection in Louisiana, the British struck their first blow. A few days before they had entered Lake Borgne under convoy and captured six American gunboats. Jackson on his return declared martial law, and assumed dictatorial powers. The British lost no time. Seven thousand men were transferred from their ships to the island in Lake Borgne. The British line of advance was selected six miles down the Mississippi from New Orleans. A force of 1,688 British soldiers was landed three miles from the Mississippi. They commanded a point which Jackson *British attack New Orleans* recognized as one of the three necessary approaches. News arrived that the British had entered the nearest plantation. Jackson had 2,000 men, with two field pieces, immediately available. In the river lay an American war schooner, the "Carolina," armed with one long 12-pounder and six 12-pound carronades. The British had no artillery beyond two 3-pounders. The Americans advanced along a narrow road through the plantation. Colonel Coffee, with 732 men, marched around to attack the British from the rear. Commodore Patterson on the "Carolina" opened the fight at seven in the evening. A quarter of an hour afterward Jackson struck the British outposts while the main column was resting. The Americans rushed in on them and a brisk fight followed. At the same time Coffee struck the British flank opposite the "Carolina's" fire. Within an hour the British were forced to seek protection on an old levee. Their casualties were 277 men. Jackson lost 214 of his soldiers. The moral effect of the fight was greater than the actual military results. Jackson's next position was chosen behind an old dry canal three-quarters of a mile in length.

Preliminary fighting

Major-General Sir Edward Pakenham was in command of all the British forces. They numbered 6,500. The Americans deepened the canal and put up a parapet behind it. Pakenham was reinforced by two howitzers and a mortar from the British fleet Under the fire of his artillery, the "Carolina," lying off in the river, had to be abandoned. Early in January, the British attacked Jackson's line with heavy artillery fire. The fire became general and lasted until noon. It proved so disastrous to the

British that they abandoned their position with their guns at one o'clock. The British commanders attributed their defeat to the American superiority in the use of artillery.

On January 4, Jackson was reinforced by 2,250 backwoodsmen from Kentucky, mostly unarmed. The English within a day or so were also reinforced, bringing their army up to about 8,000. On January 7, Jackson learned that a British force had crossed the river and threatened New Orleans. He could do no more than put 800 of his Kentuckians on the west bank. At six in the morning Pakenham sent a force of 5,300 men to the attack in two columns. Jackson, with an extended line of picked riflemen, awaited the attack behind bales of cotton. When the British lines came within musket-shot the fire that met them was so deadly that they faltered, and after a few rods of struggling advance, wavered and broke. General Pakenham fell at the head of his troops, and General Gibbs was mortally wounded. A British column, under Keane, meanwhile marched along the road between the river and the levee. The concentrated fire from the whole American right wrought havoc among his troops, and Keane himself fell wounded. On the west side, too, the British were repulsed, and had to be recalled from under fire. Next day, General Lambert, who had succeeded Pakenham in command, began preparations for a hazardous retreat. On January 27, his troops were re-embarked. Of their total force of 6,666 men, 2,000 were lost. The total American loss was 71.

(margin note: Both sides reinforced)

(margin note: Battle of New Orleans)

When the news of peace reached New Orleans, and was communicated to the newspapers by M. Louaillier, member of the Louisiana Legislature, Jackson had him put under military confinement. Judge Hall, who issued a writ of habeas corpus for Louaillier, was haled before a drum-head court-martial on the charge of "abetting and inciting mutiny.' For this contempt of court, Jackson subsequently had to pay a fine of a thousand dollars.

British attempt on Mobile

General Lambert, after withdrawing from New Orleans, decided to attack Mobile in Alabama. This plan was frustrated by the landing of an American brigade in the rear of Fort Bowyer on February 8. The British position was so ill chosen that they had no choice but to capitulate. They surrendered on February 11, while their fleet withdrew to the West Indies.

Surrender of Mobile

There were several actions at sea during this period, which added new laurels to the American navy. Decatur, in the "President," fought the "Endymion," and reduced her to a wreck, when, three other ships coming to her aid, he was compelled to surrender to this overwhelming force.

American naval exploits

The last two naval actions of the war were no less brilliant for the Americans. These were the capture, in February, 1815, by the frigate "Constitution," Captain Stewart, of two British sloops-of-war, the "Cyane" and "Levant," off the island of Madeira, and in March, by the "Hornet," Captain Biddle, of the brig "Penguin" off the coast of Brazil. "Thus terminated at sea," says Alison, the British historian, "this memorable contest, in

which the English, for the first time for a century
and a half, met with equal antagonists on their own
element; and in recounting which the British historian, at a loss whether to admire most the devoted
heroism of his own countrymen or the gallant bearing of their antagonists, feels almost equally warmed
in narrating either side of the strife."

On the same day that the British surrendered at
Mobile, news arrived in New York of the conclusion
of the peace negotiations at Ghent. The American
Senate unanimously confirmed the treaty on February 16. A special message was despatched late Peace
on Saturday evening to Boston. By making special in America
welcomed
haste the messenger reached Boston in thirty-two
hours. The Boston bells were set ringing early on
Monday morning, and schools and shops were closed,
while British and American flags were hoisted in
honor of the event. In the South the relief was
even greater. Along the entire coast, from Maine
to Mississippi, the news of peace was received with
transports of joy.

Yet peace was still delayed. In midsummer,
Captain Warrington, in command of the "Peacock,"
captured the "Nautilus" in the Straits of Sunda.
On the next day, July 1, 1815, he learned of the ratification of peace; so he gave up the "Nautilus" and
sailed for the United States. When he reached
home he found that every cruiser, both public and
private, had returned to port some time before. To
Warrington, therefore, belonged the distinction of The last
having fired the last shot of the war between Amer- shot
ica and England.

Peace found the United States in a deplorable condition—trade was ruined, commerce gone, no ready money, banks without credit, and a general depression. In shipping alone it had cost America 1,683 vessels and the lives of 18,000 sailors. Yet, such were the resources of the country, that the United States almost immediately entered on a career of unexampled prosperity. Cotton rose from ten to over twenty cents per pound.

At Vienna, during this same time, the diplomats of the allies had virtually finished their labors. The Polish and Saxon difficulties were settled by Prussia contenting herself with a portion of Saxony on the right bank of the Elbe, while Russia consented to maintain Poland as a separate province and relinquished her claim to Cracow and the border fortresses. The German states were united in a confederacy, with a diet in which Austria and Prussia each had two votes. Belgium was joined to Holland in a kingdom to be ruled by the Prince of Nassau. He agreed to maintain the great fortress of Luxembourg and its surroundings as a stronghold of the German confederation. Holland likewise had to relinquish all claim to her colonies, Demerara, Essequibo, Berbice, and the Cape of Good Hope, forfeited to England during the years of war. In a measure she was compensated therefor by England's restoration of the rich island of Java. The various cantons of Switzerland were all made part of the Swiss confederacy on an equal footing, and the Pope's dominions were restored. At the request of Great Britain the allied powers joined in a declaration against the traf-

Readjustments in Europe

The Dutch colonies

fic in black slaves. There remained only the question of Naples, where King Murat still ruled over the former possessions of the Bourbons. The unsatisfactory drift of affairs in France and Spain under Bourbon rule left the representatives of the other powers lukewarm toward Talleyrand's pro-Bourbon representations. When Metternich sent secret inquiries to Fouché, his spy in Paris, asking what would happen if Napoleon should take it into his head to return to France, Fouché replied: "Should a single regiment of an army sent against Napoleon declare for him, the others would surely follow the example. In case nothing of the sort happens, France of her own volition will soon seek refuge in the dynasty of Orleans." *Slave trade discountenanced*

Fouché's prophecy

It was at this juncture that a report suddenly reached Vienna that Napoleon had left Elba. The effect of this startling news was magical. All differences were sunk in the common desire to meet the situation. Talleyrand, to be sure, expressed a conviction that Napoleon would only cross into Italy, and there combine with Murat; and Wellington added his contemptuous opinion that, "Even if Napoleon should venture into France, he had acted upon false information, and the king would speedily destroy him." *Wellington overconfident*

Others knew better. The sovereigns of Austria, Russia and Prussia had learned from their own bitter experience whom they had to deal with. Alexander sent immediate orders to mobilize his army of 280,000 men in Poland, and declared that he would throw all his resources into the balance to "put an

end to these revolts of Pretorian Guards." The
Czar was the more aroused, since it was he who
had saved for Marie Louise the principality of
Parma, and who had opposed all projects to remove Napoleon from Elba, on the ground that he
had given his imperial word that he should be left
undisturbed. "We can have no peace now," exclaimed Alexander. "There is a mortal duel between me and Napoleon. He has broken his word
with me. I am freed from my engagement to him,
and Europe shall have an example."

Napoleon in Elba had been kept well informed of
the happenings in France and at Vienna. For several months all his old followers in France were looking forward to his return. "The soldiers plotted
openly," says the Duke of Roviga, in his memoirs,
"even at the corners of the streets. Every one, except perhaps the Ministers, knew what was going
on." Napoleon in Elba rallied about him his favorite
veterans as a bodyguard. With the three million
francs he had been allowed to keep he purchased four
coasting vessels. "When do we set out for France?"

was the standing question of his officers. On February 22, Fleury de Chaboulon, formerly an auditor
in the French Council of State, landed at Porto
Ferrajo. On his own initiative he had undertaken
the mission to urge the Emperor to return. In ardent words he informed Napoleon of the latest signs
of discontent in France, and of the reported dissolution of the Congress of Vienna. "Then they still

remember me?" inquired the Emperor. "My soldiers have not forgotten me?" Napoleon's resolu-

tion was soon taken. He despatched Fleury to Naples, while he gave orders for a final ball at court. His mother, then residing with him, was alone informed of his determination. The old woman, who had steadily followed her son's course with misgivings, trembled. Then she kissed him and said: "I see you cannot remain here. Go, and may God protect you!" On the night of the ball, while Napoleon's mother and sister directed the festivities, the little garrison was ordered to march to the quay for embarkation. At four in the morning all the other vessels in the harbor were embargoed. The Emperor left his guests in the assembly room and, hastening to the quay, embarked with 900 of his followers. By sunrise the little flotilla was under way, with Napoleon leading on the brig "Inconstant." As the ships drifted in the uncertain breeze, they fell in with a royal French brig. Napoleon ordered his soldiers to lie down, and his ship saluted with the flag of Elba—white, strewn with bees. The French captain hailed: "How is the Emperor?" "Very well," answered the pilot. We are for Genoa." "We go to Leghorn," answered the Frenchman, and so they parted. On the morning of March 1, a landing was made in the Bay St. Jouan, three miles out of Antibes. The troops went ashore with a cry of "Vive l'Empereur!" A detachment of guards who proceeded to Antibes were not admitted within the gate, but the inhabitants readily sold them provisions and horses. That night Napoleon and his men bivouacked among the olive trees of the Provence. The next day the Emperor,

Napoleon leaves Elba

Landing at St. Jouan

after a brief study of the maps, struck out across the hills in the direction of Grenoble. What guns he had brought with him he left behind in the ships. "It is not with cannon shots that I will win this campaign," he said. Over muddy roads and snow ravines the column pressed onward at the rate of forty miles a day. Not until the close of the fifth day's march did the mounted men riding in front come upon a detachment of royal soldiery in the village of La Mure, twenty miles south of Grenoble. Napoleon's Old Guards and the soldiers wearing the **First bloodless encounter** white cockade mingled in the streets, until their officers were filled with apprehension and drew them off. The next morning, as Napoleon's column advanced on the road to Grenoble, they found the full regiment drawn up to block their passage. "Never mind, they won't shoot!" said the country folk. "Maybe we have been deceived," said Napoleon to Bertrand; "but, no matter, forward!" He himself rode forward, and, addressing the royal troops, called out in a loud voice: "Soldiers of the Fifth, do you recognize me?" "Yes, Sire," said the men. "I am your Little Corporal. What man among you would fire on me? Here is my breast!" "Vive l'Empereur!" shouted the veterans, and rushed forward to press his hand. Their commander, left alone, saw the ranks broken and his soldiers trampling their white cockades underfoot. Napoleon rode toward him. "I know you well, Monsieur Lassard," he said. "Who made you **A Napoleonic effect** lieutenant-colonel?" "You, Sire." "And before that—who made you captain?" "You, Sire."

"And you wish to fight against me!" "Only because it was my duty." So saying, he tendered the Emperor his sword. Napoleon took it and pressed his hand. "We shall meet again in Grenoble," he said. Then turning to Bertrand and Drouot, he remarked: "There, it is settled. To-night we shall be in Grenoble, and in ten days in Paris."

All was settled, indeed, and the famous period of the Hundred Days was well under way. The veteran regiments of the various royal garrisons joined Napoleon's column in a body. As they approached Grenoble, Colonel de Labédoyère called out his regiment, and raising the eagle of the seventh, marched to meet the Emperor with flying colors. Napoleon embraced the young officer and the old flag. "We are tired of seeing France humiliated," explained De Labédoyère; but, Sire, everything is changed. A new reign must be inaugurated." "I know it," answered the Emperor, "and am resolved to do so." This was likewise the keynote of the proclamation he issued after he entered Grenoble in triumph:

The Hundred Days

"Soldiers! In my exile I heard your voices. I am come through all obstacles and dangers. Your General, summoned to the throne by the prayer of the people, and raised upon your shields, is now restored to you. Come and join him! Tear down those colors which were proscribed by the nation, and which for twenty-five years all the enemies of France have rallied round! Display the tricolor which you carried in our great battles! Win back those eagles which you won at Ulm, Austerlitz, Jena, Eylau, Friedland, and Wagram!

Address of Grenoble

"Come, soldiers! stand by the banners of your chief! His life is only yours; his rights are only yours and the people's; his interests, his honor, and his glory are only your interests, your honor, and your glory. Victory will march at the double; the eagle, with the colors of the nation, will fly from steeple to steeple, even to the towers of Notre Dame! Then will you be able to boast of your deeds, then will you be the liberators of your country!"

The wonderful personal magnetism of the great captain once more exerted its full influence on his soldiers. The rhapsody of the Hundred Days was its token. In its most poetic expression this frenzy of France has come down to us in the immortal lyrics of Béranger. The wild loyalty of the French soldiers of those days, curiously enough, has still better been rendered by a German poet. It was Heinrich Heine's famous song of the "Two Grenadiers" that afforded to Schumann an opportunity to let his stirring music hark back to the forbidden strains of the "Marseillaise":

France in frenzy.

"The Two Grena-diers"

Straggling to France went two grenadiers,
    Who were taken captive in Russia;
Hanging their heads to hide their tears
    They crossed the frontier of Prussia.

'Twas then their spirits were saddened most
    When they learned how France had been shaken—
Defeated and scattered the valiant host,
    And the Emperor, the Emperor taken.

Full bitterly wept the two grenadiers
    When they heard the woful story,
And one of them said: "How salt are my tears—
    How burning my wound and gory."

The other muttered: "'Tis the end of the dance;
    I am sick of life and aweary:
But I have a wife and child in France,
    Without me their lot will be dreary."

> "What care I for children, what for a wife!
> A heavier care has arisen.
> Let them beg for bread to keep up life—
> The Emperor, the Emperor in prison!
>
> "Oh, grant me, brother, but one demand,
> When life's last hours I number;
> Take with you my corse to our native land,
> In French soil let me slumber;
>
> "My Cross of Honor and crimson band
> Place next to my heart for a neighbor,
> And put my carbine in my hand,
> Then buckle on my sabre!
>
> "Thus shall I lie still to watch and peer
> As a sentinel stands o'er the forces,
> Until the roaring of cannon I hear
> And the hoof-beat of neighing horses—
>
> "Then will my Emperor ride over my grave
> While sabres glitter and rattle,
> Then armed to the teeth shall I rise from my grave
> For the Emperor, the Emperor to battle!"

On March 8, Napoleon set out for Lyons, at the head of seven thousand men ready to die in his cause. A semaphore despatch, giving the news of Napoleon's landing, reached Paris on March 5. At first only the king was troubled. While the matter was kept a profound secret in Paris, *Paris alarmed* the princes of the royal house hastened to Lyons, Bordeaux and La Vendée, to see to the army. Marshals Ney and Macdonald, who were held to have compromised themselves with Napoleon when they prepared the way for his abdication, were despatched to Besançon and Nîmes to take charge of the troops there. Marshal Soult, in his capacity as Minister of War, issued an address to the army denouncing the Emperor. Mortier was placed at the head of the troops in the north of France;

Augereau was despatched to Normandy; full powers
were transmitted to Masséna, at Toulon; and Oudinot took direction of the forces at Marseilles. In
the meantime, Napoleon's advance was unopposed.
Defection after defection occurred in the army; and
it was soon learned that the corps of 30,000 men,
posted by order of Soult on the frontier between
Besançon and Lyons, were in large masses deserting
the royal standard. The Count of Artois, the Duke
of Orleans, and Macdonald could make no impression either on the troops or on the mass of the
people. They returned discouraged, and Napoleon,
on the 12th of March, took possession of Lyons.
This great success at once gave him command of
the centre of France.

When Marshal Ney took leave of the king at the
Tuileries, he kissed his hand and said: "Sire, I will
bring Bonaparte back in an iron cage." At Aux-
erre, Ney was sought out by Gamotte, his brother-
in-law, a great admirer of Napoleon. He intro-
duced to him emissaries from the Emperor, who
beset him with such arguments as Napoleon knew
would appeal to his warm-hearted lieutenant and
comrade-in-arms. These appeals from his former
chieftain proved too much for Ney. As he himself
explained at his subsequent trial for high treason:
"I had indeed kissed the hand of the king, his
majesty having presented it to me when he wished
me a good journey. The descent of Bonaparte appeared to me so extravagant, that I spoke of it
with indignation, and made use of the expression
charged, relative to the iron cage. In the night

of March 13—down to which time, I protest my fidelity—I received a proclamation, drawn by Napoleon, which I signed. Before reading it to the troops, I submitted it to General Bourmont, who said it was necessary to join Bonaparte, and that the Bourbons had committed such follies that they could no longer be supported."

On that occasion some of the royalist officers broke their swords, saying: "You might have spared us that," but the bulk of the army hastened in eager marches to join their Emperor. Napoleon received Ney with open arms. He cut short all Ney's explanations, saying: "Do you think I could ever forget Friedland?" The defection of Ney, followed by that of the whole army, opened the way to Paris and drove Louis XVIII. from his throne. Ney's defection

When the news of Ney's act reached the capital, the king called for a review of the garrison in Paris. Only a small part of the National Guard responded. Another review was ordered for March 19, and those of the troops that put in their appearance, consisting largely of the royal guards, were drawn off to Beauvais on the other side of Paris. The significance of this manœuvre was made plain that night, when the king with his household left the Tuileries and drove to Beauvais. Thence he took post to Lisle, and fled across the border to Ghent in Flanders. Flight of Louis XVIII.

Napoleon arrived at Fontainebleau on the 19th, and proceeded to Paris next day. He reached the Tuileries at nine o'clock in the evening. The moment his carriage stopped at the gates, he was seized by his waiting friends, borne aloft in their arms amid deafening cheers, through a brilliant throng of officers, and hurried up the great stair into the reception hall. Here, an array of ladies of the Imperial Court received him in state. Later, at St. Helena, Napoleon described this day as one of the most delightful of his life.

On the morrow the Emperor set himself to work to form a Cabinet. Fouché was summoned and demanded the portfolio of Foreign Affairs. He was persuaded instead to resume his functions as chief of police. Coulaincourt, though plainly reluctant, was made Minister of Foreign Affairs. Marshal Davoust, who had been under a cloud during the Restoration, readily agreed to be Minister of War. Cambacérès, Carnot and Benjamin Constant made up the Council of State. It was plain that a return to republican principles was unavoidable.

Napoleon in Paris

The threatening attitude of the great powers and a series of royalist risings in the south of France soon convinced Napoleon that he need not hope to enjoy the fruits of his last *coup d'état* in peace. His envoys to the Emperor of Austria were turned back at the frontier. Caulaincourt's efforts to procure a hearing for his master failed utterly. Secret emissaries who tried to rescue the Empress and the King of Rome from Vienna could not induce Marie Louise to risk the loss of Parma. Even Napoleon's decree abolishing the slave trade fell flat on the statesmen of England.

War inevitable

On March 25, the allied powers, reconvening

their Congress at Vienna, concluded a new treaty on the basis of that of Chaument. The Cabinets of Russia, Prussia, Austria and Great Britain engaged to "unite their forces against Bonaparte and his faction, in order to prevent him from again troubling the peace of Europe; they each agreed to furnish 180,000 men for the prosecution of the war; and, if necessary, to draw forth their entire military force of every description." By a secret treaty, concluded on the same day, it was stipulated that the contracting parties should not lay down their arms until they had effected the destruction of Napoleon; and that England should supply the funds. All the lesser powers of Europe acceded to these treaties within a fortnight after their ratification.

Congress of Vienna reconvened

An international declaration was issued:

"The powers which signed the Treaty of Paris, reassembled in congress at Vienna, being informed of the escape of Napoleon Bonaparte, and of his entry with an armed force into France, owe it to their own dignity and to the interest of the nations to make a solemn announcement of their sentiments on the occasion. In thus breaking the convention which had established him in the island of Elba, Bonaparte has destroyed the sole legal title which is attached to his political existence. By reappearing in France with projects of trouble and overthrow he has deprived himself of the protection of the laws, and made it evident, in the face of the world, that there can no longer be peace or truce with him. The powers therefore declare that Bonaparte has placed himself out of the pale of civil and social relations; and that, as the general enemy and

Joint note of Powers

disturber of the world, he is abandoned to public justice."

The instrument bore the signatures of Metternich, Talleyrand, Wellington, Hardenberg, Nesselrode, and Loevenhielm. On all sides they began to mobilize. Even in Switzerland and Holland the militia were called to the frontiers.

General mobilization

Napoleon realized that all hopes for peace were illusory. He himself informed the reconvened Chambers of the coming storm. The utmost exertions were made for defence. The veterans, but lately returned from their imprisonment in Germany and Russia, were called from their homes. Arms and ammunition were turned out at top speed. Napoleon's splendid genius for organization, now put to the last strain, appeared at its best. Within a month he had an army of 120,000 veterans under arms. In the meanwhile, the new French Constitution, the "Acte Additionnel," drawn up by Benjamin Constant, was breeding trouble at Paris. The Republicans, feeling themselves in the saddle, insisted on curbing the Emperor's despotic tendencies. Surrounded by such irreconcilables as Carnot, Constant, Lafayette, and his own brother Lucien, not to mention the treacherous Fouché, Napoleon had to fight for every one of his measures. When Carnot finally raised the threat of civil war, Napoleon broke out: "See here, Carnot, with you I have no need of disguise. You have a hard head, and can see through the shell of things. Let us not sow the seed of discord when the closest union is needed to save the country! Let us first save France: after

New French constitution

that I will accede to everything." Carnot gave in, and from that hour left Napoleon free to pursue his measures. When Fouché was informed of this at the next Cabinet session, he said without reserve: "If that man should attempt to curb the Jacobin principles we will overturn him at once, and forever." Napoleon, who knew that Fouché had entered into relations with the royalists in the Vendée, and who had lately been placed in possession of one of Metternich's secret despatches to Fouché, summoned his Minister of Police before the Council and, disclosing his treason, declared that he should be shot the next morning. Carnot told the enraged Emperor that this was no time for shooting cabinet ministers, and that such measures, now, would compromise him before the whole nation. Napoleon yielded with ill grace. His last words to Fouché were:

Fouché unmasked

"Like all other persons who are ready to die, we have nothing to conceal from each other. If I fall, the patriots fall too; you will play your game ill, if you betray me. Your party will perish under the rule of the Bourbons: I am your last dictator—remember that!"

The first blow was prematurely struck by Murat. On the last day of March he crossed the Po with 30,000 Neapolitans, and called upon all the Italians to assert their independence. After some indecisive encounters, the Austrian generals Bellegarde, Bianchi and Fremont united their forces, and, on April 9, fell upon his at Tollentino. The Neapolitans took to their heels, and Murat fled to France.

Murat's premature stroke

Ferdinand VII. promptly returned to his lost throne in Naples and was there reinstalled with the help of British cruisers. Napoleon was so incensed at this stroke of ill-fortune that he would not even appoint his veteran cavalry leader to a command in his own army.

Next, hostilities broke out in the south of France. Louis La Roche Jaquelein landed on the coast of La Vendée and raised the people to revolt. Napoleon, in just alarm at this menace of civil war, despatched a force of 20,000 men under General La Marque and Travot to that region. The first battle was disastrous for the royalists. Auguste La Roche Jaquelein lost his life. This ended the revolt.

Vendeans revolt

At Vienna, in the meanwhile, arrangements had been made to form forthwith three great armies from the allied forces; the first, of 265,000, chiefly Austrians and Bavarians, to be stationed on the Upper Rhine, and commanded by Schwarzenberg; the second, of 155,000 Prussians, on the Lower Rhine, under Blücher; the third, of 100,000, composed of English, Hanoverians and Belgians, in the Low Countries, under Wellington. It was further resolved that military operations should be commenced early in June; previous to which time, the Russian army, 170,000 strong, might be expected to reach the Upper Rhine from Poland, and, entering France by Strasburg and Besançon, to form a reserve for the invading armies from the east. In addition to the operations of these large masses, lesser movements were to be made on the side of Switzerland and the Pyrenees.

Plans of allies

From this plan of the campaign, it was evident that the British troops in Flanders would first be exposed to the shock of war; and the British Cabinet made exertions proportionate to the emergency. On April 6, a message from the Prince Regent formally announced to both Houses of Parliament the events which had recently occurred in France, the measures adopted by the Congress of Vienna, and the necessity of augmenting the military and naval forces of the kingdom. The supplies of men and money requisite to the undertaking were immediately voted by Parliament; and in addition to the enormous sums wherewith to support her own naval and military establishments, Great Britain granted and paid to the several allied powers, within the year, subsidies to the amount of more than eleven million pounds. *England's preparations*

Wellington, after careful deliberation, resolved to invade France directly from Flanders, between the Maine and the Oise; but, in order to conceal his design, he recommended that the Austrians and Russians should first cross the French frontier by Befort and Huningen, and, when this was accomplished, that the British and Prussians united should march upon Paris by Mons and Namur. He had 80,000 men under his orders, of whom 46,000 were British. Twelve thousand of these were veterans of the Peninsula. The rest were Dutch-Belgians under the Prince of Orange, Brunswickers under their Duke, and the Hanoverian Legion under Wallmoden. Wellington himself, rather ungraciously, described his force as an "infamous army." Blü- *Wellington's forces*

Blucher's army cher had an army of 108,000 men, all Prussians, and burning once more to avenge the injuries to their country.

Napoleon hastened to take command of his army in that quarter. The Emperor's plan of campaign was based on the necessities of his situation, and the imperative need of an early success, so as to enable him to meet the advance of the Russians and Austrians from the other side. For the direction of Napoleon at the front public affairs in France during his absence Napoleon appointed a provisional government, including his brothers Joseph and Lucien, Cambacérès, Davoust, Coulaincourt, Fouché, Carnot, Goudin, Mollien, and Décrès. This done, the Emperor left Paris on June 12, and joined the army on the 14th.

Forthwith he moved his men into camp at Laon, behind the screening chain of fortresses on the Belgian frontier. Blücher's army lay on the bank of the Sambre and Meuse, from Liège on his left to Charleroi on his right. Wellington covered Brussels. It was on Charleroi that Napoleon resolved to direct his first attack in the hope of cutting the two armies apart.

French movements On June 10, Wellington received information— which proved to be misleading—that Napoleon had reached Maubeuge with his troops. Yet neither Blücher nor Wellington took steps to concentrate their forces. When the French troops crossed the frontier near Fleurus on the 15th, Wellington's men lay in cantonments from the Scheldt to Brussels, Allies inactive and Blücher's extended as far as Namur. This inactivity would be inexplicable but for this account of the matter given by Fouché in his memoirs.

That arch traitor had promised to furnish the British commander with a detailed plan of the campaign. Wellington was in hourly expectation of this intelligence, and quietly awaited its arrival. Why he did not receive it, Fouché thus explains:

"My agents with Metternich and Lord Welling- Fouche's explanation ton had promised everything, and the English general at least expected I would give him the plan of the campaign. I knew that Napoleon would attack the British army on the 16th, or, at latest, on the 18th, after having marched right over the Prussians. He had the greater reason to expect success, inasmuch as Wellington, deceived by false reports, believed that the opening of the campaign might be deferred till the beginning of July. Napoleon, therefore, trusted to a surprise, and I arranged my plans in conformity. On the day of his departure, I despatched Madame D—— with notes, written in cipher, containing the whole plan of the campaign; but at the same time I sent such orders to the frontier as would prevent her reaching Wellington's headquarters until after the catastrophe. This is the true explanation of the British generalissimo's inactivity, which, at the time, excited such universal astonishment."

The French army crossed the frontier at daybreak on the 15th, and moved upon Charleroi. The Prus- Charleroi sian force, which occupied that town, was driven out, and fell back on Fleurus. Thus, Napoleon's first object, that of taking his enemy by surprise, was accomplished, and he now confidently expected to separate the two allied armies. For this purpose he despatched Ney with the left wing, 46,000 strong, to Quatre-Bras, a point of intersection of the roads from and to Brussels, Nivelles, Charleroi and Namur; while he himself, with 72,000 men, pushed on toward Fleurus to assail Blücher, who was concentrating his army with all possible haste, and falling back upon Ligny. Wellington received word of these movements at Brussels on the evening of the 15th, and he immediately sent orders to his troops to concentrate at Quatre-Bras.

Blücher's army, excepting the fourth corps, which had not yet come up, arrayed themselves, on the 16th, on the heights between Brie and Sombref, and strongly occupied the villages of St. Amand and *Prussian position* Ligny in front. The position was well chosen. The villages afforded an excellent shelter, while the artillery, placed on a semicircular ridge between them, commanded the entire field, and the elevation in the rear, surmounted by the windmill of Bussy, formed a good rallying point in case of disaster.

Napoleon afterward recorded in his memoirs that he attacked Blücher first because he well knew that Blücher would not be supported by the overprudent English commander; whereas, if Wellington had been attacked first, the Prussians would surely hasten to his support. As a matter of fact, Wellington himself rode over to Blücher's lines on the morning of the 16th and promised him his support. Apart from that, it is on record that Napoleon attacked both commanders almost simultaneously, for the distinct purpose of preventing them from detaching troops in aid of one another. Only, in accordance with his oft-tried strategy, he endeavored to crush each of his opponents successively by a rapid concentration of superior numbers.

In the fight at Quatre-Bras, in which the British held their ground, the Duke of Brunswick fell a sacrifice. At Ligny, by a series of superb manœuvres, Napoleon completely routed the Prussians. They lost 1,200 men and 21 guns. While trying to stem the onslaught of the French cavalry, Blücher's horse was shot under him, and two successive cavalry charges passed over his senseless body. After nightfall his aide-de-camp, Count Nostitz, returned to the battlefield and succeeded in drawing the field marshal from beneath his horse. When Blücher revived it was only to find his army routed. A characteristic anecdote is that when the surgeon attempted to rub his injured leg with spirits, Blücher exclaimed: "The stuff is of no use taken outside," and drank it down.

Blücher's second in command, General Gneisenau, saved the situation by conducting the retreat northward. Thus he brought the shattered Prussian columns once more in communication with the British. Of the three Prussian army corps that had figured in the battle, two were so speedily rallied at Wavre that Grouchy's division, later, was not strong enough to prevent their junction with the British.

The ill success of Ney's attack on the British lines at Quatre-Bras was attributed by him to the fact that the army corps of General d'Erlon, which Na-

[margin: Quatre-Bras]

[margin: Ligny]

[margin: Gneisenau's strategy]

poleon had placed between himself and Ney, was first withdrawn from Ney to assist at Ligny. Later, when d'Erlon was recalled from that battlefield to succor Ney, he could not reach Quatre-Bras until it was too late.

Much has been written of the scenes and incidents at Brussels that preceded the Battle of Waterloo. When the news of Napoleon's first advance arrived the flower of the British army was assembled at the Countess of Richmond's ball at the British Embassy. The Duke of Brunswick was the first to hasten from the ballroom to his death. William Makepeace Thackeray, in his novel "Vanity Fair," has brought the brilliant scene to life again in the chapter de-

voted to the eve of Waterloo. More famous still are Byron's immortal stanzas in the third Canto of "Childe Harold's Pilgrimage":

> There was a sound of revelry by night,
> And Belgium's capital had gather'd then
> Her Beauty and her Chivalry, and bright
> The lamp shone o'er fair women and brave men;
> A thousand hearts beat happily; and when
> Music arose with its voluptuous swell,
> Soft eyes look'd love to eyes which spake again,
> And all went merry as a marriage-bell;
> But hush! hark! a deep sound strikes like a rising knell!

> Did ye not hear it?—No; 'twas but the wind,
> Or the car rattling o'er the stony street;
> On with the dance! let joy be unconfined;
> No sleep till morn, when Youth and Pleasure meet
> To chase the glowing Hours with flying feet—
> But, hark!—that heavy sound breaks in once more,
> As if the clouds its echo would repeat;
> And nearer, clearer, deadlier than before!
> Arm! Arm! it is—it is—the cannon's opening roar!

Within a window'd niche of that high hall
Sate Brunswick's fated chieftain; he did hear
That sound the first amidst the festival,
And caught its tone with Death's prophetic ear;
And when they smiled because he deem'd it near,
His heart more truly knew that peal too well
Which stretch'd his father on a bloody bier,
And roused the vengeance blood alone could quell:
He rush'd into the field, and, foremost fighting, fell.

Ah! then and there was hurrying to and fro,
And gathering tears, and tremblings of distress,
And cheeks all pale, which but an hour ago
Blush'd at the praise of their own loveliness;
And there were sudden partings, such as press
The life from out young hearts, and choking sighs
Which ne'er might be repeated; who could guess
If ever more should meet those mutual eyes,
Since upon night so sweet such awful morn could rise?

And there was mounting in hot haste: the steed,
The mustering squadron, and the clattering car,
Went pouring forward with impetuous speed,
And swiftly forming in the ranks of war;
And the deep thunder peal on peal afar;
And near, the beat of the alarming drum
Roused up the soldier ere the morning star;
While throng'd the citizens with terror dumb,
Or whispering, with white lips—"The foe! They come!
      they come!"

.   .   .   .

Last noon beheld them full of lusty life,
Last eve in Beauty's circle proudly gay,
The midnight brought the signal-sound of strife,
The morn the marshalling in arms,—the day
Battle's magnificently-stern array!
The thunder-clouds close o'er it, which when rent
The earth is cover'd thick with other clay,
Which her own clay shall cover, heap'd and pent,
Rider and horse,—friend, foe,—in one red burial blent!

During the night of June 15, Wellington learned
of the defeat of the Prussians, and that they were
falling back to Wavre. As this exposed the British

flank, Wellington, too, ordered a retreat through
Genappe, with orders to come in touch with the
Prussians. Throughout the 17th, the British retreated, followed closely by the French. Half way
back to Brussels, when in line with the Prussians at
Wavre, Wellington halted his army near the valley
of Waterloo.

The field of Waterloo, or La Belle Alliance, as it
is called in French and German annals, stretches not
quite two miles in length from the hamlet of Hougoumont on the right, to the hedge of La Haye
Sainte on the left. The road from Brussels to
Charleroi runs through the centre of the field, less
than three-quarters of a mile south of the village of
Waterloo, and three hundred yards in front of the
farmhouse of Mont St. Jean. The British army occupied the crest of a range of low hills crossing the
highroad at right-angles, two hundred yards in the
rear of the farmhouse of La Haye Sainte, which
adjoins the road to Charleroi. The French troops,
on the other side of the valley, were posted along
a corresponding line of hills, stretching on either
side of the hamlet of La Belle Alliance. The summit of these hills afforded an excellent position for
the French artillery; but an attack across the valley would necessarily be exposed to a severe cannonade from the British batteries.

Wellington had stationed General Hill with 7,000
men at Hal, six miles on the right, to cover the
road from Mons to Brussels. Early on the morning of the 18th, he despatched letters to Louis
XVIII. at Ghent, recommending that monarch to

retire to Antwerp on the enemy's approach. Blü-
cher, during the night of the 17th, sent word to ^{Blucher's}
^{promise}Wellington that he would join him at Waterloo
with his whole army, and that his men might be
expected to fall upon the right of the enemy early
in the afternoon.

Of the two armies thus facing each other, the
French felt more confident of victory. The British officers and soldiers, after the manner of their
kind, despised their allies. Wellington himself
ordered his Dutch troops out of the line of battle,
remarking wrathfully, " 'Tis the worst army that Wellington
ever was got together." Napoleon had reason to doubtful
expect that the English would give him a hard tus-
sle. "The British infantry are the very devil to
fight!" said Foy on the morning of the battle; and
Soult, too, with his bitter memories of Spain, uttered
a note of warning: "Sire, I know these English,
they will die on the ground on which they stand
before they lose it." But Napoleon knew that he Napoleon
confident
had the advantage of numbers, and counted especially on the great strength of his artillery and
cavalry. Moreover, he believed Blücher to be thoroughly beaten, and did not think that the Prussians
would prove so troublesome to Grouchy that he
could not count on the support of Grouchy's 35,000
men. He was borne up, too, by a strong belief
in the unfailing superiority of his own military
genius.

It was a beautiful June day, after a wet and chilly
night. As the ground was still too soggy for rapid
movements of artillery or cavalry evolutions on any

grand scale, Napoleon put off the fight to hold a
final grand review of all his hosts in battle array.
On the plain of Waterloo the crops that Sunday
morning stood high, with bright patches of pale
green rye and red clover. On the other side of the
vale, the British soldiers, lying cramped in their
damp ditches, could see the sun glittering on Napoleon's martial columns, and heard the stirring strains
of the "Marseillaise" wafted across the waving
wheat fields. When the men, at last, heard the
roar of a hundred thousand French throats yelling
"Vive l'Empereur!" a stir ran through their ranks.
The auxiliaries appeared ill at ease. "The mere
name of Napoleon," said Wellington, "has beaten
them before they have fired a shot."

Opening of
the battle

Shortly before noon the battle began with heavy
artillery fire from the heights of La Belle Alliance.
Immediately Reille's corps, 6,000 strong, advanced
on Hougoumont. As the column swept down the
slope a mass of French tirailleurs skirmished into
the adjoining wood, and thence up to the orchard
and garden of the chateau where the British lay.
They were picked off from the windows of the chateau, while the British Light Foot Guards, seeking
shelter in the hollow of a road between the orchard
and the house, from that line of vantage repulsed
all French attacks. Müffling, the Prussian aide-de-
camp on the British general staff, doubted whether

Impor-
tance of
Hougou-
mont

Hougoumont could hold out, but Wellington expressed confidence in MacDonnell, the Scotch officer
in charge of that point.

While the fight raged in that quarter, the French

his prostrate lines. "Let us see who will pound the hardest."

By this time the fight around Hougoumont had reached a crisis. The upper story of the chateau was riddled with solid shot and the roof caught fire. From the blazing windows the Light Guards continued to pour their unintermittent fire, while the wounded lying behind them were suffocated in the smoke. Once, the French broke in the main gateway, but were bayoneted on the threshold. MacDonnell, who was of herculean proportions, with a cluster of his officers, by sheer force shut the gate again in the face of the frantic Frenchmen. Mercer, an eye-witness, declared later that around this spot the dead were heaped up as thick as on the breach of Badajos.

the afternoon, when the British line sufficiently shaken by the prolonged Napoleon meant to let Ney try a n masse. Ney moved his columns Emperor's orders.

barely one thousand yards came of cuirassiers and nineteen rs, trotting down the slope. lines sounded the bugle call, ceive cavalry!" The men formed in squares, or, rather, oblongs, behind the crest of the hill, while the horse artillery came dashing up and unlimbered on the ridge before them. The gunners were ordered to keep up an incessant fire of grape and canister until the French horsemen should be all but upon them. Then they were to

artillery played havoc with the British
The gunners had been ordered to hold their
a general attack. About two in the afterno
dark mass was seen moving in the woods of Oha
The French officers turned their glasses on it, and
expressed a joyful hope that it was Grouchy's
corps. A reconnoitring party returned with the
unwelcome news that they were Prussians. Napoleon instantly despatched a part of Ney's troops to
hold them in check, while he made haste to launch
his great infantry attack. Seventy-two guns prepared the way with a torrent of grape shot.
D'Erlon with four divisions of sixteen thousand
men flung himself against La Haye Sainte on the
British left and drove in the thin red line of Picton's division which had already suffered hea
losses at Quatre-Bras. A Dutch-Belgi
took to its heels and swept through
ranks followed by their curses. Bari
rians, on the other hand, stoutly held
At last, under the terrific fire of the
the farmhouse of La Haye Saint
as the French attack had sp
Uxbridge with his cavalry fel
infantry and threw them in dis
cuirassiers, skirmishing on the othe
pit, could form for a counter charge. Picton's in
fantry followed with a bayonet charge and regained
the crest. There they were swept by such deadly
artillery fire that the men flung themselves flat or
their faces. Picton was killed. "Hard poundi
this, gentlemen," said Wellington, as he rode

vy
ian brigade
the British
ng's Hanove·
their ground.
· French gunners
· caught fire, just
ent its force. Lord
· upon the French
order before the
· side of a sand

sp…

great br…

At four in…

was held to b…

artillery fire,…

cavalry charge…

in advance of the…

Through a gap of…

twenty-one squadrons…

squadrons of lanc…

Along the British…

"Prepare to rec…

in square…

Ney an-
ticipates
orders

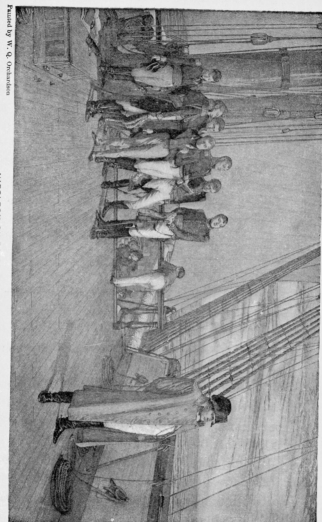

Painted by W. Q. Orchardson

NAPOLEON ON BOARD THE BELLEROPHON

run for shelter under the bayonets of the nearest square.

At an even gallop the French squadron came thundering up the slope—a solid front of flashing swords and gleaming breast-plates. Within a thousand feet from the British guns they put spurs to their horses and charged madly forward at full speed. As they beheld the gunners running for life, and saw the smoke drifting over a long row of field-pieces standing silent and deserted, the French cuirassiers became drunk with the rapture of victory. Rising in their stirrups at mid-career, they broke into a hoarse cheer. The fate of a few unfortunate squadrons that crashed into a sunken road traversing the field was scarcely heeded. *The great cavalry charge*

As the horsemen swept over the ridge through the abandoned batteries, they beheld the double line of British squares. At the same time they received a volley full in the face, and the leading squadron went down, man and horse. The maddened steeds of the following squadrons swerved sidewise and swept past the flanks of the hollow squares. They were instantly charged by the British cavalry stationed behind the squares. In confusion the French went galloping back over the slope. *French horsemen repulsed*

The scattered squadrons reformed in the valley. Ney, who had taken his ill success at Quatre-Bras deeply to heart, called in the whole of Kellermann's division—thirty-seven squadrons; eleven of cuirassiers, six of carbineers, and the Red Lancers of the Guard. Thus enforced, the French charged again.

The same scenes were enacted once more. The gunners stood by the guns until the last moment, and the British squares stood immovable, sending volley after volley into the demoralized horsemen. Occasionally some French leader would succeed in riding home to the very bayonets, there to discharge his pistol into the face of some British fusilier, but as a rule the horses refused to run into the fringe of steel. From four until six o'clock these scenes were repeated. The French rode up again and again, through the batteries and around the squares—"For all the world," to quote Wellington's words, "as if they owned them." As the horsemen reappeared over the crest of the hill the British infantry, levelling their muskets, would mutter scornfully, "Here come those fools again!" and let them have it. At last the horses themselves were so worn out that they could only be brought up on the trot. The British were careful to hold their fire until their assailants came within pistol shot. "The English squares and the French squadrons," said Lord Anglesby, "seemed hardly to take notice of each other."

Charge on charge

For two hours, 15,000 French horsemen made thirteen distinct charges on the British squares, but the British line of battle remained unbroken. One of the most realistic pictures of the fight at this stage is given by Captain Mercer, in command of a battery of horse artillery. Mercer was on the extreme British right during the first parts of the battle, and only got occasional glimpses of the ridge where the fight was raging—intermittent visions of

Mercer's description

French cavalry riding in furious charges, and abandoned British batteries with guns, muzzle in air, against the background of gray and whirling smoke. About three o'clock, in the height of the cavalry struggle, Fraser, who was in chief command of the horse artillery, galloped down the reverse slope to Mercer's battery, his face black with powder, his uniform torn. He brought the battery at full gallop to the central ridge, explaining as they rode Wellington's orders, that, when the French cavalry charged home, Mercer and his men should take refuge under the bayonets of the nearest square.

As they neared the crest on a gallop, Mercer describes the humming of the bullets as of "innumerable gnats filling the air." Through the smoke, a few hundred yards ahead, were the French squadrons, coming on a gallop. Mercer's guns were swung around, unlimbered, and fired with breathless speed. The French cuirassiers still came on.

"They moved in profound silence," writes Mercer, and the only sound that could be heard from them, amid the incessant roar of battle, was the low, thun- The sounds der-like reverberation of the ground beneath the of battle simultaneous tread of so many horses, through which ran a jangling ripple of sharp metallic sound, the ring of steel on steel. The British gunners, on their part, showed a stern coolness fully equal to the occasion. Every man stood steadily at his post, "the guns ready loaded with round-shot first, and a case over it; the tubes were in the vents, the port-fires glared and sputtered behind the wheels." The French column was led on this time by an officer in a rich uniform, his breast covered with decorations, whose earnest gesticulations were strangely contrasted with the solemn demeanor of those to whom they were addressed. Mercer allowed the leading squadron to come within sixty yards, then lifted his glove as the signal to fire. Nearly the whole leading rank fell in an instant, while the round shot pierced the column. The front, covered with struggling horses and men, was impassable. Some of the braver spirits did break their way through, only to fall, man and horse, at the muzzles of the guns. The British guns were served with astonishing activity, and men and horses tumbled before them like ninepins. Where the horse alone was killed, the cuirassier could be seen stripping himself of his armor with desperate haste to escape. The mass of the French for a moment stood still, then broke to pieces and fled.

All this while the French artillery played on the British guns. At the end of the day Mercer's battery had lost two men out of every three, and of 200 horses sheltered behind the ridge, 140 lay dead or dying.

Marshal Ney, who was probably the officer whom Mercer described, had one horse after another shot under him. With his hat and coat riddled with bullets, he still led charge on charge. "The madman!" said Napoleon, who watched the struggle through his field-glass, "he is massacring my cavalry!" All Ney could think of was to send for new reinforcements. "If we don't die here, under the English bullets," he said to General d'Erlon,

A glimpse of Ney

Losses of British artillery

Ney desperate

"there is nothing left for you and me but to lose our heads on the scaffold." Napoleon, with his eye on the Prussians, reluctantly despatched his Guards to help Ney. General Friant led forward the Old and the New Guard. Ney gathered his squadrons for a last charge, and flung himself on the British centre. It was a decisive moment. General Hill, who had just joined Wellington, said, "You may be killed here, what orders do you leave me?"

"To die on the spot to the last man, so that the Prussians may be all on the ground," replied Wellington. *Wellington's determination*

As the French Guards charged over the crest, Maitland's regiment, which had been lying flat on the ground where the guns had stood, fired a point-blank volley in the face of the dense columns. The first line of the French went down, and those behind wavered. General Friant was shot from his horse. The British cavalry came forward at a gallop. Then it was that Wellington, reining in his horse behind the crest, gave the famous order: "Up, Guards, and at them!" The British charged down the slope. All the squares, relieved of their terrible waiting ordeal of the afternoon, broke ranks and charged forward with a hoarse yell. Wellington, smiling grimly, sent orders after them that every command should move forward as it stood. The last brigade of fresh cavalry was sent forward to retake La Belle Alliance. The Prussians at last came upon the battlefield. Grouchy, pressing upon their rearguard, insisted that he had never received the Emperor's orders to join him. Buelow's *Grouchy's part* *"Up, guards, and at them!"*

Arrival of the Prussians

corps of Prussians, relieved of pressure in front, immediately flung itself into the battle. The men had been floundering over soggy forest roads for hour after hour, harassed by Grouchy in their rear and Ney's detachments in front. Blücher himself had to urge his men to do their utmost, crying, "Boys, don't make me break my word to the English!" When Wellington caught sight of the first Prussian platoons, he shouted joyfully to Müffling, "Well, you see MacDonnell held out to the last."

The last stroke

The united hosts of Englishmen and Prussians now pressed forward and completely overwhelmed the French. Ziethen's Hussars charged into their broken infantry. Napoleon's Old Guard was the last to make a stand, forming in solid squares long after nightfall. Called upon to surrender, they made the historic reply: "La garde ne se rend pas; elle mort." Of 10,000 of their men, only 150 still stood. The British and Prussian cavalry finally overrode them. Long after darkness the men were still fighting hand to hand. Napoleon escaped in

Flight of Napoleon

the confusion. He spoke first of dying on the field, but Marshal Soult seized his white Persian charger by the bridle and turned him round, saying, "Is not the enemy lucky enough as it is?"

Wellington's aides-de-camp on their side tried to draw him out of the danger in which he stood of being shot by both friends and foes. "What does it matter?" said the English general. "Let them fire as they like, the battle is won!"

La Belle Alliance

At the farm of La Belle Alliance, Blücher offered his hand to Wellington. "I will sleep to-night in

Bonaparte's last night's quarters," said Wellington. "And I will drive him out of his next!" replied Blücher. "Leave it all to me!" Favored by a moonlight night, the Prussians so hotly pursued the French that an immense number of prisoners and a vast amount of booty fell into their hands. Napoleon narrowly escaped being taken prisoner. At Genappe, where the bridge was blocked by fugitives, the pursuit was so close that the Emperor was compelled to abandon his carriage, leaving his sword and hat behind him. Blücher, who reached the _{Hot pursuit} spot shortly afterward, sent Napoleon's hat, sword and star to the King of Prussia, retained his cloak, telescope and carriage for his own use, and gave up all the money found to his soldiery. The whole of the army stores, two hundred and forty guns, and an innumerable quantity of arms thrown away by the fugitives, fell into his hands. As Lamartine has said, "The defeat left nothing undecided. The war _{Lamartine's dictum} began and ended in a single battle."

The battle of Waterloo cost Wellington nearly 15,000 dead and wounded. The losses of the Prussians exceeded 7,000 men. The full amount of Napoleon's losses could never be estimated, since his _{Casualties of Waterloo} army practically dispersed after the fugitives crossed the Sambre. Immediately after the great battle the Austrians, under Schwarzenberg and Fremont, advanced as far as Lyons. The Prince of Wurtemberg defeated General Rapp before Strasburg, and _{France reinvaded} the Swiss, under General Bachman, poured over the Alps. France was lost.

Napoleon reached Paris alone on the night of

June 20. He burst in on Caulaincourt at the Tuileries, but his agitation was so great he could scarcely speak: "You have heard the news? All is lost. The army did wonders, till they were seized by a panic terror and gave up everything. Ney acted like a maniac and threw away my cavalry. I am done for, and must have a bath and two hours' sleep. I am choking." During his bath the Emperor announced: "Nothing but a dictatorship can save the country. I have no longer an army, or a single musket. My only resources are the people. I hope the representatives will stand by me if I convoke the Chambers."

Napoleon's return to Paris

The Deputies, however, had resolved on a different policy. Davoust and Lucien Bonaparte urged a dictatorship; but Fouché, Lafayette, Dupin and other leaders of the popular party were determined to establish the absolute sovereignty of the National Assembly. "The House of Representatives," moved Lafayette, "declares that the independence of the nation is menaced. The Chamber declares its sittings permanent. Every attempt to dissolve it is declared high treason. The National Guards have, for six-and-twenty years, preserved the internal peace of the country and the persons of its representatives; and the means of increasing the numbers of that force must be now considered." This resolution was carried by acclamation. Lucien called Lafayette an ingrate. "I wanting in gratitude to Napoleon!" exclaimed Lafayette, indignantly: "Do you know what we have done for him? Have you forgotten that the bones of our

Opposition to his plans

Lafayette asserts himself

brothers and our children everywhere attest our fidelity to him—amid the sands of Africa—on the shores of the Guadalquivir and the Tagus—on the banks of the Vistula, and in the frozen deserts of Muscovy? Three millions of Frenchmen have perished for one man, who still wishes to fight the combined powers of Europe. We have done enough for Napoleon; let us now try to save France."

The call for Napoleon's abdication now became universal.

"I propose," said General Solignac, "that a committee wait on the Emperor for his immediate decision." The emperor's abdication demanded

"Let us delay an hour," cried Lucien.

"An hour, but no more," replied Solignac.

"If the answer is not returned at that time," said Lafayette, "I will move for his dethronement."

When Lucien went with this commission to Napoleon, he found him in the utmost agitation, debating with himself whether to commit suicide or to dissolve the Chambers by force. Lucien told him impressively that he must either abdicate or dismiss the Chambers and seize the supreme power.

"Dethrone me!" said Napoleon. "They dare not do it!"

"In an hour," replied Regnaud de St. Angely, "your dethronement, on the motion of Lafayette, will be irrevocably pronounced: they have given you only an hour's grace—do you hear? Only an hour." Lafayette's ultimatum

Napoleon turned to Fouché and said with a bitter smile: "Write to the gentlemen to keep themselves quiet! They shall be satisfied." He then dictated to Lucien a formal act of abdication in favor of his son.

"My son!" he repeated two or three times, "my son! What a chimera! No, no. It is not in favor of my son that I am abdicating, but in that of the Bourbons. They at least are not prisoners at Vienna!"

Generals Lafayette and Sebastiani, with three others, were despatched to the headquarters of the allies to announce the Emperor's abdication and to sue for peace. Napoleon withdrew, almost alone, to Malmaison, where Queen Hortense had been living since the death of her mother, Josephine. On June 25, he said farewell to his officers and guards.

Blücher, in the meanwhile, had pushed forward without loss of time and stood before the gates of Paris. He summoned the city to surrender. When

Davoust, commanding the National Guards, held off the capitulation, and spoke of making a last defence, Blücher wrote him a curt note in ill-spelled German: "Take care what you do. If we must take the city by storm, we shall remember how you dealt with Hamburg."

On July 3, Paris surrendered after a futile combat in the outskirts at Issy. Davoust's troops had

three days wherein to evacuate the city. On July 7, the Prussians entered, and General Müffling was appointed military governor. Blücher, who was incensed at the destruction of the stone column of Rossbach, and the disappearance of Frederick the Great's sword and watch, placed cannons at the important points, and gave orders to destroy the most galling of French trophies—notably, the Bridge of

Jena. By this time the allied troops had come up, and with them King Louis XVIII. and his counsellors, the Count of Artois and Prince Talleyrand Benevento.

Return of Louis XVIII.

Talleyrand begged Count von der Goltz to use his influence for the preservation of the bridge. Blücher replied to his entreaties: "I will blow up the bridge, and should very much like to have Talleyrand sitting upon it at the time!" An attempt to blow it up was actually made, but was given up when Wellington sent one of his aides-de-camp to prevent it. The King of Prussia himself rode to the spot to remonstrate with his field marshal. For this and other acts of interference Blücher openly upbraided the diplomats: "I should like you gentlemen of the quill to be for once exposed to a smart platoon fire, just to teach you what perils we soldiers have to run in order to repair your blunders."

Prussian reprisals threatened

It was at Wellington's great banquet in honor of the surrender of Paris, a few days afterward, that Blücher proposed the famous toast: "May the pens of the diplomats not undo what we have won with the sword!"

On the same day that Louis XVIII. entered Paris, welcomed by Fouché and other self-constituted spokesmen of the people, Napoleon withdrew to Rochefort. There various plans were proposed for his escape. Lafayette offered to have him conveyed to the United States on an American merchant vessel. The Prefect of Marine put a government cutter at his disposal, wherewith to elude the British man-of-war in the offing. "Since the society

Napoleon at Rochefort

of men is denied me," wrote Napoleon in a mawkish mood, "I will take refuge in the bosom of nature, and there I shall live in the solitude which harmonizes with my last thoughts."

Projected escape to America

It was arranged that all of Napoleon's brothers, as well as Hortense, with others of his close family circle, should meet him in America. By this time two British cruisers drew close into the mouth of the harbor, and it became plain that it would be next to impossible to foil their vigilance. As a last resource, Napoleon, on July 9, sent Las Casas to Captain Maitland, commanding H.M.S. "Bellerophon," to sound him as to his probable line of conduct. The British officer sent back word that he would stop any ship attempting to force the

Strict British blockade

blockade. In regard to the granting of a safe conduct for the person of the Emperor, Maitland added he had received no instructions, but felt sure that England would always show Napoleon the respect due to the high position he held. After this setback a few more days were wasted in vacillating projects. Napoleon resolved to gain a last point

Napoleon surrenders

by throwing himself upon the generosity of his victors. On July 14, he wrote to the Prince Regent of England:

"YOUR ROYAL HIGHNESS—After being aimed at, both by the factions which divide my country and by the enmity of the great powers of Europe, I have finished my political career, and now come, like Themistocles, to sit down by the hearth of the English people. I place myself under the protection of their laws, which I claim from your royal

highness as the most powerful, the most steadfast,
and the most generous of my enemies."

The next day he went on board the "Bellerophon." In accordance with his request, Captain
Maitland forthwith set sail for England. Ten days
later he brought his illustrious prisoner into Plymouth. This turn of affairs put the British Government in extreme embarrassment. It was proposed
in the Cabinet to deliver Napoleon to the King of
France as a state prisoner, but in the end it was
determined to put the outlaw out of harm's way on
the distant island of St. Helena, a solitary rock
lost between Africa and America.

Lord Keith, the admiral in command at Plymouth,
was instructed to inform Napoleon of his deportation as a prisoner for life. The Emperor received
the news with an impassive countenance. When
he learned that only three of his old servants were
to accompany him, and that he was to be deprived
of all personal resources, he made a motion as if to
surrender his sword. Lord Keith awkwardly turned
his back and retired in silence. On August 9, the Exiled to St. Helena
"Northumberland," bearing Napoleon to his exile,
sailed from Plymouth. With the deposed Emperor
went Generals Bertrand, Montholon and Gourgeaud,
with their families, and Count de Las Casas. Rear-
Admiral Cockburn, who commanded the squadron,
has left the most interesting account of the voyage
and Napoleon's frank disclosures in his conversations with him.

The tragic fate of this greatest of modern conquerors made a profound impression on Europe.

Goethe, at Weimar, said to his friend Eckerman:
"They have chained down another Prometheus.
For the sake of a great name he knocked half the
world to pieces. All romance, all illusions, all
poetry are as nothing before the brute strength of
such a character. But as a hero he will grow more
gigantic in his proportions the further he is removed
from us."

In a similar strain is Victor Hugo's immortal
verse:

> Angel or demon! thou—whether of light
>   The minister, or darkness—still dost sway
> This age of ours; thine eagle's soaring flight
>   Bears us, all breathless, after it, away.
> The eye that from thy presence fain would stray
> Shuns thee in vain; thy mighty shadow thrown
>   Rests on all pictures of the living day,
>   And on the threshold of our time, alone,
> Dazzling, yet sombre, stands thy form, Napoleon!

For most Englishmen, Bonaparte, with his dreams
of British conquest, was still too threatening a reality to be regarded from an abstract point of view.
For English children the dread name of "Bony" was
still a nursery bogie. Thackeray has reported how,
when as a boy he was returning home from India,
and his ship stopped at St. Helena, the black steward showed him a short, stout man walking in a
garden: "That is he," said the negro servant in
an awed whisper; "that is Bony. He eats three
live sheep every day and all the little children he
can lay hold of." Even Byron, cosmopolitan genius
that he was, wrote his "Ode to Napoleon" in a
strain of ringing British invective:

'Tis done—but yesterday a king!
    And armed with kings to strive—
And now thou art a nameless thing,
    So abject—yet alive!
Is this the man of thousand thrones,
Who strewed our earth with hostile bones?
    And can he thus survive?
Since he, miscalled the Morning Star,
Nor man nor fiend hath fallen so far.

Ill minded man! why scourge thy kind,
    Who bowed so low the knee?
By gazing on thyself grown blind,
    Thou taught'st the rest to see.
With might unquestioned—power to save—
Thine only gift hath been the grave
    To those that worshipped thee;
Nor, till thy fall, could mortals guess
Ambition's less than littleness.

.   .   .   .

Where may the wearied eye repose,
    When gazing on the great;
Where neither guilty glory glows
    Nor despicable state?
Yes—one—the first—the last—the best—
The Cincinnatus of the West,
    Whom envy dared not hate,
Bequeath'd the name of Washington,
To make men blush there was but one!

Byron's
ode

The same obvious conclusion was reached by Chateaubriand in his famous essay on "Washington et Bonaparte," published with his "Mémoires d'Outre Tombe."

Washington *vs.* Napoleon

One of the truest estimates of the great conqueror's character is that of Guizot, who served at that time in the French Ministry of Justice. In his "Memoirs for the History of Our Times," Guizot wrote: "The genius and renown of Napoleon have nothing to fear from the light of history; justice is done him and will be done every new genera-

Guizot's estimate

tion. Illustrious in the foremost rank among the
greatest conquerors of enslaved humanity, whether
subduing, ruling, or organizing, equally great by
military genius, and by the supreme instinct of
national government, he was constantly carried
away by selfish passions and desires, whatever their
importance or unimportance might be, and took no
cognizance of the eternal laws of duty and justice.
Corrupt, he corrupted others; despotic, he subdued
minds and debased consciences; all-powerful, he
constantly made a bad use of his power. His glorious and blood-stained traces remained soiled not
only by faults but by crimes. The startling dream
with which he dazzled France has disappeared; the
memory still remains, weakened, but always fatal
to our unhappy country."

With Napoleon out of the way, the rule of the
Bourbons, in France, Spain and Naples, was carried along its fatuous course as if the tremendous
events of the French Revolution and Napoleonic
Era had never happened. After the second restoration of Louis XVIII., Marshals Masséna and
Oudinot, as spokesmen of the National Guard, implored the king to permit his soldiers to retain
their tricolor standards. Fouché advised against
it, and the king peremptorily refused. "What a
race!" said Wellington. "It is easier to make them
accept a regicide than a new idea." It was at this
time that the saying arose: "The Bourbons have
forgotten nothing and they have learned nothing."

Thanks to the intervention of the Czar and Wellington, France at that time was spared the humil-

The Bourbon restoration

iation of losing the strong line of border fortresses in Alsace-Lorraine which Louis XIV. had wrested from Germany. Negotiations concerning the details of peace dragged on for months. Special rancor was created in France by Blücher's levy of a hundred million francs from Paris, and by a general demand for the restoration of pillaged art treasures. The bronze horses of St. Mark's had to be sent back to Venice. The sword of Frederick the Great was kept hidden; nor did the Germans succeed in raising the column of Rossbach out of the Seine, where it had been dumped by the Invalides. On the other hand, most of the valuable manuscripts of the University of Heidelberg, which Napoleon had placed in the library of Paris, had to be restored. While the foreign armies still held the territory of France as a hostage for the payment of a new war indemnity of 1,000,000,000 francs, the royalists inaugurated their work of vengeance. On July 24, two lists of proscription were issued. They bore the names of nineteen persons to be tried for high treason: notably, Marshals Ney, Grouchy, Bertrand; Generals Lallemand, d'Erlon, Lefebvre-Desnouettes, Clausel, Drouot, Cambronne; besides Labédoyère, Lavalette, and Rovigo. Among those that were to be banished were Marshals Soult and Bassain. Davoust handed in his resignation as Secretary of War and commander-in-chief of the Army of the Loire: "It is my name that ought to be substituted for theirs," said he, "since they only obeyed the orders I had given them as Minister of War."

Alsace-Lorraine spared

War indemnities

Napoleon's generals proscribed

Thus encouraged, the royalist faction of the popu-
Brune and
Ramel
murdered
lace went to worse excesses. Early in August,
Marshal Brune was murdered by a mob at Avignon. The government affected to believe that he
had committed suicide. At Toulouse, General
Ramel was beaten to death at the threshold of his
house. Riotous mobs burned the houses of reputed
Bonapartists at Nîmes, and lynched several innocent persons. In August, Marshal Ney was arrested at a friend's house. At the same time,
Lavalette and Labédoyère were placed before a
court-martial. "L'Independent," a new journal,
which dared to publish an article in their defence,
was suppressed. Labédoyère made his last plea:
Labedo-
yere con-
demned
to death
"I protest that there was no express conspiracy to
bring Napoleon back from Elba. So far as I was
concerned, I was misled by some glorious memories
and some new illusions." It was in vain. Labédoyère was condemned to death. His wife threw
herself at the feet of the king, but her appeal was
refused: "I appreciate your sentiments, madame,"
said the king. "Never was refusal more painful."
Labédoyère was shot August 19. On October 13,
Murat, having been betrayed into the hands of the
Murat shot
Bourbons, was shot at Pizzo in Calabria. When they
wished to bandage his eyes he said: "I have braved
death too often to fear it now." Then he himself
gave the order to fire. He died on the same day
that Napoleon landed at St. Helena.

Ney's turn came next. His trial became a *cause
célèbre*. A military court-martial refused to try him
on the ground that he was a Peer of France. Placed

on trial before the Chamber of Peers, Ney, while admitting everything, appealed to the amnesty act extended by the allied powers to all persons comprised in the capitulation of Paris. He proved that Ney's trial he was within the city at that time. The Duke of Wellington and the other ambassadors of the great powers refused to interpose in the marshal's behalf, and Ney's lawyer, Dupin, was enjoined from resting his defence on that point. Ney himself refused to take advantage of the fact that he was an Alsatian, and should therefore come under the special act of amnesty which sheltered from prosecution all the inhabitants of ceded provinces. "As a Frenchman," he said, "I fought the battles of France. Now let me die a Frenchman. Since this is not the place to invoke the faith of treaties, I lodge my A last appeal appeal with Europe and posterity." Late in the year the Chamber of Peers pronounced the condemnation of Ney. Among those that voted for the death sentence were several former officers and marshals of the empire—his comrades in arms. The young Duc de Broglie alone made a strenuous protest, but in vain. At two in the morning, December 7, the sentence was read aloud to the marshal in his prison cell. As the court officer sonorously rolled off his titles—"Maréchal de France, Duc d'Elchingen, Prince de la Moscova," etc.—the prisoner stopped him: "Say Michel Ney, and soon no more of him."

Madame Ney brought her children to the prison, and from there ran bareheaded to the Tuileries to throw herself at the feet of the king. She was re-

fused admittance—"her demand not having sufficient object." While she was still entreating an
audience, her husband was marched to the entrance of
the Grande Avenue de l'Observatoire. With his face
to the gray light of dawn, Ney himself commanded
End of Ney the fire: "Now, soldiers, straight to the heart!"

After the execution of Marshal Ney, a story became current that the soldiers had only fired with
blank cartridges and that Ney had been spirited
away to America. This story has since become one
of the legends of Louisiana.

Now it was Lavalette's turn. Though he had
never sworn allegiance to the Restoration, he was
sentenced to die on the scaffold. In vain did Madame Lavalette implore the Duchesse d'Angoulême
for interposition with the king. Even a last request that he might be shot like a soldier was
denied to Lavalette. On December 20, Madame
Lavalette came to bid farewell to her husband.
While alone together they exchanged clothes.
Lavalette, disguised in his wife's skirts and hold-
Lavalette's ing her handkerchief to his face, escaped through
escape the prison portals. For five days he was hidden in
one of the offices of the Ministry of Foreign Affairs.
Sir Robert Wilson, an English officer, finally got
him out of the country. Sir Robert was cashiered
for this offence. Madame Lavalette as a result of
these trying circumstances lost her reason.

In the midst of this reign of reprisal the final
negotiations of the Second Peace of Paris were completed. On November 20, the treaty was signed.
The war indemnity was reduced to seven hundred

million francs. Pending its payment, seventeen
fortresses on the northern frontier were to be gar- Treaty of Paris
risoned by German and English soldiers. The
French frontiers were pushed in to the old limits
of 1790. Five of the eastern frontier forts were surrendered to the German Confederation, Saarbrücken
being taken by Prussia. The stronghold of Huningen in French Flanders was razed to the ground,
and the French possessions in Savoy were ceded to
Sardinia. All that Talleyrand's diplomacy had
won during the negotiations at Vienna was lost to
France. Talleyrand himself, realizing his impotence, resigned his ministry before the final conclusion of peace.

While the affairs of Europe were thus rearranged
by the powers, the American people were striving American affairs
to readjust their own affairs. Shortly after the
shooting of a number of American prisoners of war
in an English prison at Dartmoor, hostilities with
England reached their definite end on June 18.
The first peace society of the world was founded
at New York. The war had left a heavy legacy.
American shipping as such was ruined, involving Ruin of shipping
the ruin of the once thriving trade of the New England States with the West Indies, and almost all
foreign commerce. Nearly all the banks throughout the country, including the great national bank,
had suspended payment. The national debt was
increased to $99,833.60. To raise any revenue
whatever the Federal Government levied taxes on
such personal property as hats and caps, leather
boots, gold or silver watches, and umbrellas.

The work of reconstruction began at once after the re-election of Madison to the Presidency. This election was the last stand of the Federalist party in the United States. New England's opposition to the recent war, culminating in the Hartford Convention with the hue and cry against the hated "Blue-Lights," brought about its political downfall. Once this was accomplished the bitterness of factional dissensions ceased. The people of New York provided for the construction of the great Erie Canal from Albany on the Hudson to Lake Erie. Robert Fulton, who died that year, still had the satisfaction of seeing his new steam ferry in operation, and witnessed the launching of the first steam frigate of the world. It bore his name. In Philadelphia, the great Fairmount water-works, which supply that city with water, were brought to completion, while the people of Baltimore were laying pipes and mains to make their city the first municipality lighted by gas.

In the midst of these labors of peace came another ruffle of war. The Barbary pirates, little heeded as they were during the preoccupation of the recent maritime war, once more grew troublesome. The Dey of Algiers compelled Lear, the American consul, to pay a ransom of $27,000, under threat of slavery for himself and all his household. The American Government paid over the money, but Congress immediately followed the matter up by a declaration of war upon Algiers. On May 19, Commodores Decatur and Bainbridge, with a squadron of nine ships, sailed for the Mediterranean. De-

Madison re-elected

Death of Fulton

Barbary war

catur arrived off Gibraltar in June. Learning that
the "Mashoda," an Algerian forty-six gun frigate,
was in those waters, he set out to find her. On
June 17 she was sighted, and the American squadron immediately gave chase. Decatur's flagship,
the "Guerrière," was in the lead, and soon came
within range. The Moors fought with great bravery, and did not surrender until the other American ships brought their fire to bear on them. One
shot cut the Algerian admiral in two, and thirty of
their sailors were killed. The "Guerrière" had
three killed and eleven wounded. Two days later,
Decatur captured an Algerian twenty-two gun brig Sea fights
after a short but fierce fight. Then he set sail for off Algiers
Algiers. The American squadron came-to off Al-
giers, and Decatur sent in a demand for an immediate settlement. The Dey came in person, and a
treaty was negotiated on Decatur's quarterdeck.
The Dey offered to cease his depredations on American ships if the United States Government would
help him maintain his prestige by sending him a
mere handful of gunpowder, in semblance of tribute. Decatur cut him short: "If you want powder you will have to take our balls with it." Once
the Dey had come to terms, Decatur next called on
the Pasha of Tunis, and made him pay $46,000 for
American ships in his waters betrayed to the English during the late war. The Bey of Tripoli had
to pay $25,000 for similar breach of neutrality and
to release all Christians he held in slavery. Hence- Piracy
suppressed
forth, absolute immunity was granted to American
ships sailing in the Mediterranean. This put an

end to the anomalous submission of civilized nations to the insolent demands of the Arab chieftains of northern Africa.

About the same time that security was thus reestablished in the Mediterranean, England made another great stride toward the abolition of slave

Partial abolition of slave trade trading. Through Lord Castlereagh in Paris she won for this the consent of all Christian nations, excepting only Portugal and Spain. The Prince Regent of Portugal, with whom the interests of Brazil, just elevated to the rank of a kingdom, counted for more, now, than those of the mother country, agreed to restrict Brazil's thriving slave trade to southern waters. The statesmen of Spain obstinately declined the English demands for reform on this score. They justified their refusal by the fact that Great Britain herself did not suppress her own slave trade until all her colonies had been supplied with slaves far beyond the possibilities of her colonial rivals.

With this question thus temporarily settled, Metternich set himself to weld together the pieces of the old German empire in the new form of a Germanic confederation. The terms were finally settled at Vienna, in June. The confederation consisted of thirty-five States, thirty-one of which were ruled by sovereigns. The States comprised the empire of Austria; the five kingdoms of Prussia, Bavaria, Saxony, Hanover, and Wurtemberg; the electorate of Hesse-Cassel; the seven grandduchies—Baden, Hesse-Darmstadt, Mecklenburg-Schwerin, Mecklenburg-Strelitz, Saxe-Weimar, Luxemburg, and Ol-

denburg; the eight duchies—Holstein with Lauen-
burg, Brunswick, Nassau, Saxe-Meiningen, Saxe-
Coburg-Gotha, Saxe-Altenburg, Anhalt-Dessau,
and Anhalt-Bernberg; the five principalities—
Schwartzburg-Sonderhausen, Schwartzburg-Rudol-
stadt, Schaumburg-Lippe, Lippe-Detmold, Waldeck;
the four dominions of Reuss, Hesse - Homburg,
Neuburg, and Lichtenstein ; and the four free
cities of Hamburg, Bremen, Luebeck and Frankfort. The confederation, as now constituted, had
sufficient cohesive force to endure for two generations. Yet it fell so wofully short of the more
progressive ideals of German unity that the "good
old times" of the Bund have become a by-word
of outraged German liberalism.

Friedrich Anton Mesmer, the originator of the
pseudo-science known as Mesmerism, died during
this year in Meersburg. His alleged discoveries in
animal magnetism and planetary influences, at the
close of the previous century, had made a great
stir. Through the agency of a " Secret Society
of Harmony," founded by himself, Mesmer's pretended achievements gained such vogue that he
was able to amass a fortune of 400,000 francs. This
he lost again, owing partly to the formal condemnation of his teachings by the French Academy; but
he protested so vigorously that the French Government eventually granted him an annual pension
of 3,000 francs. Mesmer's discoveries, while they
gave a certain impetus to the use of electricity
in medicine, proved of no permanent value.

It was late in the year, during the interval pre-

[Death of Mesmer]

ceding the conclusion of the second treaty of Paris,
that the singular compact was made between the
sovereigns of the Continent which has come to be
known as the "Holy Alliance." It originated
with Czar Alexander. This monarch, though loose
enough in his private morals, was deeply imbued
with religious feeling. At this time in particular he
had fallen under the sway of Mme. Krüdener, who
dabbled in mysticism. With her help he drew up
a document which read like a profession of faith,
and this he presented to his fellow-sovereigns. The
King of Prussia, who was a simple-minded ruler,
signed the paper in good faith. Emperor Francis,
who had the comfortable sense of humor of the
Hapsburgs, said that if the paper related to doctrines of religion, he must refer it to his father
confessor, if to matters of State, to his Prime Minister. Metternich pronounced the paper a mere
mass of verbiage, but advised his master to sign it
for policy's sake. The treaty practically renewed
the pledges of Chaumont, though couched, this time,
in the terms of a religious declaration. Article II.
of the treaty is a characteristic instance:

Holy
Alliance

"The three Princes unite in confessing that the
Christian People, of whom they and their nations
form a part, have in reality no other Sovereign but
Him to whom alone belongs Almighty Power; to
wit, God the Father, our Divine Saviour Jesus
Christ, the Holy Ghost and the Word. Their Maj-
esties therefore recommend to their peoples to for-
tify themselves each day in the principles and
practice of those duties which the Divine Saviour
has enjoined on Mankind."

Pious
declaration

Since the King of England was mentally unfit, an invitation to join the Holy Alliance was issued to the Prince Regent. That frivolous-minded prince, engrossed as he was with his marital troubles with Princess Caroline, left the matter to Lord Castlereagh, who was then in Paris. "The fact is," Lord Castlereagh wrote home, "the Russian Emperor's mind is not quite sound." Apart from that, he and the Prince Regent were well aware that the constitutional form of their government would not permit them to commit England to such a compact without the sanction of Parliament. Accordingly, Alexander had to content himself with a personal letter from the Prince of Wales containing a cordial approval of his good tenets. The Bourbon rulers of France, Naples, Sardinia and Spain subscribed to the treaty as a matter of course, as did the Prince Regent of Sweden, Bernadotte. The Alliance, as finally concluded, comprised all the principal rulers of Europe, with none left out but the King of England, the Pope, and the Sultan of Turkey.

England not a party

The Pope left out

Such was the famous Holy Alliance, which, though conceived by a liberal-minded enthusiast in a desire for universal peace and brotherhood, was destined to fall under general execration, as an unholy league for the suppression of the highest human liberties and free thought.